M000266665

THE PERFECT WEAPON

THE PERFECT WEAPON

The Obama Cabal's Phony National Security Prosecution of J. Everett Dutschke

By
Felicia Nona
Contributing Editors
Dana James, Laura Gomez and Rachael Goldsmith-Jackson
©2020 Chain Bridge Media

The Perfect Weapon by Felicia Nona
Copyright © 2020 Chain Bridge Media

All rights reserved. No portion of this book may be reproduced in any form or by any electronic or mechanical means, including information and retrieval systems, without permission from the publisher, except as permitted by U.S. copyright law. For permissions contact: Felicianona21@protonmail.com

Contributing Editors:
Dana James, Laura Gomez and Rachael Goldsmith-Jackson.

Hardcover ISBN: 979-8487305329
Paperback ISBN-10: 1735980315 / ISBN-13: 978-1735980317

2nd Edition

Table of Contents

What follows is an analytical work product of the Dutschke ("DUS-key") Report in long-book form with additional information, interviews and commentary added. It is not a textbook. It is not a reference book for other "journalists" to use. They had their chance in 2013-2014 to search for the truth and inform the public, but failed.

Although two names have been altered, several names, dates and other details have been redacted in compliance with CI laws and the panel. No information or conclusions of the Dutschke Report have been changed or misrepresented. A particular date (not included in the Dutschke Report) has been changed to protect identity, but is a change of no consequence as this published analysis has not received public approval from the Publication Review Board.

Additionally, "Operation Dojo" (as used herein) was not the actual name of the overall DOJ operation, but was the actual name of one of the single FBI operations against Dutschke (of numerous names) in the larger 2013 scheme of the Obama Administration.

INTRODUCTION

Throughout American history, there has been an enumerable abundance of massive and scandalous atrocities. More often than not, the list of egregious and monstrous deeds bears ties to government apparatchiks of these criminal conspiratorial operations. Most involve the American Department Of Justice and its badged agents of the Federal Bureau of Investigation.

The list of outrageous sins committed by the United States DOJ and FBI is a long one and easy for blind-apologists of law enforcement officers to excuse until one begins to look into the details of each case. Even a cursory glance at any single event is enough to prevent even the most intransigent of minds from being an agnostic on at least plausible malfeasance on the part of American law enforcement and its system of government prosecuting solicitors and even the criminal judicial system itself.

No one would believe that the FBI's Hoover aided in the cover-up of the assassination of JFK that installed LBJ; a cover-up operation that lasted for years, unless one takes the time to dig into the details. This is not a JFK book.

No one would believe that the FBI was guilty of multiple counts of manslaughter and a massive cover-up operation, which, if any other private citizen had done would be a prosecutable "obstruction of justice;" of their monstrous deeds in Waco Texas, a cover-up operation that lasted for years, unless one takes time to dig into the details. This is not a Waco book.

No one would believe that the Boston Bomber, Tamerlan Tsarnaev, was actually an FBI asset, a cover-up they actively ran for years, unless one takes time to dig into the details. This is not a book about the Boston Marathon bombing.

Those events, as well as many others, have already been exposed in one way or another; the complicit law enforcement, the details and connections which negate any accusations of being "a conspiracy theory." This is not that book, nor is anything that follows a "theory" but are real and documented events that are so remarkably unbelievable that not even the most creative or confused movie script writers could conceive.

Sometimes reality transcends fiction. And in this tale, the roles are not played by actors but by the highest office holders in the free world. And yet, this is not a tale at all. This all really happened and the way in which it is presented and with the cast of characters that are as presented, some who you know and some who will be hard to accept as real. This book covers the

1

accounting of the actual record, forgotten and ignored (and other documentation and interviews) that, if the proper contemporary media had bothered to do its job of telling the truth at the time, should not have now been necessary.

This book details several illicit schemes of an administration over a period of years, to destroy, discredit, silence and imprison an allegiant man who was doing his duty. It details the conspirators by name, role and dates. It details the lies told to a complicit press, a blindly naive public and an accomplice of a judge. It details the weaponization of the DOJ and the FBI.

There is no version of the truth that can be imparted as one imbibes a fizzy lemonade, for even the capsule version requires a slow, careful read. Some of the "short version" details may ring familiar, most of the full version will not.

Whatever is ever an "official version" by the US government, particularly the Department of Justice is *never* the actual truth of a matter. The same holds true here.

Abstract—there was, in fact, a cabal during the administration of the 44th President, Barack Hussein Obama, that consisted of a group of men and women who regularly met as if holding court to further their schemes and eliminate threats to their image, legacy or power. Sometimes such public destruction of individuals was plotted out of sheer hatred, animus or even retaliation. These meetings were not of people who were "behind the scene'" They were overt and documented and occurred often with all of them in attendance in the same room at the same time. Not just any room would do for this syndicate of conspirators. Their meeting room was oval.

This book is about the prolonged targeting and fraudulent prosecution and public making a terrorist of J. Everett Dutschke. A travesty of justice that is inconceivable and unbelievable and yet to this day he sits in a very believable prison for "developing a biological weapon."

This is a true story of the fraudulent prosecution of the 2013 KC letters, and all the deep background which led to it; who led it, who was involved and why.

The story that you think you know is but a thin veneer of what it really is. Here follows the capsule version—.

Chapter 1

What was the "Official" story?

This is not so easy to answer since the "official" DOJ story changed numerous times but the capsule version spun about it all landed roughly on this iteration.

America was on edge in April of 2013 because of the Boston Marathon bombing, a terrorist attack launched on American soil by a Chechnyan Muslim extremist and his brother that rattled American citizens to their bones, reminding them of September 11th, 2001.

This shocked the United States. Terror attacks were supposed to be a thing of the past. "How could this be?" Americans asked themselves. "After all, Barack Obama is the president and everyone loves us." Even the Fort Hood attack (Hassan) had been characterised as a "workplace violence" incident. And just like 2001, there followed a government claim of a chemical weapons attack and new footage of buildings being evacuated. Three, possibly more, letters were received that were "laced" with "ricin".

"Ricin" the media pointed out as frequently as possible, was "a deadly poison with no known antidote." That description was repeated a billion-fold by every "reporter" in the universe. The targets of the "ricin attacks" were President Barack Obama, Senator Roger Wicker and some judge in Mississippi.

Capitol Police, Senator Wicker's office and Secret Service immediately identified Paul Kevin Curtis as the mailer through an overwhelming amount of irrefutable evidence. He was arrested and his initial defence seemed to be that he'd recently stopped taking his antipsychotic medication. His family did not deny what he had done but instead made the case that Paul Kevin Curtis's mental delusions were at fault, thus he could not really be held responsible for his actions. The world learned then that Paul Kevin Curtis was a long unemployed recipient of Social Security disability (on account of his mental capacity) and therefore was "officially" more than a bit of a nutter. The government had officially granted him loon status and was, in fact paying him monthly because of it. Additionally, the man lived on the government's dole in a government housing project for low or no income. Despite that he subsided parasitically on the government handouts, it was revealed that he was rabidly anti-government, anti-CIA, anti-political in every way and was not only quite vocal about it but extremely paranoid and angry, having often written to the very same victim recipients of the "ricin" letters. In all of his previous correspondence to his targets, he had signed off as "KC". In the "ricin" letters, he had written the same. The KC letters.

The world, almost amused by this cartoonish figure who called himself an "Elvis impersonator", soon learned that Paul Kevin Curtis had been expressing his angry delusions for quite some time to anyone who would listen—radio, telly or print and internet, claiming that the CIA was poisoning the American population with commercial airlines and other strange fabrications from his medicated mind. His pet and primary tale was one he frequently told of a black market body parts conspiracy run by the funeral homes, politicians and the local hospital that had fired him as a janitor when he heroically stumbled upon the sinister plot and "blew the whistle" on it. This pet tale of his seemed to have tendrils that reached everywhere as he often hounded countless media, politicians and influential people about it for years.

One of those people was James Everett Dutschke. During the criminal proceedings against Paul Kevin Curtis, Curtis's attorney Christi McCoy deftly steered the focus of the courtroom testimony from the mailing of the KC letters to the making of what the Mueller FBI was calling a biological weapon. She mentioned the name of James Everett Dutschke during the hearing and the hearings abruptly came to a halt. The Magistrate Judge, Susan Alexander, announced that the hearings would resume after a break.

The hearings did not resume. Instead, the US Department of Justice, under Attorney General Eric Holder and the FBI under Robert Mueller III, completely switched their focus from "who was the mailer?" to "who was the maker?" and all discussion to the obedient press of the mailing vanished. The mailing became, magically, unimportant as well as all the overwhelming evidence the FBI had presented and their numerous under oath testimony that Curtis was undeniably the mailer. "Forget all that, pretend it didn't happen," became the message, "we now have a new target."

Curtis, after a few days, was released from jail on a deal with his attorney, Christi McCoy, to hit the media trail with an ongoing new narrative that "Dutschke did it."

Curtis actually claimed, on national news programs, in magazines, radio programs and more, that he didn't "know anything about anything," that he was completely clueless, but "Dutschke did it."

Not a single person in the press had either the will or the brains to ask, "Well, if you don't know anything and are clueless, as you claim, then how is it you can blame any person at all?" To this day, not a single interviewer from 2013 has bothered to think of that obviosity or revisit the tale.

One reason the media did not bother to delve into the realm of logic is that the already strange tale was getting more interesting. Mueller was seemingly embarrassed for arresting and prosecuting the "wrong man", just as he had done in 2001 with the anthrax attacks. The media portrayed the Mueller FBI and administration as having "egg on its face", which was a criticism that neither thin-skinned Mueller nor Obama would bear.

The new (third) narrative was that Paul Kevin Curtis was the innocent victim of a rogue operation to "frame" Paul Kevin Curtis for the "ricin" attacks that was actually masterminded by the mysterious and shady James Everett Dutschke.

Someone, somewhere had misspoken to a reporter that there had been some sort of "online feud" between Dutschke and Curtis. Despite that there were zero details of any alleged feud, it sounded interesting enough to the reporter to run with it which quickly got repeated by the other parroting press since secondary sourcing is what they do—merely repeating each other ad nauseum.

There was some chattering that Curtis, himself, claimed that Everett Dutschke was aiding in a government cover-up of Dutschke's political friends when he refused to help Curtis in exposing the alleged "black market body parts" scheme. Curtis' interviews indicated that he had felt resentful that Dutschke, Senator Wicker and President Obama had oft ignored his strange accusations of the "body parts" schemes (that he, in part, blamed the targeted judge for). The press, however, seemed more delighted to present the entertaining spectacle of this cartoonish man and his conspiracy theories than in presenting or inquiring as to those obvious resentment which exactly mirrored the resentment expressed in the KC letters themselves.

Instead, the world, the press and the prosecution itself was now aiming at Dutschke. The FBI claimed it had a discovered "dust mask" that was suddenly found by an agent of the Department of Homeland Security that bolstered the claim that Dutschke was guilty of "Developing a Biological Weapon" in violation of the international treaty against biological weapons development (the Biological Weapons Convention) which made such development a war crime, as signed by hundreds of different nations including the US and ratified by the US Senate.

(As a brief aside—President Obama's close White House advisor who was the head of the Department of Homeland Security's measures for counterterrorism, the man who held Obama's ear inside the Oval office, itself, was John Brennan. This fact is relevant-mark later)

This "dust mask" given to the FBI by Brennan's Homeland Security counter-terrorism agent, was claimed to be the "smoking gun" damning evidence. The Mueller FBI reported to the worldwide press that the dust mask, which they claimed was recovered from a public rubbish bin from just outside of Dutschke's office building, had tested "positive for traces of ricin".

As if this was not damning enough, they then claimed that the connection of this "ricin-laced" dust mask to Dutschke was inarguable because it also contained traces of J. Everett Dutschke's DNA on it.

End of case. Open and shut. This was their "slam dunk" evidence that would guarantee a conviction. How can anyone possibly argue with DNA "evidence" or FBI claims of any kind whatsoever?

Dutschke was then arrested and indicted. Although he pleaded not guilty, nothing was heard from Dutschke or his appointed lawyer for a long time. Neither Dutschke or his attorney refuted the evidence or any of the other newly alleged claims that seemed to slowly enlarge even after indictment. In fact, he and his attorney had gone strangely silent.

Eventually the DOJ announced it had secured a plea agreement from Everett Dutschke, yet when he appeared in the media-packed courtroom the following year to submit the agreement, and the judge asked if the prosecutors' accusations were factually correct he answered "not at all". Nevertheless, the plea was accepted and a sentencing hearing was scheduled. During this also packed sentencing hearing, J. Everett Dutschke refused to accept any responsibility for the actual mailing attacks themselves, informed the court and the standing-room-only press that they'd "all had been lied to" then actually read directly from documents which, if one actually listened, proved exactly that. He professed that he was not guilty, despite the signed plea agreement, and numerous times (over 20, in fact) flatly stated that the Mueller FBI knew that not only were all of their claims of evidence false and fraudulent, but that there never was any "ricin" in the first place and that the FBI had known all along that the product of the KC letters mailed by Curtis not Dutschke, was a decoy rendered as harmless as "fertilizer", and the entire prosecution was a sham.

Nevertheless, the judge convicted him anyway, sentenced him to a 25 years prison sentence and the media moved on. That was the official narrative.

Chapter 2

Who is James Everett Dutschke?

That is a multiple part question as it really asks "what is his background?" and "what is it about Dutschke that caused whoever to paint a bull's eye on him?" and "who is whoever?" and "what made him dangerous to who?" and "why did he need to be silenced and disappeared?". This last question is paradoxically both irrelevant and supremely crucial at the same time. The background came easily enough in one sense because many of those records have been made public, and during the 2013-2014 coverage there was a constant flood of revealing interviews; but also not easy in the same sense because a majority of those who were being interviewed by one media broadcaster, newspaper, magazine or another simply did not know him. Countless examples were found, during the years of research and writing of this book, of people who at the time of their interview claimed to know some sort of fact or another about Everett Dutschke that were simply not true or never actually knew him and in many cases, had never even met him yet claimed some sort of knowledge; all this resulted in making background more difficult since unvalidated claims that the press blindly ran had to be independently validated, each one—and there were hundreds of examples.

The "easy" background is compounded further by another social anomaly which is that the vast majority of those who were known and verified to have been closely associated or even loosely associated with him directly, seemed reluctant to talk. Some of those profess an unidentifiable and still persistent fear, as if they've been told not to (and even expressed that explicitly, "I don't think I should say".) Some of those who were actually close enough to know him remained muted by suspicion of any questions, even after all this time. And some express that it was impossible to know him.

Indeed there was revealed an odd phenomenon—the closer one was with Dutschke, the more determined they are not to talk; yet the further away an interviewee was from him, the more they are willing to prattle on in their own opinion of someone they barely knew or, in some cases, did not know at all. This means that the only easy background comes from established court or government records, and was quickly compiled. The rest, which is what reveals the true underlying issues behind the remaining questions, were developed over the years. A lot of time and effort over more than four years resulted in what can be printed here and some which cannot be—and even then there are still FOIA, questionnaires and interviews outstanding and probably many more years of deep digging still wouldn't uncover the rest including the rest of what is relevant and it is the author's thinking that, in this case, it is almost all relevant and practically from birth.

Court records and interviews with Dutschke's mother tell us that Dutschke was born in the dawn of the 1970's. Newspapers and social media posts claim Everett attended elementary school in Texas, Florida and in Mississippi, in schools both private and public. In fact, a newspaper from Palatka, Florida ran a 2013 story that he was a student there, as did a newspaper in Meridian, Mississippi. As it turns out, all of them are true. Everett as a child moved around more than most, so it's difficult to find anyone who got close to him until he settled into the Meridian, Mississippi outskirts where some even still had school and college yearbooks with him in it. Teachers almost all remember him and described him as "bright" and "intelligent". One elementary teacher, now retired, recalls him in the "gifted" program as early as 1980, just before such programs became mainstream, and one other teacher who taught him in his later, high school years called him "troubled" following the death of someone close to him. The most curious description by a former teacher expressed that, "It was like he didn't want to be bothered with us," implying that education, at least in the way that it was delivered, was extraneous; and this was at an early age. His overachiever friends recall that he never acted like a kid, did not enjoy "kiddie" things, which he found patronizing. In other words, he did not seem to want or have a childhood so much as a very early on-set adulthood. He would rather spend the time with adults in an adult world than be insulted by surrounding himself with child-centered activities, entertainment or conversations. Even his peers at church were the adults, often the older, greyer members, over the church kids. There were two exceptions to this—a boy named Van and a girl named Regina.

From third grade until Everett's junior year in high school, Van was the one person he let close. As friends recall, that was the one person who could make Everett laugh and the only person Everett would "cut-loose" and goof off with, showing that this part of Everett *did* exist. Van was among the very few that saw it. The relevance of this could be that this may have been part of the "troubled," the later high school teacher remembers, as Everett was devastated when his closest friend Van, was killed in an auto accident by a train. The other reason Everett was never particularly child-like is because he was raised early on (and lived his life) under dojo discipline. In fact, Van and he started karate classes together. It is important to note here, that in the 70s and 80s, American Karate dojos were serious business and not the family-friendly kid-hospitable system that developed in the 90s and continues. A dojo at that time in America was not a place for frolic. Training then, not as organised and systematic as today, was almost hostile to even its own students and attrition rates were incredibly high, but that's just how it was. Serious business and serious training. Floors weren't padded, neither were hands or feet. Air conditioning or heat in the winter was considered "soft", and if a child was in the class, was never treated like a child and had to do the same as everyone else, since a majority of the students, in 70s and 80s America, were young adult or older (16 to 60) not age 7 or 9. This fit Everett mentally, from the start, so it is no wonder why he never stopped training, even decades later. This becomes relevant since it actually becomes part of the path that led Everett eventually to the later moral hazards of dangerous politically-charged terrains.

A commonality amongst all those still alive who knew him either in childhood or adulthood is the feeling that no matter how close their daily proximity, no one was ever really allowed close. Some recall a high-school sweetheart, Polly, who was able to get within his protective barriers but his adoration for even her was not matched with an equal level of confidence or trust. There is more than a suggestion from most everyone that his attentions were primarily focused on the disciplines of martial arts or music. Even as far back as elementary school, those who met him remember him, but responses range from characterising him as aloof and distant to intense. No one described him as friendly or gregorius and a few (though not those who were close to him) referred to him as arrogant, one going so far as to say "he seemed like he'd get frustrated that everyone else was stupid".

Also, as a high school Junior, Everett began working in radio broadcasting, a career he kept coming back to. This sustained him even through his college years as he attended Livingston University on various scholarships, one of which he'd have to pay back to a hospital in Meridian that helped pay for his tuition, all this while still working at a radio station and teaching at a local Taekwondo dojang (the Korean word for dojo) and even raising a newborn son with his university sweetheart, a beautiful redhead who was simultaneously paying the same hospital back the same scholarship as a neonatal (NICU) nurse.

As Barbara advanced in her NICU career, Dutschke seemed to stall in his, in a telemetry (cardiac patients) unit. In a dramatic change he began teaching Taekwondo full-time, leaving both the hospital and radio behind. Business records show that he opened his own commercial dojang with an absent partner in Hattiesburg, Mississippi after his grandmother gave him $5,000. 1994 gave him an opportunity and a daughter. His wife Barbara sought out a newer, bigger opportunity in Hattiesburg but did not move right away. In the meantime—Hattiesburg Taekwondo Plus grew from 0 students to over 130, surpassing even his instructor and business partner's Meridian location.

In 1996, Everett was by all accounts, full steam ahead and established and began making plans to buy out his partner's 70%. He became part of the 1996 pre-Olympic Training committee and this was the first year that Taekwondo would be featured in the Olympics, not a medal sport, but an exhibition sport. If all went well, Taekwondo would become an Olympic sport permanently (which it did). At the same time, disagreements with his partner, who began demanding more and faster money in the buyout, began to escalate as Barbara found her way to reunite the family in Hattiesburg taking a NICU position at the hospital there, just as the Olympics were happening in Atlanta (as well as the Atlanta bombings and the United States Department of Justice wrongful persecution and destruction of Richard Jewell, the wrong man). 1996 was a busy year, following a US military bombing in Riyadh, the beginning of the trial of Timothy McVeigh for the Oklahoma City bombing, the targeting of Americans in Saudi Arabia at Khobar Towers, two very public convictions in the Clinton Whitewater scheme as the American DOJ waged an 8 day war, reminiscent of Waco, against its own citizens, on the Freemen in Montana. It was against this backdrop that Everett was again presented with an offer to serve his country, having gone through extensive testing years before only to ultimately decline; but this time was not an offer from the Air Force, as before, but in the intelligence profession. On this whim he applied, interviewed and the security investigation began. But things were going well and he knew he couldn't do two things at once. He decided during the prolonged clearance process that he would, if called back, likely decline.

Life, however, had other ideas.

Upon his return from Atlanta, his relationship with his money-peckish partner took a turn for the worse when he demanded of Everett that he immediately buy him out, which Everett lacked the funds to do. Exerting his majority stake, Everett's partner ousted him and denegrated him, taking over the school that Everett had built from scratch and never even bothered to return the $5,000 investment money given to Everett by his "Nana" as a startup. The partner almost immediately and illegally sold the business to a Tuscaloosa senior-level instructor. Everett had been betrayed by his partner who stole his students, his business, his future and his Nana's (June Chewning) money. He kept the book keeper's records, stock equity statements, financial statements and even the original cashed check his Nana had returned to him as a reminder of the betrayal, that someone he'd trusted so much could violate that trust. He vowed to never let it happen again, even as he returned to radio where he quickly found himself at the top of his profession. Indeed, 1997 records show that it was Dutschke that won "best of show" and numerous "gold" Awards by the Association of Broadcasters. However this wave crashed onto a shore of further misfortune as Everett's wife, who had twice won him from another woman decided that she, too would expel him. Meanwhile, the security clearance from 1996 now complete, Everett sought a deferment hoping he could ride out life's turbulence and advance his radio career further, but the opposite happened and he finally capitulated to the idea that his star had burned out and the best option was to rebuild his life surrounded by the invisible unknown who prided themselves on hiring only the nation's best and brightest, albeit at the time when the Central Intelligence Agency's recruitment was at an all-time low.

Class 97D was very small, especially by today's standards when the CIA receives 50,000 applications a year. The Directorate of Operations (now called Clandestine Services) was the smallest it had ever been and was comprised of a much wider spectrum of personalities than the Directorate of Intelligence's mixture of hyper-intellectuals with Masters and PHDs. The Directorate of Operations recruits, though all extremely intelligent and pedigreed in their own right, seemed rag-tag compared to the DI analysis, some of whom were family legacy. The D.O., however, had special plans for 97D, and more than half of the class of just a few dozen were educated in the medical field like Dutschke, though in various disciplines.

There is a feeling upon beginning a career in CIA, especially during the two-week initial orientation where all the recruits are together surrounded by the elite, when one says "How the hell did I get here? There must have been some mistake." But after a while of working in the intelligence profession surrounded by co-workers, that phrase morphs into, "How the hell did *these* people get here? There must have been some mistake."

Nevertheless, once orientation and interim Report Officer desk assignments were over, the next nine months or so to Everett probably seemed just like black belt camp; only much longer and loaded with more activities like "Crash and Bang," (stealing, driving and literally crashing cars), and language classes (the more intensive language training comes later), navigation, survival, communication, jump school, maritime, self-defence, firearms and the most important The Recruitment Cycle.

Recruitment training, which teaches case officers how to make and development agents, is another name for "Making friends and getting them to do what you want." Though this was never Dutschke's preferred training, it was instilled in him that "everyone has a price" and "everyone has an Achilles heel." All one has to do is find it and leverage it. Recruitment was a 'critical' element, which means it must be passed, unlike some of the other elements where a recruit could get one, perhaps two lesters and still make it past the next scheduled "Murder Board" (such as a lester in maritime).

The thing about CIA training, especially when followed by work in the field, is that it changes you; changes the way you think. This is true of all intelligence services worldwide—you "think" a certain way and that becomes permanent. You will never again think like other people. You become like a GPS that has taken a wrong turn and is always "Recalculating." That isn't to say intelligence officers are somehow "scarred for life", or that they are somehow unstable, but spies of all kinds, and all fields, and all countries have the highest divorce rate of any profession (including, most likely, prostitutes) and will never be normal. This is doubly so as a Case Officer (a spy "in the field"). And that effect is permanent. Even though the average career-span of a Case Officer is five years (often less), and those effects, this idiom of thought, lingers. To this day, it is likely that if anyone asks Dutschke the simple innocuous question "What's up?", he would likely think "Why? Who wants to know?." Or if someone asks, "How's it going?" his thought would be instinctively "Why? Who do you report to?"

Nevertheless, as some of the graduates of 1999 chose their preferences of foreign divisions Dutschke finessed a way to not jump into the "friend making business" and into the more technical embedding as he learned from, and was surrounded by, the best of the best of the persuaders of whom Dutschke later wrote "The best CIA officers, some of my friends, could convince someone to chew his own arm off".

Whether he lacked the stomach or the confidence for recruitment, or both, does not matter. In Everett's mind, there was still as much value in SIGINT as in HUMINT and he followed that interest. As he put it so in one interview years later, "We are all awash in a sea of waves. Swimming through frequencies. You can't see them or feel them, but they are there. Tides of them by the hundreds all the time and each one has a meaning, purpose sometimes in multiples. More and more these are becoming digital...ones and zeros all around us, through us. There are more ones and zeros going past you and straight through you right now than there are cells in your body. And although they are invisible, with the right tools, the right net, you can catch them, every single one and match them and make sense out of them. You each do it every day, to some extent every time you turn on your radio or your cell phone, but that's just a couple, out of thousands. And those thousands are all tangled up and multiplied and compressed from thousands more. Untangling it all and labeling it all is an impossibility, but we do it anyway. We do the impossible and then we make sure no one knows we just did the impossible."

Dutschke's direction led him to work closely with the Directorate of Science and Technology and various private contracted companies that could aid him in sorting out the invisible ether to snatch from it then make sense of those ones and zeros, including creatively intercepting microwave transmissions (not as simple as it sounds), satellite KU and Ka band, eventually with the assistance of brilliant technical engineering staff of the DST, software engineers of the Israeli 8200 and a few private contacts, developing a method of identifying by signal properties every single satellite transmitting anything back to Earth, now commonplace. Digging through air like an archaeologist searching for treasure, he mapped out the entire footprint over the Middle East of Inmarsat1 and set up capture and relay stations of every Inmarsat spot beam; stole line-of-sight microwaves, then uplinked to friendly geo–stationary birds the embedded and multiplexed transmissions in compressed files as burst and even mapped out 802.11/g wireless Wi-Fi long before it gained widespread use in the United States, sometimes operating on US soil in places like Dearborn, Michigan; aided in interfaces in the construction of a massive 40 ft satellite dish at Ramstein, Germany working alongside the professionals at

General Atomic Technologies Corp; and aided in the monitoring of a new Chinese uplink centre bullied onto Kiribati soil with an FSP agent.

CIA, at the time, valued recruitment of foreign agents highest. And although Dutschke's Bird-Dog team (signal sniffers) would have then been useful, it still does not carry the same prestige as the uber-salesmanship of recruitment of assets. Case Officers generally feel that Technical Officers are just "too chicken shit" to deal with people, thus a support role is often considered a relegation. However, Technical Officers often have a recruitment advantage with certain types of people who also work in certain technical fields because they can speak the common language of scientific interest, as with employees of foreign telecoms and events when launching their own satellites, usually from Kazakhstan. It is easier for like-minded people to "make friends" (recruit agent assets), though that sometimes works both ways. These skills and technologies were taught to field Case Officers as well as other skills such as how to tap into a fibre optic line with little more than a paperclip and parts from a DVD player. But because Case Officers don't pay attention to things like that, those lessons were pointless—especially since if they wanted something like that done and their station or division technical officer didn't feel confident that he (or the support officer) could handle it, they could just call in the bird dogs to do it, (why bother cleaning your dishes when you can just call the maid). And they did. The Near East Division, the Subsaharan division and others. A lot of this type of service was needed in Liberia and in Mumbai which is essentially the world's fibre optic hub. Practically every communication in that hemisphere is distributed out from Mumbai (just like MAE-West and MAE-East is on the Western Hemisphere).

When not TDY, Everett found himself visiting Tupelo, Mississippi as much as he could make time for, as that was the nearest dojang to Meridian with an instructor that was high enough rank to train him. This is relevant because it was during these visits when he met who would later become his second wife and considered opening his own business. One would be tempted to ask, "How is this the least bit relevant to anything that happened in 2013?"

On the surface, it is not relevant at all. It is only when one searches through the entire history and searches through thousands of other seemingly irrelevant known documents and events that a tiny piece buried here and there can be assembled into a picture that when reviewed, leads to answers that are far from speculative. One who is trained to think like a cryptographer can spot these individual trace marks scattered and varied over a decade-and-a-half that, these random-appearing dots are connecting, do not seem so random but create a clear mosaic that is complete with names, dates, times and even likely motives. Presented by a Unit 8200 officer highly skilled and trained in pattern recognition, as well as actual Mensa associate of Dutschke himself, have assembled from the known and recorded evidence and interviews all that is needed to arrange an unabridged cogent thesis of events, supported by known historical evidence, from the mist. Great care has been taken and years of interviews and reinterviews sometimes, with people afraid to talk, to ensure that there is little left for interpretation and that the total picture is not circumstantial, although it may appear so if one ignores any one data point. In this, all the relevant data points must be visible—which is to say that one must take an epic "10,000 metre view" to see that clear connection. It is almost easier to work backwards, from the conclusion, to see the individual data points in much the way that dot-painting, pointillism portraits are made. Zoom in too far, and all you see is a dot, maybe two, but no picture until you pull back from it. However, this is to be the careful reassembly of all the dots, all the data points. This book puts you in the head of the dot-painter, creating a yet unseen image one dot at a time, instead of the head of a viewer of a pointillism masterpiece.

And one critical dot, that on its own it seems irrelevant, is the original format of 97D that, remember, was loaded with not merely "America's best and brightest" but who were medical professionals as well. Though that dot was made in 1997, it later leads to the events of 2013. Another seemingly disjointed dot was the conjectures of Everett's associations with his own network of both martial artists and International Mensa members and his travels within Israel and Mumbai, leading to known encounters cooperating with agents of 8200 (who were more than just agents of 8200) but in particular meeting with and becoming friends with a former Cesarea officer whose newer cover was that of an American insurance agent (common).

While these events, these dots, were long before 2013, are the first small stones on the labyrinthine road leading there and the common element in the pavement of that road is a name you will need to remember for the rest of this book. *Rabita Trust*. This is a name no one has ever heard of, certainly not the common American, but in some ways, Rabita Trust is the very glue holding this pavement together, even when the individuals involved, each an important dot, have no idea that of the role played by either themselves or Rabita Trust.

To get to Rabita Trust from CIA recruitment of 1998/1997 one has to relive one of America's most memorable tragedies. The terror attacks of 9/11. That's the day that the CIA began to change when 19 hijackers (15 of them Saudi) stirred America's anger. By July of 2002 America had gone through its own PTSD cycle. It had experienced its collective shock, then grief, but now had settled into a new stage...America was feeling vengeful.

And the CIA was actually feeling the scorning fingers of blame from the events of previous years. Some even blame the CIA for "missing the signs", mostly an unjustified attack, since any significant failure was that of the American FBI. There was a psychological need, on a visceral level, for the CIA to somehow redeem itself, a social/political need to justify its existence.

Any specialised teams (GRS & SAD) and practically any C/O with a military background was ripped from what and whereever duty they were individually serving and taken to the field (such as Afghanistan) to lay the groundwork for the DOD to later arrive and hunt down anyone who can make America feel better, feeding their vengeance militarily. Regular CIA business had not only been put on hold, but the primary view of the mission seemed to become holding the DOD's hand. At any rate, the bird dogs, stripped of personnel, were forced into disbandment, so history tells us.

But here is where public and known history goes seriously black. The next dot is so difficult to find that one almost would need special lenses to see it. It was so buried and so clandestine that no one involved is willing to overtly or even covertly discuss. Even some of the records that once revealed this dot, this data point, once already made public through previous disclosures and court documents have entirely vanished even after discovery. Some court documents suddenly sealed and some, previously seen, vanished. An entire section of a completely declassified document remains heavily redacted, even AFTER "declassification," and that was the version that was made public. Some of this cloaked information was obtained from a former congressman's former staffer and from a different former congressman with U.S. State Department connections, some from former INR staff (U.S. State Department's analytical wing) and some from current NSC staff. Because it is of a CIA led operation, it is curious that far fewer people at CIA know of the operation than those connected to the State Department. This is the testament to multiple things. First—the US State Department, from top down, was very interested in the clandestine operation, though not until much later. Second—someone in the State Department had to begin digging to find any details on any operation they had no business knowing about. Third—the fact that no one in CIA would talk about it (FOIAs "neither confirm nor deny"), yet, since those connected with the Department of State at the highest level would (albeit off-the-record), is confirmation that CIA is far better at compartmentalization than the Department of State, which was "leaky." One thing is certain, not the Department of State, nor anyone else outside of CIA (save four other people) was ever supposed to have any knowledge whatsoever of the event. Because the actual name of "Operation Vengeance," remains unknown, if it ever even had a name, the authors will refer to it herein as "Operation Vengeance" as that describes its essence. Keep in mind as you read the rest of the book that the name "Operation Vengeance" is an entirely made-up name. And unless there is further declassification (of an assignment that never officially happened), or unless someone talks (which is unlikely), then the true name, as well as the details and specifics of how "Operation Vengeance" occurred will remain unknown.

Within a month of the September 11th attacks, it was a CIA deep investigation that had identified where some of the financial support for the

Al-Qaeda affiliated hijackers came from. One of the original founders of Al-Qaeda and a close associate of Osama bin Laden (UBL) was a man named Wael Hamza Jalaiden (WHJ). WHJ headed a funding channel for Al-Qaeda operations named Rabita Trust. Rabita Trust would be filled with operational cash by funnelers who would gather money from supporters and surreptitiously steer it to Rabita Trust which then distributed operational fundings, or to the Institute of Muslim Minority Affairs (IMMA), the World Muslim League's propaganda wing. The Institute of Muslim Minority Affairs (IMMA) is described to us by Andrew C. McCarthy as a primary tool "for the propagation of Islamic Supremacy," a key creed of Al-Qaeda (and WHJ and UBL). One of those "funnelers" and founders of Rabita Trust and its promotional sister, IMMA, was a man named Abdulla Omar Naseef who had developed close ties with UBL as far back as the 80s. Abdulla Omar Naseef was vice president of a major university, so the money he collected and steered to IMMA Rabita Trust came from his prestigious friends. Although Naseef was successful, his ability to be the benefactor to IMMA and Rabita Trust wasn't the result of his own salary. The coffers of IMMA and Rabita Trust (millions) came in part from three men. Those three men were partially responsible for the funding of IMMA and Rabita Trust, an operational fund for Al-Qaeda, which included the 9/11 attacks. Remember the name WHJ, Naseef and one other—Syed Abedin, the man who was brought in by UBL associate Naseef to run IMMA. The names of the three men:

They were the men who helped pay for the events which triggered America's Vengeance and led to the CIA backed "Operation Vengeance." Of all the above names, only one of them change, the man who was the benefactor to Rabita Trust and IMMA. Naseef, needed a replacement for Syed Abedin when his friend Abedin died. So Naseef, replaced Syed Abedin with Saleha Abedin (Syed's widow) who continued to advocate for Muslim extremist and continued to depend on her benefactor, including the same very wealthy three men Naseef collected from.

Who were those three men? Who were the three who helped pay for 9/11? *This* is where the blackout begins, and these three men, funders of IMMA and Rabita Trust, are key—so why the blackout? These three men, it was quickly discovered, were all high government officials in the ███ government.

- ███ ███ ███ ███ ███ ███-███ was the ███ of ███ ███

But that was only the half of it; all three men were also members of the ███ ███ family. If there is ANY family on the planet that one should never cross it's this family. However, that is exactly what the six-person team of "Operation Vengeance" was about to do. Revenge must be doled out, and it must look like natural causes if possible. Although Operation Vengeance and its results and aftermath have been written about and eluded to elsewhere, this will likely be the first book to name the names. Names that were not known by anyone until 2011 and the conditions under which the names were discovered were sinister.

However, Operation Vengeance, which took place in July of 2002, after only minimal preparation, was not a military mission, and this was prior to any DOD operation in nearby Iraq, as that war had not yet started. This was all about payback and retribution with only three targets, and that is what burned in the specialized team, made (in part) of members of 97D, medically trained CIA officers and their support. Though there were only six members of Operation Vengeance, there were several assets that they had been recruited in ███ ███, mostly hospital staff, to ensure it went according to plan. The end result is that one of the three related financiers who was undergoing a routine appendectomy, which is normally a simple outpatient procedure without any complications, suddenly developed inexplicable complications and died within three days in one of the most ultra-modern hospitals in the world. Simultaneously, the second family member also developed mystifying symptoms, then random organ failure. Within three days, he too, was dead and the baffled medical examiner's post-mortem diagnosis said simply "he died of thirst," which is not even an actual diagnosis and practically unheard of. The third family member was in a 'sudden car accident' and was pronounced dead at the scene. All three men, all within just a few days. Al Jazeera and a few world-wide newspapers reported the coincidental deaths, including a few leading American news outlets. Three people, same city, same extended family and all in a very dangerous place. Soldiers could not have done it, but a team of six people had held the three men to account on a dangerous and officially unsanctioned operation for the sole purpose of…payback. For it to be completely successful, it had to all be timed perfectly. It almost was. Almost. Things didn't go exactly according to plan and there was no safe exit—one member was trapped inside the hospital, put on lockdown and under constant search. For three days (rumour has it at the bottom of a ventilation and lift shaft), hiding until he felt it was safe; emerged on day four, weak and expecting to be shot, into the moonlight. From a nearby asset's apartment he violated protocol by using unsecured communications and couriers to make contact with the remainder of his team who had secured themselves into similar temporary safety. The highways out of the city where shut down or were being watched and random-search and some house-to-house searches had begun, so it was a matter of time before they would all be caught, yet there were no viable roads out of the city, out of the country. The separated team member contacted a friend of his in ███ ███ Iraq and asked for his help. This man's name was Sa'ayd Al-Sayidi, who made a back-door arrangement for the American team, stuck in ██████ to extricate themselves if they could all meet up at the right time and place, the only problem being that it was very near the same hospital. Within hours, at nearly 2 A.M., an air-ambulance lifted off the pad without its usual pilot and without authorization. This helicopter was a Eurocopter 350 and was not properly flight-checked for a journey, at low altitude, of nearly 700 miles. The roads to ██████ and ████████ may have been closed but the Operation Vengeance team did not need the roads anymore, piloted (barely) by an unqualified team member.

At this point, it is worth interjecting that under normal circumstances, one wouldn't need to use his own network for an emergency extraction. Under normal circumstances, one would contact the CIA's Chief of Station who would follow a PACE solution whether for his own people or for a CT. However, this was not the *normal* circumstances. The team had been told "under NO circumstances are you to contact the COS here." The COS at the time was a man named ███ ██████. This caveat meant several things, one of which was that ██████ had not been briefed on the operation.

This is almost entirely unheard-of! What is it that could possibly be that would cause the highest (small handful) of CIA to not trust ██████ with one of the most crucial ops in his purview? Why would they choose not to trust the COS to know in advance? Perhaps it was because ██████, had converted to Islam. Perhaps it was some other reason which would give ██████ plausible deniability in the matter. Regardless, the team was on their own and kismet was not yet finished with them. Perhaps the Eurocopter AS-350 was not designed as well as advertised. Perhaps the particular aircraft had seen its better days. Either way, the stolen helicopter did not make it, and despite two makeshift refuelings, it went down. It may be that the crash happened because something that *could be* constantly operated for 6 hours plus does *not* mean it *should be* operated for 6 hours plus. But the result was not good, and one team member had already had a very bad four days.

What was reported in the news at the time was that a small number of "US servicemen were killed in a helicopter crash in Jordan during a routine training flight from Israel," a passing story.

That report is not quite how or what happened.

First off, "servicemen" is misleading. Not a single member of the team was active DOD at the time. Second, no one in the crash died, they just probably thought they had. Third, they weren't flying from Israel. Fourth, there was nothing "routine" about it. And it was definitely NOT a "training exercise" as reported. And fifth, it is not entirely clear, and to this day no one can state whether or not the team even made it all the way into Jordan.

18

Here is what *is* known (as gathered many years later, 2011, from insurance records and hospital records when the 2011 State Department began unlawfully digging into this July 2002 event): six John Does were soon admitted to Ramstein. One of those six had a small skull fracture and his scalp was stapled shut, a broken right hand, right thumb, right big toe, right ankle, left lower rib, right fibula and nose. He was unsure he'd ever be able to walk again. While there, he asked questions of attending medical staff while still under the influence of anesthesia from the ORIF surgeries. Questions the medical staff was not even cleared to hear, much less answer, though the staff was likely all Air Force. All six were quarantined from everyone else in the hospital until their release, four months later.

They were beat up. They were broken. But somehow, the vengeance that was doled out, that Americans were never going to find out about, was supposed to make Americans feel better. The CIA's briefer to the president was a man named Michael Morell. Remember this name.

If Operation Vengeance was what it looked to be, then it both "took care of" a problem (for two countries) and created a problem at the same time. It took care of or fixed a problem in three ways. One: it eliminated three major financiers of Naseef who were the benefactor of IMMA and Rabita Trust, crippling the propaganda of Al-Qaeda and removing a source of operational income. Two: it sent a hell of a message to other would-be funders AND to Naseef himself. Three: the ▇▇ family itself, including ▇▇ ▇▇, was embarrassed to have not just one but three members within their own ranks that may have aided in the 9/11 attacks on the Americans and even feared that Islam had now "been publicly hijacked" by the crazed Jihad-types (certainly it was the jihadis that got all the attention and there was nothing the average Muslim could do to stop the louder extremists). Indeed it had been speculated that members of the ▇▇ ▇▇ family, even with ▇▇s knowledge and blessing, aided in the logistics of Operation Vengeance and might have even been the ones to support that ▇▇ ▇▇ not to be informed until afterwards. However Operation Vengeance created a problem as well: the three financiers were not just family members, they were also government officials. By definition, an act of assassination, thus illegal.

In 1981, President Ronald Reagan issued amended execution order 12333—"no person employed by or acting on the behalf of the US government shall engage in or conspire to engage in assassinations."

In fact, this is (currently) part of CIA Charter. Listed as executive order 13284, section 2.11 is "prohibition on assassination" and is covered under 50 USC§3001. However that executive order was not officially entered into registry (68 Fed Reg 4077) until 6 months later (January 23rd 2003) And not codified into statutory law until the Intelligence Reform Act of 2004.

And an illegality is still an illegality. Some future Department of Justice wallopers could later decide it would be the grounds to prosecute any known team members. All it would take is one corrupt or unethical FBI agent or DOJ prosecutor (and they are all corrupt and unethical). Nor is this speculative. In fact, the Clinton Administration FBI (Janet Reno—AG), had actually arrested a noted CIA C/O Bob Baer in 1995 and accused Baer of "Crossing Interstate borders to commit murder, to wit—Saddam Hussein." So there is, in fact, an actual history of FBI LEOs going after a CIA officer for that very thing.

Now if Operation Vengeance had been a military operation, (which it could not be; this was not the "drop a bomb" or "shoot a bunch of guns at people" kind of thing). Then, the solution to the problem would be—just label the targets as "enemy combatants." That solution usually results in the target being eliminated in an explosive ball of fire. And indeed, five months prior to July of 2002, DOD had begun such a tactic, arming predator drones to accomplish this. Then it isn't called "assassination" and it is almost celebrated.

However, Operation Vengeance was *not* DOD. The only solution for the team was to "make sure it doesn't look like an assassination." This translates, literally, to "however you do it, leave no trace."

Although every CIA CST goes through "poison school," it is a short course and the American public has always been led to believe that such a thing is exclusively the domain of the Russians. It is *not* inconceivable, however, to determine that the class of 97D was primarily medical professionals for a reason, that the CIA wanted a better working understanding and a better operational understanding of how to utilise a person's extensive medical knowledge. (If you want to have someone around who can fix cars, you hire a mechanic, not a painter or a cop.)

This created problems for Dutschke. Because now he had done it or seen it done. He returned, off crutches but still using a cane to walk. A fifteen year old, two-seater Fiero that he'd purchased in D.C. was not an ideal automobile for someone with mobility problems. And he still wanted and needed to continue training even as he considered making his injury hiatus permanent.

During his recovery, records show he opened a business of his own, and this time was not merely a front to be used by the Central Cover Office. This time it was to be for real, which meant he'd chosen a location to be permanent. He chose Tupelo. This same city where he met a woman earlier that summer and soon they'd moved in together; not in his tiny, previous side street apartment, but a rented house where they planned a future together and even wed. His company, not surprisingly, started from scratch, was a satellite company that provided a high-speed hybrid (Broadband downlink/dial-up Uplink) developed with former associates in the Directorate of Science and Technology (DS&T) leasing unused satellite bandwidth from another company. In 2002, the vast majority of ISPs were dial up, so all Everett needed to do, in his mind, was reach those users. The equipment and marketing cost to do so required him using a cooperative of funds received from Dish Network and Wireless One (being liquidated by the failing giant Mississippi Telecom company WorldCom) and Dutschke launched eLocity.

On the surface, eLocity seemed like the perfect DST product for a marketplace that was ripe to begin switching from dial-up to high-speed.

It sounds innovative. And in his mind, it probably was. But at a satellite industry event in Hollywood, Florida, Dutschke met with billionaires Charlie Ergan (Dish Network) and Mark Cuban (who had launched and sold HD Net). While the meeting seemed to be pleasant, Everett came away from that Summit with the realisation that he had made catastrophic mistakes. Mistakes that would cost him. Ergan's people showed him their new product in partnership with Echosphere—a satellite broadband that was a two-way system; both uplink and downlink. Cuban informed him that DirecTV was also releasing a two-way system ("Direct PC") with Hughes and reminded Dutschke that they already had an existing customer base to market to... cheaply, something Dutschke did not have. What Dutschke DID have was overly ambitious plans, three offices (Tupelo, Laurel and Huntsville), a growing staff and overhead, but a product that would be obsolete in two years because of his disastrous decision to opt for an internally installed satellite modem and a hybrid (downlink only) system that still needed dial-up for sending. While Dutschke's choice to develop an "expansion card" type satellite modem might have been based on the idea that fewer external boxes made for a "cleaner" looking install, it was disastrous since once installed, no other computer could use it (now high-speed modem boxes are ubiquitous, making Cuban right). And the one-way hybrid system required a proxy server and would soon be antiquitated by the broadband two-way systems on the horizon. Though Dutschke's decision to develop the one-way hybrid system was based on his low entry cost, since he only paid via contract lease for the amount of bandwidth actually used, it was clear he was taking the quick and easy way.

When a business owner or CEO makes a mistake, it affects everyone. A CEO that makes a catastrophically bad decision is putting everyone at risk, letting everyone down. His own family, his employees, their families, the office workers, sales people, all the businesses, landlords and others, that service that business and even any existing customers. A CEO's failure jeopardizes everyone, including the children being raised by the parents who work and believe in the company. When an employee makes a mistake, it is a ripple that can be smoothed out. It can be fixed. But when a CEO makes a mistake, he has failed everyone, and there is no "do-over." So Dutschke's decisions were all on him, and would lead to a dog's breakfast of events that gave eLocity a limited lifespan if he could not correct the problems. But to fix the problem he needed an infusion of cash.

Although he was now married to the daughter of a multi-millionaire financier, there was absolutely no way he would allow his new father-in-law into any part of his life or business. So he traded in his blue card for a green one, as the intelligence world was growing leaps and bounds through contracting and began a contract as a training T/O hoping to develop new bird dog teams. But the CIA was becoming less and less reliant on SIGINT, almost exclusively NSA territory now as NSA director Michael Hayden was quickly growing his agency, the NSA, from a support agency to an out-of-control, monstrosity. During the period of time that Hayden was making himself the most powerful man in the world. CIA almost became but an errand boy for NSA and DOD; it certainly had much less use for signal interception of its own accord, like it used to. Plus everything was moving rapidly to fibre optics so there were not as many transmissions that needed sniffing out. Specialised bird dog teams (and the advanced skills of it) were simply not needed and companies like SWS and Airmax, with their highly advanced technology, all wrapped up in suitcase-sized units, begin seeing their field equipment just collect dust. With diminishing sales came a diminishing need for training and Dutschke failed to get enough money in time to rescue eLocity, then sold to a company in Birmingham (later sold to Wild Blue, then to a few others). The forced sale and loss of three offices and every single employee stressed his marriage to his second wife. On top of all that, police reports reveal that one of his office managers had been embezzling tens of thousands of dollars from him, a woman he trusted to handle things when he was away and what's worse he had been blaming the revenue shortage on a sales manager, Manuel, instead; who might well have been the only honest employee in his organisation.

2003 might have been a year of his physical recovery, but it laid the groundwork for 2004 and his fall from grace; which, just like the last one (1996 to 1997) resulted in divorce. But before 2003 was over, he began to be ensnared by yet another woman. Janet was catching Dutschke on the rebound and it seemed to be the historical consensus that he could never say "no" to beautiful women, something which no doubt, might have troubled all his previous relationships; so there was no way in which he could have resisted Janet's immaculate Russian face, even before the ink was dry on his divorce from his second. Janet found him an inspiring figure and latched on, even as Dutschke was in the process of losing it all. She did not mind or question Everett's absences, often prolonged. As it turns out, she too, was in a "rebuilding" phase. Even though their lives were separate, they would find a way to rebuild together. Upon returning from an extended contract assignment he made a decision to make a new life with Janet concrete instead of migrating to a different city, as he was want to do. He moved into a new house and started a new business, the kind of business that required physical geographical presence (or at least looks like it). A newspaper. This suggests he intended to put down roots and try for a normal life. Janet even helped create the illusion of "normal" by moving into the new house with him, though, perhaps showing her incertitude over either him, herself or them together, she actually held onto her own apartment at the same time—maybe a "just in case" move subject to whether or not the two of them could make a go of it in Tupelo, Mississippi.

CIA requires that anyone staying with you for longer than a certain period (days not months) requires a background check. The problem is that getting someone cleared to actually live with you actually takes quite a while. Because both CIA and USIS were particularly lax about these things, no one bothered to follow those protocols anymore (CIA took forever and USIS was fudging numbers and files even despite that this was a post 9/11 world), certainly not for a T/O and most definitely there would be no rush or sense of urgency for a green-badger. So Dutschke's reporting of his now live-in girlfriend would not have gotten approval for up to 18 months, which is why he moved her in anyway and without approval.

Owning and running a newspaper sounds rather boring and tedious, but Everett probably welcomed the idea of boring and tedious. He was probably weary of looking over his shoulder, all the time, wondering if someone from the other side of the planet was coming for him. A lack of too much excitement probably suited him well. Irregular contracts floated the newspaper's income as Dutschke's hired sales people, he found, were generally not consistent or reliable. A voiced frustration was that hiring in Tupelo is not like hiring anywhere else. Elsewhere, a person hired for a job actually worked; that is not the case in Tupelo, Mississippi, though no one could ever convince a Tupeloean of it. All are convinced that they are salt-of-the-earth workers, a regional notion that is the furthest from the truth. Having seen workers from around the world, Dutschke knew that Tupeloeans would be shocked to learn that they are the least hard-working and least reliable on not just the planet, but even in the same state. But since there was no changing that truism and no convincing them to be otherwise, because they would never believe it of themselves, he just let them be who they are—a population who would quit the moment they felt like work was too "worky." He supported the lack of advertising with his own income from the odd intelligence contract, supplementing the paper when it needed it.

In 2004, George Tenet, who—despite his own issues—was a DCI that Dutschke and most C/Os respected for at least trying to hold on to the CIA's mission, a man who actually seemed to care about preventing employee "burnout," a man who had done his best to fight the minimisation of the agency relative to the growing monster being created by Michael Hayden at NSA, was replaced.

Though Everett was technically in training during the later part of John Deutch as the DCI, Tenet was really the only DCI that Everett had ever known and had successfully rebuilt and steered the agency from the morass created by Deutch (a Clinton political appointee).

The agency should be run by people who are familiar with every tiny aspect of the agency's mission and never by someone who is a mere political appointee who has zero experience with anything intelligence related, such is the point of view of every qualified person working for every intelligence service in the world. Only in America can someone who has not "come up through the ranks" of the intelligence agency be put in charge of it. Often (too often) a president will appoint someone as Director of Central Intelligence not because he is the most qualified, but because the president wants to ensure that they can use a CIA as a tool to do their bidding, and to control the CIA to ensure there's no political threat and to clean up the president's political messes, keeping him out of trouble.

President Clinton's choice of politician, Deutch, was one such example, Tenet cleaned up Deutch's mess. So who would George W. Bush select as a Tenet replacement? A qualified person who at least went through CIAs two-week orientation ("This, students, is what a classified document looks like and why it is") or some politician? Unfortunately for America, and to Dutschke's now revealed chagrin, George W. Bush appointed a politician. The 7th Floor became staffed with people who had never before generated a classified document, never worked out logistics of an operation, had never learned the recruitment cycle for recruiting an asset and had no idea what the intelligence cycle is. In short, blue badges were issued for people not qualified for even a brown badge. Dutschke was not alone in his knowledge that Porter Goss, skilled former C/O but still a politician, and Dusty Foggo (his deputy) were not qualified to run the motor pool (actually, the woman who DID run the CIA motor pool was one of the most amazing, nice, experienced, adept and capable CIA employees.) Seventh floor vaults should not become the site for "deal making," yet that's what they became. Foggo became the worst employee to roam the "blue highways" since Nora Slotkin, and appointing Goss was the one mistake Bush had made (so far) in his wartime presidency, in Everett's estimation.

Through still sensitive, still classified channels, Everett discovered that a man associated with companies called Radiant, Ntera and World Quest Networks, Inc. (NASDAQ: WQNI) had been funneling money from terrorist associated companies to the election campaign of John Kerry in the 2004 election against George W Bush.

Though "W" later personally wrote thanking Dutschke (which Everett and Janet later framed) nothing was done about the American culprits behind the foreign election tampering scheme except that Robert Farmer (John Kerry's campaign Treasurer) claimed he "returned" the terrorist money (or at least that part which was discovered). The reason there were no real consequences is because a senior-level CIA C/O, Larry Kolb, retired, maintained a different assessment of the intelligence. Kolb complained, though likely with some "coaching" by Robert Farmer, that the meddling and tampering in the United States 2004 presidential election by an actual terror supporting group was some sort of plot masterminded by Karl Rove, a close

24

advisor to the President. This, Dutschke thought, was absurd—the intelligence shows what the intelligence shows because it is real, not because Karl Rove "framed" John Kerry to win some election they were going to win anyway. However, above-deck Kolb had gravitas, Dutschke didn't (except with Bush) and Kolb's theory seemed to be what prevented any consequences. Additionally, it may well be that nothing happened because it was politically inconvenient for the agency since two of the men particularly responsible for the terrorist collusion with the Kerry campaign were also CIA affiliated, one a former known asset named Richard Hirschfield, the other a long-time CIA asset named Bob Sensi who had convinced "The Turk," Engin Yesil, to move money around to help fund their schemes. The other reason there was no fallout is likely because the media was squarely behind their Democrat candidate, John Kerry, thus willing to ignore anything potentially problematic for Kerry. This was an opportunity for the FBI to actually do its job of enforcing the law (start with, campaign contribution violations), yet when the criminal referral was made, they did nothing, likely because Kerry was involved. This showed Dutschke that LEOs will sit on their hands and choose not to prosecute what they don't want to and prosecute only when they wish. Justice in America was not blind. If one had the right political connections (i.e.: John Kerry, Robert Farmer) then you can get away with whatever you wish. The FBI, the same organisation that failed America on 9/11, led by Bob Mueller, practised selective prosecution. The law did not apply equally.

Everett, two years after the cripplng crash, was feeling not only fully recovered but eager to resume training. He resolved to open a Taekwondo dojang again and did so even attempting a "comeback" competitively by the 2005 nationals inching out a first place performance, but he never regained the title of grand champion. As some others in the organisation who were of high enough rank to recall, he lacked the "wind" or the "stamina," some identified, to last longer than one match or even past one minute and was often lectured by the other high ranks on exactly that.

Unlike his previous school in Hattiesburg and Laurel where he tested 130 students regularly every two months, he kept his student assemblage smaller and tested them only every three, still accepting the odd contract and running his growing but still manageable newspaper. Janet had committed herself (as fully as one can commit to Everett—which is, it seems, like grabbing at smoke) and was along for the ride, even joining the class, herself.

His other life had slowed to a trickle, which, again, seemed just fine with him. The agency (which had fewer than 50 new recruits in 1996) was now, and continues, to have 50,000 applicants per year (doctors, lawyers, military and college degrees all) and another 50,000 specialised contractors moving from civie to government and back to civie. It was and continues to be, very well staffed… but with Goss at the helm, was going steadily downhill.

There are indications Everett was still active, opening numerous cover businesses as needed, never intended to become profitable, then closing them when they got burned. Secretary of State records to this day still show 18 corporations on which J. Everett Dutschke was the CEO of the company or was on the corporate board. Some included Airmaxx, Starmaxx, Tri Clean, Aon Marketing, Digital Satellite Telecomm, eLocity, Comm Craft, Aon Publishing, Tupelo Taekwondo Plus, Aon Media Grapevine (a newspaper), Progress (newspaper), Pulse (another newspaper), Aon Biolabs Research Network, Aon State Health Exchange (insurance—a common CIA cover), SMA7 (Secretary of State paperwork lists as vague "consulting"—another common CIA cover), Fastaxx (tax return assistance) and Easy File (another tax return consultancy). The majority of these each had corresponding websites, physical location and mailing address to look or appear authentic. Most however, were only as real as they needed to be until they were "burned' by someone "checking up" on an "employee" and at that point is no good anymore unless someone wishes to try to then make the business legitimate. For example, "Progress" records are wiped so clean its as if it never existed, indicating this "newspaper" was burned quickly. However, "Aon Media" records showed nearly 80 employees; 12 of them share the same first name but different last names. 80 employees would be something that would be notable to anyone who knew Everett, but not only does no one recall him having 80 employees, they insist he worked alone and no one can recall Aon Media. Yet there it is, right there as obvious as the sun in the Secretary of State's records. And that is just Mississippi and only the registered business. There are more in Alabama, Virginia, Massachusetts, West Virginia, Delaware, California, and New York.

Aon Biolabs Research Network is a curious one. Filings indicate that it consulted on the creation of new laboratories and that is it. Tracking down the address of one of the 34 laboratories revealed a farm that leased biodiesel-making equipment from Dutschke and reported its monthly production and use to Dutschke on a website he created, a very streamlined system. This appears to have been a legitimate and clever business that sold what's called "RIN's." In America, these Renewable Energy Certificates (each given a Renewable Identification Number) are bought by (mostly energy) companies in order to get tax credits. At some point some politicians must have successfully sold the legislation in order to punish the "evil" energy companies. Dutschke's primary product of Aon Biolabs Research Network was a bunch of "laboratories" that he never had to operate; in fact the operators paid *him*, for a product they use and a by-product that he then sold on RIN speculation and auction sites in batches, getting paid twice for a lab he never had to operate. Once set-up, it was basically a steady, hands-free income stream practically on auto-pilot. One farmer (sunflowers) suggested that fertilizers and even pesticides were often included in the numbers, though it would be hard to fathom how to include a pesticides, even on an industrial crop-dusting scale, that could qualify—that idea may have been suggested by the former DST friend, Ben Morris.

As to the bulk of the other businesses, however, Dutschke had no intention of working them once they became burned, so they became but a flash in the pan, except for the insurance brokerage. Back in 2004, the Athens Greece Olympics comprised much more than just athletes in each nation's delegation it was also the scene in which ██ ██ had been turned over to the ████████ by the American ██ instead of handing him over to the American LEOs of the FBI as a normal CT operation may have done. ██ ██ was suspected in coordinating the UBL bombing in Riyadh, but he also knew of how the team of Operation Vengeance escaped █████████ and he was so brutally beaten and tortured that he told the █████████ what he thought were the names (covers all) of the 2002 operation and the name of the man who had aided in their escape—the name of Iraqi Sa'ayd Al-Sayidi who, at the very moment, should have been competing for Olympic gold representing his newly liberated country, Iraq. Sa'ayd Al-Sayidi did not win 2004 gold but his new country was proud of him anyway.

Later, at the moment Dutschke was preparing for black belt camp in 2006, the Iraqi National Taekwondo team was on a bus in a small convoy traveling from Sadr City to training camp in Jordan. Though the US military initially offered to escort the team through Anbar province, that escort through that conflicted territory never happened. When the bus did not arrive at training camp like it was supposed to, one of the Jordanian Taekwondo team members called for Haidar Jabbar of the Iraqi team and Jabbar's family assured him that the entire team had gotten on the bus. They called the bus charter company who had lost contact with the driver. The Iraqi team never arrived. The bus had never made it to Jordan.

Al-Sayidi; (the man who had saved Dutschke in 2002) along with the entire Iraqi National Taekwondo team had vanished.

On the other side of the planet, at a later white tablecloth, high level event, Everett was taken aside and shown a photograph of a grey-haired grey-bearded man who had been so badly beaten that he was barely recognisable as a human being. It was a photo of ██ ██ when he had been finally turned over to the American FBI by the █████████. What little there was left of the man would be prosecuted in Virginia claiming that this once ██ asset was also a UBL conspirator, an accusation Dutschke refused to believe as he was also an asset that aided in the Operation Vengeance which targeted the three financiers Naseef used for WHJ's Rabita Trust and Saleha Abedin's IMMA. The update informed Dutschke that because of the "aggressive" interrogation of ██ ██ there was a high confidence that Rabita Trust and IMMA might know at least the cover identities of Operation Vengeance; and that they were at least asking questions about it. The junior Senator of New York, Clinton, seemed to be making simultaneous inquiries as well. The relevance of this concurrence will become apparent later. The briefing C/O, who was taking a "hand-off" from Dutschke at that event and did not seem to fully understand the message she was delivering, stated that most everyone felt that ▇ would be convicted, even if by a "show trial." When Dutschke asked if ▇ had mentioned Sa'ayd Al-Sayidi by name—the answer was "likely." When asked if it had anything to do with Al-Sayidi disappearance—the answer was "I'll have to ask ▇ Devermont keep you posted."

The following year, 2007, Dutschke himself was in a fierce political campaign against a 30-year incumbent of the House of Representatives and on June 14th, his birthday, he received an early morning call to rush to ▇▇▇ immediately to a flash level SCIF. Hours later he was watching a real time live feed of an intelligence asset that was also a ▇▇▇ for Reuters in the inside of a hallway and Imam Ali Hospital in Sadr City. The video showed a massive white bag in the hallway. As they watched live footage, those watching the feed realised what they were seeing. A hodge-podge mix of bones, skulls—some jawless, some with tufts of black hair stuck to it. Dirty t-shirts, pants, sandals and more bones. About 10 hands sifted through the clattering bones as kneeling family members, numbed by their duty, tried to sort out who was who. Dried, decomposed tissue glued some of the parts together.

Others stood behind or around those doing the sifting and hoped to recognise the pieces of someone they loved. On the video, the asset narrated in her British accent. At least 13 bodies, all decomposed, had been found by the Anbar Salvation Council after a Saudi AQAP captive told them where the Iraqi National Taekwondo Team had been killed, in a ditch in the desert about a hundred kilometres west of Ramadi, in Anbar Province not far from the highway to Jordan. It appeared that all had been shot and killed about the same time they went missing. Sa'ayd Al-Sayidi's T-shirt was in the mass of clothes and remains. The man who had arranged the escape of the American Operation Vengeance team–Or what remained of him–was mixed in with the pile of jumbled decaying pieces of his teammates, indignantly tossed into the hallway of a slum hospital. His fragments were probably separated as best as they could, but the only thing the grieving family could be certain of was probably his shirt. His beautiful daughter, Maha Al-Sayidi, who had herself become a black belt, would never be able to see her father compete in Beijing in 2008.

It was known that the team had been specifically targeted. It is known that ▇▇ ▇▇ had told his torturers that Al-Sayidi had heroically arranged the rescue of his friend and his 2002 associate. It was unknown if other connections have been made which could eventually point to anyone specific. Now might not have been the best time for Everett Dutschke to raise public profile.

Nevertheless, he threw himself back into the political campaign in a district that was heavily skewed Democrat (the previous governor's election showed a 60% Democrat/40% Republican split), but lost causes are worth fighting for. On July 4th 2007, his son, while staying with Everett's mother, had been very badly burned from a combination of excessive amounts of hand sanitizer and fireworks and was being flown from Meridian, Mississippi to the nation's top burn center in Atlanta. Dutschke's campaign came to a halt. His opponent, the 30-year incumbent, actually began openly advocating for a burn center in Mississippi. Though Dutschke still received thousands of votes, he would have needed a 14-point swing in a swingless district.

By the end of the year, Dutschke ceased publication of the newspaper, but it was not all bad news. His son was going to survive (though more skin grafts were necessary) and after years, his fiancé, Janet, was finally "cleared." There had been security concerns that took a long time for anyone to bother addressing, involving whether her father, a defector from the old Soviet Republic of Ukraine, was her father or her grandfather and his association with a man named Djuseppe. Everett could marry Janet without any concerns and so she (after years together) became his third wife.

(Records confirm that two of his marriages occurred in Tennessee, the other is unclear.)

It was during this period that George W. Bush made the second catastrophic mistake of his presidency, at least in Dutschke's mind. That decision had to be the result of a constant buzz of the Cheney/Rumsfeld/Pentagon faction of the White House which had been pushing for winning territory against civil liberties. For years, the NSA had been turning the outward-looking intelligence apparatus searching for specific threats to the American way of life into an inward-looking apparatus seeking everything. The man who had been silently building the NSA monster with a philosophy of "know everything about everyone everywhere" was Michael Vincent Hayden. And his influence and the machine he created from what was once more of a supporting agency made him into "the most powerful man in the world," according to Dutschke, who was not alone in his opinion. Thus, the only person on the planet least qualified to become the Director of Central Intelligence, the only person a worse choice than Porter Goss, would have been Hayden. Yet, under the immense pressure from the faction, that is exactly who Bush appointed as DCI. Dutschke was not the only one who understood this.

For decades, the philosophy of the CIA was to collect certain specific intelligence and from certain specifically recruited sources. An entire protocol called the intelligence cycle is indoctrinated into every single head of a CIA employee from a senior-level 7th floor careerists to the brown badges working the Dunkin Donuts cash register in the Langley cafeteria. Intelligence is looking for a very specific needle and a very specific haystack then letting the analyst PhDs figure out what it means when a C/O's R/O delivers the analyst that needle.

Hayden's working philosophy throws out the entire CIA mission as evidenced by his generalship of the NSA. Hayden's philosophy is—everything is a needle—everything is a haystack. This creates a practical impossibility since now you have an infinitely large and growing haystack to search through and only one needle is significant. In addition, Hayden did not care if the haystack was in China, Afghanistan or Des Moines. It did not matter to him if a 12 year old girl was sending an email to her grandmother on her birthday—in Hayden's mind, he needed to know that. Exactly what was written by whom, what time and the entire circle of influence (COI) of both the girl and her grandmother, what medication the grandmother takes, what physician prescribes her those medications, who else the physician treats, where his patients go to church and what TV channels each of those church members subscribe to, where they do their banking, what deposits and withdrawals were made by the bankers, the names of the banker's pets, (which could also be their password for their email service) and if any of them also got an email from a 12 year old granddaughter and if so what did it say and so on. This is not an exaggeration, it is real and that is just what Hayden called "intelligence" and that is just in the United States, where the CIA did not like to have to operate. Every email, every phone call, every text and every citizen has his/her own parted profile/dossier. *Plus*, Hayden was very, very Pentagon-centric. In fact, the NSA director is *required* to be DOD or ex-DOD. The CIA, however, should not be Pentagon-centric. CIA serves the president, NOT the Joint Chiefs. Sometimes it is the military that is the problem and the civilian intelligence agency has no business thinking of itself that it is an army. Furthermore, Hayden's granting access of NSA to law enforcement and steering CIA gathered intel INTO the repository of NSA is a disaster.

Think of it like this, the NSA traditionally, has been a repository of intel, a library where the various intelligence agencies stored all their books. DIA had its aisle that only DOD could peruse. The CIA had its aisle that only the CIA could walk down. Using this analogy, Michael Hayden's history was that he opened up all the shelves to all the agencies, including law enforcement (Carnivore). The result is that the FBI now had access to the CIA shelves. This is the worst idea in the world for any country that does *not* want to become a North Korea-like police state. Plus it is a strict and explicit violation of the CIA Charter, section 1.8 (50 USC, chapter 44§3001) and under 50 USC§403 (D)(3) clearly states: "provided the agency shall have no police, law enforcement power or internal security functions," Hayden's wholesale granting of access to FBI of even the smallest bit of CIA-gathered intel means that CIA-collected intelligence could now be used for law enforcement purposes. The FBI (as well as all LEOs, from federal down to the local level) has an infinitely large and long history of misusing and abusing its power and authority. To trust a LEO with any information at all is an egregious mistake. Cops aren't even very good at what they do, so trying to pretend they'd be good as an intelligence officer is folly. Cops aren't intelligence officers, they have proven themselves not good at it, and intelligence officers aren't cops. A CIA officer does not care one bit if someone speeds or someone bribes someone or if someone steals the car. In fact, a good Case Officer is someone who has *done* all those things. It is none of his/her business because the CIA is not law enforcement.

A cop on the other hand, local or federal, gets a great deal of personal affirmation when he sees someone go seven miles over the speed limit. It gives him a reason to assert himself.

Giving the FBI access to CIA-collected intel, no matter how innocuous it seems, is not only against the statutory law, it violates common sense, and there is no way that a true security-minded society could stand for long Hayden's philosophy (though there seems to be a higher acceptance of the still-existing Hayden doctrine that Dutschke realised).

Besides, if a LEO wants to know something, he should do what the CIA does and go investigate it for himself; instead of being lazy and tapping into Carnivore's vast data.

In short, everything about Hayden's doctrine was completely antithetical to the CIA's mission (which was damaged, not even begun to be fixed until the appointment of Gina Haspel as DCI actually DID come up through the ranks and unlike political appointees to DCI, does understand and "gets" CIA's mission; from the top to bottom. Though few will ever know, it is SHE, who has actually been in the "trenches," that will be the greatest DCI ever).

Nevertheless, Bush (who Dutschke greatly respected) had been pressured into the Hayden appointment, and whether Dutschke liked it or not, Hayden would spend 2006-2009 decimating the HUMINT component of CIA. About the only thing Dutschke would credit Hayden for was understanding the value of contractors and his ability to squeeze money away from Congressional "Pet Projects" and election-oriented pork into CIA instead.

As a result of the ██ ██ "disclosures" (under foreign torture), the hit on Al-Sayidi and the bus, and probing being done by organisations in DC, Dutschke began looking over his shoulder again. With Hayden as DCI, any contract work seemed unpalatable. 2008, it seemed, would be it. The last year of "service" so that he could begin a transition into a normal uncontroversial life. But his past wouldn't let go so easily. 2008 was an election year and though Dutschke openly supported Huckabee ("open" support is not supposed to happen), it was discovered while advocating for a US project in Western Africa, that a US senator and her staff were directly interfering on behalf of the Chinese government and were, in fact, leaking sensitive (to the project) intelligence to them so the Chinese could gain a competitive edge on securing

31

"dibs" on an industrial site. While digging further, it was discovered that the Chinese (and others) using intermediaries, were illegally donating to one of the presidential candidates (who went on to win) and that foreign organisations had been set up specifically in order to bundle and funnel that money to both the campaign directly *and* to PAC and 501c(4) organisations inside the US supporting that same candidate. When that intelligence went up the ladder, just like in 2004, nothing happened. There was probably even no criminal referral to the DOJ, or if there was (which is equally as unlikely), the Mueller FBI stalled and it went nowhere; perhaps because deals had already been made ("Hey Bob, if I win this election, I plan to keep you on as FBI director. So...make sure I win").

Also during this time another relevant event had happened that, again, involved criminal activity and that same campaign. In order to protect that candidate, specifically, from the "foreign influence" charge, a "security consulting firm" that had been hired by the presidential campaign "hacked" into the database of the US Department of State passport records. The passport database of the candidate was "scrubbed clean" by the "hackers" of the candidate's foreign travels that could have become a problem (as well as another candidate, Hillary Clinton). The CEO of the "consulting group," therefore the one behind the "hacks", was none other than John Brennan, the same man who was the ███ of ███████ in ███ years earlier, when Operation Vengeance occurred. The same ██ that the ██ kept in the dark about the operation until after it was done. The news media reported "hack" was no hack. It was not authorized access, true, but the company (Brennan) did not need to actually "hack" the passport database, since it is common knowledge that the ██ has always had backdoor access to the database. Something a T/O and the ██'s Central Cover Office knows well; and uses every day. Thus a company run by Brennan, former ██████ ██ ███████ had no problem making the alteration to the candidate's file. That might have been part of the reason that inexperienced candidate trusted and hired Brennan's company in the first place. It was likely that the senator/presidential candidate simply made another deal: ("Hey John. You know if I win, I'll make a place for you. So make sure I win and handle this for me").

And so it was done (and such a position was, in fact, created for Mr. Brennan as he was post-election immediately made the "assistant to the president for the Department of Homeland Security for counterterrorism").

Although the FBI prosecutes "hackers" willy-nilly, treating them as if they are the bane of all existence; especially anyone who accesses government servers without authorisation, in this case (once again) the Mueller FBI chose to look the other way. Brennan got a famous Mueller pass.

CIA rules allow work affiliation disclosures to a cleared spouse if it would not endanger either the agency, the employee or the spouse herself. In this case, Everett likely felt his wife did not need to know since the bulk of his affiliation was long past, despite that he had introduced her to several still active officers (she would not have known their affiliations) passing them off as if someone else. And he had previously involved her (unwittingly) in a single contact operation of a potential high-level asset (potential agent) owner of a foreign telecom company at a large, formal banquet. Everett passed himself off as a telecom lobbyist for a later hand off to a C/O. Without warning preparing her in advance, Janet went along gracefully and perfectly with the ruse and did not ask any questions. The later report did not even mention her presence at the introductory meeting.

It is extremely helpful to understand the networks surrounding Rabita Trust and not only who created and kept it full but who taps into it for resources and exactly who they are, because in 2009 following the inauguration, the networks involved with it would be viewed differently.

Rabita Trust was created in 1998 by (as previously mentioned) Abdulla Omar Naseef and Al-Rabita Al-Alami Al-Islmiya or, the "World Muslim League". The World Muslim League (WML) is a primary coordinating "government" (a state without borders) that controls everything else. It was established long ago by the ██ ██ family (the same family as the three targets of Operation Vengeance) and the person Naseef chose to run it was, as previously mentioned, Wa'el Hamza Jalaiden (Abu Hamza), Osama Bin Laden's former logistics chief. Naseef and the Muslim World League's goal is the promotion of wahhabism even through radical means and coordinates global operation. A special division of the World Muslim League called simply "The International Relief Organization" or the IRO was founded to fund al-Qaeda and UBL specifically. All of this, to the vast majority of Americans, may sound as if it is a loose collection of bearded, armed cave dwellers in some vast but harmless desert on the other side of the planet. As if all these bizarre and funny sounding foreign names has nothing to do with them or is far removed from American lives or interests. That thinking would be horribly mistaken.

The Muslim World League setup SAAR network, also known as Safa group. SAAR is a vast and very complex collective of "Islamic charities" and "nonprofit organisations" with a labyrinthine ability to conceal the financial activity of its members and its contributors. United States Customs and Immigration Enforcement Agency has publicly alleged that SAAR network is just a giant money laundering operation to finance terrorism operations and is completely comprised of nearly 100 different almost cellular groups. SAAR network (Safa group) is not some far away imam or bearded guy in a cave with a laptop and a checking account in the Middle East. SAAR Network is based in Virginia, right in the heart of the center of America's politically influential, and plainly marked offices. Osama Bin Laden's Al-Qaeda operational fund, the above-mentioned IRO was founded in 1992...in Virginia.

SAAR Network (The Muslim World League's complex financial group) also supports the American Muslim Alliance and shares common members. The American Muslim Alliance (who support the terrorist-designated Hamas) espouses Muslim "resistance" and is actually a registered political action committee that was funded in 1994 in California. They are not some distant, sandal wearing, robed crazy-people. They are a part of a network in America and exert political influence, donating to political campaigns. And not obscure candidates or small paltry either—for example, the American Muslim Alliance contributed $50,000 to the Hillary Clinton campaign.

The Muslim Public Affairs Council (MPAC) is affiliated with the Muslim Brotherhood and shares many SAAR and MWL members supporting Islamic Supremacy and is a registered PAC, a 501c(4) listed entity, though it has sponsored terrorism support rallies. It actually hosted Hillary Clinton at its convention.

Their physical presence is in America's own yard and its own house as they have influence over certain candidates and high officials, not just as groups, but even as individual donors. For example, SAAR donor Tariq Ramadan (called a Muslim scholar) who helped to fund terrorist activities was banned from entering the United States in 2004 by the Bush Administration; however in 2010 that ban was inexplicably removed by Secretary of State Hillary Clinton.

Why were the Islamic causes of Muslim World League and its progeny organisations able to exert influence over Clinton?

It would be too easy to simply answer—money. The more complete answer goes much deeper than that and takes us all the way back to Rabita Trust.

Again, the MWL and Abdullah Omar Naseeff set up Rabita Trust for the promotion of Islamic supremacist ideology and chose Jalaiden to run it (who was later designated as a global terror entity by the US Treasury and Jalaiden's assets were frozen) and did so with the money from the three financiers. Think of every one of the MWL's organisations, hundreds of them just through SAAR, including Al-Qaeda as franchisees of MWL. Think of each of the hundred of organisations in the network as a small-business franchise that operates with a local soft drink bottling company supplying your local petrol stations, restaurants, grocery stores and vending machines.

Each one of these businesses, Islamic supremacist organisations in this analogy, depends on the bottling company. In this analogy The Big Three (the three financiers who supplied Rabita Trust) were like Coca-Cola, Pepsi and Dr Pepper. Imagine every restaurant, store, and vending machine suddenly being devoid of Coke, Pepsi, and Dr. Pepper products. Without the Big 3—sodas simply don't have any market. Those three financiers, the three targets of Operation Vengeance, were market force drivers, hence their importance. So their (sudden) 2002 absence was a *massive* problem for the entire Islamic supremacy structure: with the major three financiers gone, a sudden emphasis was placed on the billions of Muslims worldwide, 5% of which are fundamentalist in some fashion still leaving millions that are told constantly that they must give money to the "cause" because, apparently, Allah needs the cash.

When looking at the full picture, though everyone knows the name, Osama Bin Laden, the reality was that UBL was in a sense but one hired hand of Abdulla Omar Naseef, the benefactor of Rabita Trust and IMMA (Institute for Muslim Minority Affairs), with or without the unlimited cash the major three funders supplied. Of all those Muslim World League organisations, the IMMA is the promotion and advertising department. Think of IMMA as the press secretaries of MWL and the Muslim Brotherhood at large. Naseef had put Syed Abedin in charge of the IMMA until his death when his wife took over, Saleha Abedin. Wa'el Hamza Jalaiden (Rabita Trust), Saleha Abedin (IMMA) and Naseef himself were incredibly dependent on the three men of the ██ ██ family. Losing those three financiers in 2002 created a gaping hole which was immediately filled only with questions. Their first step towards answers was the custody and torture of ██ ██ who led them to Sa'ayd Al-Sayidi. Naseef, Abedin and Jalaiden were not the only ones trying for answers (and revenge) even years later, it makes perfect sense that they continued prying and trying to connect their own does oddly, though, questions were pouring from another side of the planet as well. Other than John Brennan, who might still want to know why and who cut him, the ██ in ██ all those years ago, from the BIGOT list, who and why were querying from within the United States' own governmental structure?

The six members from Operation Vengeance could not possibly have known how far along the inquiries were but they were sure by now that someone (multiple someones) both in ██ ██ (Abedin, Jalaiden and Nassef), *and* the United States itself were trying to find out their identities.

Why?

In retrospect, it was clear they were all getting warmer. Brennan might have learned of the CIA's affiliation even back in 2002. Then there was the "escape" connection to Iraqi Taekwondo Olympian Al-Sayidi, as well as whatever descriptions ██ ██ could provide. That, alone, really narrowed it down. All the probers needed was a very clear way to fill in the blanks. They found that clever way. As it turns out, aside from John Brennan, they had someone on the inside. Very high on the inside.

To get to how this is the least bit relevant to 2013 and the KC letters, one must keep in mind that this was <u>never</u> actually about the KC letters of 2013 from the instant that Curtis' defence lawyer mentioned the name J.Everett Dutschke in court. It was about 2012 and about 2002 and it was an opportunity for that administration to protect itself. But to get to 2013 or 2012 or 2002, one has to go back further and into the 90s and even before that, to a time and place far away... A place called Jeddah. This is where Syed Abedin and

Saleha Abedin raised their children as Syed (recruited by Naseef) led the IMMA (with the immense money of the 3 rich men). It's helpful to remind the reader that Saleha Abedin took over her husband's position upon his death. She is a sociologist and an administrator of Dar Al-Hekma Women's College and a board member of International Council for Dawa and Relief—a pro-Hamas organisation and part of the "Union of Good" (listed by the US government as a terrorist entity) which is run by Yusuf al-Qaradawi. Saleha Abedin is also a member of the Muslim Sisterhood (the women's division of the Muslim Brotherhood) and as the leader of IMMA has a key role to the al-Rabita al-Alami al-Islmiya (MWL and Rabita Trust). Saleha's family business' primary project has always been the publication of the Journal of Muslim Minority Affairs so it was not a surprise that she would be among the multitudes trying to uncover what happened to her three rich benefactors who funded her family business—but she was also a firm believer in the Islamic Supremacy that the three rich men were purchasing, such a strong believer that she published a book about it. The name of Saleha Abedin's work is titled quite simply "Women of Islam" and, as Andrew C. McCarthy describes it, actively justifies Sharia Law such as death to anyone who abandons Islam and the participation of women in violent jihad. So her interest in the 2002 loss of her family's benefactors was not merely personal (though it was), the radical Islamic world, the world as controlled by the Muslim World League, just lost their sugar daddies (in 2002) and now they wanted to know the names of who was responsible—and when it comes to vengeance, Muslims have a very long memory which, unlike Americans, does not fade.

CIA had tried for years, mostly unsuccessfully, to get someone on the inside, to infiltrate all these different cellular networks and it was nearly impossible. However, it was a piece of cake for the Muslim World League, specifically for Abdullah Omar Naseef and Saleha Abedin to penetrate the highest level of United States government.

The spy, the one in a position to convince all the right people to make all the right inquiries who would not be refused, was none other than Saleha's very own daughter. Though raised in Jeddah, the spy was already there—already in position. Her name—Huma Mahmood Abedin. As has been revealed by Daniel Horowitz, Huma Mahmood Abedin has perfectly executed her role as an infiltrator, an agent for the network, and her mother is the perfect handler, both seeming so innocuous and innocent. At age 20, Huma Abedin gained top-level proximity in the White House itself, attaching herself as an intern to the equally ambitious Hillary Clinton at a time when President Clinton was attaching himself to another intern. First Lady Clinton quickly made Huma Abedin her special assistant. Throughout the years, Huma Mahmood Abedin became more and more a fixture by Hillary Clinton's side, even though she was still an editor of the IMMA's Journal of Muslim Minority Affairs. *Just prior* to the final stages of planning the 9/11 attacks Huma

Mahmood Abedin, now an assistant to Senator Hillary Clinton, had her mother remove her name from the Journal of Muslim Minority masthead. When 9/11 happened—and it was discovered that the IRO, Rabita Trust, Muslim World League and the three ███ family benefactors of the Abedin family were defiantly involved in providing material support to the UBL operation of the 19 (15 Saudi) hijackers, both Huma and Senator Clinton stayed completely silent on her direct family connection and support of those exact organisations responsible. That silence, many would admit, would be unthinkable to a patriotic American, but just as Abedin had protected Hillary in 1998 (as she would do many times later), in 2001 Hillary protected Huma. Also, Horowitz revealed that following 9/11, Saleha Abedin enlisted her son Hasan (Huma's brother) and her daughter, Heba (Huma's younger sister) to work with her on the Journal. So the family did not cease its involvement in the IMMA after 9/11. It increased its involvement.

Often when the CIA, CEG or the joint CIC considers a possible espionage agent or spy investigation, the subject's finances are among the first red flags. In 2006, Huma Abedin's salary was less than $30,000 per year. 2006 is the same year Sa'ayd Al-Sayidi (Dutschke's 2002 rescuer) and the Iraqi National Taekwondo team had been targeted and assassinated. Yet, somehow, with the salary that is less than a DC cop, Huma Mahmood Abedin purchased (in August) an expensive apartment in DC ($650,000). There was no CIC investigation.

By the 2008 presidential election, Saleha Abedin's daughter, Huma, had become candidate Hillary Clinton's traveling chief of staff. As part of (another) deal made by Hillary Clinton's opponent, he appointed her (Clinton) to Secretary of State after his 2009 inauguration. She, in turn, designated the former editor of the Journal of the Minority Affairs, Huma Abedin, as the United States Deputy Chief of Staff in the US Department of State. Now—there would be no inquiry into world affairs that Saleha Abedin's Daughter, Huma, could not make or cause to be made. At the same time, the man who had (through his "consulting" firm) hacked and scrubbed clean the State Department files of the new president was rewarded with the appointment to a newly created position as a special DHS "Presidential Advisor" (and would later be appointed by the same to be DCI, in charge of the very agency that had kept him in the dark in 2002 when he was a ███. Both John Brennan and Huma Abedin had an intense interest in the who and how of 2002, and both Muslim (Brennan had converted to Islam during his CIA tenure, and Abedin born into it) in a new administration that suddenly went Muslim-friendly.

In 2009, just months after inauguration the administration announced, through DOD, they believe that the US military had captured the "man" responsible for the 2006 assassination of the Taekwondo team (and al-Sayidi), though intelligence agencies (including America's CIA, Britain's MI-6 and

Israel's 8200) had but moderate confidence in the absurd claim (the idea that one man with a gun, representing Al-Qaeda, could stop, kidnap and assassinate 15 of the most formidable men on the planet all at the same time is almost laughable if not so serious). Nevertheless, the American military turned the "suspect" over to the new Iraqi government for prosecution. According to the public voice of the administration, it was case-closed. Meanwhile, behind the scenes, it was *not* case-closed. There were a multitude of organisations, all considered "friendly" now, that still wanted to know the details (who and how) of 2002 and their three ████ financiers. Some of these organisations were worldwide, some are based inside America and some have such innocent and friendly sounding names that no one could object to them, yet every single one was connected to Naseef, the MWL, and Rabita Trust, and ultimately to the three money men and terrorism. Most Americans had no connection to the names—Abu Nidal Organisation (ANO), Al-Qaeda, HAMAS (Islamic Resistance Movement), Armed Islamic Group (GIA), Harakat Ul-Mujaheddin (HUM), Al-Gama'at AlIslmiyya (IG), Hezbollah (Party of God), Jaish-e-Mohammed (India), Al-Shabaab, Taliban, Tupac Amaru Revolutionary Movement (MRTA), Al-Aqsa Martyrs Brigade (AAMS), Palestine Liberation Front (PLF), or the innocent sounding United Association for Studies and Research (UASR-SAAR branch in Springfield, VA), Global Relief Foundation (GRF—connected to UBL), Benevolence International Foundation (BIF—supports terrorism in Sudan and is located inside the US), Muslim Arab Youth Association (MAYA) or those inside the US such as the Holy Land Foundation for Relief and Development (HLF-in Richardson Texas), American Muslim Council (AMC—supports Humas), Islamic Society of North America (ISNA—Publishes the militant Islamic Horizons), Ba'it ul Mal, Inc. (BMI—a SAAR firm in New Jersey), Kind Hearts (supports Hamas—in Toledo, OH, OK, NV, CO, PA and IN), Mercy International (funded in Denver, CO, offices in Garden City, Michigan). But now all these organisations, most importantly Saleha Abedin's IMMA and Naseef, had someone in Brennan and Huma Abedin that could finally get results. Yet not even Brennan, close advisor to the President himself, nor Huma Abedin could get much traction to their CIA inquiries other than to learn that there had possibly been a helicopter involved in the escape, which they already knew from the 2004 torture of ██ ██. Finally, someone making inquiries on behalf of Naseef and Saleha Abedin (it could have been Huma or John Brennan or someone else) discovered records of the stolen air ambulance and that the helicopter had been discovered crashed. This caused inquiries to hospitals, eventually leading to Ramstein which became a dead end as the six "John Does" of 2002 left absolutely no DOD records of ever being there and no one fessed up to the four months of treatment.

Either Saleha Abedin's daughter, Huma, or John Brennan then had the very savvy thought that anyone who would be returning from Ramstein from a helicopter crash in late 2002, would also be undergoing some follow-up visits and/or rehabilitative physical therapy and would leave insurance records. There was just one problem, no one, not even the Secretary of State—could access the insurance records of ███, the primary carrier of the ██, at least not without a warrant. What the Rabita Trust/IMMA probers high up in the administration needed was a vehicle for such a warrant to search for the identities of those receiving physical therapy at the correct time and for the correct injuries and with people aboard (Secretary of State Clinton, Brennan and even the President himself) who could simply ask (exert pressure) FBI Director Bob Mueller. Getting a sponsor for the warrant wouldn't be a problem as long as they had a case to tie it to. Any case.

That case was not hard to find since the Obama Administration DOJ began prosecuting CIA cases like it was their new sport. It is almost as if the Obama/Holder DOJ needed to flex its muscle and whip the CIA into shape; First, by prosecuting every CIA case they could find and second, by the appointment of politician Leon Panetta as DCI (since he would be passive and compliant) and third, by unmasking any CIA holdouts (who—once burned—could cause no problem for the administration). Because of the nature of CIA, once a CIA employee is attacked by the (Eric Holder) DOJ, they could not really defend that employee. So the vehicle they needed, to sponsor the warrant they needed (in short the case they needed) was already in their hands. An ex-NSC staffer believes she has discovered the case which was used. The case of Jeffrey Sterling and Operation Merlin.

It must be noted here that the reality of the background—simply answering the question "Who is J. Everett Dutschke?" just to this point, is already far too complicated for a "criminal trial", such as the 2013 KC letters. Americans can not follow it, as they prefer a much more simple narrative. Americans can grasp something like—"President Clinton had sex with an intern and then lied about it under oath." But that is about their limit. Much more than that and their eyes glaze over. So when there is no "microwave version" of the truth, very few Americans are capable of following anything with any complexity to it. And already there are so many details, so many people involved (with strange names no one has ever heard of, so many moving parts occurring over so many years with only millimetres of progress that it just isn't "sexy" enough for them, certainly not for the massive spectacle of a criminal show that administration's Department of Justice (under Eric Holder and Bob Mueller) put on for a national press corps that needed to fit the entire story on the front page above the fold. So even if any of the American (or worldwide) press could possibly have known or discovered all of the names and details revealed here in this book, they simply would not have had either the opportunity or the inclination to bother to try. Details, especially details that require a very deep dive and over six years of research and fighting sometimes for every detail and dead-ends, are just too much work for the media that wants everything simply handed to them, and in nice little, bite-sized pieces that satisfies their viewers/readers craving for keyhole melodrama. To CNN and its viewers, a reporter's two-minute recapitulation of whatever the Holder-Mueller yarn is in the DOJ press release that still leaves room to squeeze in a commercial for Depend Diapers or AARP or reverse mortgages, is practically erotica, especially if they have some footage of the defendant being walked in shackles, chains and orange jumpsuits so that he just "looks" guilty.

If they wish, they can try and do the same research that was done for this book (good luck finding the sources or getting anyone to talk to you), but they would never attempt such an endeavour (though some of it was simply not available during the actual periods, 2002-2013). For journalism is dead.

But there are a few exceptions. One of these exceptions is a man named James Risen. And even though this history is already complex, it is about to become even more so, with more players and more details.

The Obama DOJ (Holder/Mueller) were gearing up a prosecution against former CIA officer Jeffrey Sterling.

Their premise for demolishing this man's current life was Operation Merlin and their attempt to frighten the kinds of reporters that actually dig up details, even the hidden ones (like James Rosen, Sharyl Atkisson and James Risen), away from ever exposing anything negative about the administration. The objective was to send a message to investigative reporters to forgo investigative reporting during that administration's term ("play ball our way, or we will sic the dogs on you and your stories").

The CIA senior staff had concocted a plan and instructed CIA officer Jeffrey Sterling to deliver blueprints of a thermonuclear device to Iran through an intermediary that was a Russian scientist. The plan was for the Russian scientist (turned agent) to simply walk the nuclear bomb blueprints through the office door to the Iranian Embassy in Vienna in exchange for money. So far, this part of the story, as movie-like as it seems, is simple enough that even CNN could follow it. However, here is where they cut away for a Metamucil commercial, because it gets complicated. The Russian scientist convinced Jeff that the plot would not work and was too risky because the defects in the phony decoy blueprints were "easily identifiable". Operation Merlin was to sell the dumb Iranians a fake nuclear bomb they would work on, since obviously the CIA thought that the Iranians were so dumb they couldn't discern the difference between a thermonuclear weapon and a mini-fridge. Well, the Iranians are not that stupid and the Russian scientist and Sterling knew that this was, in part, why Operation Merlin was deeply flawed. Jeff's reservations inevitably lead to his exit in 2002.

In February of 2003, CNN wrote an article on its website about the Iranian nuclear program (because if they had broadcast it on their networks, there wouldn't have been enough time left for a Viagra commercial) and soon after, Jeff called James Risen. They spoke numerous times and discussed Operation Merlin.

In April, James Risen called the OPA for CIA and NSC staff asking about the Iranian nuclear operations and Merlin. Not long after, Risen, with New York Times, Jill Abramson, got a visit from George Tenet (CIA-DCI) and Condoleezza Rice (National Security Advisor) for the purpose of convincing the two reporters not to publish the story. In August, Jeff Sterling, who had moved out west and was now selling health insurance (common), decided to make inquiries to send to staffers about any inquiries being made into Operation Merlin.

Flash forward a few years, 2010, and James Risen's book, "State of War" is creating quite a controversy. In the book, Risen reveals Operation Merlin, the operation that caused a row between Jeff Sterling and CIA senior staff. Since the Mueller FBI (under Holder's DOJ) had already begun an investigation for the purpose of prosecuting Jeff for...something, whatever they could come up with, they could piggyback Operation Vengeance inquiries into Operation Merlin inquiries as long as they were vague enough and clever enough with their rationale and language of the warrant applications. The warrant applications, which have been seen but since disappeared post-2015, would need to go to a friendly court, a special court, the kind of court where a judge never really questions federal agents and approves 99% of all warrants because they are afraid to stand in the way of "National Security". The trick of using a warrant to get OTHER information outside the scope of one investigation to pry open another, is one of DOJ's most commonly used tactics, so they are incredibly skilled at controlling the warrant process; judges know they are no match for the FBI. This warrant would have the premise that—If CIA officer Jeff Sterling talked to this guy, Risen, about a CIA operation, we suspect he may have talked to ██ ██, a previous CIA operational asset, who we know disclosed to the ████████ his association with Americans who had been in a helicopter crash, so the DOJ was seeking the health records to confirm who was ██ ██ American contact. A serious stretch.

It was a very novel and clever idea, but there was absolutely no basis, no proof to it at all. ██ ██ had absolutely no connection whatsoever with Operation Merlin or to Jeff Sterling. One of the things that federal judges do to provide cover for themselves is to lecture the agents that they "don't want agents to go on 'fishing expeditions' with the warrant." Once they *say* that canned warning they feel they are off the hook and issue the warrant anyway, nearly every time. Then the fishing begins.

It's doubtful that Bob Mueller was informed by the curious cabal as to why and how this information was to be used, simply instructed (asked) to hand it over once the insurance company, ██████, returned the relevant records. The curious cabal has since been identified as: the Secretary of State

(Clinton/Abedin), the DHS counterterrorism adviser to the President (Brennan), the President himself and Susan Rice, the National Security Advisor, with an additional possibility of DCI Leon Panetta and Michael Morell as well as other potentials of the 7th floor vaults.

When information is provided by one of these special court's warrants, any actual name of an American citizen is supposed to be redacted wherever it shows up in the requested records that are produced, except for (if necessary) the name of the target of the investigation, the target of the warrant. The (normally HIPAA protected) names that resulted did not span all six but the insurance records provided three files which fell within the parameters that were presented in the warrant, but the names (which were not either ██ ██ or Jeff Sterling) were not redacted as the law requires. When an agency or a warrant exposes those names, this is called unmasking. It means that a CIA employee has been burned by his *own government!* At that point, the moment at which a CIA officer has been burned (usually by DOJ), there is nothing the CIA can do about it. Unmasking is an instant career killer. In that administration, the designated person to do that "killing" was National Security Adviser, Susan Rice. Usually, unmasking is some political retribution against a specific CIA officer (i.e.: Valerie Plame via Armitage/Cheney). However, in the Obama Administration, it may be possible that National Security Advisor, Susan Rice herself, might have been unclear as to what she was doing and certainly as to why she was doing it. Nevertheless, three of the six of the Operation Vengeance team were burned and publicly exposed. Two of the unmasked were already out. The 2011 unmasking did not much upset Dutschke who had been already transitioning to a normal life for at least two years (perhaps since the appointment of Hayden) and telling his own mother for decades he was on the verge of quitting. The problem for these three was not really so much a problem with public exposure as it was their own personal safety. This is because they knew the inquiries of injuries were being made for a reason, and this was the third and final step that was needed for Naseef, Saleha Abedin and Wa-el Hamza Jalaiden to finally learn, after all these years, who are at least some of those responsible for Operation Vengeance. From this point forward, the unmasked three and their families were at risk. To the rest of the world, the only thing exposed (unmasked) is that three people received physical therapy. But to those very few that knew the significance of the crash also came the surety of the significance of those unmasked three.

Everett had never wanted any part of any controversy and was trying since 2009 to maintain a tidy and conservative reputation, having returned to teaching and family life. He had been a lily-white for years, but now his being burned put himself and his family at risk to anyone who could figure out how to connect the dots. The only ones who could do so were at the highest levels of his own government and those in the MWL or Rabita Trust who still lamented the loss of their three ████ ultra rich financier's still existing connection spanned the globe. Suspicions arose when a known member of that network, who actually lived in Tupelo, began to penetrate into Everett's very small inner circle. The man's son began getting very close to Everett's stepson and soon the two boys were even spending the night at each other's homes. Then that man inserted himself into a romantic relationship with one of Everett's few close friends, Angela, the daughter of a radio network mogul.

About that same time, the public shoe dropped. Following the unmasking, Dutschke became fair game to anyone and numerous, sometimes random people would make contact with Everett about some problem or issue they thought Dutschke could do something about. Often, even anonymous mail, even a radio talk show host sending middle-of-the-night texts. Dutschke viewed all of these as simply potential probes and accordingly responded without any detail whatsoever. Meanwhile, the prosecution of CIA officer turned insurance agent, Jeff Sterling, ramped up and the administration began investigating CIA officer John Kiriakou, with other former officers coming under the same destructive scrutiny. To add petrol on the fire, anti-CIA, anti government conspiracy flake Paul Kevin Curtis began to distribute his own book in which he named Dutschke as aiding and the cover-up of a Bizarre "Black Market body parts" conspiracy of government officials, a hospital and a funeral home.

Curtis's associated stories claimed that CIA was dumping "chemicals" on to the American population (no truth to that) and that agents "blew up" his car among other strange claims. Everett knew in 2011 (after Curtis's book) that all of Curtis's claims were dangerous. It was reckless to make people believe that hospitals are unsafe or are funeral homes for deceased loved ones. It is dangerous to convince people that their own government is dumping toxic chemicals on them from airlines. It is dangerous for the population to distrust an agency because they are convinced that agency goes around blowing up automobiles. (Quite frankly, it was equally dangerous, in Dutschke's mind, for people to think that the same agency would fail to blow up the occupant. If Dutschke's friends had actually tried to blow up Paul Kevin Curtis's auto, Curtis would simply no longer be around to complain about it.)

Nonetheless, Everett had never asked for any of this. The stress and worry about the potential retribution from anyone connected, even remotely so, to Naseef, Rabita Trust or Saleha Abedin or even possible agents of the ███ government were mounting and that stress showed. Janet, his wife, began to think Everett was having an affair, withdrawn and acting suspiciously. At one point, after arranging a meeting with a female CIA C/O who was still connected and was delivering Everett with the only intel she had on how this all happened and who was involved (it was not CIA), Everett's wife Janet directly accused him of an elicit meeting. It was an elicit meeting, to be sure, but not the kind Janet had feared. To allay her concerns, Everett convinced Janet to come with him to meet this alleged paramour. She was fearful, but

Janet capitulated. The meeting itself dispelled that particular accusation. But Janet was often given such false intel of "affairs" Everett was indulging in with women who he'd never met. Everett had dealt with such malicious accusations most of his life, but Janet had not. Because she maintained a very cheerful, very public face in Tupelo, this was one of the attacks to which she was vulnerable.

Conversely, as Everett Dutschke and his wife struggled, Saleha Abedin's daughter, Huma Mahmood Abedin had no fears at all, as she, herself, got married to New York Congressman Anthony Weiner. Professionally though, she was still Deputy Chief of Staff to Secretary of State of the United States (Clinton), she was still moonlighting as a "consultant" for Teneo, which is a "consulting firm" whose sole relevant client is the Clinton Foundation. She was also still receiving a salary directly from the Clinton Foundation directly as well as salary for being Hillary Clinton's personal assistant.

The kind of "quadruple dipping" caused the Senate Judiciary Committee to cry foul as Senator Chuck Grassley proved that Huma Mahmood Abedin had committed embezzlement, even filing false timesheets. However, just as expected, no criminal referrals to the FBI on the fraud ever went anywhere and was swept under the rug. The Secretary's solution to dodge any future scrutiny? Simply award Huma SGE status, making her (officially) a government contractor. An unheard-of step that the Deputy Chief of Staff of the United States State Department is its contractor. Yet no one dared question it.

Unlike in the movies, CIA work is quite mundane. It can be downright tedious. It can, of course, have incredibly intense moments, but those rarely happen. The idea that something from nearly a decade prior—that was supposed to be a single fleeting moment, a moment that creates problems, scrutiny, chagrin, personal stress and controversy is an unthinkable notion—or at least, should be unthinkable. Just because of one moment, one thing, a singular point and time when America's blood was afire, people in very dark and very high places were still digging around to find out names and details years later, causing stress borderlining on paranoia. This was not what Everett had signed up for. It was just one single thing, a thing that was just a one-off, a never-again gig that was not even part of Dutschke's normal realm. He had not given any thought or consideration to Rabita Trust, or Saleha Abedin or Naseef or any of those hundreds of foreign names of the Muslim world, for most part of that was somebody else's job, someone else's "beat". He wasn't Arabic fluent. Dutschke was not a part of the NED (Near East Division) and had very little connections to it (other than his friends in Cesarea and within his own network of people). He cared only about Northern Africa, Sub-Saharan division, South Africa and India and those divisions never gave him any trouble nor did any other operation.

No one was digging around to find out who installed a VHF transmitter in an African lawmaker's guitar. No one was digging around to find out who assisted in an uplink centre on an equatorial island. No one was digging around to find out who had climbed a frozen tree in a frozen land to raise a frozen MARTI antenna between two foreign microwave relays. No one was digging around to find out who trained multiple groups of bored, glassy-eyed intelligence officers how to capture and uplink burst transmissions of intercepted signals. No one was digging around to find out who ghosted a hard drive (multiplexed) using regular electrical lines of a foreign agricultural minister at a conference. No one was digging around to find out who spent two weeks assembling and taping the shredded bank records of a Liberian lawmaker. Yet there seemed to be no escaping the events of July 2002.

He needed a distraction, and found one in returning to one of the past loves of his life. He began to relive his affections for his mistress's long slender neck and perfect curves. He had picked up his guitar again, and dove head-first into music, recording almost right away. As one can hear from the early recordings (2009 to 2010), his skill with the studio software left a lot to be desired. This was all songs written by others recorded as "demos" for producers looking to match an artist with a song that fit them. Everett compiled a vast production library which included instrumental pieces successfully marketed and used in commercials and even full-length movies, all this while making definite progress in the art of recording. He and his ever-changing band quickly began making themselves a national presence selecting from key, high-profile performances (Six Flags, colleges, Hard Rock Rising tour, Atlanta Pride, city festivals, television appearances, Bud Light Port Paradise and countless more) seeking out indie radio airplay and winning regional and national contests and even a 2011 nomination for an Indie (the Hollywood event right before Grammys). The later and final recordings, produced solely by him—released by Florida's Melodic Revolution Records— were a quantum leap better than the early production and is as good as, in many ways, even ahead of, current-day radio production in both songwriting, performances, even the sound itself, and is still available to this day (Big Bad Wolf Album) with all major digital and CD retailers.

While his new life's "distraction" seemed to be successful, the world seemed to be on fire and in various shades of chaos. Everett no longer needed to care, so long as he had his guitar. The only way in which his rapid music success is relevant to the 2013 KC letters was the suggestion an FBI agent made under oath that there was some sort of music rivalry as part of some sort of feud between Dutschke and Curtis. That under-oath testimony, widely reported by the blind media, is as fake as it gets, and is just another of many, many myths that surrounded (and still does around) the case. There was no such "rivalry" or "feud". Paul Kevin Curtis was not in any way any sort of "competition" for Dutschke's band in any way. Curtis was not at all part of an actual music "scene" since he merely considered himself to be an "Elvis impersonator," which is not exactly sought-after by radio, colleges or anyone, really. The music industry and its consumers pay absolutely zero attention to someone who "impersonates" a musician.

The reported "feud" was a phrase used by Curtis's ex-wife, who knew next to nothing about Dutschke (who had hardly given her the time of day). It was likely SHE (Curtis's ex-wife) who helped coordinate the now-infamous confrontation, of Curtis crashing a meeting he was not cleared to be at to print Curtis's bizarre conspiracies in Dutschke's newspaper which he refused to do. SHE... The agent, dragging her ex-husband into a group meeting that was presumed to be about insurance coverage and policy changes was way out-of-line, since her (crazed) anti CIA, anti-government ex-husband who was not an agent had absolutely no business whatsoever to crash this meeting for the (admitted) explicit purpose of meeting and pressuring Dutschke. Not once, since 2013, has even a single member of the media even bothered to question her about it-no one-though it is clearly obvious that the ONLY way that Curtis could even have known about the meeting (which did not involve him) is if SHE told him. Her absolute dishonesty knew no bounds. It was the press' job to query her then. They failed.

Meanwhile, the Mueller FBI spent its days destroying and demolishing the life of Jeff Sterling. The media helped. The Mueller FBI began to plot the destruction of NSA's Thomas Drake. The media helped. And each of these cases, the men whose lives were destroyed were men who had served in the shadows to protect the American way of life. And in each of these cases the Obama administration with Eric Holder at the helm of the DOJ and Bob Mueller as the hands, set out with the political purpose of demolishing the lives of the people America should be thanking. John K had a family, a wife and young daughter that were equally devastated when Holder/Mueller dropped the full destructive force on to him. And that is all the American FBI and DOJ is, nothing but a destructive force that publicly justifies its existence through self aggrandizement and a willing popular entertainment industry determined to constantly rehash the tired-old inaccurate plotlines that LEOs (federal or not) protect lives. They do not. Their statutory function is that they protect statutes and policies.

The very word "police" stems from and is etymologically the exact same as public administration (policy) (from the Latin politia). Thus, their actual purpose, as defined by both statute and practise, is to help prosecutors build criminal cases against people—to find some statute (policy) that could be used to criminally convict someone. The job of a LEO, one must keep in mind, is to convict someone, whether they are actively pursuing a person to do so or not. Police (local or federal) are simply the hands (tools) of prosecutors and American prosecutors view their job simply as this: put as many people in prison for as long as possible while inflating and seeking vainglorious personal affirmation for doing so.

Thus, whether Americans want to admit it or not, wishing to pretend it is not so and feigning blindness to the reality that cops, by actual statutory definition and practise, are not heroes (as portrayed in popular culture), they are simple tools of administrative policy used to secure convictions at all cost. The tactics used in doing so are specifically designed to get a conviction. And though those draconian tactics are best described elsewhere, it resulted in John K's inability to gain employment to support his family or to keep a job, as he began to bleed financially, losing his home and going into debt (it is not only a common tactic but a trained tactic for the FBI to financially "break" someone into signing a plea—one of many tactics). In fact, this veteran, above-deck CIA officer, in seeking a job, discovered that prospective employers were even intimidated (crime) by badged FBI thugs in pursuit of that standard, "tried and true" tactic. They even intimidated his attorney's employer forcing her out of her firm for daring to represent him. Because the Obama Administration through the tactics of Holder/Mueller DOJ/FBI, very publicly painting John as a traitor, he was a poison pill no employer would have around; though he found a temp job stacking shelves after hours at Toys R Us until the FBI found a way to ruin even that.

Jeff Sterling found that his post–CIA career selling health insurance was also jeopardized by the FBI's similar tactics, and he was similarly branded a "traitor".

And for what? The worst the administration could come up with was akin to a CIPA violation-disclosure of "classified information." In this case, this was "disclosure" of an operation (Merlin) that DIDN'T happen! The Iranians' failures in their nuclear program is due to them and their complex designs, not because of "Merlin". And to the extent that any misinformation even could have contributed to their failures then it should be celebrated, not prosecuted. Even if "Merlin" had been a successful operation (it really wasn't), that wouldn't make CIA (Sterling) a criminal, it would be a heroic act, even "disclosure" of it. The Obama Administration seemed to be sending a new message—anything that upset the Muslim tyrants of Iran "or any other country" also upset the new American President who wouldn't stand for it. And, as has been done with past presidents, the FBI would be the enforcer of the unwritten policy which is but a symptom of that president's general leaning. The FBI would be used to "whip" any maverick intelligence officer back into shape if they wanted to work on the Obama Plantation. To prison with the rest.

For a brief moment, there seemed to be a light at the end of the tunnel with the new DCI appointment. General David Petraeus (replacing Panetta) would finally begin to undo some of the damage done to the minimisation of the agency by Hayden (who increased staffing but decreased real HUMINT), as the agency, within the CS (formerly DO) had lost its original mission, now playing a supporting role for NSA and DOD. The CIA had morphed into an airline, but without passengers and flying only Predator and Reaper drones from Tampa. Perhaps Petraeus would be the one to restore CIA's original mission. Let the BOP run the prisons and let the DOD make war and let the NSA do whatever unconstitutional collecting of data that they do; it is not CIA's job to hold their hands—let the CIA get back to its mission. But such hope was short-lived as Petraeus, before he could make any meaningful restorations, was replaced. And who did Obama later appoint to act as the interim director of the agency? The man who was the CIA presidential briefer when 2002 Operation Vengeance occurred, Michael Morell. This was, later, a disastrous choice, but for the agency, not for the President.

(Petraeus's exit was not an accident. He was forced out because of his disagreements over how Benghazi was handled and it was Mueller's FBI that forced him out.)

CIA and Department of State always had a good working relationship. But THIS was something else, something far beyond two agencies working together for a common goal of the American people who generally have no idea what either agency does. This was a personal partnership between two people as Morell is/was/always has been a Clinton minion. While this, alone, could be (and likely will be) a topic for another book, suffice it to say that there is a reason that Morell publicly endorsed Hillary for president and why when he left the CIA he went to work for a Clinton Foundation "consulting" firm.

In the summer of 2012, Everett would have thought he'd finally found "normality" in a simple and routine life with Janet (though still not as "routine" as most families); that is until he received two phone calls that reminded him that his forgotten past would not let him go and was not forgotten. The first was regarding a previous contact from the ████████████████ a professor of ██████ that would meet only with "Mr. ███", a previous Dutschke alias, about a past (and ongoing) "issue" involving U.S. ███ Department officials and their direct involvement in a "██ █" ████████ in ██████ and other countries. This would require activation and travel to Libya which could take a while and be problematic since the unmasking. A special green-badger scenario could be arranged if Dutschke would act as an interim contract T/O in Tripoli, to which he agreed since it should only take a few days, if it could be arranged by September. And he could use the money.

The second phone call, confirmed by a simultaneous email by someone else, was to inform him that ███ ████, a former CIA TISO (a DS computer whiz) Everett had a long-term friendship with and had relied on heavily during, often and after 2002 was dead. The conveniently believable autopsy concluded it was a massive drug overdose. Although Everett had not seen his friend in six years, both he and the family (who saw him often) were dubious since ████ ████ or "██" had been clean and sober for years since his stress-filled days helping Everett were over. The call and email were specifically and explicitly asking if Everett was going to make it to the funeral.

This would be the second funeral of someone associated with a team member of Operation Vengeance and a third, ██ ██, had been tortured then imprisoned and this was happening at the same time the President, running for re-election, was using Holder/Mueller's DOJ/FBI to demolish Jeff Sterling and John K. Everett told his wife he could not attend the funeral, though he expressed feeling guilt for not doing so. In the back of his mind, surely he had to be troubled that several things seem to be simultaneously bubbling back up. Surely something did not sit quite right.

Nevertheless, as arranged, records show that Everett left before dawn on Monday the 10th and was slated to return on Friday the 14th. He would resume teaching new classes the following week, the 17th. However it did not happen that way and he returned early, late at night, on the 12th. It is not clear whether or not he met for certain with this contact during his trip, cut short. But what has been learned is that there seems to be some sort of kerfuffle over an accusation that was required to produce a digital file first to DOD then to State Department, which he refused to do as he practically fled home.

Because Michael Morell was senior 7th Floor CIA under Petraeus at the time, he would have easy access to any specific list of all persons working Libya, and his level of access would not have excluded anyone, even if that person was Dutschke. Secretary of State Clinton (and her deputy, Huma Abedin, Daughter of Saleha Abedin) would have also had almost the same level of access though her (their) list would only show who is coming in as a contract T/O, and would not have been immediately privy to Dutschke's meeting or any content or purpose of that meeting.

Court filings and a sealed Capitol Hill hearing suggest that Dutschke created a file from the contents of the meeting in Tripoli AND all communications and the personnel along with their assigned duties, not just those in Tripoli, but Benghazi as well. Just the files alone, of all the communications have been potentially a massive political problem to the administration who not only chose to do nothing during the 9/11/12 Benghazi attacks organised by Kassim Soleimani (Iran's powerful proxy war wager), but an administration that did less than nothing ("Stand Down—Let the CIA guys get killed") from the highest levels, actively *removed* assistance at the very moment when it was most needed. However, the other part of the file, the intel from Everett's meeting, was, in Everett's mind, even more devastating. Since DOD claims he did not give it to them and the State Department says he also refused to give it to them, what happened to it?

One thing is clear, no matter what was on it or what he did with it, those aware of the Tripoli File's existence certainly thought Everett had the Tripoli File and very much feared what he would do with it and were about to prove they would stop at nothing to force it from him so they could deny its existence. In the meantime, they needed to not only begin the pressure on him, but to completely discredit him at the same time. The small cabal, though occupying the highest offices in the land, had other friends also in high places that could bring down a wrath of biblical fury that were confident they could not only discredit J. Everett Dutschke (until now a patriot) but could tarnish him so badly that when they were finished no one would believe him if he said 1+1=2! The cabal's friends also had a media machine behind them that could slander him so severely that it would make even Paul Kevin Curtis look sane by comparison. The machine began to slowly roll.

To answer the question "What happened to the Tripoli File?", one must flash to 2013 as Congress reconvenes, finally ready to publicly dig into the Benghazi fiasco of the administration. In her interview, Jennifer Williamson was one of the very few who credibly claimed to be an ex-girlfriend (the majority of similar claims were not authentic) who had known Everett for nearly twenty years. "He called me the night of January 10th and said he was in DC until Saturday or Sunday for a hearing in ▮▮ ▮▮, which made me inquire no further. I told him to swing by and pick me up, then we could go pick up Aimee and go get some Middle Eastern food in Tysons Corner. He laughed because he remembered the place and showed up in a white Maxima that was all cluttered inside. He told me he'd borrowed the car from a student so it wasn't his car or his junk. I asked if he still drove a convertible and he told me he drove a minivan now, like a soccer mom. When we got to the spot, Aimee and I ordered drinks, alcoholic of course, but he never drank. I remember he had chocolate milk and lamb, which he called camel-hump."

"Aimee and I are catching a buzz, but Everett wanted to talk business and just straight-up asked me, if I could get him a meeting with John Mills before he was to testify unofficially before HPSCI". This was a bit irregular as it suggested Everett may have been having second thoughts about a closed-door hearing or that he wanted to leak something in advance to control the inquiries or maybe just wanted to know which member of the HPSCI could be trusted. "I won't say he's paranoid but he does not trust just anybody with intel, even if that person is cleared for it. Part of that is that he'd been burned several times before like in Mumbai. The other part is that he thinks most others are either compromised or just plain stupid."

The Mumbai incident to which Williamson refers was a rainy August 13th, 2004. He was to meet with two recruited 'Chinese' assets (agents), both young Manipurese women. Yet, someone that Everett suspected was actually connected with the SSCI, perhaps even someone on a Senator's staff, tipped off the Chinese and when the sun finally came out and he emerged from the Taj Mahal Intercontinental to meet with his contacts at the Gateway (which was practically outside his hotel window) he discovered that the two Manipurese girls, essential agents to the assignment, had been violently stabbed, one practically decapitated. Law enforcement in India never knew anything about the connections or Dutschke and called it the act of a crazed attacker, even arresting a suspect, Uzar Patel, then closed the case.

As Williamson explained, "Everett always hated going up against the Chinese. They beat him every time so he always thought someone on the inside was helping them. Because there's no way anyone could outsmart him, right? But the truth is, they are real professionals, maybe the best in the world at some things. And they only just keep getting better. And if they had someone on the inside, well that's part of the game, isn't it?"

When asked how it ended, she answered, "I just never could... get a hold of him. I think he had a thing with some perfect blond-type, but also all he'd ever talked about was his ex-wife, the redhead. A girl really doesn't want to hear those kinds of things, you know? So competing with some woman that's around, that makes sense, like the blonde or that translator from their (their "hometown" of Meridian, Mississippi). But how can you compete with some chick that's not even there? The redhead? You can't. Anyway, his interim was up so he went off to Chiggerville (the Farm), so it took care of itself."

Williamson told Everett that she could probably set up a private introduction and meeting with John Mills, "but not before tomorrow", and Dutschke's hearing was for tomorrow. "So then he asked me about Turry. He said he should speak to Turry before tomorrow's hearing. When I asked him what this was about, he didn't really answer. He said a deal was made to get stuff from Russia to Iran's Soleimani. Turry and McCain were involved as well as State." "McCain sat on the SSCI and Everett did not want to face McCain about whatever it was and he didn't say what stuff was going to Soleimani through Russia, just that it was with money going the other way, and that his guy, a Qatari, was certain and reliable. He then lectured me and Aimee about how the NSC staff shouldn't believe anything that came out of that State Department. Which was weird since he'd never thought that way before. I asked him why he doesn't go to the CIA with his concerns. Maybe ████████. He said 'I'm out' and he said he couldn't because Morell is DCI and there's nowhere higher to go. He looked helpless yet determined at the same time, even though I told him there wasn't time to get with Turry either. Aimee and I were nearing tipsy, I always wondered if the two of them had a thing way back, and Everett, and his borrowed Nissan, dropped Aimee off at her apartment. She teased at me, 'don't do anything I wouldn't do', which isn't much. I invited him in to my place. And he did and he took out his laptop. It was exactly like mine, a Toshiba. He tried to connect to the neighbour's Wi-Fi and couldn't get past the password. He didn't want to use my connection, so right there, in my living room, he made an antenna out of a cereal box, aluminum foil and the USB cable and the USB Wi-Fi modem and pulled in someone else's unsecured and went on the whole time about ██████ stuff that his Libyan guy had put together with this Qatari guy. I reminded him gently that since he'd been burned, so none of it was his problem and he stopped his kicking (literally kicking) around the living room and looked at me and said 'Jenny, it's *because* I was burned. All this is my problem.' Meaning it is all related, on this end, he said."

At one point he asked her about the Secretary of State, "Do you know she met personally with Saleha Abedin? Not a conference call. Not a rope line, but she MET with her."

Of course Williamson had no idea why Everret would be concerned with Saleha Abedin, which really means why Saleha Abedin, Naseef and the entire MWL network was concerned about J. Everett Dutschke. But she *did* know that the Clintons were not to be crossed. The Clintons can get to and "eliminate" their problems no matter the circumstances, and a Clinton target is not safe even inside of a federal prison. Everett reminded her of what happened in late 2004 as little Richard Hirschfeld was getting ready to spill the beans to federal prosecutors about the foreign money, some from Hillary Clinton's SAAR affiliate in the 2004 campaign to Democrat candidates (including Hillary and Kerry) when Richard Hirschfield (as federal prisoner 24226-083) was found "hanged" in the laundry room of the Miami Federal Detention Center (Epstein style). Good people put their lives at risk to get this information to Dutschke, who is the same person whose life is potentially at risk from those the information is about.

When she asked him what he was doing on the laptop, he told Williamson, "I am burying this file so deep in the internet that I'm the only one who will be able to find the bits and pieces," or something to that effect.

This seemed to be of particular interest to the Holder/Mueller DOJ/FBI much later in the case as it was discovered that on that very laptop and other desktop (though the laptop was illegally obtained and searched) that there was, indeed, a file which had absolutely nothing to do with any evidence of the 2013 KC letters whatsoever. Additionally, it was discovered that in 2013, the Mueller FBI sent a full search team to the Texas ranch of Dutschke's father, a place Dutschke had never been. To the national press, it appeared as if they were searching the father's residence for any evidence of Dutschke developing a chemical weapon and under that pretense. They even went so far in the search of the home to stage and enter while wearing full biohazard suits since it looked good for the camera, to aid in the illusion. But they knew they would find no such chemical weapon development evidence there; they knew Everett had never been to this place and had no idea where it even was. FBI evidence logs show their real intentions. Though making a show of it to make it seem like a real search, the real thing they were after was his father's computers and any and all possible memory storage devices. The log shows they made mirror images of everything—every hard drive, memory card, USB drive. Why? Is a USB drive a chemical weapon? It is not. They were on a data search disguised as chemical weapons search, of a place Everett had never been, but a place where Everett could have sent a digital file for safekeeping. One does not need to wear biohazard suits to search data. That was all for show, as it is clearly shown in the only relevant "seizure." According to the FBI's very own file, it is the mirror image data stolen from the Texas residence. The summary is that they were looking for a specific data file they had concluded Everett had stashed. They did not find it in the Texas "evidence."

But they didn't stop there as Everett's own mother became the next target, this time of a remote attack. It's unclear exactly who was doing the snooping, but it is clear that the initial trojan was through a Windows exploit known only to NSA. It was discovered that at night, that someone presuming that Everett's mother, a woman in her sixties at the time, would have long since gone to bed. She had not. She is an owl. As she described it, though other incidents must have happened based on other evidence, the one that made clear to her what was happening is this late night event where the sleeping desktop computer woke up by itself, and the mouse cursor began moving around clicking on things while no one was even sitting at the desk. In her words, "the computer had a life of its own and was searching for something." Being Everett's mother, she knew to immediately disconnect everything and took it to a trusted resource who told her he'd heard about what he'd encountered on her computer but he never seen anything like it. He didn't need to review his logs to recall the incident for this book. As he consulted, both at the time and even afterwards, with other senior level cyber-security technicians, they confirmed that what he was dealing with in cleaning her computer was not standard to any hacker and was specifically used only by two entities, both of them government. He had never had such difficulty in clearing out a system, and he sent her home with a clean system, a new browser and firewall protections. If there had been a file on her computer that she'd stashed for Everett, when the government hackers were remotely probing around, they didn't find it.

Moreover, the DOJ accidentally let it slip to Everett's appointed attorney, Ken Coglan, that they were after the file when they revealed to him that they had indeed encountered a "file" on Everett's computer that was so heavily encrypted that even they could not open it. Their November 2013 ruse was to suggest to the lawyer that he should help them "recover the data," and they might go lighter. Not Everett nor his attorney believed that for half of a second and refused. The FBI even let it slip in documented form. And in their discovery report they admitted they were after that data file and that they, the US GOVERNMENT, could not crack into. They even made the mistake of admitting it in a court filing. PACER documents revealed that an opposition motion filed in late November, 2013 mentions it specifically. Most of the filing (#48) is the DOJ false claims of "evidence" that simply was not true, trying to present to anyone following the case (including the judge) that there was just such overwhelming mountains of evidence that fighting would be futile, a very common, though dishonest, tactic of the FBI. For example, they mentioned that "FBI reports" "have been provided to the defence," ignoring that the actual analysis behind the report had not been.

(The tactic here is that often the "FBI reports" simply make a claim and that claim is the exact opposite of what the analysis actually shows. So they bury the actual analysis, concealing it illegally and only make available the claim. In other words, if the "FBI report" says that your client's fingerprints were on the knife, wouldn't you demand to then see the actual fingerprint analysis? So whenever a document, such as is, states that they have supplied the defence with "a report" but does not specifically state that the actual lab work was included, then that is indication that the "report" is completely false and the FBI prosecutors know it. The sad thing is that though all parties know the common scheme has been deployed, judges usually just play along. In this case, the Dutschke case, the prosecutors had done exactly that and one can plainly see that "reports" are what is listed as provided discovery, not the actual analysis, or "evidence," which was concealed)

On page 3 of that filed case document, they made the same mistake as they did in their discovery "reports," admitting that the "FBI is attempting to break the encryption code." This filing was in late November more than half a year after they arrested Everett and "seized" his computer. Several months later and the United States, supposedly with the most advanced technology in the world, with what is supposed to be the preeminent law enforcement agency in the world, the Federal Bureau of Investigation with nearly 80,000 employees and Bob Mueller who had called for special assistance in this case from the Department of Homeland Security, where John Brennan led as a special counterterrorism advisor to the President himself in the initial stages of this case and even elements of the United States military, and yet none of them were capable of breaking Everett's encryption? Yet there it is, in writing and their own document, drawing attention to it. If their case was so overwhelming, and so egregious of an assassination attempt on a U.S. President and a traitorous act of terrorism, as they reported to their parroting media puppets, then they would not have cared a pinch about cracking that file, and they wouldn't have needed to. Nor would they have approached his attorney with a deal if he would have cracked it for them or even have offered any of the plea deals. If it was truly a deadly biological weapons attack, an act of terrorism as they presented, they would have gone straight to trial. Was Dzokhor Tsarnaev offered a plea? Ramzi Yousef? Timothy McVeigh? John Wilkes Booth?

Their inability to access the encrypted file, a file which was not actually relevant to whether or not "Dutschke developed a biological weapon," unless they had more knowledge than they admitted meant that whatever ever he did that night in Jennifer Williamson's flat on a stolen Wi-Fi signal was a triumph, but it only raised their concerns later, after his arrest. They might have presented that that file was relevant to the case because both Morell, Brennan and possibly even Secretary of State (Clinton/Abedin) knew that the "Qatari," who gave him some of the intel, that he later made into the unified Tripoli File, was a professor of ███████ and that Dutschke's "loose end" in Libya, was his unfinished (pre 2009) ███ consultant and a suspected unreported association with a former Cesarea member. But they could not do such a thing without revealing that the Tripoli File exists (though inadvertently, they did). Still it was not a bust for the cabal because if the only copies that existed were on Everett's computers, then they had the copies of the Tripoli File when they "seized" his computers and since *they* had his computers, he didn't have access to the file. As long as they could keep him in jail or prison, the Tripoli File would never see the light of day as long as they could ensure Dutschke didn't either.

They likely knew that Dutschke had indeed stashed a digital copy somewhere, they just didn't know where. In addition to the remote search of his mother's computer and his father's, all in different locations separated by many miles and hours, they returned back to Everett and Janet's home, this time raiding the house to confiscate the kid's gaming units (PS3, Nintendo, Wii), DVR units, camera, anything with any kind of memory, still searching for the likely stashed copy of the Tripoli File. But still, as long as they could keep him in prison, he couldn't access it no matter where he hid it. The executive SAM order personally written by the hand of Eric Holder himself would be designed to keep him from accessing it by proxy, but that wouldn't come until later. The only person who might have seen where the Tripoli File was sent, other than Everett himself, could have been Jennifer Williamson—that night in early January 2013, just before the Benghazi hearings.

In fact, it might be that she is the only one who knew for sure that it was sent anywhere, though she denies telling anyone, nor has anyone ever asked her, "I hope Everett doesn't think I told somebody, I didn't. I really wasn't paying much attention to exactly what he was doing. I was focused more on what he was going to do. What he planned. He told me he didn't have a plan for this, yet. He was either frantic or a little intimidated."

She explains that she tried to distract him by asking "about the interpreter" from their hometown, prying a bit. "He answered that he was very sad about ████ ███ more than anything who strangely had lashed out at HIM when *her* daughter wrecked one of *his* cars. Strange, sure, but it was easy to see he adored her. He probably always had, going back 25 years I don't know if she knew it...They might have even had a thing. But even if they didn't, she was one of the few people he responded to."

While Everett's attention was probably focused on how to play offence against both an external force (Naseef, Saleha and Rabita Trust) seeking retribution against him and an internal force at the highest level of government who were content to see good dedicated CIA (contract) officers die in Libya (as well as State Department men including an ambassador), and

55

furious at the administration's instinctive immediate cover up, which (typical to that administration) sought to blame America and to distract from anything "Muslim-negative" about the Soleimani-militia organized Benghazi attack. (It is entirely possible that his stresses were contrivances from within his own head resulting from undue, unwarranted but typical paranoia. Just because a shadow exists does not make it nefarious)

"Everett was furious," Williamson reminds us, "that it was Americans who had left American patriots out to dry having to be rescued by a cobbled-together group of non-Americans".

Williamson did not know that in 2002, Everett had personally lived through that very thing before. "and he was animated, mad that Soleimani was getting ███████ for Iran from Russia in part of the same deal cut by ██████████ that was, according to his Qatari, enriching her." Dutschke expressed that he wouldn't be surprised if ███████ had some back-channel to Solemani himself and even postulated, "what if the T/O that was killed was supposed to be me?"

"Everett always got huffy with people who couldn't quite understand or see what he was able to see. He didn't have any patience in that way. When someone wasn't following him fast enough, instead of explaining it step-by-step, he just talked really slow to them, like talking down to a child. As if he was being insulted when somebody wasn't getting it. I reminded him that, you can't talk to the committee like that tomorrow. They aren't children. And he shook his head. He understood, probably, but he said, 'What's more important? Their egos or the truth?' But we both know it's their egos."

She went on to warn him again, "You won't be able to bring your own agenda into the room. They are going to want to get their talking points out and they'll probably spend more time talking than listening or asking." He reminded her, "Jenny, this is a closed-door, classified SCIF meeting. Vault-style. No formalities at all. They only posture like that for the camera, when cameras are present to posture to."

She still had concerns, "you can't come at them with anything too complicated." He understood and agreed, but then did the unthinkable, asking, "What about the press? There have to be some, not many, journalists that all they do is the complex and detailed."

She was shocked, but he quickly seemed to retreat from the idea. She still needed to soften his edges, "still, don't treat them like they're stupid. They are US Congressmen you have to treat them with respect."

Apparently, Dutschke did not listen.

Without the coaching Everett had hoped to get from John Mills on what to expect, how to handle whichever members of the committee bothered to show up, and more importantly—how not to feel overwhelmed. Jennifer Williamson had heard that he had gone in as if in adversarial mode, telling one questioner, "Did you not hear me a moment ago? I just answered that question," pointing, "He just asked me the same thing." Apparently he realised his tone might have seemed a little condescending to the safe and clueless men who always had the benefit of hindsight; and more importantly always had some party-driven agendas, because he cut out of the capital before the actual "scheduled" hearing began. In his mind, probably, he still did not know who could be trusted since their already predetermined minds were constantly calculating the political advantages of how to use information as weapons to wallop one another. What he needed to do was get the relevant information into the hands of the right person but *without* being the courier so as to remove himself from the mix.

A portion of the Tripoli File, which purportedly deals with some matters leading up to the Libya Solemani-controlled Ansar Al-Sharia attacks (Benghazi) which was of the short-term and immediate public interest, would be the bait that would lead to the longer-term, bigger picture details that involves the same people and extends all the way up and as far back as 11 years prior. And he needed to do it in such a way that once done he could not step away from it and NOT be caught in the ensuing chaos the way Jeff Sterling and John K. were, whose lives were ruined as the administration used them as public-target-practise to send the CIA men to prison.

The way John K was treated by the DOJ and the press goons in his Abu Zabeyta disclosures (which was not even really *his* doing), one would think that it was John in some black site somewhere, laughing as he waterboarded and tortured some innocent man.

Hollywood in modern culture spends far too much effort into brainwashing and force-feeding the public that the CIA are the bad guys and that all law enforcement or military are the good guys. But the fact is that law enforcement and military are only called in when bad things happen. CIA prevents bad things from happening in the first place, or try to, and to look at it in a bigger, longer-term picture; not just an event to "first respond" to.

In books, movies and culture, the gun-toting FBI agent is some hero who runs around shooting people without consequences and is never outsmarted by the "bad guys," in the end. America (the same holds true for many other countries) holds these people in an almost religious reverence and reinforces the image that LEOs are of a morally superior cloth, expertly trained and skilled and always with the best intentions. None of those attributes are universally true. Not one. The American military man has been equally elevated in structure in an almost automatic and presumptive fashion, though are much more deserving (generally) then LEOs. American military are skilled and expertly trained, but while there's plenty of evidence they are not universally "Men of Honor," they'll most certainly deserve some regard and deference above the non-duty-bound population and definitely more than LEOs. However, the point is, there is an automatic and programmed reaction by the at-large public to uniforms, whether it be with a badge or military insignia. In airports, people stand and applaud when they see someone in military garb. Soldier's seats get upgraded. People buy them drinks and cover their meals. They are made heroic figures in movies, books and television. Police get free coffee and donuts. Droves of programmed people are constantly compelled to approach and say, "Thank you for your service," or "Thank you for your sacrifice."

Even the hyper conservatives and politicians know they are required to pay the price of obligatory gushing, ad nauseum, when referring to either group as, "Our brave men and women in uniform who put their lives on the line every day."

If Americans were all in a drinking-game where they had to swig a shot every time a pundit or politician uttered verbatim, "Our brave men and women in uniform who put their lives on the line every day," then it would need to reinstitute Prohibition because there would never be a sober person in the land. Do a push-up every time some predictable politician or pundit heaves out "Our brave men and women in uniform who put their lines on the line every day." and you would be Atlas in no time.

First of all, one should never put a prosecutor's tool, an FBI agent or local cops, anywhere near the same category as the men and women who actually ARE trained and actually DO live by a code and actually WILL return from their deployment with some physical or mental malady. Some shell-shocked kid who is now missing a leg is now paying an incalculable price for the rest of his life just to humbly make it through the day is NOT the same as some lesser-mettled FBI man whose job and personal affirmation is his daily hope that today is the day he gets to put someone away in jail or prison, begging for the excuse to pull his gun for firing upon a victim or intimidating and demanding respect.

The two are *not* the same.

Secondly, the CIA is never given the same treatment. No one applauds as an intelligence C/O or T/O walks through the airport. No one buys them drinks or pays for their lunch. No one says, "Thank you for your service." They are made the "bad guys" in the movies and culture and aren't allowed to publicly defend themselves. Conspiracy nut-jobs (like Curtis) spread distrust and paint the CIA as sinister and they cannot publicly defend against it. LEOs and prosecutors target them for public ridicule and imprisonment, knowing that they cannot publicly defend themselves. They are never given even a shred of the respect that every badged LEO demands. CIA officers don't run about with guns (that would be dangerously stupid and problematic) or badges to flash around that earn them free coffee. They pay for their own donuts and they fly coach. And yet it is they, CIA, that sees the bigger picture. They don't react. They act (PROactively). Methodically and long-term strategically, they prevent war. They preserve the American way of life, sometimes down to the details and no one thinks of them at all. They don't intrude on you or invade your life (as NSA does), they don't wait by stop signs or speed limit signs hoping to catch you speeding past. They don't drop bombs, missiles or drone strikes on birthday parties causing collateral damage. They just quietly make the micro adjustments needed to ensure *you* still have a job, can put food on your table and don't have to send your children into some war that you don't understand.

They know that while you sleep soundly, there are a lot of bad actors in the world plotting that you can't. Their job is to make sure you and your family can continue to sleep soundly, and you never have to think about it or ask how. It does not matter how. It may be way too complicated to follow. It may not always be pretty. You should never want to know how—just enjoy your life the way it is, the way you envisioned it to be and don't ask who is keeping the demons at bay. In your world, you don't ever need to recognise that the demons are there (sometimes even within your own government). Because the CIA is who protects you. But don't ask how. You do not want to know how the sausage is made, it is far better for you if you don't. Just enjoy the sausage. Yet for whatever reason, CIA is often treated like it is the IRS or NSA. It is known that those frustrations were all part of Dutschke's perspective because he has publicly voiced exactly that, nearly verbatim.

So Everett felt he was the wrong messenger. How, then, could he start the right inquiries into the right matters and still avoid all scrutiny? Especially when the enemies of the state, the enemies of the Constitution are at the very top of government and are allied with foreign enemies, even making financial deals (especially in regards to political campaigns) with them. The Oath of Service requires "protect...against all enemies" whether foreign or domestic. And another oath Everett repeated and lived by, daily since age seven, requires in part to "be a champion of freedom and justice." Neither oath had an expiration date. The only question, since violating oaths was never an option for Dutschke, "is the optimal course a direct action or a passive action?"

"Passive" being finding and trusting the right journalists who will hopefully magically fix everything. Direct being handling it himself since others just cannot be trusted. His usual option, even recently, is direct action—though by the time PACE get to C or E, it has usually morphed into a more passive or defencive option.

Doing his own unsanctioned op was not really an option as it could lead to trouble and requires resources (time, money, personnel). The money he'd been trying to collect was going to a specific purpose since 2012. He was going to launch a new radio station in Tupelo with his wife and relaunch his original career that he loved. Records show that in October of 2012 he paid a large deposit with an engineering company to begin all the required engineering studies and documentation complete with site survey and construction specifications that the FCC required prior to the deadline for the scheduled 2014-2015 LPFM frequency auctions. He had already been assigned a frequency and call letters (by the engineering research) and would begin acquiring equipment as he could afford it. The week after his 2013 return from DC, the following Friday (January 18th), Everett took his stepson to the dentist in Grenada, Mississippi; then on his return to Tupelo met with his engineering consultant to do the site survey for the transmitter and tower. At one point, they were near the office building of Jack Curtis, the brother of Paul Kevin Curtis. Everett was reminded that for weeks he'd been putting off telling Jack something important about Jack's brother, so Everett and the engineer stopped. Jack was not in, but there was a man there with a pickup truck that was collecting a chair from Jack's office. Everett's later testimony matches the phone records obtained by the FBI. Since Jack wasn't there, Everett sent a text.

This is relevant because Everett maintained (in 2013 and 2014) in letters snuck out of the jail to reporters that the text voiced concern over something Jack's brother (Paul Kevin Curtis—the actual mailer of the 2013 KC letters) might do and concerns for Laura Curtis's (the ex-wife of Paul Kevin Curtis) safety (because Everett was unaware that Curtis thought of others as his "enemy").

The FBI records, in fact, DO show the warrants to Verizon to track Everett Dutschke's mobile phone activities. And they, in fact, did get both the records of his BlackBerry and his wife's smartphone—*including* text messages. This means they knew of and had the very text that Everett sent to Jack Curtis on January 18th, 2013 around 3 pm. Yet the message itself, the FBI has, for years now, concealed (the FBI does not often produce that which they wish hidden).

It is not and cannot be that they did not have it; they did. The FBI's concealment isn't because they are generally afraid to use it; it's because any text that they can twist to damage Dutschke in any way they would most certainly use, even if innocent and innocuous. In fact, they went out of their way to twist meanings of texts that Everett's wife, Janet (who is *not* Everett), sent to someone *else* above "burning stuff", taking texts that *she* (not he) sent entirely out of context and to use *her* texts (of which he was entirely unaware) against *him* in the indictment. So it is public record that the FBI had all the texts from the mobile phones. It is also public record that the FBI was not afraid to use (or misuse) those texts (even if agents, like Thomason, had to lie to make her texts somehow relevant to the KC letters) and, in fact, *did so*. Yet the *one* text that is directly relevant was the one "missing" from their records. They were willing to lie to misrepresent the meaning of the wife's (who is *not* Everett) texts, but they were not willing to tell (show) the truth from Everett's own text. The text sent that day, the day of the site survey, was the only meaningful one. And it was the one that "vanished".

There may be plenty of FBI or general LEO apologists that will stretch to make any excuse possible for it, but this missing text alone should have damned "the case against Dutschke", but taken with everything else—the cumulative effect adds up to the biggest manifestly unjust prosecution in American history. However, just judging it as a singular event, there are only two possibilities:

One: the FBI is entirely incompetent—even on a case this high-profile, and genuinely was never provided the text, itself, by the phone company who was issued the warrant and didn't bother asking Jack Curtis about it...
Or
Two: the FBI *did* know all about it and concealed it from everyone, making them corrupt liars.

There is no third choice. Either they knew (making them corrupt) or they didn't (making them stupid). It is one or the other. Considering that they *did*, in fact, lie about everything else, a logical and reasonable person will conclude one possibility, but the reader shouldn't feel free to consider that it is the other, for neither option reflects well on Mueller's FBI.

And *that* should be his legacy.

On the other hand, while very far fewer in number, there are CIA apologists too. Unlike the LEO apologists, who are all programmed blindly by culture to automatically elevate anyone with a LEO badge to a near god-like status, there are those very few people (likely only those who have some sort of direct association with the IC) who might automatically mentally default to an idiom of thought that the CIA, generally, can do no wrong. And it is obvious that this kind of thinking, which Everett had already expressed, could easily qualify Everett for this small category.

That kind of thinking extends past what an agency does or does not do to also reach what an agency knows or does not know, even though agency action (or policy) and knowledge (intel) must be evaluated completely separate from each other because the intel simply is what it is. However, policy (directions, action or inaction) is not an objective thing. Policy (what or how agency acts upon knowledge) is often based on the administrative preferences of both the seventh floor and the president they serve. And the president they were serving (2013) was changing the entire perspective of how the world was supposed to look in his eyes. The president, then, would necessarily skew his actions to base policy around how *he wanted* people (not just people in the IC, but people of the world) to see things. He did not want to base policy on how the world actually looked, but instead on how he wanted people to look at it.

While it is obviously very dangerous to place such naiveté in charge of a whole lot of administrative agencies (the entire executive branch), one agency's founding charter (the CIA) specifically and statutorily states that the purpose of CIA is to serve the president.

So to someone like Dutschke, who is of the general mind to give CIA the benefit of the doubt, at least as far as the intel was concerned, at least two of the (known) five or six elements of the Tripoli file had to already have been known.

- 1.) The entire and full records around Libya both before and during the Soleimani organised Ansar al-Sharia Benghazi attacks.
- 2.) The Qatari's intel of back-door sales of ███ ██ material to Solemani and Iran through Russia to enrich the ███ ████ ███.
- 3.) The Rabita Trust money trail and its direct connections to highly placed spies in the ████ ████ and elsewhere.
- 4.) How that money trail endangers anyone associated with the 2002 Operation Vengeance and how it already led to two deaths, one torture, 15 execution-style assassinations and three unmaskings.
- 5.) Illegal foreign 2012 presidential campaign contributions of scores of millions of dollars from hostile governments and organisations, including from China and terrorist designated organisations through high-profile bundlers and even a high-profile American entertainer.
- 6.) Unknown.

It would seem nearly impossible to Everett that Alec Station would not have known the Rabita Trust and Muslim World League money trail backwards and forwards. It would have been impossible to think Saleha Abedin (and Naseef) connections to the Secretary of State (Clinton/Huma Abedin) were unknown to CIA and/or considered harmless.

And surely the Soleimani connection both to the Russian ████ ███ deal by the US and to the Benghazi attacks and every detail of and behind those attacks was all intel that CIA definitely learned (even if after the fact). The only things that may not have been entirely known in detail would be the Rabita Trust money trail connections to the killings, tortures and unmaskings following 2002 Operation Vengeance, which had been largely forgotten even by those very few who knew and were still around. Because the CIA (esp. the DI) is loaded with PhD and Master's degree adriots unmatched in their ability to see all the patterns in the intel, surely they must have recognised that there is someone that is in common with four of the elements of the Tripoli Files. The one thing that all four have in common is the Secretary of State (Clinton/Abedin). That is not an opinion. It is not an assessment of the intel. It is the intel. It is the intel as it is, no matter the "meaning" or how someone chooses to look at it (or excuse it). The commonality is a fact and it is so glaring that it cannot be missed. So while it seems that Everett's natural propensity had always been to assume that others can see what, to him, is obvious, it was also his propensity to presume that anyone who turned left off Route 123 and carried a little blue ID badge around was smart enough to see it.

So the "knowing" wasn't so much in doubt. The problem is/was the "doing"—The action, the policy, the "what to do about what we know" bit. That was the question. Here's why. The Tripoli File, while it addresses and details other critical issues of national security, in relevant part implicated the Secretary of State (Clinton/Abedin) and exposes a network of not just people, but cash and very bad acts which could be considered a betrayal, treasonous, and a long-time consistent pattern going back years. The Tripoli File was not merely a postulation, as it presumably includes exact names and details. All of the elements of it which circle around the Secretary of State (Clinton/Abedin) including the two Soleimani-Iranian elements which have little to do with Rabita Trust.

(Always follow the money.)

But by law (50USC§402) the CIA is under the National Security Council, of which the Secretary of State is the third ranking member, just after the President and the Vice President. The Vice President at the time (Biden) was such a non-factor (as pertains to those two sections of the Tripoli File) that it meant the Secretary of State was effectively the co-president as far as National Security Council (the NSC) was concerned (in stark contrast to previous administrations where the NSC was a primary focus of the VP). This structure *usually* leads to a very, very close relationship between the CIA and State Department. However, it is obviously *not* the optimal structure for when the ranking member of the NSC (Secretary of State), is compromised and implicated (both by office and personally), and certainly not when the President (of the NSC and of the US) is as well, in matters that are diametrically opposed to *actual* national security; except that "National Security" is whatever the President says it is since the national security policy is set by him. Not only is a president the President of the United States that by charter the CIA serves directly (50USC§3001,1.7(a)(4) and Exec Order 12333). But it also serves under the NSC structure (under the third ranking member Secretary of State), and who is the chairman of NSC? The POTUS is. So there is no bypassing either the ranking member of the NSC (Clinton/Abedin during Obama administration) or the chair of the NSC (POTUS) because there literally is no one higher.

Therefore it could be safe for Everett to have assumed that any above deck CIA staff who recognised the furrow would necessarily be unable to escalate it to the NSC as it would be such an untouchable subject that could not be addressed or even mentioned at all in an NIE or PDB; for when the devil is the boss, then you cannot complain to the boss about the devil.

Compounding the problem is that it was Michael Morell that was the acting DCI at the time (2012 to 2013) who was also the CIA presidential briefer in 2002 (during Operation Vengeance) and was a long time Hillary advocate (and not just a little bit of an advocate either). If CIA employees are discouraged from declaring any political affiliation it is in part because of people like Morell who had proven his allegiance to the Hillary party (note that this is not to necessarily say the Democrat Party, but specifically the "Hillary party" of which he would, along with Huma Abedin, be one of the founding members). Thus, it was definitely not the right time for anyone, especially a temp green-badger civvie to take to the seventh floor anything that revealed anything about that particular Secretary of State. As long as things were known, and they had to be, keep quiet about it and don't complain—lest POTUS or USSOS hear you.

Then there was the additional glaring issue that Morrell was acting DCI during the Benghazi hearings, and it was a massive act of betrayal, especially in the minds of the military-oriented GRS officers, that the American CIA personnel and diplomatic corps were left (albeit late) for rescue by *foreign* assets (which wouldn't have come at all but for quick, unauthorised CIA arrangements). Someone had committed the egregious act of NOT acting— leaving someone(s) to be responsible (almost as complicit as Soleimani) for new stars on the wall. Unforgivable.

It is (almost) understandable that Morell did not defend CIA (as Petraeus would have done) and loudly oppose the false narrative being fed to the administration's press goons by the likes of Samantha Power and Susan Rice (the serial unmasker) and even Hillary Clinton of the "video spurred spontaneous protest"; understandable only because CIA is in many ways unable to and structurally forbidden from defending itself or its heroic personnel. But it is absolutely unforgivable that Morell aided in covering for Hillary (and POTUS) who became the puppet master of events that night, leading to two new stars and a dead ambassador.

Therefore, when Everett finished with the hearing it is not inconceivable he thought the most prudent choice would be to wait. After all, he had waited since September anyway and the only thing he did was meet with Congressman Nunnelee to seek a meeting with Mark Turry (Nunnelee, new in office, did not know who Turry was which was probably why the meeting had not happened by the time of Everett's asking Jennifer Williamson the same thing as late as January 2013).

The possibility that Everett was content to do nothing, though, seemed unlikely to Jennifer Williamson, "When I asked him to stay, and he didn't, I could tell he was in that mind that he was going to do something. He was determined. You could see it on his face, in his eyes, his body language. He has this intensity when he's like that, that's, I don't know but it's serious. That was the last time I saw him. He held my hand a minute and said 'wish me luck,' then was gone. Next time I saw him was all over the news. Every channel. Claiming that they (Muller, Holder and the press) thought HE did what that other guy had been arrested for. It was nonsense and everybody knew it. But once it got going, it got bigger and bigger and couldn't be stopped. That's when I knew it was all wrong and that they were just using all *that* to shut him down, like the others. He must have gone to somebody. I warned him. I did."

Whether he was warned or not it is exactly what he did. Starting the week of January 14th (and continuing through SAM imprisonment as he found ways to sometimes defy Holder's SAM order) he reached out both directly and through surrogates to Sharyl Atkisson (CBS), James Rosen (FOX), Emily Waggster-Pettus (AP) and Patsy Brumfield as he took his cues from Jeff Sterling and John Kiriakou (though it might be as easily said that "Not having learned a lesson from Jeff Sterling and John K"). It might have also been specifically calculated in order to pick a public fight, as he was often want to do; thinking it best that such a fight had better be in public since fighting in the shadows is a good way to end up lying cold in one.

The problem was, again, that there were so many details and people and connections that the issue is too complex for a press that likes a simple to follow, three-paragraph story. The larger problem was simply one of credibility. A sitting president (especially that one) and his sitting Secretary of State (especially that one—counting Huma Abedin) had a considerable and measurable advantage with the (2013) press. Which is why Everett sought out those he thought could be trusted to dig without ever needing to even mention or know the name J. Everett Dutschke at all (two of them were already familiar). The facts are the facts, whether Dutschke was involved or even existed on this earth or not. His presence or involvement is meaningless to the facts. Facts don't care about "credibility" of a source, they are simply facts. This invisible hand off was likely what he was hoping for.

That is not what he got.

While he was focused so intently on how to pursue an offencive strategy, he completely ignored defence. Thus he was shocked and surprised when the attacks on his credibility began. Just about the time as the public Benghazi hearing at which Secretary of State Hillary Clinton replied to questions about the death of CIA contractors (and an ambassador) with the shocking phrase—"What difference, at this point, does it make?" Everett recognised that he was going to be forced into a corner and that the unlimited power of the executive branch would have no problems extending its tendrils into even Tupelo, Mississippi to reach him and would, at some point, result in a literal and inevitable very public battle for his life.

Thus at the (later) point in April of 2013, when his attorney, Tony Farese, told him, "the noose is tightening and it is tightening around you," Everett already knew it had been tightening for a while.

Again, some might still ask "What does any of this have to do with the 2013 KC letters?" To some readers, the answers by now should be clear; others who may not be very good at visualizing completeness from mere abstract framework might require more direct connections. Of this latter group of people, it is a strange phenomenon that, though their mind needs to see a completed picture in order to recognise the picture, they often ask about or they assume motives to affirm their belief in what they are seeing (and yet actually dealing with "motive" at all is a drastic swing *from* the objective and *to* the murky land of the subjective). Truly knowing "motive" of anyone or any group of people is completely impossible, even in hindsight as one cannot ever really "get into the head" of another. It is an entirely speculative exercise and actually requires *more* imagination than the ability to visualize a completeness from only the framework, without the taint of the speculative "motive." Also, "motive" is irrelevant to the facts and events. That is to say that—"this FACT exists and this *event* occurred thusly" is what it is, completely regardless of motive (which can taint the math of it); which is asking "why" did a person do or not do something, the same as inquiring what is in his head.

Take for example that a fact based case could be—A man was shot in his home by a .25 calibre pistol, the same kind of pistol owned by his wife that also bears her fingerprints and was missing one bullet. The pistol was found in her pocket when the police arrived who "sprayed" her for powder burn traces that they observed on her right hand. Interviewed neighbours state that they heard the man and wife in a heated row just prior to hearing a single gunshot. When the constables arrived, the wife stated, "I have just shot my husband." She was immediately arrested. In dealing with the case only using the facts in the case to arrive at any conclusion, untainted by "motive", one draws from this example their conclusion *only* from the facts and events. The conclusion is that she is guilty of the murder of her husband, with her gun, in their home. Nothing else is needed for that conclusion. She, no one else, is clearly "the bad guy."

But when one begins down the foggy road of the subjective instead of the objective, then the conclusions become equally as foggy. It is *those* minds that deal in speculation, which is often dishonest to the facts and events.

Using the same above hypothetical—facts are not ever enough for the press, who seldom wish to simply connect the dots of details (facts and events) in a way that is accurate. And prosecutors do not operate in a fact-based world either since they know the "Best Story Wins" (an actual name of an actual prosecutor's handbook on how to gain convictions by contriving stories and narratives). So they cherry-pick and misconstrue any fact and/or event that can be twisted to sell their story (to the public, judge and jury), concealing any fact that does not help sell their tale. Conclusions can be altered by the subjectives.

Using the same hypothetical example—suppose the news reports that neighbours have been told by the wife for years that the husband, an overweight, unemployed ex-con, had been beating her and threatening her for years. Suppose the neighbourhood preacher told reporters and an investigator that she'd show up to church alone, sometimes in tears and that the liquor store proprietor saw her frequently as she purchased as much alcohol as she could claiming she "had to hurry up and get home with it before *he* got mad." Suppose the wife had wept to her sister and mother that the husband had been molesting their young daughter for years and that she was afraid to confront him. Suppose that she had told her boss, who in turn told a reporter that she had to be paid in cash as she had to give it to her husband each night as soon as she returned. Suppose that a neighbour recalled to police an incident when he asked the wife why SHE was cutting the grass instead of her husband, she answered, "Because he is passed out in the bathroom." And when the same neighbour asked how is the puppy her daughter got for Christmas, the wife answered, "My husband threatened my daughter and then strangled the puppy to death in front of her on the dinner table." Suppose a reporter wrote that the husband had previously been in prison for drugs, burglary and arson and that three girls had accused him of rape and an old man from the trailer park the husband had lived long ago, a neighbour of the husband who had complained about the noise, had ended up dead in his small garden as he tended to his marigolds. Suppose the wife, when asked by her mother to leave her husband, told her mother as well as the later investigators, "I was afraid to leave. He said he'd not only kill me and my daughter but my mother as well. And I love my daughter and my mother. But I just couldn't let him keep doing...what he was doing. He said he'd had enough, he was going to kill me, so I had to protect my family."

Now... Does your conclusion change? Is the wife a cold-blooded murderer? Is she still the "bad guy" or isn't the husband now the "bad guy"? Can you see most people would at least soften their previous conclusion?

Note that in this second, amended version of the example, there are *no* facts, nothing that is directly related to the actual details of the actual shooting. In fact, if one goes back through and reads it, every single bit of it is from her projected cunning. None of that was actually observed by anyone. Yet her disclosure of it all ascribes a motive, A *justifiable* motive in the minds of most people for her actions. At no point in the amended story was the actual motive explicitly assigned, it was implied; but that was enough to sell the story that SHE wanted told the way in which she wanted it. Because the subjective can evoke emotions, it is far more powerful, sadly, than actual facts and events.

American prosecutors know this. American press knows this. The American public at large, however, does not and buys the tale as sold based on their emotions (created by the crafted narrative) instead of the details and facts. The actual facts and events, at this point, have become secondary props to the emotional ("motive") narrative. In the factual recounting, the facts were all that was necessary to reach a logical conclusion. Yet after the *non*factual, anecdotal telling of reports of events that may or may not have happened, it is only the sum total of the anecdotes, the narrative which becomes the priority and the facts are merely incidental to the tale the tale of "why" she did what she did, sadly becomes more important than the simple determination of whether or not she did it.

It may well be that *not a thing* that she told the neighbours, the police, the proprietor of the liquor store, her boss, the minister, her mother and sister or what any reporter said is true. There is an equal, maybe even more likely chance that her claims damning the husband are false. She could be a serial and pathological liar and everyone knows that reporters generally care little for the truth and will dutifully report anything any official (especially a LEO) claims as if it is unchallengeable. It could well be that the husband is entirely unaware of anything that she was saying to all of those people, just as he was unaware of her torrid affair with the minister, since he was too distracted by caring for their special needs daughter and making sure their daughter did not know about her mother's drug and alcohol addiction. But even if this was the reality, it would still never gain any traction in the minds of the American public since the other story has now become the "official" narrative and the husband, now dead, is incapable of telling it. So the truth remains forever hidden away and the tall-yarn of the wife replaces it. Told by enough of the press and the wife's tale (like many wives-tales) "becomes" the "accepted truth" since the public believes whatever is reported on the internet, newspaper, and especially television. Besides, there seems to be an (unfair) inherent propensity to want to believe that the wife (any wife) was horribly abused and protecting her family from the evil husband. *That* seems to unfortunately fit the predetermined tastes of the media-programmed American public—so the press and prosecutors are simply catering to the monsters they created.

And then there is the reality that (especially when the "battered wife" story is so much more palatable to the American taste) there is no appetite for the majority of Americans to look *past* a well-sold story that they want to buy anyway, since the truth is much more complex and involved than her false narrative and they would have to spend too much in trying to intellectually grasp it. This is another way of stating simply that when the general public is too lazy to think or follow (which is always) it is just so much easier to believe the lie. Besides, the perception is—"well, everyone else believes it, so I will too."

It is because of all this (the lie was told first, the public's taste, media salesmanship, group think pressure and intellectual laziness) that the press and prosecutors (often one and the same) seize the advantage and why Winston Churchill (though credit is often disputed) said—"A lie can circle the world three times before the truth has a chance to get it pants on."

And Sir Francis Bacon—"What a man rather were true the more readily he believes." And Elizabeth Bowen—"Nobody speaks the truth when there's something they must have." And Janet Frame—"In an age of explanation one can always choose a variety of the truth." And Adolf Hitler— "The broad mass of a Nation will more easily fall victim to a big lie than a small one." And Destouches—"The absent are always in the wrong." And even the Bible—"You are being fooled by those who deliberately twist the truth." And "He who speaks first SEEMS right, until cross-examined." And Carlyle—"History is a distillation of rumour".

The press and prosecutors know they will automatically be trusted, no matter if they say 1+1= 85. And if enough say it enough, then 85 "becomes" the accepted "truth" And judges (who are also human) are *not* immune to the virus of the contagious lie. In fact, they are *more* susceptible than most because they gravitate toward whatever position holds the most power and control, which is rarely the position of skepticism. As such, judges will look for novel legal ways to support whatever is the popular position, over the truth, most often by not even addressing a raised factual or legal truth and by misconstruing the issue. Then, once the judge makes a decision in court, even if the decision is based on a bold-faced lie, it is forever magically whatever they say 1+1 is now 85! And there is no appealing their decision to a higher court because higher court judges cannot be bothered to actually *read* every case that comes before them, especially if it means overturning a lower court ruling; that would mean taking the *un*popular position. And they won't stick *their* neck out for that.

So since the popular accepted tale of a battered wife was the one first presented, so then bought by the public in drone fashion, and the murdered husband cannot counter it with the truth, which wouldn't be accepted anyway since *her* narrative is the one the public *wants* to believe, then history will record the lie as if it is so.

This is shameful, but it is the way of the human world. Anyone who dares be skeptical of the "official" tale is branded as a crazed "conspiracy theorist". How dare someone question the "official" tale. How dare someone think outside of the accepted communal story. How dare someone step off the plantation.

Therefore, it is unfortunate, but that growing lack of independent thought and judgment which is now endemic in America is a most Un-American trait; one which they would each deny, as long as they are sure everyone else in the herd is denying it too.

The sad phenomenon is why "motive" seems to matter to the masses in the case of the KC letters. This is, in part, because (although the "official" tale has changed numerous times) the facts were deemed unimportant. In this case, the events and facts of Dutschke's past life and the hard-to-follow, hard-to-pronounce names and connections and the escalation of events are so much more complicated than simply saying—"Dutschke 'framed' Curtis for the ricin attacks as part of an on-line feud."

That "feud" story, originally propagated by a speculating press was a fueled spark set off by Curtis's ex-wife and is utter nonsense. There was no "on-line feud." But reporters world-wide repeated it, then each other ad nauseum without bothering to look for a single fact that would verify the tale. Without details, the story should have died. But it did not, thus ascribing (phony) "motive" which somehow became widely accepted despite that it is devoid of logic. It was simple, so it served the public's purpose.

Therefore, Everett's past is equally essential to those who require "motive" as part of their calculus for dealing with the much larger and correct truth. Details are important to the truth, and in this case, that is where the real motives are found. It is easy to fall into the media and prosecutor-driven trap of not accepting the truth (since it is laden with actual burdensome facts and details), which means denying reality, simply because one does not *want* to accept motive. This is why, in the long-run, motive should be meaningless. In other words, the what, when, who and how are far more important than the "why" because what, when, who and how are questions that deal with facts and details (objective) and they are what they are—unchangeable, unaffected by perspective, preference and speculation (the definition of subjective).

Thus, what _really_ matters is where and what details there are. As in, using the hypothetical example, the details that lead to the conclusion that the wife shot her husband. Nothing else really should matter since nothing else has any _real_ details to it. Questioning "why" does not change the details one bit.

However, for those who need to factor in the subjective ("motive"), then it is much wiser to see the motives of _everyone_, which is why the historical details are important. The claim of "retaliation" by Everett against Curtis, for a non-existent "feud" was the (phony) ascribed "motive". But if that is a valid subjective consideration, then the (not phony) "motive" of "retaliation" and the drive of it is just as real and powerful for Rabita Trust, Saleha Abedin and Naseef as is and was America's drive of retaliation felt after 9/11.

It is a _fact_ that there was no "on-line feud" between Dutschke and Curtis, but that is not what _was_ reported. It is a fact that there _was_ definite animus and a thirst for vengeance that America acted upon (in sometimes uncomfortable ways) against those responsible in any way for 9/11 and equally as much animus in return when some of those people were neutralised. The difference is that the details, events and connections have remained mostly unknown, therefore also not reported. It is a documented fact that the details show, at every turn, a very specific and extreme targeting of Everett through the most serious national security tools available from the highest levels of government, which, by itself, demonstrates that the developed decade-long details of Everett's history are relevant and more so because of the "perfect storm" of exact people that all attained power at the same time, and the long-established connections of those very people to Rabita Trust, Naseef, Saleha Abedin. And ultimately the three financiers and benefactors to the Abedin family and Muslim World League network.

The unpalatable fact is that when an administration, particularly that administration, feels the least bit threatened, or even if it is in the interest of maintaining their official image (illusion or not), that administration will go to extreme measures, no matter the human cost to those measures.

And that particular administration has a documented history of lies, deceit and destruction of lives and families in pursuit of their cover-ups. This was just another, controlled from the very top, and in the end they kept the Tripoli File from being made public (for now) *and* protected themselves while giving the country a boogeyman "bad guy" to hate as they simultaneously endeavoured to save face and to redefine what one expects a "terrorist" to look like (Dutschke is a white, Christian male).

So anyone interested in the true story of the 2013 KC letters cannot ignore the history of J. Everett Dutschke, or the details and connections of the Muslim World League (as part of it), as inconvenient as it all may be to some who wish it all stay hidden forever. These things, because integral to the history, are in fact, integral to the entire story, especially so for those who are tempted to ask—"But *why* would that administration lie about… (the evidence, the connections, the money trail, the names and details of the office holders who involved themselves, the tactics, the law or any number of concealed issues)?"

In the end, the asking of "why" is meaningless since the why does not matter to any details, just that it is. *why* the DOJ chooses to lie for its masters is secondary to the fact that it does, demonstrably so. This tendency to lie was not merely given a pass by that particular administration, it was encouraged. Holder, Mueller, Yates, Comey, Strzok, Sigler, Thomason, Lamar—none of them had anything to fear about lying to the court and to the public as long as their lies served the political purpose of that administration. Lie to the public about your target, break them financially, intimidate them and their family and anyone that would dare defend the target...then smear. Most people, certainly most Americans, do not know that the FBI and federal prosecutors actually train and teach each other such tactics. The American public, at large, does not know because the American media is aware that the American public does not WANT to believe it.

But it is true, nonetheless, especially of Holder or Comey or Mueller. Just ask James Risen, James Rosen, Jeff Sterling, John Kiriakou, General Michael Flynn, Roger Stone, George Papadopoulos and even the 45th president, Trump. If there is no case, the prosecutors (and the cops who serve them) will invent one.

And it is very arbitrarily selective as to who gets prosecuted since certain people are immune from their grave offences; among them Jim Comey, Bob Mueller, Eric Holder, Sally Yates, Stephen Thomason, Huma Abedin, the Clintons and others...proving there really is no justice since it is selective.

After September 11th, 2001, America proved it could grieve better than any other country. It proved it could seek vengeance better than any other country. It proved it could strengthen itself better than any other country. By the time 2012 arrived, it had also proven it could completely forget better than any other country. It took only a year and a decade for America to announce (September 11th, 2012) that it had surrendered, when it left its citizens (patriots who still believed in the America of September 12th, 2001) to die—having to be rescued (and too late) by foreigners—then blame *its own* (American) citizens and chastising them for being mean to Muslims in some video that no one ever saw.

But no amount of pretending otherwise could actually sever the factual ties between the Deputy Secretary of State Huma Abedin and her mother, Saleha Abedin, nor the ties between Saleha Abedin and Rabita Trust and Abdulla Omar Naseef or the three financiers that funded the Abedin family legacy (IMMA), the Muslim World League network, therefore its operations. People can pretend those ties were not real or ignore them as they did during that administration, but pretending or ignoring does not change the inconvenient truth. No amount of pretending or forgetting, even now, can bring back to life the three financiers, benefactors for the Abedin family.

The matter was compounded when President Obama finally repaid his debt to the man who "hacked" (unauthorized entry) the State Department's passport database (2008—Analysis company) to conceal Obama's controversial travel; Obama appointing that man, John Brennan, to become Director of Central Intelligence. Brennan, the same man who had left the agency during the previous (W. Bush) administration and then founded the "security consulting" company to get Obama elected, was also the same man who was the Station Chief in ███████████ and was never informed of the 2002 operation, was just as eager to see some payback on anyone who took out his fellow Muslims and ██████ friends. John Brennan, a follower (converted) of Islam, was now in charge of the CIA. What would the Muslim, John Brennan, do?

It is known that one edict he quickly instructed was to remove the word "jihadi" or "jihad" from CIA vernacular. No longer, according to the commanding DCI (Muslim, John Brennan) was any C/O, R/O or analyst (or even a brown-badger working in the agency Starbucks) allowed to refer to any Muslim terrorist act as an act of "jihad" or as a "jihadi"; (equally eschewed was identification of "Muslim terrorist" or "Muslim extremist"). The CIA just became Muslim-friendly.

But it did not happen in a vacuum.

That particular administration, notably anti-Israel, even actively tampering in the Israeli election to aid Netenyahu's opponent, issued an order that the extremist terrorist group (partly funded by Rabita Trust and WML) ISIS, was not to be called ISIS in the Obama administration. The President and everyone in that administration must instead refer to them as "ISIL" (substituting Levant for Syria) which is a slight against the existence of Israel.

Disgustingly, the cowardly sycophantic press went along with it and it was not long before the Obama-worshipping reporters began to shamefully change their language to "ISIL", clamouring for his approval. The near animosity of the American president could not have made Everett's Cesarea friends happy.

The man who would never have dared to stand up to Hillary (the way the DCI Petraeus would have if he had not been "scandaled out" by Obama/Mueller's FBI), Michael Morell, was now the ongoing (2013) DCI upon Brennan's appointment. Morell was the presidential CIA briefer during the '02 operation (even if he, personally, was outside the BIGOT list), perhaps had even seen (but not archived) the operational names (CIA Alias and AIN). He would have been seventh floor during the (2011) Susan Rice unmasking and the now missing Sterling warrant (missing perhaps because illegal, violating HIPAA, not CIPA), *and* during Everett's acquisition of the Tripoli File. What would HE do now that he was finally leaving the CIA? Brennan gave Morell an example to follow. Morell immediately joined a "security consulting firm" that was working for—guess who—the Clinton Foundation and to elect the next president (Morell hoped), Hillary Clinton!

Hillary did not need Huma Abedin's powerful influence (though she had it) in order to paint a target on Everett Dutschke's back. The Tripoli File was enough impetus for that. With so many people at the very top of government aiming for Dutschke, it was as if they were all one and the same.

(In 2015, which is *after* Everett's SAM "conviction" and disappearance into the bowels of the National Security Unit in the US-ADX Supermax, the HPSCI issued a subpoena for all of Hillary Clinton's correspondence during Secretary of State. This makes the Tripoli Files' value much higher since she, through surrogates, defied the subpoena and destroyed anything and everything that might have held any correspondence. Later it was learned she forgot some. They were discovered on the laptop of Huma's ex-husband, Anthony Weiner, in a New York State investigation which forced FBI director Jim Comey to pretend he was "reopening" the Clinton email investigation for a spell.)

To suggest that all of this is irrelevant to the 2013 KC letters prosecution of the so-called "ricin attacks" would be folly. But even assuming arguing that it is irrelevant, some readers might still ask and want to know, "Who is J. Everett Dutschke," and rightly so.

Though this comes after Everett's arrest, it was revealed to Mueller's FBI by a different agency and by some working locally, that Everett kept safe deposit boxes at bank branches in three cities. Normal (warrant) practises aside, the FBI must have been saddened and confused when they did not discover the Tripoli File in any safe deposit box, as they were undoubtedly hoping to do, this time unencrypted. It is possible, but unknown if his wife, Janet, aided them as they had begun to pressure and manipulate her and would have been curious when they discovered credit cards, travel documents and visas, and various names, that did *not* bear the name "J. Everett Dutschke". The aliases and passports perhaps were supposed to have been returned to the central cover office long, long before, or still active, or there may have been other reasons or uses. It will never be known. One thing is for certain, they are now burned.

Several news outlets have referred to Dutschke as a "ghost." The "men's" magazine GQ in 2013 called Dutschke "a mysterious figure." And one of his previous wives' sister said in an interview, "No one really knew anything about him" and "it was like he kept a separate life or family somewhere."

This, however, can only be part of the circumstances that is unique to any interviews involving Dutschke, which is that the only people that *will* talk are the ones who really did not know him. In fact, such descriptions are in stark contrast to the reality that both he and his wife kept a very public face. YouTube was once rich with videos of Everett, some giving large public speeches. All those videos but one (of him solving a Rubik's Cube with rapid speed) have vanished. People recall television commercials of him during his campaign against the 30-year House of Representatives incumbent. His former students all seem to have had easy access to him, thought very highly of him (at the time) and were heavily influenced by him, but that is very nearly all most will say. They are, in fact, probably the key to understanding him—but the problem is, most behave as if they've been forbidden by someone to talk to him.

But the commonality is that every single one, all of them, thought so highly of the man, almost an inspirational figure—*until* the 2013 news coverage (by people who did *not* know him). In other words—those that actually knew him only changed their mind about the man they (personally) knew *after* being *told* to do so by people who did not know him; based entirely on reported alleged events that not a single one of them ever witnessed or could conceive possible. They were the ones who were around him daily, and in very close proximity, and not one ever actually witnessed even a hint of any of the alleged criminal behaviour. However, the news of something is considered more credible than first-hand experience with the person...somehow. If NBC or CNN say Dutschke did...whatever...then it must be so, right? Even though they, the ones around him daily, knew better. Just shut up and believe what you're told. No matter what, no matter who.

Regardless, the Dutschke they knew was *not* how someone who is "mysterious" (using the words of GQ) carries himself. By all accounts Dutschke was an open book, unless those accounts are by those to whom he wasn't. It is that simple. If it ever was that Dutschke was comfortable living in the shadows, he stepped out of the shadows once he moved to Tupelo (mostly). If ever, as happens in the normal course of life, he encountered conflicts, he did not seem to deal with those conflicts secretly and in some sneaky fashion, but rather boldly, direct and often very, very public, making sure that everything was known and disclosed to everyone so that there would never be any misunderstanding or misconstruing of any accusations of hiding anything. He taught his students to be the same (a lesson, based on their still scared silence that they must have unlearned). In fact, he seemed to prefer to take his battles public and never be cowardly and indeed almost welcomed public confrontation.

If there was to be debate, then air it in sunlight. No matter with who, no matter how powerful or perceived as knowledgeable. Direct and bold action was very much his trademark. Often the battles seemed as if David was picking fights with Goliath, yet the objective almost always appeared to be to expose Goliath as hypocritical or fake. Whether positive or not, the reality is that people remember that Everett must have gotten some sort of joy from challenging bullies as if he was still taking down dictators, often coming across as arrogant or gleeful in demonstrating mental superiority, especially in the face of his supposed "superiors." So the claims of his being "mysterious" (a la GQ) do not look to be supported by fact. But it is, again, another case of: if you repeat a lie often enough, people believe the lie. The details of Dutschke's life, at least post 2005, however, are details that suggest otherwise.

That isn't to propose that he was gregarious; he was reserved, but approachable. The only thing that bolstered that general (GQ et al) claim is that although the actual inquiry into his 2005-2012 life reveals someone who does NOT seem to be trying to keep a low profile, even those who know him still feel like he kept everyone at a distance. The best way to describe him sounds self-contradictory, but it is not—that is "Public, but personal."

Yet again, the media (people who did *not* personally know him) needed to obediently destroy Everett, because that's what that administration wanted (also a trained DOJ tactic), and because sensationalism sells. So the truth of the man, known to some, became unimportant; replaced with a fiction that was unrecognisable to those that literally knew him ("I do not recognise the person you are describing as the man that I personally know"). But that did not matter to the press...so just shut up and believe what you're told.

In military terms this is known as a force multiplier. The cabal needed to attack someone. Dutschke. He seemed to be withstanding the earliest attacks and almost welcoming the battle, turning the attacks around on to the weaponized system itself. So at their first opportunity (the instant Curtis uttered Dutschke's name) they weaponized the entire DOJ, mobilizing the overwhelming force of the DOJ/FBI which, though the most formidable force in the world, Everett looked to thwart as well.

So then, in typical fashion, the Holder DOJ/Mueller FBI weaponized the full force of the national and international media with its relentless swarms of constant poisonous attacks, attacks that Everett is particularly sensitive to. The weaponizing of the press is the strongest, as it influences everything else.

A family member, friend, spouse or any other loyal person, who knows the target better than anyone else, still sees the global hostile coverage and cannot help but to be swayed by it.

For example—A wife, a mother and a brother who all know very well that their loved one is not a cult leading, drug dealer, who also did not kidnap the Lindbergh baby, suddenly sees that the rest of the world believe that their loved one IS a cult-leading, drug-dealing kidnapper of the Lindbergh baby, because the worldwide press says so, will likely begin to think, "Well, maybe my loved one actually IS a cult-leading, drug-dealing, Lindbergh baby kidnapper and I just never knew it. Everyone else (who don't even know the guy) seem to think it, so now I must believe it, too (even though I know better). After all, the media says so."

This common, practised and taught, DOJ force multiplier tactic, is powerful because it works almost every time. It works because the loved ones, who are really the ones who should advocate *against* the accusations and tactics, since they know the person better, simply do not know and do *not* realise that it is just a force multiplying tactic. The loved ones do not know that it is just a ploy and it is (in this) *they*, not the accused, that are the targets. Part of the objective of the scheme is that it severs any support that the accused *should* be able to count on from the loved ones, The advocates who actually *know* better, but were cajoled away from what they know, to accept what they don't— simply because the media said so (because the weapon of the press has been deployed).

The weaponized press is not merely targeting and deployed against the accused to poison the population (therefore any potential jury pool); the scheme is deployed against the wife, the mother and brother—to poison *them*. The FBI and prosecutors have stuck with this scheme of collusion for so long because family members of the accused do not know it is just a (practised) weapon—they just don't know better.

In the Dutschke case, the force multiplier scheme was maximized like never before in history with the imposition of the executive order of the Holder SAM, the order that Eric Holder personally penned with the endorsements of Bob Mueller (2013) and Jim Comey (2014), which involved "National Security" and ordered extreme solitary confinement with no communication with any person, including the press; meaning that Holder, using the executive power that the President granted only to him (under 28CFR§501), was *not* going to allow *any* counter to whatever narrative they had presented to the press who, without question, dutifully parroted to the public—no matter that their narrative was physically, scientifically, temporally and utterly impossible. The strictures of SAM also prevented, in writing, and by the order of the Attorney General, that Dutschke's appointed lawyer, Ken Coghlan, was not allowed to communicate with any person on Dutschke's behalf either, which necessarily included the press. Meaning that, again, there would be no dissent allowed of the official Holder/Mueller DOJ and by the team of the original arrested suspect—the mailer, Paul Kevin Curtis and his lawyer, Christi McCoy—not a single one of them actually knew Dutschke; McCoy, Mueller and Holder had never met him, and Curtis and Comey only briefly, nor any of the FBI agents. Yet these people, with not a clue about the man, were the ones telling the press what to trumpet about him.

Along with personal pressure directly applied by "investigators," this scheme worked, ensuring that those who actually knew him—too afraid or ambivalent to help—would stay silent. The usual scheme involves the FBI agent or officer acting as a "trusted" person who "just wants to get to the bottom of this thing" or "just want to keep people safe." The FBI does this in every single case (calling someone they do not know a "monster") because it usually works. It, like the weaponization of the press, works because those who actually know the accused are unaware it is a ploy, a tactic, part of the routine scheme. With this kind of applied personal pressure, the "trusted" investigators contact the accused's loved ones (people who know him best), as if reaching out- even on a personal level (i.e.—"I'm just calling to see if you're okay") or a simple text ("hang in there") to gain trust. This is called "working the relationship." And though the FBI is a very practised amateur in this compared to CIA, the scheme often works, eventually manipulating that loved one, that trusted advocate (the person who knows the accused better), to turn against the "monster" and "give us something that will help" convict him. Of course they do not use the words "convict him", though that is their actual and only goal. Instead they replace "convict him" with phrases like "keep everyone safe" or "do the right thing"—neither of which is truthful, but truth does not matter when they are executing the scheme. Only conviction matters to LEOs.

Because only conviction matters it does not matter then if the person they "turn" or "flip" is telling the truth or not. The FBI, in this case especially, will always take a well-crafted and convincing lie if it will aid them. Whether the one who "flips" tells them the truth or not is meaningless so long as LEOs can spin or twist it to fit their narrative. This makes the "flipped" a force multiplier.

In the Dutschke case, and from early on, teams and teams were sent out to "flip" Dutschke's people, the people who actually knew him. Secret Service, FBI, JTTF and even local badged LEOs "worked" scores of people, often meeting with them at their home, waiting for them at their work, calling, sending texts and emails and social media messages—all the things that would be considered stalking or harassment if committed by another non-badged person. But what are you going to do—call the cops and tell them you are being harassed by the cops?

The conviction-hungry officers/agents harassed scores of Dutschke's people and in typical fashion presented themselves as "just trying to help figure it all out,"; presented themselves as friends or buddies, just as the LEO textbook requires. And it usually works.

However this time, it did not.

After months of sometimes near constant harassment by the badged "buddies," not a single one of those who actually knew Dutschke "flipped". Most eventually told their armed harassers to leave them alone, some had to go as far as to say, "Talk to my attorney. Leave me alone." The reason for this, in part, is because not a single one of them ever had or knew anything to "flip" about. They all knew nothing because there was nothing to know. These were the people who knew him personally and to them Everett Dutschke was a pillar of the community, so it all came as a sudden surprise when unfamiliar accusations began flying in 2013. It came as a sudden surprise to them that they (those who actually knew him) were being told by the LEO controlled press (who didn't know him) to think differently and change their own mind. None had ever seen even a trace of anything he was suddenly being accused of. Thus, even if they have *wanted* to feed anything to the conviction machine, there was literally nothing that those who knew him could contribute. The only people willing to cast stones with those who were *not* close to Everett and did *not* know him.

With one meaningless exception. There was one person the FBI agents wanted to "work" but could not because he was underage and his mother had forbidden them from her son. So they waited.

The moment the boy turned 18, they waited until his mother went to work, then they snuck over to the boy's grandfather's house so they could "go to work" on the boy.

Because the boy was not savvy enough to *not* be intimidated by their badge, gun, credentials and the national media firestorm surrounding the case, and because they manipulated him from the highest (literally) level of government, he fell victim to the "caring buddy" routine and he "flipped".

What he disclosed to them was earth-shattering and would surely make it into the next Presidential Daily Briefing. The information they squeezed from the tyke was bigger news than Pearl Harbor and 9/11 combined. It was so devastatingly crucial that it may have saved all of civilization in the entire universe.

The new prise informant-turned-rat for the FBI told them that he had once personally seen Dutschke toss out his old GPS system after he bought a new one. Earth-shattering! Damning! Who in their right mind would replace their vehicle's GPS with a newer, better model? Why...any person who could even conceive of such a monstrous deed *must* surely be guilty of violating the international treaty against the development of biological weapons, right? Replacing your Tom-Tom has just got to be indicative of a war-crime. It's just got to be! No one who has ever gotten a newer GPS system could be anything other than an international terrorist, right? It's treasonous!

The scared recent-minor cornered by the world-savvy FBI agent grown-ups also informed the men that he had personally thrown the cardboard box of the new computer Dutschke had bought into a neighbour's rubbish bin. This claim was something any sharp FBI man would know could not have been true since they already knew that Everett's wife, Janet, had stuffed that box full of old bills and bank statements and burned it during the bonfire gathering, as evidenced by *her* text to someone *other* than Everett; a text which *predated* the KC letters in the first place. Nevertheless, throwing away the box in which your new computer was once packaged is *not* a violation of the biological weapons treaty or any federal law. Who on earth keeps their old boxes piling about? Hoarders? Whether the boy tossed it (which did not happen) or Janet burned it (which did) full of her silly old bills and receipts (as it seemed her practise to do), neither scenario does anything to bolster the FBI's case. There was nothing at all related to ricin (or any biological or chemical weapon) on the computer, nor the letters themselves. The new computer (box), just like the new GPS, was irrelevant.

What IS relevant is that the same exact agent who had stalked and harassed Janet and others in Dutschke's circle was the same exact agent who waited until that day the child turned eighteen so that his mother's boundaries no longer applied (then waited until she was not around to pounce on the boy) to ambush the boy in order to turn him into their snitch—and that this FBI agent was the same exact shameful cretin (Stephen Thomason) who had lied from the stand to the magistrate judge, Susan Alexander; lied and misled in the arrest affidavit, lied to the grand jury and was eventually taken off the case (replaced as lead agent by Grant).

Their newly-made, recently-minor FBI informant was, like most Americans, naïve to the schemes and regularly deployed tactics. He was unaware that when he fell victim to the FBI, he was just being used as a tool for that administration (and more-so, that if he had stuck by his claim would have, and later did, legally imperil his mother). Holder, Mueller and everyone involved, including the criminally corrupt FBI harasser (Thomason) had to be horribly disappointed—but really should have just been ashamed that they rested their high-profile national security case on the testimony of a badge-intimidated naïve boy. Since the badge-intimidated naïve boy really gave them nothing of value (though they did try to use his testimony, looking foolish in the process), all the special prosecution team had left was their fabricated testimony of the lab results to rely on—and that would inevitably be a problem since the final lab analysis contradicted their initial and public claims.

Since the conviction, the only narrative being perpetuated is the ever-changing and constant prattling by Paul Kevin Curtis which is always such rubbish and in always Curtis's self-interest and self-aggrandizement. And always as rapidly hostile and demonizing of Dutschke as one might expect.

However, the history books, almanac and ever-present internet still present Everett as having committed a war crime that he did not, in this case, commit. Radio talk shows—such as Glenn Beck and Coast to Coast AM have referred to Everett as an assassin. None of that is helpful. Because he was locked away in the National Security Unit (the ADX SAM unit) which restricts all communication, there was no possible means for him to correct the false narrative; and who would believe him anyway since he has been convicted and labeled; wrongfully so, but convicted nonetheless.

General Michael Flynn (National Security Adviser) was convicted (via plea) by some of the same exact cabal, including Jim Comey, and it is known that the FBI lied, fabricated documents and even misrepresented documents to the federal judge who seemed willing to always look the other way at the FBI's constant frauds. Precisely the same exact thing is true in the Dutschke case and with many of the same exact people (even Mueller/Comey). Yet the difference is that Dutschke did not have a high-profile attorney who is not afraid to take on the corrupt FBI/DOJ, Sidney Powell (if you want someone familiar with the FACT that the FBI lies and prosecutors use fraud to feed their "conviction machine", she's your girl because she once *was* one). The difference is that Dutschke, unlike Flynn, did not have someone like Glenn Beck, Sean Hannity, Mark Levin and a justice-hungry alt-media to pound the drum of justice constantly. When Dutschke was finally convicted, he was quickly disappeared into the ADX SAM unit to sit silent with the 29 other spies and "terrorists" that make up that unit, unable to communicate with anyone, including his own attorney of record.

When Manafort was temporarily placed under similar conditions, though *not* as harsh or as long as Dutschke and dealing with the same corrupt DOJ cabal, the same radio and alt-media raised hell, calling Manafort's conditions draconian and a violation of the 8th Amendment. Yet not a single one of them responded at all the same way (2013 to 2017) when it was Dutschke—and by the personal hand of Eric Holder (SAM order), Mueller and Comey (even *pre*-conviction). This high pressure tactic is one of many (often) used by the DOJ to force a plea, but it was magnified x100 with Dutschke. If a little of it was so outrageous when it was DOJ vs Manafort or Stone, then why wasn't a whole lot of it at least just as outrageous when it was the very same cabal vs Dutschke? Especially when, with Dutschke, it was personally ordered from the very top (Holder) and with the full knowledge and executive power of the President (Obama. 28 CFR§501.2 and .3) as a matter of record.

In the recent case of Carter Page, his unmasking, costing him his career was lamented by the same alt-media (as the same was by the unmasking of Valerie Plame by the mainstream media). Yet when Dutschke was unmasked (2011) no one in the press batted an eye. In the recent case of General Michael Flynn, the fact that he was forced to sign a plea because agents threatened to prosecute his son (a very commonly used FBI tactic), the alt-media acted livid and expressed an outrage shared by the half the country that did not obediently follow the cues of CNN and read the New York Times or USA Today. Yet when that very same cabal of corrupt FBI agents and DOJ puppets did the very same thing to Dutschke (threatening to prosecute his wife, Janet, who actually had to get an attorney appointed), there was no such expressed outrage. No one even noticed. Rush Limbaugh, Mark Levin, Sean Hannity, Glenn Beck, Fox and the few websites and journalists who are principled—were right to give voice to the injustice of the tactics used to coerce the plea from General Flynn, because it was morally, legally and shockingly an egregious tactic. The broadcasters and journalists should be commended for doing what the rest of the media was either too yellow to do or chose not to because political allegiance of the plebe-press requires that the spineless ignore the FBI's wrongs because the weaponization of the FBI is within their party interest.

But still, if those FBI collusion schemes, used by the same people against Flynn, were so outrageous that everyone should be outraged, then how can those same exact schemes (by the same exact people) have been acceptable against Dutschke? Especially when so much *more* was at stake with Dutschke? The truth-media was in the right to call out and ridicule the plebe-media hypocrisy as they did when they saw it (with Flynn). But the truth-media OWES it to themselves and the rest of the world to avoid accusations of that same kind of hypocrisy.

The Flynn case and Dutschke case shared, at least in ancillary fashion, some of the very same characters of the scheming cabal—Comey, Mueller, Clinton, Yates, corrupt individual FBI agents including from the National Security Division, plus Brennan and more. Dutschke even had the benefit of adding one more to the cabal—Eric Holder. And, both Dutschke and Flynn share the former president himself, Obama, as their persecutor. Dutschke had so much *more* at stake and against a greater involvement of people for an even longer period of time. In short—the outrages against Flynn were but a diet version of the same, and by the same, against Dutschke. The difference—no 2013 media was interested because no Trump was involved. The idea that there even is a difference (intense interest with Flynn yet apathy with Dutschke) is disgusting. It is as disgusting to be selective with one's concern as it is to be selective with prosecution. Either it is real and outrageous, or it isn't.

While Everett may have been better able mentally prepared to persevere then most, he never should have had to. But if the more recent media attention on the FBI's wrongs committed against Flynn tell the public anything, it should be this:

No one, not even a DOD General, can withstand the assault and schemes of a determined DOJ/FBI.

The common temptation for the American masses is to think that the system works the way it appears to on the telly. "If he is innocent, then it will be shown in court," and "well, if he signed a plea—then he must be guilty" and "If I was innocent, then there'd be *no way* that I'd cop to some plea." That thinking is childishly naïve, as real-life is *nothing* like the TV shows. The reality is that no one has a chance against the monsters who run the conviction machine and they do not care if someone is innocent. It is not a coincidence that the only people naïve enough to think that "the system works" are the same people who have never really examined its workings.

What the Flynn case did do is reveal to the masses that the FBI is a corrupt tool of a particular political bent (especially in the Obama era), that has long since been weaponized (along with the plebe-media) which is something the masses would have refused to allow themselves to even see before. It spurs people to rightly ask—"If the FBI/DOJ was willing to do this to Flynn, of all people, why on earth would they *not* do the same to everyone else?" Is there anyone dense enough to believe that with Flynn was the first time that DOJ/FBI used such fraudulent tactics? Both are precisely the right questions to ask. The fact is, they DO all this to everyone else, and always have. The FBI is actually *taught* to lie, misrepresent, twist and manipulate. They are encouraged to do so by judges and media who allow them to operate in such corrupt fashion without any consequences

The FBI and DOJ, who are supposed to be stewards of the law, as well as their only equivalent, *know* they are free to violate law in pursuit of convictions since no one will ever hold them to account. Who are you going to call? The police?

This acquiescence by cowardly judges and press only guarantees future misdeeds by LEOs and their Prosecutor Kings. The American public, however, is so indoctrinated that they refuse to see that American LEOs are the same as Hitler's brownshirts; not wanting to believe that things are not as they appear to be on American television programming where the police are all noble heroes protecting them from the "bad guys". This intentional self-blindness is but a psychological self-defence mechanism to avoid guilt. For if people saw that their own "justice system" is anything but that, they might be expected to care, or feel strongly, or worse yet—*do something about it*. And caring and doing are just too much "work". Besides—what can *they* do? It is much easier to just believe that the FBI is full of movie-worthy heroes. Rubbish.

This is no different than those who turned their heads during the Holocaust. Such refusal to accept reality and bury one's head like an ostrich into the sand of media indoctrination, and intentionally believe the current "system works" or "trust the system" is exactly what the FBI/DOJ prey on. They count on any kind of willful blindness as it empowers them to treat anyone like Flynn. They may not have to go as far as they did with Dutschke, but no one is immune so they know they can throw their weight around. To continue to stay willingly blind is an egregious sin of mental and moral laziness.

Dutschke and Flynn had, in different fields, at one point taken an oath. That Oath of Service required of them that they protect and defend the Constitution of the United States and against enemies whether foreign... or domestic. What does one do when it becomes obvious that the enemies really ARE domestic?

The "foreign" part is easy; if not in the defence itself but at least in the recognition by the masses and an accord as to what/who the enemies are. It is not so easy when it is "domestic", because most Americans are, again, willfully blinded from the possibility. So how does one fight a *domestic* enemy of the Constitution?

In General Flynn's line of work, one cannot launch a missile at said domestic enemy (that would be considered "terrorism" or sedition by some who actually support that domestic enemy). So how is it done? Because there really IS no answer to that, the result is nothing but despair, frustration or just doing nothing like everyone else—and turning a blind eye. Before considering the possibility that someone could just—"Expose it. Report the enemy and the wrongdoing to the authority," one must keep an open mind that the enemy *is* the "authorities". And exactly the same "authorities" that one would report to, at that. In the mind of the authorities, the law is not the law—*they* are the law. And don't you forget it.

While Flynn, going through what a thousand other victims of the FBI and DOJ go through daily, was shocked that "the system" (he means the actions of the people who control it) operates and schemes the way it does, he was only learning what others already knew, and he learned it *after* his indictment. He was not faced with having to fulfill his oath against domestic enemies. Dutschke, however, had to deal with both. He had already seen (in 2004 and in 2008) that using "the system" to prosecute "the system" does not work.

The modern American vernacular now includes "the swamp" as a reference to its entrenched "system" workers who protect their other swamp monsters. In 2012, when it became obvious and documented that the swamp monsters all protected their swamp overlords and even at the cost of American lives (Benghazi). Dutschke *should* have been livid. It would only have been right for him to be so. And it mattered that the lives so casually disposed of by the swamp ruler were other men who had taken the same oath. That *should* be infuriating, indeed.

Not only were the monarchs of the swamp saying that "America's best and brightest" were not worth a single rupee—but the cover-up afterward and the ongoing concealment designed to constantly protect the swamp rulers was not merely an affront to the Constitution and oath of service, but an all-out assault on it.

So men like Flynn, and Page, Sterling, Kiriakou, and Dutschke who have taken the oath, and the second oath of Dutschke (that reads, in part, "to be a champion of freedom and justice") learned that their oath, the very thing that controls their lives and actions (sometimes against their own conscience), was meaningless—which makes them men who suddenly have had their purpose yanked from them. They saw and learned that there was no more room left in the world for silly principles and childish oaths, making the lives they lived until now a fog of lies that they'd believed in. All that they believed in and lived for was no longer valued or wanted by the world anymore. America had become no different than the criminal thugocracy of Russia. Those who control the "justice system" also control the media—so going to them is not an option either.

It is controversial but, sadly, accurate to say the swamp rulers are willing to not only allow but to actively cause the deaths or destruction of human lives to simply serve their own greed. And yet each time someone (especially during that administration) proves this to be true, the collective group-think American public is eager to blind themselves from such procrustean; and the American media is willing to aid in that blindness. Americans like to reflect back to their revolutionary roots as if those courageous figures of their history are somehow familiar to them. The truth is they are so far removed from their "treasonous" forefathers that they share more commonality with the monarchy-worshippers that they claim they split away from—as long as they get "the right" monarchs. With the behaviours exhibited by the administration towards its enemies, and the media/public willingness to not only ignore the injustice and personal destruction and character assassination of Dutschke, but the piling-on to it as well, it would be easy to conclude they would accept monarchs who practise such (of the same) tactics in the past such as: Hitler, Stalin, Chairman Mao, PolPot and all the other dictators they claim to hate. Where were the "Civil Libertarians" in 2013? 2014? Even now? Or to some, how can they justify that the Constitution they claim they hold so dear only applies to those who really don't need it, and does *not* apply to those who actually need it, to call upon its constraints of government?

Any man can call himself a patriot. James Comey, one of the perpetrators of this (and other) cabal has called himself a patriot in his autobiography. But being a patriot and *actually* being patriotic is not about espousing platitude-ridden ideas or in his case, regurgitating rationale for his destructive actions in the same manner in which all prosecutors (remember he *is* one). Since they have no other way to justify their own tactics, no other excuse for their self-aggrandizement. Being a patriot is not at all about merely expressing beliefs. Being a patriot is not about shouting platitudes from behind a political podium that have been focus-group tested to evoke emotions to a rally or supporters in the press.

No.

Being a patriot is about showing you are willing to sacrifice yourself for your country's best principles, whether you announce those principles or not. One cannot pronounce oneself a patriot because words are not part of the equation, words only add to the illusion—or delusion; it is about deeds.

Patriotism is not an award. It is not a plume, ribbon, medal of distinction, it is not a badge. Patriotism is a condition. It is a state of being only truly recognisable by a person's actions. Being a patriot is not about what a man says, it is about what a man is willing to do...sometimes in the dark, when no one is watching. Real patriotism has nothing to do with those—"Hey everybody, look at me. I am being patriotic. Is anyone seeing this?" moments. It is about what a man does, not what he announces. It is about the "slings and arrows" he endures while swimming against the stream in defence of sometimes unpopular principles that actually confers the status upon him. It is about what pains and risks a man endures preserving those principles. It is about what he does, his actions. It is not about any action he commits *against* others (such as putting others into a prison—i.e. stifling someone else's liberties and rights) which is why a prosecutor (Mueller, Comey, Holder, Lamar, Sigler) or a prosecutor's tool (Thomason, McCabe, Jim Johnson or other LEOs) can *never* be truly patriotic in that capacity no matter how many help them pretend, as it is their common goal and practise to stifle people's rights, even as they wrap themselves in the flag. They are anti-patriots.

And no one should make the tragic mistake of automatically thinking that a defence attorney is patriotic for defending the client's rights against the state solicitor either, because most (not all) defence lawyers are just donning the hat, wearing the disguise. Wearing the disguise of a patriot while simultaneously aiding the machine of the anti-patriots to stomp out some person's liberty is still but aiding in the illusion. There are some, a few defence lawyers who qualify for the title, but those few often get beaten probably more than they are victorious in preservation of the rights they believe in.

Still, that sentiment, combined with actions is required to actually be a patriot. A patriot, then, is a man who has proven it by what he has done (and not *to* others but *for* others), not by what he said. He cannot pronounce it upon himself, nor can anyone else award the title to him. Patriotism is not a costume competition who's prise is glory, it is humble... and often unrecognised. It is an "earned" state of being. Nelson Mandela, imprisoned for decades, was a patriot for his country. Is that a price that a single LEO or prosecutor has proven they are willing to pay? Would Comey, Lamar, Holder, Yates, Mueller, Clinton, Thomason, Sigler, Jim Johnson or Obama himself be willing to endure the decades in prison that were pronounced upon Mandela or Dutschke? What about the half a decade the cabal took from Sterling or Kiriakou or the much smaller time stolen from Flynn or Papadopoulos? Would anyone in the cabal be able to endure the losses each of their victims suffered, the loss of every single possession, dollar, relationship, job, family photo and their own names and reputations? Has a single one of the Obama syndicate proven it in their deeds? Has any of them ever truly put their lives in real peril, in the dark, risking themselves putting everything on the line to preserve their beliefs? The answer is a resounding, "No".

(Not one of them could survive even a weekend in jail for a DUI)

The clear and inarguable fact is that they have proven they are willing to sacrifice others to their own self-serving course. That is antithetical to Dutschke's oath and principle-driven thinking and acts. Acts that were often done in the dark, beyond the reach of public recognition—immune forever from accolades. There is not a single person interviewed who knew him at any stage of his life that can describe him as without principles. Dutschke lived his principles from the beginning and all the way to the sentencing hearing where, while still proclaiming his innocence, as the transcripts show he said—

"I would rather go to prison for the next 25 years with (everyone) knowing the truth, then walk out the door right now a free man with anyone believing a single thing that *they*" (the Obama cabal and prosecutors) "have said!" (2014)

One of the few things that the one ex-wife who reluctantly agreed to limited questions did say was roughly that—"there is a lot that he did elsewhere and here (America) that nobody else would do or have the courage to do. A lot of things that he and his friends risked their lives to do. To protect our way of life here. Things no one will ever know or admit happened. But that wasn't just work time for those guys. They were the job all the time. He was like that here. Every minute. It's not like he needed a thank you, he wasn't angry about it. But sometimes he'd see someone on (the tele) or hear someone bad-mouthing CIA, or media glorifying or excusing some court-case or law enforcement wrongdoing or sometimes even some Hollywood celebrity mouthing off and he'd say—*their* world only exists because of people like US. Not like he was angry, but like he was disappointed. That was just him."

So the simple answer to this original, the simple way of putting it all is like this—

Everyone who actually knew Everett Dutschke, who *actually* knew him, thought he was an inspiring, intense and good-hearted person that they'd follow. Those people, the ones who actually knew him, unanimously and conclusively thought he was a great man…. until they were told not to (2013) by people who didn't know him.

The 2013-2014 picture painted by the administration and its press was not only inaccurate, it was unparalleled in its magnitude and in its egregious and destructive intent to be as dishonest as they could in their misportrayal. The reason those who knew him did not recognise the 2013 portrayal of him was that it wasn't him. As it will be shown in later chapters, including the next, the reality of both the man and his known character was rewritten by those who had no clue of either and was then propagandized by the administration's colluding weaponized press. That unholy syndicate then did the same with the actual facts, casting to the side for what really was an unbelievable and completely contrived case designed not just to sensationalise and convict but to smear.

Some history books, articles and news have called Dutschke an "assassin" and point to the 2013 KC letters. This phony narrative, as you will see in the following chapters, is false. The only assassination attempt in 2013 was the character assassination committed by that administration's obedient weaponized press. In 2013, they proved themselves to be the grandmaster of the assassin's guild. It was messy, and they didn't mind the mess (good for ratings), but because no defence was allowed it was the most foul and thorough character assassination in history by those who have had decades of practise.

It was also a gross failure of media morality. It was in fact, the pinnacle of a perfect example of media malpractise and will likely never be topped. This is exactly why the (later) Attorney General of the United States described in late August of 2020 the tactics this way:

"The so-called watch dogs of the system became attack dogs"
—William Barr.—

Chapter 3

What did the evidence REALLY say?

It's now known that the product of the KC letters was simply not the "deadly poison with no known antidote" that the Mueller FBI had the worldwide press proclaiming that it was, for a year. It is now known that they concealed the knowledge that they'd known, since even *before* the Dutschke indictment. It is now obvious that a primary reason for the SAM order was to conceal the actual toxicity analysis from the press, the public and the court (as well as Dutschke). The actual and final toxicity analysis would have been exactly what Dutschke and his appointed counsel were waiting for, to prove that the FBI's primary claim was rubbish the entire time.

The world was told that the KC letters, all three, were "laced with ricin, a deadly poison with no known antidote." Yet the actual analysis from the National BioForensics Analysis Center (Ft Detrick, MD) as well as the FBI's very own internal email from CBRNSU to the FBI's very own laboratory (Rebecca Reynolds) dated April 27th, 2013 proves that the FBI knew the claim they had been so publicly making was entirely false. Three claims actually.

The first was the claim that the letter (that Curtis sent) to the judge was "laced with ricin". That document shows they'd known since as early as April 27, 2013 that the KC letter to the judge was *not* (listed as evidence number Q-11 or NBFAC,130418.0001.0004).

The second was that the other two "tested positive" (the KC letters to President Obama and Senator Wicker). This analysis memo does not even show that either the Wicker or Obama KC letters were even tested by the National BioForensics Analysis Center for the presence of ricin. So the public claim the media parroted (that the FBI claimed their labs "confirmed the presence of ricin on the three letters) was also completely fabricated. The only KC letter tested was the one (Curtis sent) to the judge, on which "ricin was not detected", quoting directly from the lab report. So with "ricin not detected" on *that* one (Q-11), nor on the others, since they were not even tested—not a single one of the three "was confirmed for the presence of ricin."

The third, as explicitly indicated on the FBI's very same memo from *their own* laboratory and the National Bioforensics Analysis Center (Ft. Deitrick, MD), is that the smoking gun claim of the Mueller FBI and Holder DOJ that the now-infamous "dust mask", the thing which triggered the Stephen Thomason signed arrest warrant, contained traces of ricin, was entirely a fabricated and false claim. If the April 27, 2013 National Bioforensic Analysis Center at Ft. Detrick, MD (which is the U.S Government's top-notch and ultimate laboratory and facility for biological and chemical weapons. It *is* the

U.S. bioweapons facility) analysis actually had confirmed that ricin was detected on the dust mask, and *if* the April 27th internal FBI memo from Neel Barnaby to the FBI labs actually had stated the same, then that would be particularly damning to Dutschke and would have bolstered their public claims of their smoking gun claim. Because they repeated to the world, through the obedient media that the dust mask (that they magically found outside Dutschke's building in a public garbage bin, giving them reason to get the arrest warrant) contained Dutschke's DNA, and ricin. So people who had known and were close to Everett Dutschke suddenly believed that there was a ricin laced dust mask with Dutschke's DNA on it, even though those people had never seen such a thing. The rest of the world believed it, too. After all, they heard it or saw it or read it in the news, who got their information from FBI agent Stephen Thomason, who swore to it on the arrest affidavit. And since Thomason works for the FBI, then gosh; it must be true, right? The FBI agents signature, along with the media tidal wave and the weeks of dealing with the case with Curtis (as the *mailer*) was enough to convince Judge Susan Alexander to sign the warrant, not that she needed much convincing as she was embarrassed already since she was under the (false) impression that she'd already signed a warrant previously to arrest the "wrong guy" (Curtis). To Judge Alexander, like to the rest of the world, the dust mask claim was a conviction. She, like the rest of the world, actually believed it. She should not have. It was all a lie. It was yet another Stephen Thomason lie.

The very same April 27th notifications from the NBFAC (which IS the government's bio weapons laboratory) and April 27th Barnaby internal FBI memo explicitly indirectly list the "dust masks" as evidence items Q-420 and Q-422, and explicitly states "ricin was *not* detected on any of these items."

Stephen Thomason lied. He lied, under oath, on the arrest affidavit to a federal US Magistrate Judge who then signed the warrant based on the LIE which was then repeated by the worldwide press and then was believed by the public at large. That one document exposed three lies, sworn to by Thomason, announced by the administration and perpetuated by the plebe-press. It is a critical document and one that was hidden away, concealed from Judge Alexander (a federal crime) and the press, in part because of the date. The date, clearly marked at the top, and in plain view, is designated as April 27th, 2013.

But J. Everett Dutschke was arrested April 28th! This means that the DOJ, from Attorney General Eric Holder and Bob Mueller down to FBI agent Thomason all knew that the April 28th arrest warrant, the arrest itself and the news they'd been feeding the press was *false* information. *This* is why they concealed this document from the press and Dutschke, because it exposed them as liars, and they could not afford any more embarrassment from Dutschke.

Moreover, this means that they then lied to the grand jury (x2), also with Thomason under oath, in order to get the indictment; and continued to hide from the grand jury anything (including this document) which might have given any reasonable grand juror a reason to *not* indict. This is called exculpatory information, and the grand jury has a right to see it. But they did not.

Of course the press did not know of the FBI's very own lab document, so they had no idea the claims were lies, and they simply ran with and reported the lies as if it was true, and the world bought into it. This document would not be discovered until after they had forced a plea from Dutschke. By then (the following year) it was too late. The history books had already been written and people's minds were made up, based on the FBI's false claims.

Those documents, directly from the NBFAC (Fort Detrick), the nation's top bioweapons lab, and the FBI created a bigger problem for the FBI in the future. Because if this, the trace analysis, showed (in April) "Ricin was not detected," then what would the final *toxicity* analysis show? There would be time before the FBI would have to deal with that, since the toxicity analyses of the KC letter would take months, but they needed to ensure there were no set-backs for their (false) story in the meantime; otherwise they may have to lie about something else… again.

Which is exactly what they did.

Recall the "smoking gun," slam-dunk claim that Mueller FBI and Holder DOJ fed to the hungry press: the dust mask. Their claim was that Q-420 (the dust mask from the conveniently timed "trash-pull") contained traces of ricin and Everett's DNA. It is now known and shown, and anyone who is capable of reading can see, that "ricin was *not* detected" on the dust mask, though the DOJ propaganda claimed the opposite.

But what about the DNA? That was the other part of the FBI claim of the infamous dust masks. Once again, however, the media was reporting a lie to the public, eager to convict Dutschke. The fact is that the order had come down from the very top (literally) of the government that though Dutschke is not actually guilty of developing a biological weapon, to "make him guilty." The DNA claim that the public bought, because the administration sold it through their media proxies (as a force multiplier), was a false claim. Moreover, the FBI knew it and knew it *prior* to the grand jury. While Stephen Thomason's arrest affidavit (April 28th) had already been sworn to and signed, he still testified at the preliminary hearing to judge Susan Alexander, under oath, that the DNA on the dustmask matched Dutschke. That testimony was *after* the date of the later discovered email from the FBI's Constance L. Fisher to special agent Brandon Grant which explicitly states that Dutschke "was *ex*cluded as a source" of the DNA on the dustmask. (a cheek swab or "buccal sample" was taken from Dutschke *during* the arrest for DNA comparison). Connie Fisher's email from the FBI's very own DNA lab to Brandon Grant was dated May 2nd, 2013, 4: 37 PM, which meant that they knew this (including Thomason, who testified) *before* the preliminary hearing and hid this email from Judge Alexander (and the press and Dutschke) while representing exactly the opposite. Furthermore, the grand jury (there were two) testimony by Thomason was also an absolute lie, as he again concealed the exculpatory May 2nd email from the FBI's Connie Fisher to the agents. This is not speculative, it is documented. This is perjury and, just as with the trace evidence analysis are the dust mask showing "ricin was not detected," the grand jury (x2) had a right to see this exculpatory information in order for them to have a choice *not* to indict. They did not.

When DNA analysis is done, certain alleles or fields are isolated and amplified using polymerase chain reaction (PCR). Those specific sections of the DNA sequence, in this case, actually showed that the dust mask DNA source was an "XX" chromosome. For those unfamiliar with the basic biology, Everett Dutschke is a male (born that way, not some bizarre modern conflation of how someone "identifies"). This means that Mr. Dutschke's DNA sample (the buccal swab; FBI evidence #K24) returned as an XY chromosome—male. Thus the mismatch of the DNA samples between Mr. Dutschke (K24) and the dust mask (Q-420) was obvious, hence Constance Fisher's email that Mr. Dutschke had been "excluded" as the source. The (XX) was that of a *female*.

So one obvious question would be, "Well, if that isn't Dutschke DNA on the dust masks, then whose is it?" A sentence he posed verbatim according to the transcripts of the 2014 sentencing hearing. Good question. But no one will ever know. "Because when the FBI discovered (May 2nd) that it was not Dutschke's, they stopped looking!" Although really it does not matter, in truth to whom the dust mask DNA really belongs since the reality is that there was no ricin on it anyway (See Barnaby memo/NBFAC and DOJ). Without ricin, the dust mask is really entirely irrelevant except to show that Thomason lied under oath (x3) and that the press repeated that lie, ad nauseam, without question and for the sole purpose of convincing the populace eager to convict Dutschke. This document was also concealed from Dutschke (and the press) until after they forced the plea. But, again, it was too late.

This was another massive problem for the Mueller FBI and Holder DOJ who had been instructed to ensure a conviction. The "DNA and ricin on the dust mask" was a critical claim, both parts of it. And people believed it. The Obama-worshipping press would never forgive them if they found out the truth. No, wait. Of course they would forgive them. In fact, they would even help the administration cover it up, by simply not raising any questions and by accepting whatever the administration said, no matter how untrue, bizarre, impossible, unlikely or in conflict it was with the Curtis/prosecution-proven facts. What any administration of integrity who had found themselves in such a muddle would have done, would be to release Mr. Dutschke along with an apology "Gosh, we are so sorry we got it wrong and lied to the world to demolish you, your family and soil your reputation forever. We apologise for this mishap and pledge never to let this happen again." But that would be what an administration of *integrity* would do. This was not an administration of integrity. They did not. Instead they chose to continue to lie, ensuring the press did the same, and hoped that the coming (but slow) toxicity analysis did not come too soon since they knew that the final toxicity report would likely show there simply was no toxicity at all. They needed to secure a signed plea from Dutschke before that inevitability, so hopefully, for them, there would be no setback for their (false) story in the meantime. Otherwise they'd have to lie...again...again.

Which is exactly what they did...again.

One of the claims Thomason made (under oath to a federal Magistrate) was that three "swabs" were taken of Dutschke property and "tested positive for ricin." This includes a drain trap from under a wash basin in the restroom of his previous office and a hammer that his wife, Janet, (not he), had some people pack, and move, from that office building into a storage cabin of a friend (of hers not his). The "positive swab" items were those two and some other unconfirmed item. Those three swabs, Thomason and the FBI announced, had "tested positive for ricin." Once again, this is another thing that the media mindlessly reported as if true. After all, when the government, especially that particular administration, reports something to the press—then it must be true.

This was the same administration that told the press repeatedly that some evil Americans had been mean to the poor Muslims with a YouTube video that no one in the world watched—so the poor, innocent and repressed Muslims who lived in Benghazi, Libya just had to finally rise up like magnificent patriots and grab their trusted family heirlooms (grenades, automatic rifles, mortars and mortar rounds, RPGs and night vision goggles) that they had lying around and spontaneously protest against the mean old American YouTube video that no one watched. So this was an administration that could be trusted, right?

What Mueller/Holder/Lamar/Thomason did not do is plan anything beyond their initial statement on these three "positive swabs," because in their experience they did not need to. The press would do it's damn job and just repeat that these three swabs from Dutschke's items "were positive for ricin." The American public would buy into it, reinforcing their (false) claims that the masses did not know were false. This claim was false too. In June, the Centers for Disease Control (CDC) completed their analysis of the three "positive swabs" when sent to them by the Bioterrorism Rapid Response and Advanced Technology (BRRAT) laboratory of the CDC/National Center for Emerging and Zoonotic Infectious Diseases. This "Bioterrorism Unit" (BRRAT) released the analysis in a memorandum dated June 25th, 2013 by the Director of the Division of Laboratory Science, James L. Pirkle, M.D., PhD to Dr. Michael

Farrell, the Research Microbiologist and into the general CDC/NCEZID. It explicitly states that the three "positive swabs" were, in fact *never* actually positive; the exact language that the PhD-level medical doctor Pirkle used was "analysis of the samples was NOT possible." The attached laboratory print-out from the liquid chromatography tandem-mass spectrometry (LC-MS/MS) for both a structural and activity assay was "nonreactive" (NR). This obvious contradictory lab analysis was an obvious problem for the Obama regime which had told the obedient press that "items" swabbed "positive" when an actual analysis was simply *not* possible (according to the PhD who ran the analysis). If this document were ever to be seen, it would be yet another case of the DOJ agent with a badge claiming the opposite of what the actual experts knew, and documented. And *that* could be embarrassing (again). Mueller/Holder could not have that, so they ensured that the CDC report by Dr. Pirkle's "bioterrorism" unit would never be seen—not by the media, Dutschke, a judge, any attorney or anyone ever. It would never be included in the discovery because it proves Thomason and the FBI to (again) be liars. Hiding exculpatory information is what is known in America as a Brady violation and it warrants dismissal of an indictment, even if discovered post-conviction (as this document was). This CDC document which proves the FBI (Thomason) lied (again) is but one of many, making the cumulative effect of all the primary claims, of the case that they represented to the press who diligently reported it to the trusting public, entirely empty. Their entire case was a house of cards to begin with, yet disguised as solid as long as the lies kept coming and the truth (documented) remained hidden. The etiology of the public's gullibility was the natural plebeian tendency to just follow authority, especially law enforcement which has been elevated to near-godlike status by popular books, movies and television programming; but was multiplied a hundred-fold by the simple fact that the 2013 press just was desperate to believe anything that particular administration said (plus—they simply did not know that James L Pirkle MD, PhD of the CDC, had documented the opposite of FBI agent Thomason's claim because Lamar/Sigler/Holder made sure Pirkle's June 25th memorandum vanished).

The important thing, from the Obama's DOJ point-of-view, would have been to make sure no one saw this. At this point, a *real* system truly interested in truth and justice would have let this be known, and by everyone. There are two completely polar opposite choices. Which option do you suppose they chose?

If you guessed that they chose to conceal this, just like they did the others, you are right. All they needed was to buy (more) time...just push for a plea, try to set him up in the meantime with an entrapment scheme (Dennis Montgomery) and if *that* does not cause Dutschke to crack and sign a plea, try another entrapment scheme (Christopher Stutsy/Jim Johnson of Fast and Furious) and if that does not work either then just keep lying. As long as they did not have any more setbacks, maybe they could force and intimidate Dutschke into a plea before the dreaded toxicity analysis was done. Maybe they could call the NBFAC and get them to slow down on this toxicity analysis, because they needed more time and for nothing else to pop up to ruin their false story. Otherwise, they'd have to lie again...again...again. Which is exactly what they did...again...again.

Thomason and Lamar (the prosecutor who had colluded with Thomason) had floated the information that Dutschke's hair had been discovered underneath the mailing label of the KC letter that was sent (by Curtis) to the judge. The FBI evidence number of the specimen under the address label was Q-11.2. The FBI laboratory conducted a stereo microscopic comparison and the laboratory concluded "are microscopically dissimilar" to any related to Dutschke. Another bubble of the DOJ/FBI case had popped. Does anyone recall them announcing the results of the stereomicroscopic analysis to the press? No! This is because, just like all the other analyses proving Chad Lamar and agent Thomason to be nothing but liars, this was concealed as well. So far, every single thing about the actual case had completely fallen apart. But as long as they did not tell anyone, no one would know, no one would be embarrassed (except Dutschke and who cares about him?), and the prosecution could continue. It *had* to continue, as per the orders from above.

One would think that a true law enforcement agency would be ecstatic to know that no law had been broken and then celebrate that there really was no ricin and there really was no "biological weapon" developed and everybody is safe, let's go have cake and celebrate that no one broke the international treaty to commit a war crime.

One would think so.

However, this is not what the DOJ chose to do. Instead, they hid this truth and all the others from the press while claiming the opposite and continued the pressure to get Dutschke to sign his own conviction in a plea. He did not. So they still needed to push, and harder, before the toxicity analysis was complete. By this time, Dutschke and even his putty of an appointed counselor were impatient and asking for the toxicity analysis to be completed and made public, proving that it was all a lie. So the DOJ really could not deal with anything else not going in their favor. They needed to do something before the toxicity and analysis returned or they'd have to lie again...again...again...again.

What is what they did again...again...again.

This one was not about a specific scientific analysis, it was about an entire scientific theory—and along with it the legal premise—under which the prosecution was taking place. And it was one massive lie. James Everett Dutschke was officially indicted for violating the international treaty against the development of a *biological* weapon. The U.S. statute which "enforces" that treaty (somehow) was written into effect by the Biological Weapons (Biological Weapons Convention Implementation Act) Implementation Act, specifically 18USC§175(a). Although the details of this scheme by prosecutors is best left for its own chapter, the primary sketch of how prosecuting under this statute is an illegal, therefore criminal, prosecution scheme is simply this—ricin (which is what the FBI alleged), is *not* a biological weapon.

It is *not*, in fact. It is not, scientifically. It is not, legally. A biological weapon, by scientific *and* legal definition, involves a microorganism (or virus, which simulates a microorganism) and is pathogenic, capable of causing harm or death. Now that the world has seen Covid 19, it should better understand what a "biological agent" actually is. The treaty, and therefore the statute that "enforces" it, is designed to prevent such "germ warfare". But ricin is not a germ! It is a molecule, not a living organism. It is considered a "tool of assassination" and is therefore targeted in effect, incapable of "spreading" or infecting others like coronavirus or anthrax. Common sense and science say it cannot fit under a law that "enforces" the "germ warfare" treaty.

So does the actual law. This is because there is an entirely different international treaty called the Chemical Weapons Convention, with an entirely different "enforcing statute" (18USC§229) which came a decade *after* the biological treaty. The chemical weapons treaty specifically, explicitly and numerous times identifies "ricin" as a chemical—legally. The Chemical Weapons Convention Implementation Act (CWCIA) specifically identifies "ricin" as a chemical—legally. The CWCIA specifically directs the FBI to investigate violations of chemicals (listed under the treaty such as "ricin") under §229 (chemical), not §175 (biological). (The FBI/DOJ in Dutschke, however, did *not* follow the law and chose to prosecute under §175 instead). The regulations that are CWCIA progeny specifically and explicitly designate "ricin" as a chemical (not a biological germ). The "enforcing" statute itself (18USC§229) explicitly designates "ricin" as a chemical (not biological) and even defines "biological agent" in such a way that "ricin" cannot be confused for "biological." Thus, the *law*, as written, leaves absolutely no room whatsoever to consider that "ricin" is a germ, *legally*, because it is not. It would be entirely foolish scientifically, and entirely naive in common sense, and entirely illegal to consider "ricin" is a biological germ to be prosecuted under the "biological" statute. Anyone who would try to do so is either being utterly dishonest (for a reason) or just plain stupid. Or both.

Yet *that* is exactly what they did.

It is scientifically, factually and legally a lie of biblical proportions for the either inept or dishonest prosecutors to have done so. Yet no one ever questioned it. Dutschke's appointed lawyer Ken Coghlan, had never handled a case of such magnitude and high-profile before, and never dealt with any case involving biological weapons before. No attorney alive had. Therefore it is painfully obvious that Coghlan was ill-equipped to even begin to represent someone such as J. Everett Dutschke and his case. Coghlan had absolutely no idea that "ricin" was legally (and scientifically) *not* a living microorganism or that there was indeed an entirely different statute "enforcing" an entirely different treaty specifically designed for prosecution of chemical agents called the chemical weapons treaty (and statutes). Every single court filing there is indicates that Coghlan did not even know such a statute existed, so could not possibly have known the special prosecution team and the FBI were using the wrong statute (intentionally).

The reason the special prosecution team used the wrong statute was because they knew that they were *not* dealing with an actual—functioning toxic molecule, or as they often called it "a deadly poison with no known antidote," (which would require actual toxicity under the chemical weapons statute 229), so they used a statute that has no such toxicity threshold, the biological statute instead. It was a massive lie. A serious fraud perpetrated on the court, on the public and on Dutschke. And as long as Everett's appointed lawyer, Coghlan, remained clueless to the actual law, he would never raise the point that the indictment is invalid: that if the FBI was alleging "ricin" then the legally proper charge must be §229 (chemical) not §175 (biological). Coghlan, by all accounts, stayed clueless and did not listen to Dutschke, for the most part. Perhaps if Everett had been dealing with a drug charge, selling meth or transporting marijuana or something like that, or if he was accused of stealing a car or writing fraudulent checks then Ken Coghlan might have been up to the job. But in a case like this, there was no way Coghlan could have withstood the tsunami crashing against his client. Not even a chance.

The lie, a massive one, would hold out as long as no one questioned it. All the special prosecutor needed to do was keep pressuring Everett to sign his own conviction, hoping to get him to cave before the toxicity analysis was complete. Otherwise they'd be forced to lie...again...again...again...again...again.

But they ran out of time.

Late in the evening of October 7th, nearly October 8th, 2013, the NBFAC Immunology/toxicology manager, Stephen Cendrowski, PhD, completed the toxicology analysis that Everett and his appointed lawyer were waiting for. And it was, just as Everett had said all along, devastating to the Holder/Mueller narrative that the KC letters had been "laced with a deadly poison with no known antidote." It was devastating because Stephen Cendrowski, PhD, of Fort Detrick (the highest US authority and facility in bioweapons) at the National Biodefence Analysis and Countermeasures Center of the National Bioforensic Analysis Center of the Department of Homeland Security typed out a memo to the FBI's Christa Mason and copying James Burans and personally signed the memo. Christa Mason of the FBI's CBRNSU Unit (Chemical Biological, Radiological and Nuclear or "weapons of mass destruction" Unit) circulated the memo the very next day, which was October 8th, 2013. The memo disclosed two things:

1.) That the mass concentration of toxicity was 0.0%.
2.) Only two of the KC letters were ever actually tested (the KC letter to President Obama and the one to the judge who had previously jailed Curtis).

The letter to Senator Wicker was *never* tested at the FBI lab or NBFAC for the presence of ricin (nor was the KC letter to Obama), and it was *never* tested at the NBFAC/NBACC for the final toxicity analysis. This means the entire claim about "confirming a deadly poison" lacing the Wicker letter was, in fact, a lie. A lie that the media, nevertheless, reported. A lie that the judge (Aycock) happily repeated. A lie the public believed.

It also means that the actual toxicity of the product that the FBI/DOJ claimed "laced" the KC letters had also been a lie, since the arrest affidavit and testimony to two grand juries and to magistrate Alexander at the preliminary hearing (Thomason), the indictments (Lamar/Sigler) and the public claims (Holder/Mueller/Lamar) and the reporters (CNN, ABC, CBS, AP, Reuters, every news site and newspaper on the planet) was equally as false, as the FBI/DOJ knowingly exaggerated the results.

But it also created a serious legal problem for the Holder DOJ/Mueller FBI. That is the date. Considering that the FBI and the DOJ did not even have the final toxicity analysis until October 8th of 2013, and that Dutschke had already been indicted (*twice!*) for developing a biological weapon they claimed was "a deadly poison with no known antidote,"—what, then, had been presented to the grand jury?

It could not have been the actual toxicity analysis (showing no toxicity at all) because that wasn't available yet. The grand jury certainly could not see an analysis not yet completed could they? And the only actual completed lab work actually available at the time of (either) grand jury was the April 27th Barnaby memo which had only tested Q11 (the judge's KC letter) which specified "Ricin *not* detected," that was a document the grand jury never saw because the DOJ/FBI had to conceal the truth about that letter and the dust mask.

So what on Earth had been presented to the grand jury?

The answer is shocking.

The grand jury, both times was presented with false and misleading testimony. This included misrepresenting previous statements. Dutschke had informed select members of Congress of a weapons-grade analysis (90% or higher) of a Libyan sample from a ███████ source, who alleged potential development by ██████████ for ███████.

This Libyan product was in no way related to the KC letters of 2013. And yet specifically selected, 'cherry-picked' experts from that sealed, closed hearing could be used out of context to make it appear as if any product associated with Dutschke MUST be the same (weapons-grade ricin). The grand jury would never be informed that there could be no relation between the Libyan sample and the 2013 KC letters, which were not even in the same year.

So why present the grand jury with it at all? For the specific purpose of prejudicing the grand jury, easily swayed by such conflations and manipulative tactics, that's why.

This would indicate a serious problem, street-level FBI brownshirt Thomason would not have been able to access the transcript by himself, if it existed. No staff or Congressional note could have left the room, no excerpt would have been leaked to him via anyone actually on the HPSCI ("House Intel Committee") and he does not have that level of clearance, nor does Chad Lamar. And neither Holder nor Mueller would have known to look unless suggested to investigators who briefly questioned Congressman Nunnelee, to whom it is known both Dutschke, then later the FBI, spoke. But Nunnelee was not on the committee and would not have known precisely what was said in a hearing that did not keep public records, and Nunnelee, a political mentor of Everett, would not have betrayed Everett like that—at least, not without serious cause. And the twice requested meeting with John Mills never happened, (or at least there is no record of that, which is not quite the same thing). Thus it would have to have been someone who knew of the record-less hearing and would have had clearance high enough that there is no information which they cannot pry away. The number of people in government with that level of gold-card all-access is very, very small. There are only a handful of people to whom someone would feel compelled to disclose, to, not just inter-agency group but intra-branch as well. Those who sit within the interagency group routinely do it, even with individual Congress members who are from an entirely different branch of government, and not all from within the interagency group are "gold-card" carriers. It can easily be narrowed down to four people, 6 if one counts the President (a possibility, and close to Mueller) and the Vice President (Biden not a likely factor. The VP was not known for discretion, but *did* have "friends on the hill"). The four likely candidates are Clinton (and Abedin) (which is just saying the same thing) representing the State Department, John Brennan who was a presidential adviser to President Obama with gold card access then appointed to director of CIA 2013 prior to the Dutschke indictment (both Brennan and Clinton/Abedin would have been closely curious and inquiring about Dutschke post September 2012, having interest in him prior), or Michael Morell, former acting DCI. The scenario with the highest confidence would have been a combination of Brennan and Clinton/Abedin who both had an undiluted influence over President Obama, and with Brennan doing most of the legwork for five reasons.

1.) When it comes to a "covert" operation, as the way this would have been viewed, Brennan would have believed himself the most capable and fit for it given his previous experience in CIA. That was, in fact, why Obama really needed him around.

He needed a reliable "Watergate-type" guy (especially as he had to compete with the Clintons dark operations)

2.) Brennan would have had much closer and natural access to Bob Mueller to have steered and influenced him to utilise that testimony of a secret house hearing.

3.) Brennan had closer and more natural access to the President and to Mark Turry to influence one to green-light the inquiry and another to give up, then redact implicating sections of that testimony out.

4.) Brennan had closer access to Michael Morell and in 2013 would have been able to pull any intel he wanted from the CIA's French desk (since part of the Tripoli File that Brennan and Clinton were trying to secure involves the former French President Sarkozy finances).

5.) Brennan would never allow himself to even be put in a position to ever be asked about this or any other Obama White House clandestine ops, and if he ever was to be asked, he would deny it without a second thought.

The field test results of the KC letters? By citing this, Thomason could take full advantage of a layperson's total scientific ignorance, as the grand jury (x2) was surely *not* made up of PhD-level biochemists, proteomicists, molecular pharmacologists, physiologists or really anyone who would bother to question either Thomason or Chad Lamar when they said nonsensical things like "the fluoroimmuno assay" or the "Polymerase Chain Reaction" (field-grade tests) were the "gold standard" (actual words of Lamar in grand jury) for ricin testing. The grand jurors were likely the average Joes (pulled from the average North Mississippi voter rolls) such as a retired carpet cleaner, a retired factory worker, a part-time construction worker, an unemployed and unmarried stay-at-home mom, a young retail worker and a fast food high school dropout. These are the people that would have been the standard-issue North Mississippi, Obama-friendly voter—so this was the pool which would have populated the grand jury. None of them would have ever experienced such "an important case of National Security" before or shirked "their duty" to indict this guy they'd heard so much about on the news (Dutschke). They would have been dazzled to see the inner workings of the real-life "justice system" and seeing a real-life FBI agent (not on TV). They would have been overwhelmed by the presentation of dealing with such a case of such magnitude. It would be easy to be terrified of the claim of "a deadly poison with no known antidote." Not a single one of them would have asked to see the actual mass spectrometry analysis, which was a good thing for Thomason and Lamar since they needed to (and successfully did) conceal it from the grand jury. Not a single grand juror would have known they could (or should) ask for it, especially since

Lamar and Thomason manipulated the grand jury with claims that the field test of KC letters was the "gold standard."

Not a single North Mississippi grand juror knew that the Polymerase Chain Reaction (PCR) test only looks for whether or not a certain DNA is present (in this case—the DNA for R. Communis) and does *not* test toxicity. In other words, the PCR test only determined whether or not a castor product was present.

The grand jury would not have known that the fluoroimmuno assay and PCR both simply monitor the genetic expression of two similar molecules during R. Communis seed development, which means that it only looks for a certain sequence of DNA to see if either of the molecules (one toxic, one not) *should* be there, without looking for the toxic molecule itself. The only DNA test most North Mississippi grand jurors are familiar with is the ending of any episode of the Jerry Springer or Maury show—("you *are* the father!"). So the grand jurors would not know that either a PCR or fluoroimmuno assay is inherently unreliable. Nor would they have known enough to point out that using ELISA comparison methods is a joke since ELISA can be used reliably for determining individual microscopic organisms like a bacterium or even (much smaller) virus, but not for an individual molecule (almost infinitely smaller). The average North Mississippian would never have thought to demand to see the final toxicity analysis (which did not yet exist). The average juror there would not have thought to mention that the only way to truly accurately determine any quantification of glycosidase activity of any cultivar extractions is by a particular methodology used in isotope dilution mass spectrometry followed by a comparison between the calculated A peptide and B peptide with a corresponding mass spectrography for the disulfide bond, all of which must match at 1:1 ratio or it simply is *not* the biological (actually chemical) agent they claim. Lamar and Thomason knew very well they would not be questioned, so they simply banked on the typical fact that the average juror just capitulated to whatever the two said to them. Even if it was just a lie ("This is a deadly poison. Just trust us. Don't question it. Just do as we say and indict like we tell you".)

Testimony and claims about the dust mask? With this, the most they could have done is shown a photograph of the dust masks. Not much looks more "official" than a photograph of some "evidence" with some sort of evidence tag in the shot. That would look, to the grand jurors, just like something they'd seen on the telly! Of course they would have to be merely *told* the lie that the dust mask contained "traces of ricin and Dutschke's DNA" without actually seeing the trace evidence analysis (the Barnaby memo) or the email from the DNA unit (Connie Fisher email) since both of those documents had to be concealed from the grand jury (because if the grand jury was shown the truth, they might choose to *not* indict, and that is not what grand juries are supposed to do. Grand jury is supposed to just be a meaningless process. A rubber stamp). This is why Lamar and Thomason hid these documents from the grand jury peons. LEOs and prosecutors view the grand jury as the easiest tool in the world, gullible puppets they can manipulate through lies and concealment because the grand jurors (in the minds of prosecutors) *want* to be lied to. They *want* to feel like they are "part of" the process, because (in part) they do *not* know that it *IS* a lie. This is exactly *why* the once public grand jury process has morphed through time to become a "secret" process. Where grand jurors are specifically told: "Okay now, when you leave here today you cannot tell *any*body *any*thing about all the rubbish we told you to get the indictment. You've got to keep this nonsense just between us, okay?" Wink. Wink. There really is *no* other reason. Why else must they keep "evidence" that the prosecutors are required (in theory) to disclose "by law" anyway to the defence (and inevitably in court and in public) "a secret?" The *only* reason for them *not* wanting anyone to know what was told to the gullible rubber-stamp lemmings of the grand jury is because they must hide that they lied and perjured themselves. This way, no one will know they committed a crime (perjury) and concealed the truth (hiding exculpatory information—Obstruction of Justice). Grand jury has grown by practise, not by constitutional law, into "secret" proceedings only to conceal LEO criminality. It is a licence to lie and Thomason and Lamar are practised liars, which was good for Mueller/Holder.

The video footage of Dutschke from the MQ-1 predator drone? It is unclear even still how the FBI ever secured that in the first place, but it was specifically listed in the discovery of "evidence". "Evidence" of what, exactly? It was also never quite clear how the prosecutor intended to use it, except that as a visual, FLIR (night vision) footage of the odd colored glowing figures that someone identifies as "the subject" (Dutschke) taken from 10,000 feet just looks sinister. An infrared video shot from a DOD surveillance drone *looks* just like the footage of a kinetic strike of a terrorist on the disposition matrix just before the Hellfire is deployed, the same kind of familiar looking footage often leaked to the press. It would surely *look,* to the grand jury lemmings, like "the subject" is up to no good, just like the video clips on the telly. A visual aid that provides no useful information, but is designed to prejudice the jury to view the prosecution's victim a certain way. One thing is likely, the MQ-1 Predator was procured and FLIR video cards provided "evidence" by one man. None other than John Brennan. John Brennan was Obama's first term "drone commander," in the capacity he was installed, even when Panetta was DCI. This was likely Brennan's above-board move (the majority of his deeds and dealings were from behind the curtain, as is his usual M.O., behind the scenes from even the President…"officially unofficial").

The CDC analysis on the swabs? Doubtful. There is little chance that Lamar would have allowed the (second) grand jury to see or know anything about the memorandum from James L. Pirkle, MD, PhD to Dr. Michael Farrell and Dr. John Barr that the swabs were *not* reactive during the Spectrometry Structural Assay and Activity Assay and that "analysis was not possible." Instead, Lamar just had FBI agent Thomason regurgitate the lie that three swabs have "tested positive for ricin" and that the field tests were the "gold standard" (Lamar's exact language) since the uneducated grand jury would never have any way to know otherwise. Because it was a grand jury, Lamar and Thomason could keep it a secret that they kept the actual CDC analysis and now it (on the swabs) a secret.

The final toxicity analysis (to show if it was actually "toxic" or "a deadly poison" or not) was not completed until October 7th, so the grand jury (May and September) would never have been presented with the Dr. Stephen Cendrowski, PhD Memo from Fort Detrick, showing the KC product had been specifically engineered to be *non*-toxic. As Lamar would have just had Thomason testify that it was "a deadly poison." A lie, but since it is grand jury and "secret", who would ever know?

So the grand jury, left with only Thomason's untruthful accusations, had no choice but to indict. Besides, if the grand jury members owned either a television, a radio or had internet or read any newspaper, they already knew the Holder/Mueller accusations against Everett, so Thomason was only reinforcing to the grand jury what they had already been programmed to think by the (force multiplier) media. Because all the actual and real analysis was concealed from the "secret" grand jurors, they had no choice but to buy the already popular administration myth. They saw no lab work at all, at best presented only with an FBI report (which sounds so official, but it is still only testimony typed onto letterhead) of the field tests.

So what, then, started the whole thing? Where did the "ricin" accusation come from, the original accusation in the letters (Curtis sent). The long answer is complete but is much more complex. But the short answer is the field test.

In 2011 a peer-reviewed study was published, **Anal. Chem 83,2897-2905, A research of "detection and quantification of ricin...using isotope dilution tandem Mass spectrometry"** which discussed exactly that; as a methodology, this procedure would be much more reliable than the inaccurate PCR and Fluoroimmuno assay used by the FBI. The authors of the research paper were Dr. SC McGrath, Dr. D M Shieltz, Dr. LG McWilliams and none other than Dr. John Barr and James L Pirkle, MD, PhD, the same directors of the Division of Laboratory Science at the CDC who analyzed the "swabs" to be "analysis not possible", so it is clear that he was part of the study that knew better.

Countless studies have long since shown that the antibody-based methods cannot differentiate *any* difference between the toxic molecules (AB chain with an intact disulfide bond) or the non-toxic similar RCA molecule. These methods are the PCR and the fluoroimmuno assay, known by the scientists to be unreliable. Such as Avld, Rolfe, Mckeon 2001—"J. New seeds" 3, 61-69, and Avld, Pinkerton, Boroda, Lombard, Murphy, Kenworthy, Becker, Rolfe, Ghetie, 2003, "registration of TTU-LRC caster germoplasm with reduced levels of ricin and RCA120," Crop Sci. 43,746-747—and Baldoni, de Carvalhe, Sousa, Nobrega, Milani, Aragao, 2011 "And variability of ricin content"...Pesq. Agropec. Brasil 46,776-779; Garber, 2008 "Toxicity and detection of ricin..." Journal food Prot. 71. 1875—1883; and Pinkerton, 1997, "selection of Castor divergent concentrations of RCA using radial immunodiffusion", Texas Tech University; and Pinkerton, Rolfe, Avld, Ghetie, lauterbach, 1999, "Selection of castor for divergent...agglutinin", Crop Sci. 39,353-357; the list is truly endless. PCR (Polymerase chain reaction), so it is a DNA test, *not* a test for toxicity. And the other "quickie" test, "time of flight Mass spectrometry", relies on ELISA database for comparison and is suitable only for detecting organisms and viruses, which are massive compared to the individual molecule one would be looking for in ricin, thus are woefully inadequate for such a purpose. So the real questions are (and should have been): How is it possible to design a product that would not actually be toxic and have zero ricin toxicity (as confirmed by the final analysis) yet still *looks* like it to the field test? And who could have engineered a product that field tests (and ELISA) but really isn't.

It is not helpful to Dutschke, as pointed out for the press by Jack Curtis's statement—"He (Dutschke) is a genius." Nor is it helpful to Dutschke's connection to the 2012 Libyan product or the possibility that the 2002 Operation Vengeance might have utilised actual ricin as a culprit (the cessation of cellular protein synthesis by depurination of a ribosomal elongation factor causing organ failure) through the oxygen delivery system. It is also not very helpful to Dutschke that in 2003 he penned the white paper (for the then President George W Bush) regarding the potential use of biological and chemical weapons by terrorists—"The Boom Factor." But what should have helped although it didn't, is that it is not illegal nor a violation of any war-crimes treaty to develop a product that is *entirely harmless.*

The problem is that it appears as if the product of the KC letters was a nitrogen-based preparation that seemed to be specifically designed to mimic ricin in the field test. Yet the toxicity of it, as confirmed in October, 2013, was nil, literally the signals for active ricin and RCA molecules were below the actual reliable limit of detection of 1-0 ng/ml. So the *how* it could have been designed to comport with the various analysis is both complicated and not at the same time a step by step process, for such a product does not exist. Yet the toxicology experts, proteomicists, clinical chemists, biochemists, microbiologists, toxicologists would all agree that it could be done and in the case of the two KC letters, had been done. One would need to start with the phosphate buffered extract from Macaranga grandifolia from the Euphorbiaceae family (A close biological relative to castor) and the lipid layer of the US Virgin Island Cultivar (cv:pizo9326 which is "small seed" cultivar of R. Communis) that has undergone extensive centrifugation, thermocycling and rocking in an adenine-releasing bath of ammonium citrate and ethylenediaminetetraacetic acid (PH-4.0) followed by a nebulized application of the resulting USVI cultivar product onto the macaranga grandifolia extract in a nitrogen filled chamber, infusing the USVI product into the nitrogen-rich macaranga extract. The USVI cultivar would be chosen because it has a higher natural level of RCA protein than it does ricin molecule, and the ricin molecule it has is a molecular isoform that has never been shown to be toxic ("ricin E"—has a different B-chain sequence that is derived from the RCA molecule which does not easily bind to cellular glycoproteins and glycolipids does never giving the A-chain a chance to depurinate ribosomal adenine). The thermocycling and rocking acid bath breaks the disulfide bonds which means the A chain can never gain cellular entry. The PCR and fluoroimmuno assay (DNA) test can detect NONE of this, nor can the ELISA-based (antibody-bases) TOF-MS. To those tests, it all looks like "ricin". This is why the real scientific community has time and again warned against the use of those methods. They are but quick, preliminary tests, certainly *not* the "gold-standard" as Lamar misrepresented to the grand jury. And it is exactly *why* Lamar and Thomason had to conceal the actual laboratory analysis from the grand jurors, the judge and the public, because the actual Laboratories (NBFAC, Fort Detrick and the CDC) reliably resulted in "ricin not detected" "analysis not possible," which is not what the DOJ and its obedient press reported to the American public.

That is the how.

As to the question of—"Who the hell could develop such a product?" The answer should be: "*who...* is immaterial."

The answer is immaterial because legally, such a (non-toxic) product does not in any way violate either the Biological or Chemical weapons treaty therefore no statute that "enforces" either treaty. Since it is not against the law to develop an innocuous and *non*-toxic product, there is no crime. This was specifically pointed out by Fox News legal analyst Judge Andrew Napolitano. The only "crime" might have been the letter's verbal content—written entirely by Curtis who isn't Dutschke—which does *not* mention ricin in the text of it at all. And *that* would be a matter of whether or not someone considered *text* that Curtis chose as a threat or not. According to the 2014 Supreme Court Elonis case, it is not. (But regardless, the *making* is a separate act from the *mailing*).

Therefore, as far as the actual lab work revealed, there was no crime; this should not have been a conviction. So "who" does not matter.

The Holder/Mueller DOJ/FBI did not care. They had their orders. Convict Dutschke. Damn the truth. Just hide it away. No one will ever know.

Until now.

It is important to remember exactly what happened, meaning their reaction, when the final toxicity analysis finally was complete (the Cendrowski memo). Recall that the FBI's Christa Mason first circulated the memo on October 8th, 2013. Keep in mind that the law, as written, for ricin sets a prosecutorial threshold of 0.5% purity and note that it carries into the tenths, past the decimal point (half of 1%). Remember that the National Bioforensic Analysis Centers National Biodefence Analysis Countermeasure Center laboratory under the Department of Homeland Security at Fort Detrick, MD (The nation's top bioweapons facility) announced that the toxicity of the *two* KC letters that they did test (they never tested the Wicker letter) was not estimated to be higher than the legal "round to zero" threshold (of over that of .5%). In fact, the Round To Zero rule that controls ricin and under the law means that the 0% that was the KC letter product renders both of the tested letters unprosecutable!

(How does one prosecute for the developed "poison" that isn't?)

At that point, the FBI, the prosecutors and the judge should all have gone to the press and said—"UHH-OOOPS! So sorry, we made such a terrible mistake and we all lied to you daily for half a year and destroyed a man's life and reputation in the process. It turns out that there never was any 'deadly poison with no known antidote' despite what we told you to report. We and the president regret the public lie, admit to it, ask for Dutschke's forgiveness and let him go. We are happy, however, to announce that there never was any biological or chemical weapons attack and pleased that everybody is safe and no crime was committed. Our mistake. Sorry."

But that is NOT what they did.

For by now, they were too far publicly invested so they had to bury the Cendrowski analysis to make sure it would never be used, would never be seen, would never be discovered.

The problem for Holder/Lamar/Sigler/Mueller/Comey/Thomason et al, is that this is precisely the lab analysis that Dutschke (and his appointed lawyer, lawyer, Coghlan) was waiting for. Anyone who was familiar enough with Dutschke would know that his likely response would be to shove their own lab report in front of the DOJ's face (and the press) and yell—"See!" I *told* you all along that you were all liars. Now you cannot escape it. *This* is the evidence that proves you all to be worthless liars to anyone who can simply read, if any of you in the DOJ or the press is even capable of reading at all. Which I doubt. So I'll be happy to read it aloud for you and I'll go slow enough so that even the FBI agents can understand!"

His manner of speech aside, he would have been entirely justified in thinking that way. But he would never get to parade that document (as personally signed by Stephen Cendrowski, PhD), and in fact would not even know that document existed; because the DOJ (Holder et al) knew very well what Dutschke's reaction would be and that the worldwide press would find out which would, in fact, reveal to the world that the cabal had, in fact, fabricated their claims, misrepresented the law and made up "evidence". The world would know if this (and the other) lab analysis became public, that all their claims were/are, in fact lies. The world would know that the prosecution was a complete setup, a sham. Then they might have started asking "for who" and "why", which are questions that not even the Mueller/Comey FBI was privy to. All the FBI knew was they were supposed to tighten the noose on Dutschke, with no idea why (though that did not matter because the FBI/DOJ is very skilled in sham prosecutions). This would all cause a major political scandal and the entire world was watching this case. This document (and the others) would clear Dutschke and burn the cabal.

So they could not let it be seen. By anyone. Ever.

So here's what they did. The DOJ (Holder et al) saw the Cendrowski memo on October 8th. Within 24 hours—literally the *very next day*, the Attorney General of the United States, Eric Holder, invoked the very, very rare executive authority granted *only* to him by the president called a SAM order. This act and the timing of it is an undeniable fact and a matter of historical (now) record.

The SAM order (which stands for the very, very, vague "Special Administrative Measures") is ceded to only the Attorney General of the United States (and *no* other person or designee) and is invoked incredibly rarely and for the explicit purpose of "National Security." The SAM regulations that "allow" Holder to do so are at 28 CFR§501.2 and .3 and ONLY the A.G. (no other person) can issue or enact a SAM order. 501.3 requires that "the HEAD (no other person or designee) of a federal law enforcement agency" (which was Bob Mueller in 2013, then Jim Comey in 2014) must endorse Holder's executive order; and 501.2 requires that "The *head* of (no other person or designee) a member of the intelligence community" (John Brennan) must endorse Holder's executive order. Bob Mueller (2013) and Jim Comey (2014) did endorse Holder's SAM order(s), John Brennan did not.

The SAM order itself does *not* require that anyone be convicted of anything and is an extraconstitutional (which means unconstitutional) power to imprison *any* person (citizen or not) into extreme solitary confinement restricting any and *all* communications with anyone. Think about this. This meant that the President of the United States vested the power into one man (A.G. Holder) to snatch and "disappear" any person he wanted to into prison (which is probably a bit better than the Clintons' method of "disappearing" people) whether that person is guilty of a crime or not. There is no "due process" to dispute it. It cannot be taken to court as a judge cannot effect, cannot enact and has no agency or even branch jurisdiction (Article II vs Article III power) in an executive branch's "administrative action". There is no oversight either within the DOJ *or* congressional oversight. There is no process or means or mechanism to fight the "National Security declaration" or designation.

The result was that all communication ceased. With anyone. All discovery and case files were confiscated, including privileged attorney notes, by the FBI and never returned. Dutschke no longer had contact with any person, no access to any legal resources of any kind, no discovery and no "notice" whatsoever as to how or why he was left sealed into a concrete room with nothing but a roll of toilet paper. Court records reveal that even to this day, 2020, Dutschke still had never received a copy of this supposed SAM order that Eric Holder himself purportedly wrote and signed, despite that the regulations require that Dutschke be delivered it. Though the SAM order deserves its own chapter in this book, it should be noted that because of Dutschke's ordered imprisonment into extreme solitary confinement, it means that he was not allowed any communication with the press as well—so even if he had known the toxicity analysis had been completed, even if he had been tossed a copy of the Cendrowski memo (he wasn't), he could not have trumpeted either it or its significance to anyone. Not only was Everett now in the dark, so would he and the media stay. Nor was his attorney (also bound by the SAM on behalf of Everett) allowed to speak to the media or any person on behalf of his client either. The SAM, as intended, muted and blinded Dutschke- silencing him and crippling his defence.

Think of this. As soon as the exculpatory lab work was discovered by the DOJ, Holder et al slammed down the wall of an executive order around him to prevent him from knowing it and sharing it (or anything with the public). With that abusive move of extreme executive power, the Obama Administration was free to do and say whatever it wanted and continue to advance their fake, untrue and quite frankly impossible narrative and there was no one around to counter it.

Because Everett is who he is, he still found a way to sneak letters to two reporters, Emily Waggster-Pettus (AP) and Patsy Brumfield (Daily Journal) who did nothing at the time and did not try to reply until years later, when it was too late.

The Holder/Mueller (Comey now) prosecution team fabricated to the press and others as well, new claims about Dutschke and went even quite elaborate in their staging of the contrivances, even while he sat in solitary confinement unaware of what was going on or of any of the new accusations which were being presented as new crimes. There would be no defence against the new accusations because they were bogus, contrived for the sake of smearing Dutschke and the press (and his wife) further. And because there were no indictments or even formal accusations, there was no mechanism for defence, which he could not mount anyway because of the SAM. However, because of the SAM, there was no contradiction or even a denial of any nonsensical propaganda the Holder/Mueller/ (then Comey) team fed the press. So the press (and the individuals harassed by the FBI) all assumed everything was true, smearing Dutschke without response.

The facade of the Holder/Sigler/Lamar game was almost broken at the January 2014 plea hearing. Almost. The prosecution read from a long litany of utter and object lies, including among their fictitious "statement of facts" the bogus claims of elaborate schemes they had claimed to the press of new (but uncharged) "crimes", a bizarre and physically impossible narrative and outlandish and equally impossible claims of evidence. Following this "reading of the facts" (none of which were factual), the presiding judge, Aycock turned and asked Dutschke the perfunctory question—"Mr. Dutschke, is what (the prosecutor) described about your conduct true and accurate?"

Now at this point, the proper and traditional answer by a defendant is supposed to be—"yes, your honor," and nothing else. In fact, this is what most putty-spined lawyers advise their client to say, only that. However, when the judge asked Dutschke if the prosecutor's description "about your conduct true and accurate?" Dutschke's response was, "*not* at all!"

"Not at all!"

To any person fluent in the English language—"Not at all" means exactly the same as "None of it." It does not mean, "Well, your honor...some of it is, but a little bit isn't." It does not mean, "mostly." It means what it says. And he stood and said "Not at all!" This is a matter of record.

But because he was not armed with the lab analysis, he could not explicitly confront and expose the prosecutors for the liars that they are.

That would change.

On Friday the 13th in May 2014 Dutschke was taken to the sentencing hearing and it is clear and obvious from the transcript that he was trying to push back against the forces aligned against him including the prosecution team, the judge, and, sadly even his own appointed lawyer. Dutschke spoke for himself, instead of his bumbling lawyer speaking for him, when he could, as the filled-to-capacity courtroom was wall-to-wall with media, wondering where they stood, if they would see any drama.

They did.

Without addressing most of the prepared objections to the pre-sentence report (which is designed to encourage "sentencing points" which increases the actual sentence) the judge flew through the motions of pretending she had thoughtfully considered the issues in front of her dealing with "sentencing factors". She had not thoughtfully considered anything, it was clear, because she accepted every lie of the pre-sentencing report and with the objective of seeing past the magic number that would equal a life sentence. Dutschke's objections, frustrations and even attempts to educate fell on deaf-ears as the judge's mind was already made up. The safest thing for her to do, politically, was to avoid the controversy that would come by allowing this measly prisoner-defendant to actually try to defend himself; she had never had a case with this much media interest, involving parties of this magnitude. She just needed to do what was expected of her by that administration (and the President) and get rid of the meddlesome guy. The *only* thing she could not find a way to justify was the "Terrorism Enhancement", which was among the smear labels that administration had tried to stick Dutschke with.

This time, though, Dutschke came prepared. He did not have *all* the lab reports, but it is clear from the transcript that he now had two. Two that should land a solid body-blow to the prosecution team. During the hearing he stated nearly 20 times that the entire courtroom knew that he was not the mailer and that everyone should "stop pretending" and directly called out the impossible narrative spun by the administration (and even by Curtis) for the fiction that it is now clearly seen that it was. But in reference to the lab work, he reminded the present media of the falsity smoking-gun dustmask claims they had all reported to the world (at which point he, himself, was reprimanded by Aycock that he was addressing her, not anyone else). He then held up the trace evidence analysis (the Barnaby memo) and read it aloud, demolishing the prosecution's claim right in front of them, for the press and the judge to see. He was not finished. He then read directly from the Connie Fisher internal FBI email showing that it was *not* his DNA.

These lab analyses, each, should have demolished and ameliorated the case, right then and there. Here he stood, holding up, reading and showing in writing that the administration had been making it all up. He announced, countless times repeating it, that there was no ricin toxin "and everybody in the room knows it", and showed, in writing, from documents from the government's very own lab, that the administration's claims were entirely bogus. The press, if they had any integrity, should have immediately turned on the administration.

They didn't.

They came to watch a man be hanged. And Everett's innocence and insistence on it was interfering with their spectacle. Not a single outlet bothered to run a copy of the exculpatory lab work on-air, on paper or on the web, showing that this high-profile national security prosecution was a sham and circus. Instead, they carried the Obama Administration's water and pretended it never happened.

It was not important that the entire prosecution was a pile of lies. It was only important that Dutschke be convicted and disappeared.

After a second hearing, that is exactly what was done. As expected. The entire justice system had been weaponized, and exposed for the fraud that it was, but no one cared because people had willfully blinded themselves to it.

Despite that certain lab analyses told the truth, it was an unfortunate lesson that people *don't want* the truth.

Paul Kevin Curtis had written in the KC letters—"to see a wrong and not expose it is to become a partner and its continuance." This statement may not be wrong at its essence, which is a huge irony that the mailer (Curtis) was correct in his thinking. But what Curtis did not consider, therefore one way in which he was wrong, is that it does not matter if a wrong is "exposed", because people en masse simply do not care if a wrong is occurring. It is far easier for them to just ignore it or just turn their heads.

The lab analyses prove now, to anyone who still has enough integrity to care, that the entire case was a fabrication, and that the administration knew it from the beginning. The lies told, the SAM to silence Dutschke and the truth—all of it—was part of the political weaponization of the FBI and DOJ, a conclusive fact that is indisputable in retrospect, and with a complicit press to boot.

What should have mattered to the public and the system is the (documented) proof.

It didn't.

Chapter 4

Conviction by Fraudulent Plea

At some point, Everett, just like others federally prosecuted, did finally realise that the judge does not care about truth or innocence, the prosecutor and "law enforcement" does not care about truth or innocence, and most sadly the media does not care about truth or innocence—for when the public wants to see a hangin'...well, by God we better "gibb'em a hangin."

The most unfortunate of those is the press, because this makes them complicit in the disgusting crimes of (especially that particular administration's) weaponization of the Justice Department and the FBI. The argument ends, however, the second someone capitulates to the pressure and signs the plea. At that point, no matter the circumstances, the plebian-press could say—"See! *He must* be guilty because he admitted it by signing the plea agreement" (which is precisely what the *criminals who are prosecuting* the case also say from that point forward). But to anyone with a brain—that cannot be accurate.

No one who is fighting their case, fighting, fighting, fighting, for a year just signs a plea.

Someone who knows they are guilty signs, and quickly. But someone who is innocent will fight and fight and fight until they recognise that no one cares. Someone *not* guilty will spend that year, and more if they have to, hoping that as the evidence comes in—the "Trusted fact-finders" (LEOs and prosecutors) will drop the case once they recognise that LEOs and prosecutors see the truth; a hope that always ends badly since the LEOs and prosecutors don't care about truth or innocence, which is why they hide it. They care only for conviction. No matter how long someone clings to their hope.

One of the most important things to remember is that Everett finally caved at the point when he believed they were about to prosecute his wife, Janet. One must recall that *she* had to get the court to appoint a defence lawyer to *her*, and indeed one was appointed. What did she have to do with any of the evidence?

The fact is that, Thomason's arrest warrant cited more of Janet's actions than Everett's. Thomason took *her* actions and twisted them, turning them into evidence that he claimed implicated Everett.

A common tactic—use the wife's evidence to convict the husband, then "work" the wife to turn against the husband and when that does not work, threaten to prosecute the wife and any husband worth his salt will cave and sign the plea to protect her.

What "evidence" did Thomason claim in the affidavit he swore to? According to Thomason's affidavit, Janet sent a text to someone who was not

Everett and that the text said that she was coming over to "burn some things." Somehow this meant that Everett, who was not party to that text or even present when it was sent, developed a biological weapon.

According to Thomason, when Janet received a text from Everett stating "the FBI is searching the house", that must have meant that Everett developed a biological weapon (*no* evidence of either making or mailing a bio-weapon was "seized" from the Dutschke home).

According to Thomason, the Waste Management garbage bin was filled up when Janet did her annual spring cleaning, and the FBI then "seized" that garbage bin from the Waste Management truck when they (not Everett) replaced the bin with a new one. They then searched that "seized" garbage bin (and found nothing). Thomason's implication was that Janet's annual spring cleaning must have meant that Everett developed a biological weapon.

During the preliminary hearing Thomason revealed that they had visited the second residence where Janet's "burn pile" had taken place and was shown the spot where family frequently burned their bills at campfire gatherings. The FBI sampled from the ash. When Lamar led Thomason (who was under oath) on the witness stand, Lamar asked about "evidence that had been burned." Thomason shook his head sadly and answered that the "evidence" had been rendered "to ashes." His implication was that Janet's "burn pile" meant that Everett developed a biological weapon.

At the same hearing and at a later hearing they discussed some items that Janet (not Everett) had moved from Everett's office building (without Everett present) with *her* friends to one of *her* friend's storage sheds (someone unknown to Everett). The FBI "swabbed" some of these items then claimed that one of the items Janet had moved to *her* friend's storage "swabbed" positive for ricin (it didn't—"the ricin positive swabs", sent to CDC, were *not* "positive" at all). Even though Everett had nothing to do with the item or its location, Thomason's implication was that Janet's moving stuff meant that Everett developed a biological weapon.

But Thomason's kicker is what did the trick. At the preliminary hearing, FBI agent Thomason told the magistrate that the now infamous dust mask from the "trash pull" outside Everett's previous office building yielded DNA results of two people. Not one, but two. It is now known that *they* knew the day *before* that in court, under oath testimony that the Fisher email had *ex*cluded Everett "as a source" of the DNA on that mask (which Thomason also falsely claimed had traces of ricin on it). Thomason, on *that* day, lied to the federal magistrate, under oath, and just like always, he got away with it. Everett, however, had not seen, therefore did not know, about the Fisher DNA email and *knew* that Thomason (and the press) was lying about *his* DNA on a "ricin" mask. But as Everett (later) began to see that the FBI was allowed to lie, and the judge was predisposed to encouraging FBI/prosecutor lies (as was the entire worldwide media), the FBI agents tried a new tactic-suggesting that the "other" DNA on the mask (which is, in fact, female) was Janet's; giving them rationale to indict her.

It was *that* suggestion by the FBI (a lie) that pushed Everett over the edge. The records shows that, that is when he signed the plea.

It is worth noting here that the usual FBI tactics are for FBI agents to call, email, text and visit the wife that they "are working". And in the process of "working" her, slowly gain her trust ("Just checking on you, to see how you are holding up") while poisoning her mind against her husband and weakening her resolve. If that does not work, their usual next step is to set up some staged event, an entrapment that would cause her to be furious at him. It could be an affair accusation or claims of other (contrived) crimes or something to shock her conscience. (In this case, one of those step-two tactics was to say—"Did *you* know he kept a *lock box!?*" Implying he had kept secrets). Most wives do *not* know that LEOs ("professional" agents practise it) actually are allowed to lie to the wife, or any witness, and do so as a matter of routine—because it usually works. IF THAT does not work—step three is to stop pretending to be the nice guy and threaten prosecution.

In the Dutschke case, *he* could not know if they had stopped the-"good cop" routine with Janet or not, since he was under a SAM order and had no contact. HE did not know it was potentially just a bluff since plenty of "evidence" cited by FBI agent Thomason was Janet's actions being used against *him*.

In retrospect, it is a stretch to see how Janet burning her bills (in the new computer's box) and doing spring cleaning or sending texts or moving things could have anything at all to do with a war-crimes treaty, or how on earth FBI agent Thomason got away with presenting those actions of *her* (not Everett) to be somehow a sinister act of national security worthy of life imprisonment of her husband. The fact that it is a stretch did not matter to the press who did not bother to raise a single question about it.

It is also a mystery as to what Thomason actually disclosed to Janet while he was "working" her. Did he ever show her the arrest affidavit where it explicitly used *her* actions to condemn Everett? It would be a safe bet he never showed or told her that. Did he ever tell her that he depended heavily on his testimony on *her* spring cleaning, *her* "burn pile", and her text when he was under oath in front of the magistrate? It would be a safe bet he never told her that. Did he inform her that he was going to push the idea to Everett's lawyer that *she* would be prosecuted on the suggestion that it was *her* DNA on the dust mask? It would be a safe bet he never told her that. Did he inform her that he tried a (also common) jail-entrapment scheme (twice) and was yanked off the case as agent-in-charge after the failure of a second scheme? It would be a safe bet he never told her that. (Incidentally, it became obvious *after* the plea was signed and Everett then saw in the Barnaby memo that there was no ricin on the dustmask—that it did not matter if it was Janet's DNA on the dustmask or not. There was no "ricin" on it, thus is "evidence" of nothing sinister or criminal at all. Of course, by the time he saw that exculpatory lab work, he had already signed and was not allowed to withdraw when he tried)

The DOJ/FBI uses these tactics all the time. It is so commonplace that the tactic was recently exposed with former National Security Adviser Michael Flynn, A 30+ year veteran and DIA General. People who now act shocked to discover this tactic was used with Flynn, should not be. Instead they should simply realise that—"If they would do this to *him* (and others), then they would do this to anyone." And they do. Just like Flynn, Dutschke signed it. to save his wife.

People, then, are programmed to think, "Well, if he signed it, then he admitted to the crime. He did it." This thinking is wrong. Especially here.

And *this* case, is an exception. He never admitted *anything.*

The Alford Plea

Doesn't a plea mean that Mr. Dutschke admitted to the making (count one) and the mailing (remaining counts)? No.

In this case, it is a matter of public record that Dutschke was unequivocal and vehement in his denials of guilt, from the first opportunity (the change of plea hearing) through every single post-conviction filing.

When a plea agreement is signed by a defendant, he legally then is required to admit to every element of the alleged violated statutes. This is usually accomplished under oath during the prosecution's "Reading of the Facts."

The "Reading of the Facts" by a prosecutor is supposed to lay out the factual events or behaviours which show the defendant admits every one of the statutory elements of a criminal statute. According to the law, *every single* element must be admitted. In most cases, the "reading of the facts" or "statement of facts" is a prosecutor's narrative and it is explicitly written to cast the defendant in the worst possible light. It is designed to make the defendant look like "a monster" ("monster" is the exact term FBI agents are trained to use, along with "scheme" as part of their tactics to weaponize sentiments against a defendant).

Most defendants simply agree to whatever the prosecutor's "statement of facts" says, even though the "statement of facts" is rarely true (a "fact", in criminal court, does not mean "fact", in the same way the rest of the world knows it—as in something that is true and correct. In criminal court, "a fact"—or an "established fact" is any allegation the judge allows prosecutors to make, whether true or false).

In US vs Dutschke, the plea agreement was signed (after they threatened to prosecute his wife, Janet) yet at no time did he ever accept even a single allegation—not even a single element of a single count was admitted to, as the law requires. This is known as an "Alford Plea" (when the defendant signs the plea agreement but maintains his innocence), and has only been accepted by a judge in a tiny handful of cases in history.

The transcripts show this, as a matter of record, Dutschke maintained his innocence from the beginning.

From US vs Dutschke case 1:13-CR-00081-SA-DAS, The change of plea hearing transcript of January 17th 2014:

When the prosecutor read the "statement of facts" (page 29, line 18) Court (Judge Sharion Aycock): "Mr. Dutschke, do you understand everything the prosecutor stated?"

Dutschke (response): "Oh, I understand, yes…"

Court: "Is everything Mr. Joyner said about your conduct true and correct?"

Dutschke: "NOT at all!"

Now, that does not sound like an "acceptance" of the read "facts" does it? Because it wasn't. "Not at all!" has a pretty clear meaning. The next time the public saw Dutschke was a few months later, during the sentencing hearing from May 13th 2014.

- At *that* hearing (page 20 line 6 of transcript), his attorney, Ken Coghlan, referred to the product at issue as "ricin"—Dutschke quickly corrected his attorney—"No!"

- Page 21, line 15 of the same transcript, Judge Aycock is trying to say that in sentencing, "toxicity doesn't matter" (which is simply *not* true according to the sentencing guidelines *she* is supposed to follow). Dutschke quickly corrected her—"That's not right."

- From page 21, line 20 of the May 13th transcript. The prosecutors tried to make the false claim that the product was "intended to be toxic" by the maker. Dutschke quickly corrected them—"No"

- From page 25, line 12. The prosecutors allege a false claim about a computer printer. He quickly corrected them—"Not true. Not true. Not true."

- From page 28, line 21. The prosecutor made the bizarre claim that Dutschke chose the targets of KC letters. Dutschke quickly corrected him—"They were chosen by Curtis." For some unexplainable reason, the actual transcript reads "they were chosen by courtesy." Dutschke even filed a motion asking why the transcript replaced Curtis's name with the word courtesy, since it makes no sense and asked the judge to simply correct this transcript error. The judge (Aycock) denied the motion stating in essence, the court did not want an accurate record. Seriously. Bizarre.

- From page 34, line 9. The prosecutor outlined his strange and bizarre (thrice changed) theory and claims. Dutschke replied "*Everything he* (prosecutor) said is crap!"

115

- o Note—Mr. Dutschke didn't reply by saying, "a *few* of the things is crap" or "some of the things"—but instead, as a record shows, Dutschke said "Everything…" which does not leave any room for any doubt.
- From page 35, line 19. Judge Aycock repeated the prosecutor's fiction. Dutschke immediately replied to *her*, "That makes no sense."
- From page 37, line 15. The prosecutors make false claims to Aycock about the "ricin" tests. Dutschke replied—"That's misleading and *he* knows it."
- From page 38, line 16. Dutschke plainly stated, "There was *no* ricin toxin anywhere…"
- From page 38, line 13. He repeated—"*not* toxic…"
- From page 38, line 16. "There is *no* ricin toxin".
- From page 38, line 22. "They're lying to you… it's not possible"
- Page 40, line 20. regarding the mailing. Dutschke—"I did *not* mail those letters and he knows that, too."
  - o It is important to remember that Curtis was only charged with the *mailing* and never charged with the *making* (development of a biological weapon), It was Dutschke who was charged with the making.
- Page 47, line 12.—"This has been absurd from the beginning."
- Page 53, line 14.—"You have all been lied to"
- Page 54, line 1.—"I'll start by being clear as possible. There is no poison. There is no toxin. There is no ricin. There never was—everyone in this room knows it—lab results now confirm it. Why are we all still standing here pretending? There is no ricin, there never was"
- Page 54, line 21.—"There is no poison, never was"
- Page 54, line 22.—"*not* Based on real facts, or even actual crime"
- Page 55, line 2. Regarding the mailing—"I did *not* mail the KC letters"
- Page 56, lines 9-23. Reading the exculpatory email—"Your honor, this is an internal memo to the FBI laboratory… ricin *not* detected"
- Page 58, line 16.—"There is no poison. There is no toxin"
- Page 61, line 4.—"It's twisted (the prosecutor story), it's confusing, it's illogical. The whole (arrest affidavit) should have been written in crayon…it's completely absurd. I've seen better logic on episodes of SpongeBob SquarePants"
- Page 61, Line 18.—"There is no poison. There is no ricin"

Just this list alone, from only two transcripts (and there are plenty more) are 25 different denials of "guilt"! *None* of the above sounds like an admission of guilt, does it?

This (actual transcript excerpts) shows that Dutschke tried to withdraw from the plea. It did not matter. Even though Mr. Dutschke did *not* accept even a single allegation at the plea hearing, the judge (Aycock) accepted the plea anyway (making it an Alford plea).

Then at the sentencing hearing, Mr. Dutschke continued to assert his innocence. He clearly did *not* develop anything that was "a deadly poison," but he wasn't supposed to reveal that in court...he was expected to just shut up and accept it.

He was expected to do what most criminal defendants do, which is to let the prosecutors lie and roll over him, being nice and subservient to the judge the whole time.

He clearly did not mail a single one of the KC letters, but he wasn't supposed to remind everyone of the actual mailer, Paul Kevin Curtis, either. Certainly, Dutschke was not accepting guilt and was maintaining his innocence. There is not another transcript to be found anywhere, in *all* of U.S. criminal history (*including* the Alford case) where someone was convicted by a plea deal while vehemently stating his innocence over 25 times prior to conviction. Not one single case, in history...*ever*. Yet that is exactly what happened here. Mr. Dutschke was convicted anyway.

In other words, Dutschke's case is actually *more* of an Alford plea than even the Alford case itself!

Some may query the record, recalling that the opposing judge and prosecutor stated in later, post-conviction filings, that Mr. Dutschke "affirmed his guilt" during the *second* sentencing hearing. That is a lie. He did not. A thorough review of the transcript is entirely devoid of any admission of guilt of even a single element.

The closest he came was stating that he "affirmed the plea agreement", which *not* the same as "affirming guilt", which is an indisputable matter of record that he never "reaffirmed guilt".

Any allusion that Mr. Dutschke "affirmed guilt" or admitted to even a single element (though *all* the elements are required for a plea to be valid or legal), is nothing but another lie. The record, as written, clearly shows such admission *never* happened.

Anyone claiming otherwise, whether a judge, prosecutor or any other person, is simply lying.

Yet Dutschke was convicted anyway, then sent to the National Security Unit (SAM unit) to be "disappeared" from anyone who might be curious. The administration's predetermined outcome, conviction without public trial, was successfully pulled off.

When the trustees of the justice system (as in the American LEOs and DOJ lawyers and judges) lie to an accused person, his family or a witness, in order to secure a specific result, how is that any different than when someone is accused of lying to the FBI? Lying to the FBI is considered a federal crime worthy of imprisonment (just ask Martha Stewart, General Michael Flynn and countless others) yet *they* do it all the time, as a matter of tactics.

And it is allowed, even sometimes in the very same setting that will become part of or sometimes even in legal proceedings themselves. (What do Flynn, Dutschke and Martha Stewart here have in common? Lying Comey)

For example, during the initial stages, when the FBI was questioning the mailer, Paul Kevin Curtis, an FBI agent told Curtis that because of one of the letters that he sent, someone who handled it was in the hospital in critical condition and might die. The agent even mustered a tear or two in order to "sell" and elicit emotion from Curtis (an "emotionally breaking" person will talk). It was not true. It was a blatant lie. And because it was told so very convincingly, Curtis, a very experienced liar himself, actually fell for it, and at one point (after Dutschke's name was brought up during his hearings) he agreed to work with the agents, becoming an important part of their media operation with his "Blame Dutschke" tour. In fact, convincing the press to seamlessly switch from prosecution of the "MAILER" to the destruction of the "MAKER" (in their minds), without too many questions, might have been a little harder of a sales job without Curtis and his attorney laying the groundwork for the segue. Curtis's efforts to claim that he was the innocent victim of a rogue operation to "frame" him, with Dutschke as the mastermind behind the operation is what gave his new FBI bosses cover for the Operation Dojo and the (well documented) DOJ plan to discredit and convict Dutschke. It prevented further embarrassment for them. And Curtis, thankful at the point when he was released, who was not particularly mentally acute, had no idea that he was being used by the LEOs to do their bidding. His "blame Dutschke" media tour was exactly what they wanted. As long as Curtis was out there as a lie ambassador, they had much less work to do (which continues to this day).

Even at the moment when the LEOs (FBI) are "conducting a formal interview" it *is* a legal proceeding because *anything* you say can and will be used against you...*against* you in court. So the presumption, legally, should be that those "interviews" are but an extension of the court testimony (even if *you* are not under oath, the LEO will *later* go under oath to claim your said whatever he said you have to have said). In court there are recordings and legal transcripts of each word spoken (though transcripts are routinely altered). And those interviews and statements that are outside of court *do* lead to convictions (a la Martha Stewart, John Kirirakou). Yet the FBI, as a matter of practise and policy, do not actually record any of their interviews. There is no video camera rolling, no digital recorder. Not even an old Radio Shack cassette recorder during the interviews.

Why?

This is now 2020. Is there no technology available for the "premiere law enforcement agency" in the world to use? Even though local-yokel beat cops wear "body cams" that record everything they do (except when they misbehave or abuse their trust—at those moments the "body cam" seems to always fail to record). Can the FBI, which has one of the biggest chunks of the federal budget, not afford a trip to Walmart for a $10 purchase of a digital recorder or to eBay for an old reliable cassette recorder? Do they not know that their phones now record (audio and video)? Why is it that instead of simply recording their interviews they just write little notes on paper?

The answer is simple.

They want no actual record of what actually was said by anyone during the interviews. They then take their little notes back and compile a "302" with them to reflect how they wanted it to go down instead of how it actually went down. No recordings means the "302" (a tool for prosecution) can say whatever helps their narrative and ignores what doesn't. If they want to alter it, they simply edit ("revise") their 302 *after* the fact to say what they want to say (a la Peter Strzok), and such changes ("revisions") are routine. You cannot "revise" a recording. A recording reflects the truth. And they do not want that. A recording could be played back to a judge or a jury to prove an FBI agent is lying. And although judges do not care when FBI agents lie (which encourages more of it) a jury might. And because the FBI wants no record of the truth, they do not record interviews (as was admitted by Thomason himself at the preliminary hearing).

It seems absurd. Impossible to believe until one realises that the objective of the FBI is to hide the truth; a possibility that is incomprehensible to the American culture who is indoctrinated with the religion that the FBI is pure and their justice system works as advertised to them on the telly and movies since childhood. A deeply ingrained religion of faith. When the FBI lies (which is always—they structure their system to ensure it), whether it is through the prosecutor or through its complicit media operatives or through an informant patsy (such as Curtis), the victim of that lie is not merely the person being lied to in an interview, or the judge or jury, or even just the accused himself. The victim of the *lie* is everyone. Everyone who is supposed to have faith in the FBI, in the system, all those who have been programmed into the religion to believe in law enforcement without question. Belief without question, is by definition, called faith. Because they have been allowed for so long by the court to lie as a matter of practise and tactics, they have continued to do it. Prosecutors, then, who have a duty to the courts and to the system are either corrupt (substituting their own goals in place of truth) or are just too stupid to recognise that the lies of the FBI actually harm their cause as more and more people begin to see that the infallibility of the system and the FBI is but a myth. This is why prosecutors aid and abet the FBI in hiding the truth;

the fewer people who see the lies for what they are, the fewer learn it is all but a myth.

Faith is only wrong when it is misplaced. In an ideal scenario, the people of America should be able to have faith in an FBI whose only interest should be truth. But that is not the FBI they have. They have an FBI only interested in conviction. The lack of the people's faith and trust is entirely the fault of the FBI itself.

To further complicate matters, the political party that takes a hard conservative line to automatically elevate law enforcement to near deity levels, the Republicans (although most Libertarians find a home in the same party), the party who claims to be for small government, likes to pretend the corruption is a "small percentage at the top." That is *far* from the truth. It is true that the top (usually appointed ex-prosecutors) such as Mueller, Comey, Strzok et al, is corrupt through and through, that corruption permeates every law enforcement agency at every level all the way down to the beat cop and prison guard—primarily because the pool of people from which "law enforcement" is drawn are a miserable lot of psychologically disturbed people to begin with. For example, it is not only the director of the FBI that conducts interviews without recording them, but every single "agent" in the field. Peter Strzok and Jim Comey are not the only agents who devise entrapment schemes; that is a pandemic amongst the badges. Any person who wishes to carry guns and practises shooting people hoping to involve himself and find reasons to tackle, spray, arrest, send to prison and destroy someone's life is a sick person. This is someone who psychologically needs the badge, the blue lights and the firearm as their visible decorations in order to demand some sort of respect as the self-affirmation they could not otherwise earn on their own. Only a certain kind of person—with those psychological pathologies—is attracted to that field in the first place. Conservative pundits are woefully wrong when they, representing the party of "Law and Order" fail to recognise that modern American LEOs are the exact same as the 1940s German Gestapo. Their blindness in this matter is, again, caused by how they *wish* things to be, not how they are. The problems are *not* just "at the top", as they say, but soak all the way to the very essence of the institutions, drenching the street—even in how they are trained. It is *not* the 1% that is corrupt. It is only 1% that isn't.

So when the sadism, as regularly practised by the FBI and DOJ, finally finds a way to convince an innocent accused person that innocence does not matter since *they* are continuing the prosecutorial destruction anyway, and it is *they*, not the truth, that controls the system (instead of the truth controlling the system and them), the deflated innocent eventually capitulates to the plea. The lies, misrepresentations, entrapment, fraud and manipulations to get him to that point are not merely tactical lies victimising the excused, but victimising everyone.

A common tool to pressure the accused into the realisation that the game is rigged and that there will be no fairness is to financially cripple the accused. In this, they have plenty of allies. And they train in these tactics as a matter of routine. Step one—begin to go "to work" severing any and all possible support that the accused may have. This is done by tracking down relationships and warning every person not to get involved, poisoning the minds of any friends or family that can financially aid the accused in hiring any attorney that would be good enough to actually defend his accused client. This step takes a while and it's time—consuming.

Step two—finding out where the accused banks. Then simply pay them a visit—no warrant necessary. Just walk in, and show the bank manager your FBI business card, show them your badge and smile a lot, invoke the words "National Security", remind them of the wall-to-wall news coverage and appeal to the bank manager's sense of duty. The bank will then immediately panic, seeing the gun and badge and willingly and quickly hand over all banking records, then freeze or shut down the account. All without a warrant to do so. If that does not work immediately, remind the bank that the law requires them to rat out their client and be patsies to the LEOs, no matter who the accused is or how much he trusted his bankers to be confidential. This will do the trick; again no warrant needed, because the bank manager will be intimidated.

Because a broke accused person will be stuck with a "public defender" (snicker-snicker) or an appointed lawyer who will *not* actually defend him, it is important to break him, financially.

What is described is exactly what the FBI did to Dutschke...without a warrant. There was one such attorney that Everett's trusted. A man of serious principles and drive and, more importantly, and intellect up to Everett's standard. A take-charge kind of lawyer that Everett's existing and previous lawyer Lori Basham agreed to work with who is one of the few south of Memphis that not only knows how the stacked-game is played but is also one of the few south of Memphis that has the courage to take them on anyway. His name is Tony Farese. Tony is the kind of lawyer who boldly throws elbows in the rumbling neighbourhood hoop-games of the court and unlike the appointed putty-lawyers does not allow the opposition to control the press. This would have been a challenge for Farese as, when one reviews the press at the time, it can be seen that there were two simultaneous press operations working as machinery—the machine controlled by the Holder/Mueller DOJ/ FBI and the machine controlled by Christi McCoy for the mailer, Paul Kevin Curtis. If there is a camera or a reporter anywhere, Christi McCoy, it is known, will sniff it out, which suited her guilty but released client just fine. However, that might have been exactly the kind of battle Farese would have welcomed because though the opposition was operating, in reality, two media machines (DOJ and McCoy), it did not seem to be operating in tandem. Because the problem with any interview of Paul Kevin Curtis is that he eventually opens his mouth. And even by the time the DOJ had fraudulently indicted Everett, Curtis had already given conflicting and provably false public statements. While the national media drones of the DOJ did not ever bother to challenge the absurdities of Paul Kevin Curtis's constant self-serving statements because *his* narrative was tied to the DOJ narrative, Farese is the kind of guy that notices every tiny detail and nuance that lessers (such a the press or DOJ lawyers) miss. He would have easily seen the million ways to ameliorate the narrative, showing Curtis (and therefore his DOJ allies) as full of nothing but lies. Expose Curtis and the case falls. Expose the (now documented) fraud and lies of DOJ and the Curtis narrative falls. They were inexorably bound to each other.

Farese would have instantly noticed the fraudulent bait and switch (indicting for a biological weapon when the alleged "ricin" is, by law, a chemical weapon). Farese would have understood why the Holder/Mueller prosecution team was committing that fraud (they knew there was no "toxic" product and needed to avoid the statutory threshold that the correct, chemical weapon, statute mandates). Farese would have ensured that the public, press and judge were not manipulated by the DOJ/FBI in the manner they usually are. Farese would have rallied the support for Dutschke and shut down LEO intimidation tactics. Farese would have begun instant campaigns for prosecution of the agent who sent people into the jail for entrapment schemes. Farese would have been the game changer.

In June of 2013, when Everett had a windfall that would have allowed him to bring Farese aboard (again), and needed his wife, Janet, to access it for him, an agent went to Janet to warn her not to do it, warning her not to help Everett defend himself (by Farese), which would leave him practically defenceless, dependent on an overworked, underpaid and apathetic public or appointed defender. That agent was doing the routine-tactical bidding of Bob Mueller and Eric Holder, who was rightly afraid of Tony Farese and the embarrassment that Mueller would have (again) faced—when Farese demolished the case. But it never happened. It never happened because the agent, who had been constantly "working" the wife, Janet, scared and intimidated her from Farese. Think about that for a moment. What kind of person tells a wife, "I don't want your husband to defend himself"? That is, in essence, exactly what he said by scaring her from the money Everett had specifically set aside to hire Farese. If a citizen had done such a thing he would have been charged with "witness intimidation" or obstruction of justice, a crime. Yet this harassing FBI agent was addicted to the behaviour and knew that no one would hold him to account for feeding his addiction. The arrogance displayed by DOJ/FBI, both individually and as a unit, is staggering; knowing and flaunting that they manipulate the court, lie to the press, lie to the court, hide and conceal exculpatory evidence from the court and the defence, lying to the grand jury, intimidate witnesses, intimidate and harass the wife and family; lie to them, misrepresent evidence, threaten the accused then his wife to secure a plea, strip an accused of resources (without a warrant), smear the accused in the press, issue and invoke a very, very rare National Security SAM order under the Attorney General himself with the blessings and knowledge of the President *himself*; place the accused into extreme solitary confinement disallowing him any contact with any person (including counsel); confiscating all his case work and discovery, attempt at least two entrapment schemes, sever his ties with family, begin spying and surveillance on his family (in search of the Tripoli File) which includes digital invasion and subversion, deploy a Predator drone, investigate and surveil any reporters he reached out to (Sharyl Atkisson and James Rosen) and *their* families (Rosen) and arrange to send him (Everett) for years into ADX-Supermax. All this and more, knowing they would never get caught, never be held to account and would never be convicted for it. In the process of convicting Dutschke, a thousand laws were broken and several actual criminals (not just Curtis) were released. And the FBI/DOJ knew they would get away with it. The name of the agent who warned Janet away from hiring Farese (leaving Everett defenceless)? None other than Stephen Thomason.

The reason that the American FBI knows that they can do all these disgusting things is that in their experience, as an individual, top to bottom, they know that even when their schemes are discovered, they are untouchable.

The simple unavoidable, undeniable fact that prosecutor LEOs anywhere did and do engage in concealment or withholding of *any* documentary evidence of any kind in any case anywhere means that they know that they are simply not presenting the truth. A prosecutor who does *not* disclose everything to the grand jury or to the judge or to the defence is, in fact, hiding the truth (by definition) and likely knows the accused is innocent. Any LEO (federal or local) who lies at *any* time or conceals anything at any time from any witness or accused, including during an investigative stage (critical) is, in fact, obstructing transparency and actively misleading and is therefore guilty of obstruction of justice. All of these things do, however, happen frequently as it is a matter of practise and is proof that prosecutors/LEOs are not interested in truth, only conviction (judges allow the behaviour), meaning that the process is biased and any evidence that does not fit their bias must be, in their mind, hidden. Anything else which supports their preordained conclusions becomes confirmation-bias "evidence". And if it is not then they can and will try to find a way to twist any completely unrelated issue into evidence fitting their confirmation bias.

Consider, for example, Janet Dutschke's common annual routine of spring cleaning, tossing out and throwing away the unnecessary. Stephen Thomason, the FBI agent who lied from the stand, presented to Judge Alexander in the affidavit and in sworn testimony as well as to the grand jury as evidence that Janet's common annual cleaning should lead to Everett's permanent imprisonment. This is a matter of record, sworn to and personally signed by him. Likewise, her habit of burning her bills and other sensitive documents at the campfire site, along with her text to some other person (who was NOT Everett), was cited by Thomason, under penalty of perjury, as evidence to arrest and convict Everett.

Everett had never participated in any of the campfire gatherings nor was privy in any way to her texts, ever. Yet Thomason explicitly presented Janet's deeds as "evidence" that Everett had breached national security at the highest level and violated a war-crimes treaty that is so serious that a statute was made (18 UCS§175(a)) to enforce it. Thomason was desperate to make it all look so sinister, so his scheme included using the phrase "burn pile" in both documented and oral testimony as well as the phrase—all "that was left of the evidence" was "just ashes". None of those things are related, yet he twisted their meaning to his audience (judge, press) as part of his scheme simply because the non related events fit his confirmation-bias. And because Janet, perhaps wanting to appear as if the whole thing was not happening, to somehow protect her public image, did not bother correcting Thomason's fraudulent misrepresentation. Or perhaps she simply was never shown (by Thomason or anyone) exactly what Thomason was doing and saying...using Janet to convict and smear Everett. For whatever reason, his "evidence" received no public push-back at all, at least none the many researchers of this book, over years, could find as she seemed to have made zero public statements at all after Everett's arrest.

Conversely, the documented laboratory evidence in the form of the government's own analysis (the CDC, the NBFAC, Fort Detrick, NBACC) stayed hidden. Thomason never informed the grand jury (or any other party) about it, proving bias. If a person, any person, on any matter is trying to convince *any* other person toward a conclusion on any matter at all, his hiding the truth, even if but a small bit of it, is proof that he is wrong. Anyone who knows something to be true, *truly knows it*, need not suppress evidence of any kind.

Suppression of relevant evidence combined with the twisting of irrelevant evidence by the prosecution is a sure sign that the accused is innocent.

Otherwise the prosecutors would never need to do it.

Unfortunately, the American media and the public has not seemed to catch on to this simple logic just yet. This book is aimed at revealing the truth of the fraudulent prosecution and manufacturing of a terrorist by that administration's DOJ, not to lay out a pure defence for the victim (Dutschke) of the fraudulent prosecution. The transparency must work both ways and at no time did Dutschke or his attorneys attempt to reveal any of the underlying issues or force transparency by the DOJ; and NDAs took precedence over defending against a prosecution that "did not need to go there".

But it is clear and explicitly stated both in writing and in the plea hearing that he knew that the case, itself, was entirely fabricated and left absolutely no doubt whatsoever of his claims of innocence.

Even in later-filed court documents he pushed back. In one later-filed appeal, Judge Sharion Aycock claimed that "Dutschke affirmed his guilt" in the second sentencing hearing. A simple review of that hearing transcript and subsequent filings easily proved a Aycock's statement in her order to be patently false. Dutschke never "reaffirmed his guilt" at the second sentencing hearing. The record is clear:

- At the January plea hearing, when asked—if the conduct described is "true and correct", Dutschke answered—"Not at all."

When asked in that same hearing if there was anything further specific, he told the court—"It doesn't matter, I signed your contract." He never "admitted" guilt.

- During the creation of the sentencing PSI document, on the section that demands "Acceptance of Responsibility" by admitting in writing what and how the "crime was committed" and admitting to the laid-out "Facts", Everett instead denied the facts and refused to fill out that section, leaving it blank. This fact, never reported by the press, is a very serious matter as this is the document sentencing relies on. For it to remain blank is very rare. He did not admit "guilt".
- During the first sentencing hearing, Dutschke stated his innocence nearly thirty times and chastised everyone in the courtroom for "still pretending." He did not admit "guilt".
- During the second sentencing hearing, it was stated, by his attorney (not Everett), that Dutschke was "reaffirming the agreement" (not guilt) Ken Coghlan (his appointed lawyer) asked him "isn't that right, Mr. Dutschke?" who then answered, "YES" (reaffirming the agreement—but *not* guilt) then immediately deflected and changed the subject with a rapidly returned question about "custody". And at no point during the hearing was there another "reading of the facts", nor was there any "reaffirmation of guilt" as Aycock later falsely claimed. He never admitted guilt.

So the actual record, as written, is that he could not have "*re*affirmed—his guilt" because he never affirmed it in the first place, he only

125

ever denied (and very publicly so); nor was it ever "affirmed" even at the second sentencing hearing; he and his attorney using very clever language in avoiding his admission of actions that he never did, made up entirely by the prosecutors and FBI.

Therefore, legally, because none of the "required elements" of the statutes were ever admitted, Dutschke's plea *is not valid*.

The Supreme Court has stated numerous times that a plea is only valid if each and every single "element of the offence" is admitted. Dutschke's plea, minus those admissions, is not a valid plea, therefore is not a valid conviction.

Then there is another problem, discovered only upon review of filed court documents. The CWCIA (1998-22 USC§6701 et seq) specifically states as a statutory law at 22 USC§6712 (entitled "No abridgment of constitutional rights") that "no person may be required as a condition for entering INTO A CONTRACT with the United States or as a condition for receiving any benefit from the United States, TO WAIVE ANY RIGHT under the Constitution for ANY PURPOSE RELATED TO THIS ACT OR THE CONVENTION (chemical weapons convention)."

It is a fact that ricin is a Chemical Weapons Convention annexed chemical. It is a fact that the plea agreement "which required"...waiving the right to trial and appeal is a "contract with the United States". Therefore the contract which contains this "waiver" clause is an invalid contract. The plea agreement is null and void. This is the law.

It is also equally clear upon review of the appeal record, that Judge Sharion Aycock could not give two flips about what the law actually states because when this exact law was explicitly raised by Dutschke on appeal—she completely ignored it as if it was never raised and never written by Congress; proving, in part, the judges are but rubber-stamp extensions of the fraudulent prosecutors and lying FBI. Even when the law is explicit and clear, those three equally complicit parties pay it no mind, for the actual law is not nearly as important as getting and maintaining a conviction. Only the conviction is important to them, not the law.

Dutschke's special plea, legally known as an "Alford plea" is the exact and precise opposite of saying "I am guilty of what they accuse me of." By law, this rare kind of plea (agreeing to sentencing while maintaining innocence), is the federal version of only one "admission"—the simple admission that the DOJ and judge will simply not allow anything other than what the cabal demanded. That the administration and its complicit press and judge simply would not be beaten.

The history books and news reports of 2013 presented that Dutschke admitted he was guilty. The record, however, and the special plea used proves that to be untrue. As far as the record itself is concerned, legally he is *not* guilty, yet still convicted. Let us see if the media ever corrects itself. But as of now, this moment, the people, starting with you—now know the truth.

The authors of this book have queried more than a few esteemed legal professionals that each have their own staff of highly regarded researchers. Upon consultation with them and after their team's thorough search through the entire corpus of American jurisprudence, not one, of the best attorneys in the land, have ever seen and cannot find any single prosecution that is known that comes anywhere near the injustice committed by these prosecutors and their militant LEO and media assistants. There has literally never been a case like this in history. There have never been abuses that have matched these extremes as those of the Dutschke prosecution and Operation Dojo.

Never before has there been so much pressure been applied from as many different prosecutorial tools and tactics as was in this case to force a plea. Never has a defendant endured so much to fight it.

The record clearly shows that to the end, including during both the pre-sentencing hearing and the sentencing, that he denied his guilt and even exposed a bit of the truth, challenging both the judge and the prosecution to "stop pretending", yet Everett was convicted anyway.

Those who actually knew Everett personally could not understand how the Thomason arrest affidavit/warrant was ever signed by a judge at all. Jennifer Williamson finished looking through the PACER documents and filings (which took weeks), she shook out her little brown ponytail and pushed the stacks of documents back across the table in her rented flat and sighed at the interviewer.

"The agent wrote a bunch of unrelated stuff about Everett's wife, her text about spring cleaning and bonfires, which have nothing to do with anything, and claims to have found a dust mask, which was probably hers, not his, the DNA says so...and the guy twisted it around to make it look like all that somehow means that Everett must have done the attacks! It's crazy. What judge would ever sign something like that? There's *nothing* anywhere, that has anything to do with mailing anything. Just the opposite. And the SAM order? I've never even heard of a SAM order. I didn't know something like that could be done in America. Instead of all this...bullshit, they should have just sued him for the Tripoli File, or something. But this? This is all bullshit. And the way they manipulated *her*? *She* didn't know any better. She's not one of us. She probably didn't know how they operate. She couldn't stand up to all of that. That dude (the agent) worked her over and they all, the news and everybody went after him like nothing I've ever seen. If it had been me or Rose or Dana or , I wouldn't—we wouldn't have fallen for it. There was nothing there. The stuff that *was* there was stuff they could never have used in court because it can't ever be public. And some of this stuff, even I didn't know about, and I thought I knew everything and from the beginning. But it is crazy that they even got a warrant for *him* and charged *him* for...a biological weapons attack. Most of what that dude wrote is about Everett's wife, not him, and has nothing to do with anything."

The common response when talking to anyone about the vile conviction, prior to his or her learning the details of the cabal, seeing the exculpatory evidence that the Holder DOJ kept concealed and learning of the SAM or the final threat to prosecute Everett's wife, is a shrug of the shoulder and the reply, "But he must be guilty. Why else would he sign a plea?"

The response changes when one reviews everything then reads his statement from the sentencing hearing transcripts where Dutschke mentioned his wife. On page 50 of the transcript he mentions the seizure of his letter to her. The female DNA on page 62. Her texts on page 59. FBI warnings for her not to associate with him on page 52. The other filings where it is specifically mentioned that the Holder DOJ's final leverage to sign the plea was their threat to Dutschke that a grand jury was to be convened to indict Janet in the beginning of January, 2013. An attorney was appointed by federal court to her. Just days before that grand jury, just days before her indictment, it is a factual matter of record that Everett quashed her indictment saving her, when he signed the plea.

Until that point, Everett Dutschke had already endured more than any other accused man in American history and under unique and unprecedented (SAM) conditions imposed by the (literal) highest office holders in the world and, for himself, was determined and willing to endure more, welcoming the battle. As he had learned, though, long before and in his own training—"Everyone has an Achilles heel. You just have to find it". Well, they found it. For no matter how much determination Everett Dutschke had to persevere the worst of whatever the administration could throw at him (already more than anyone else); and even though, Glenn Beck has told his millions of listeners (July 1st 2020) to respect a man who was willing to go to the gallows to tell the truth; and Everett had proven himself to be that man...he was not willing for his wife to suffer the same.

So the obvious question would follow—"Why else would he have finally signed the plea?" Like Williamson, once someone has seen the full panoply mobilized, weaponized against him, and who were specifically involved, they then offer a different response—"he did it...for her."

Chapter 5

The Impossible DOJ Narrative Buried the Truth

Pretend for a moment that you are incapable of reading. Pretend for a moment that you were unaware of the actual evidence which completely disproves the nonsensical and impossible narrative that was shoved down your throat and into your head by that administration's FBI/DOJ propaganda machine (the evidence included in this very book). Pretend for a moment that you are not willing to think for yourself...so you choose only to believe what you were told to believe. And let's explore what kind of rubbish you would have to believe in order to think that the Obama Administration's fiction could possibly be as they presented.

A warning to the readers—keep in your head that accepting of any of the DOJ variations below will require that you put logic and reason aside, shut off all cognitive function and swallow the impossible... as the 2013 to 2014 plebe media did, because the details of the actual case itself, in reality, make all of their multiple variations impossible indeed.

The FBI's first iteration of events was that Paul Kevin Curtis mailed the KC letters. The press dutifully reported this truth and not a single person was surprised by it; not his closest friends, family, associates or anyone who knew him at all, including his own brother, ex-wife and children.

Every bit of evidence of the mailing of the KC letters did and still does implicate Paul Kevin Curtis in every single way and no one else. Even to this day, there is not a single shred of evidence that in any way could point to anyone else as the mailer of the KC letters. The only sworn FBI testimony on record that reliably deals with the mailing is very clear and the FBI is a hundred percent certain that Paul Kevin Curtis mailed the KC letters. The court transcripts are easy for anyone to review—and evidence presented and revealed elsewhere is overwhelming.

For the purpose of review—

The three targets chosen in the mailing were specifically identified by the FBI, and Capitol Police and the U.S. Secret Service, for compelling reasons which it was stated as a matter of record that they had absolutely no doubt whatsoever. Starting with the three targets themselves—President Obama, Senator Roger Wicker, and a local judge who owned a funeral home. That funeral home-owning judge was named by Curtis as one of the co-conspirators (along with politicians, local hospital administrators and other government agents who he alleged tried to cover it up) of his bizarre "Black Market Body-Parts" nonsense. The same scheme he alleged in his 2011 book. The name of that book, remember, was entitled "Missing Pieces." This judge is the same exact Tupelo judge who had, many, many years before, sentenced the fellow to a year in jail after he assaulted a District Attorney. According to the FBI, Curtis's assault on the said solicitor was not merely with a weapon, but a gun. Although it was apparently more than a decade from her sentencing Curtis, his discovered online rants about that event, combined with the later (2014) revealed magazine interviews with Curtis and others are confirmation of FBI conclusion that this is clearly a guy who holds onto grudges with passion, perhaps in part because the man really had no other life whatsoever, consistently unemployed as a result of his history of psychotic mental illness and bizarre antics and behaviours.

Senator Roger Wicker, one of Curtis' 2013 targets was on Curtis's "enemies list" (an actual physical social media page featuring photos) simply because he had simply ignored Curtis's many harassments, usually about the very same "body parts" conspiracy he kept hooting about. It was revealed by the FBI that Curtis admitted to harassing this member of Congress frequently including at the very wedding ceremony of Wicker's daughter. One account of the wedding episode recalls Curtis literally cornering what he laughably boasts was a red-faced and "shaking" Senator Wicker. The Capitol Police detectives learned that Curtis had written, as part of his ongoing harassment, numerous times to Wicker. In fact, it was Wicker's Senate office staff who were the first to identify Curtis as the mailer. Even other US Senators from other states indicated their certainty of Curtis's guilt (of the mailing). There is only one person outside of Wicker himself (and staff) that could have known of Curtis's frequent contacts to Wicker or what issues those contacts were about. That is only Curtis himself.

President Obama was equally the recipient of Curtis's ire for the same reason. He simply had ignored Curtis when Curtis wrote him about the same ("body parts") nonsense. So this man who loves his grudges ensured that President Obama would no longer ignore him; and ensured it by sending him one of the same letters he sent Wicker, who had rebuffed Curtis, and the judge who Curtis held partially responsible for the same "body parts" scheme Curtis was complaining of to Obama...(Whew!). Additionally, the FBI reviewed Curtis's Facebook posts. Though Curtis maintained multiple Facebook pages (mostly impersonating other people to praise himself and "catfish" others), on one of his primary pages he had blasted Obama and his stance on gun control (a bill which would have prevented ownership by people with psychotic illnesses such as Curtis), along with a photo of Obama. A subsequent post was a photo of his pistol, along with a caption where he announced—"say hello to my little friend!" The only person outside of whoever handles the presidential correspondents that would know of Curtis's rants to Obama is, again, only Curtis himself.

Now, when it comes to ignoring Curtis when he writes to someone about his bizarre "body-parts" piffle—some have learned through experience that Curtis does not take it lightly. Just ask Tupelo's Reverend Mike Hicks to whom Mr. Curtis wrote asking to address his congregation about the evil "body parts" black-market scheme by the sinister government baddies. When the reverend refused to subject his God-fearing church-goers to such torturous rubbish from the crazed man, Curtis did what any man of God would do and promptly sent another letter to the respected clergyman, this time repeating his intent to hijack the spiritual convocation so that Curtis could replace the sermon with heaping portions of his own self glorification. But in this second letter to the Reverend Hicks, Paul Kevin Curtis attached what any devout, saintly holy-man would obviously include—an article about a minister who had been stabbed multiple times. Despite his new incentive which was quite characteristically reminiscent of a terroristic act, Hicks courageously gave Curtis's demand (including the attached article of the perforated holy-man) the treatment it so justly deserved and ignored it ("get thee behind me Satan"). The FBI spent quite a spell in recounting this example from the stand, under oath, to Judge Alexander. Yet only one media outlet recognised and understood its significance to the KC letters case which was Curtis's delivery of a simple message: he would not be rebuffed without retribution. Obama had. Wicker had. The judge was, in part, to blame for Curtis's woes. The significance? Well...he had done this all before.

As the FBI informed the magistrate, Susan Alexander, Curtis's previous correspondence to Senator Wicker had been closed with "this is KC and I approve this message." Other than Wicker (and staff) only Curtis would have known this. The FBI also revealed that Curtis, in his previous mail to Obama about his "black-market, body-parts" drivel, was also signed "this is KC and I approve this message." Though the FBI did not say in court exactly when the previous letters to both Obama and Wicker were written, it was suggested that it was over a period of years and multiple letters were involved. Indeed Senator Wicker's office seemed to be eye-rollingly familiar with Paul Kevin Curtis in large part *because* of Curtis's previous attempts to correspond with the US Senator, all of which had resulted in the Reverend Mike Hicks treatment. Which resulted in Curtis's extreme frustration, growing anger and the addition of the two politicians to his publicly posted enemies list. Everyone who was ever forced close to the psychologically-ill Curtis, primarily family, were the only ones who tolerated spending time with him, all recall (even publicly so in 2013 interviews) that Curtis was indeed obsessed with those who rejected listening to all his hallucinatory tales of lopped-off corpse appendages for sale and those rejections (by Obama, Wicker and even Dutschke) to "lend Curtis an ear" only fueled his burning anger. It was not unnoticed by the Secret Service, the Capitol Police or even the FBI, that Curtis's previous correspondence to the politicians was signed in such a manner, a manner in which (outside of the recipient) would only have been known by Curtis himself.

131

What is the relevance?

Because the three KC letters of 2013 were all also signed as such—"This is KC and I approve this message." Curtis signed the KC letters using exactly the same words as he had in previous correspondences to the exact same recipient of the exact same topic. Of course no one else could have possibly known that. Not even the recipient targets, themselves. Obama's mail facility could not possibly have known how Curtis had signed any of Curtis's Wicker correspondence and vice-versa; nor could any person but Curtis himself have known either how or who got any correspondence and signed as such. No one could. Only Curtis himself.

The envelopes themselves, according to the FBI, at least two of them, bore the imprint of previous return addresses, though the envelopes themselves had no return address printed on them. In other words, the 2013 KC letters were devoid of the return address, but the FBI laboratory discovered indentations where the return addresses should have been. Those indentations were made on to the KC letters, the FBI explained, years prior when Curtis wrote one return address on to an envelope that was stacked on top of another (that he then used in 2013). The actual addresses that the FBI laboratory recovered from its forensic analysis of the envelopes were placed where Curtis had not lived in a decade.

There is no way in which anyone else could have visited Curtis years in the past and stolen some of his envelopes for use in 2013 because no one has yet successfully invented a time machine. To discount the FBI forensic analysis, however, would require that such a contraption have been utilised because either Curtis retained possession of his old envelope until the FBI seized them or someone used their time machine to go back a decade or more for the purpose of pinching Curtis's postal supplies. The invention of such a device which has never been publicised suggests that such a fantastical apparatus simply does not (yet) exist. Or *if* such a thing does, then it actually does *not* (but will), and means that if one waits an unknown period longer—then the inventor would be the culprit. It is doubtful, however, that such an inventor of a device which is capable of violating all known laws of physics would set as his priority the thieving of an insignificant man's post supplies (perhaps there is some sort of future postal crisis that could only be averted by the pilfering and then reallocation of envelopes belonging to a professionally unemployed self-described music impersonator, however it would be wise for the reader to view such a scenario with skepticism).

The far more likely scenario is as the FBI described, under oath: At one point, Curtis filled out an envelope writing his return address where it needed to be. That envelope was atop the second envelope which received the indentations from the first. Curtis maintained ownership and possession of the stack of envelopes for later usage (and without fear of any time-travelling envelope burglar). Years later, 2013, he pulls the second envelope from the stack for the KC letters and sends it to his target(s). That is exactly how the FBI described the sequence to the magistrate. That is exactly how it happened, as they described it.

The exact text of the KC letters refer to "Missing Pieces" and Curtis's reference to his delusional beliefs about chopped-off "body parts" being sold by judges, hospital administrators and politicians and is the same topic as Curtis's previous correspondence to Obama and Wicker, something no one but Curtis would possibly have known. It also happens to be the title of Curtis's 2011 book where he alleges the same. And again, no one other than Curtis could possibly have known that Curtis had repeated the complaints of his book directly to the frequently contacted politicians, and then later into the KC letters themselves.

Then there is the rest of the text of the KC letters which reads:

"To see a wrong and not expose it is to become a silent partner to its continuance."

While the sentiment of that unique phrase is principled and true, it is his choice of its uniqueness that makes any other person as the mailing culprit an absolute impossibility. Here is why—the KC letters were postmarked with a Memphis (via somewhere in North Mississippi) postmark on April 8th, 2013. This means that exact phrase was inside the three envelopes (that the FBI would soon claim was "laced with ricin") and sealed up and beginning their transit to their destinations on April 8th. Within 24 hours of that postmark on the envelopes bearing his unique phrase inside them, Paul Kevin Curtis created a Jpeg picture file on one of the computers that the FBI would soon seize. That file was an image of text only and here is what that text in the file read: "To see a wrong and not expose it is to become a silent partner to its continuance."

He created that file *as* the KC letters, containing that phrase, were in transit. In the picture file, he even claimed to copyright that phrase with the copyright symbol and "2013". The very next day, after he creates that Jpeg file, copyrighting the same phrase that is at the moment being transported to Obama, Wicker and his nemesis judge, he then posts that very file on to the primary of his many different Facebook pages for his friends to see. This is the same page where he had just blasted Obama and posted a picture of his pistol with the "say hello to my little friend" caption. *So, AS the letters were in transit,* that has that unique phrase printed on it—his Facebook was updated to read:

"To see a wrong and not expose it is to become a silent partner to its continuance"

Then a solid line, then claiming a 2013 copyright to that phrase which was only elsewhere printed in the still traveling letters. Another way of saying this is thusly; Paul Kevin Curtis posted a picture of the phrase from the KC letters just before they hit their destination on his Facebook page to his friends, much in the same way a golfer calls out "Fore!" as the ball is in the air or a bombardier calls out "Bombs away!" as his weapons have been released and on the way to their target (only adding the exact details of the bombs).

While the FBI did identify and note this from the stand, they seemed to have been underwhelmed with its significance. The mathematical possibility, especially when one considers Curtis's number of Facebook pages in daily postings to each page, that he would have picked this one exact phrase (from the KC letters), at this one exact moment and mailed, made a picture file of it and posted it simultaneously, is so astonishingly slim that it has been calculated that one literally would have greater odds of being struck by lightning and winning the lottery on the same day, than the mailer being anyone other than Curtis. There is no magician with a crystal ball to have known in advance exactly when Curtis was going to (in the future) create a post copyrighted claim to that phrase so that the magician would know precisely when to print and get his copyrighted phrase onto it post-conveyance. Such a magician would have had to borrow the time machine of the envelope larcenist. And the envelope thief would likely not lend out its time-travel device to a magician, for magicians are as untrustworthy as elves, Santa, the Easter Bunny, the Tooth Fairy and fake Elvises. It is clear and obvious Curtis was the mailer.

Curtis had briefly floated a defence of this as a possibility that his Facebook account (that one at least) had been hacked. This weak defence was quickly shot down during the hearings when the FBI presented that the IP address from the Facebook posting was none other than one of the very computers and connections of the government assisted, low income housing project that was assigned to Paul Kevin Curtis.

No one was surprised to learn that Paul Kevin Curtis was the mailer. The mayor of Tupelo himself was quoted in the press saying, "Curtis is dangerous and he's out to hurt somebody", indicating he had long-known Paul Kevin Curtis's propensities. Congressman Alan Nunnelee's staff was quoted— "He is crazy," and that was not intended to mean that Curtis was "crazy" in the fun, partyish way. He was not a "zany" fellow, but a raging mad loony, hence the public chiding from his ex-solicitor, Jim Waide about staying on his psychopathological medications.

While there was other evidence of Curtis as the mailer, it was obvious, plain and clear that the FBI, Capitol Police and the U.S. Secret Service knew without any doubt whatsoever that Curtis was, in fact, the mailer of the KC letters. It was Senator Wicker's office that identified constituent "KC" immediately. All of that evidence is still relevant, none of it debunked in any way as those details (and more which come later) are not even debatable. Paul Kevin Curtis was and remains the actual mailer of the 2013 KC letters without doubt. This is why it was the FBI testimony and it was the first iteration.

However, this was the prosecutor's official story during the initial stage, the stage at which only the FBI was involved (with help from countless other law enforcement agencies) and at this point, there was no SAM order, no ex-Intelligence Officers or cabinet members involved and no "National Security" executive order invoked by the White House. The soon obvious problem was the first iteration of the public narrative was that the *mailing* of the "ricin-laced" letters was only half of the criminal allegation, and the minor half, at that. The FBI could press Curtis all day long on the *mailing*, but that would not solve anything about the *making* of it (development of a chemical weapon). And though they prosecuted Curtis for the mailing, at some point the making would be questioned.

So their second version was that Curtis did not act alone. This happened for two reasons. First, because the FBI was keeping the prosecution simple by (rightly) focusing on the mailing (which meant Curtis only), pressure began to be applied to FBI Director Mueller, himself, from others *outside* of the FBI (Brennan, the President's "Counter Terrorism Advisor", had the President's ear and undiluted influence) including from the President as to who was the maker. Mueller, who although would not have objected to collusion in any conspiratorial tactics with his fellow cabal members, did not need to know that the President (Obama) push of Mueller was at the influence being applied by the top of the Department of State (Clinton/Abedin) and his "Counter Terrorism Advisor", John Brennan, in part, combined with his own interest, to steer Mueller's FBI from the mailer (Paul Kevin Curtis), who the trio (Obama, Brennan, State Department) was *not* interested in, to who was the MAKER— the person that the trio *was* interested in. Second, it was rather clear that while Curtis was, in fact, without any doubt the mailer of the KC letters, Curtis was incapable of being the maker. There is little chance that someone like Curtis would have had direct access to a chemical weapon of political assassination or been able to develop such a thing. Curtis's mental issues render him as low-functional. In addition, though early, FBI was beginning to suspect, even at this stage, that their very loud, very public and repeated claims of "a deadly poison-ricin-laced" might have been overstated and that the product actually used was designed to specifically be a non-toxic decoy, though triggering the goat-antibody-based 'field tests'. So the FBI questioning, confident already in their knowledge that Curtis was the mailer, began to inquire about the maker. The focus broadened slightly to catch Curtis's "co-conspirator", and it broadened during the questioning of Curtis himself who immediately told them that Everett Dutschke was the maker.

At the exact moment that Everett was on the phone with an AP reporter, the FBI knocked on Everett's door and told him that Paul Kevin Curtis was trying to rat out Everett as the maker. Everett truthfully answered that he had not developed any chemical weapon, specifically ricin, for Paul Kevin Curtis, and that he had never purchased any castor seeds from Lowe's or any other hardware store or local nursery. Everett told the FBI that he had only met Paul Kevin Curtis on one occasion, when Curtis had entered an unauthorized meeting to convince Everett to print Curtis's delusional beliefs as an article in the newspaper Everett owned. He reminded the FBI that Curtis was nuts and reiterated that he was dangerous. The FBI agents then went on their way, confident that Curtis had (again) steered them wrong. The Mueller FBI continued preparing prosecution for what it had, which was the mailer; which would have been a sound strategy considering the FBI's growing realisation that the only real crime was the mailer since they were beginning to suspect their claim of a "deadly poison" was not what they claimed. While this left the question open—"who was Kevin Curtis's co-conspirator?", the Curtis hearing focused on the mailing.

Until Christi McCoy, Paul Kevin Curtis's defence lawyer, started. Christi McCoy knew the weakness of defending Curtis on the mailings. That element of the KC letters was clear, so she deftly attacked the prosecution on the making. In other words, she completely changed the subject from the mailing to the making, a wise move for the attention-starved barrister, and she knew exactly where Curtis wanted to go with it—which was to suggest J. Everett Dutschke was the maker. Unbeknownst to the local FBI/DOJ prosecution team, that was also exactly where Obama, Brennan and the Secretary of State (Clinton and her deputy Abedin) wanted the Mueller FBI to go as well. Although McCoy's invoking the name of Dutschke did absolutely nothing (on the surface) to deal with the mailing (except to suggest that Curtis had been "framed"), it was successful in bringing the prosecutorial proceedings of the mailer, Curtis, to a screeching halt. On day two of the hearing, just after McCoy had fingered Dutschke on Curtis's behalf, the magistrate ended the hearing and said the hearings would resume after lunch.

The hearings, however, did *not* resume after lunch.

The prosecution's focus was suddenly and abruptly switched to ignore the mailer and to focus on the maker, now with public pressure, (thanks to McCoy and the press who were now inquiring directly with Dutschke in the same manner the FBI had already done) and with the additional pressure on Mueller to "make an example out of Dutschke" from the White House which had now finally roped Holder and Mueller into the cabal. The cabal of four (Obama, Clinton, Abedin, Brennan) had briefly become six (adding Holder and Mueller) then seven (adding Department of Justice's National Security Senior Attorney Andrew Sigler) and grew to a full-on gang after that. The new narrative was that Dutschke was Curtis' co-conspirator. (This begat later variations that were bandied about.)

To the media, this began a feeding frenzy and increased the intrigue. To anyone who knew Everett or Curtis, there was no way this narrative could last. To Mueller, this was a perfect customisation of a perfect narrative that he could deliver to the President. He could give the country the mailer and the maker, and do what he thought Obama wanted which was to distract the country from the Muslim Boston bombing terrorism prosecution to give the country two white-male "terrorists" to hate, one of whom (Dutschke) is

Christian (Mueller may not have been privy at that point as to how much deeper Obama's need to convict and silence Dutschke was. Only that he was to target Dutschke.)

McCoy wasn't having it.

During the break, she made it clear that the only way her client, the mailer Curtis, was going to formally implicate Dutschke was if her client gets to walk free, and to that end they could help Curtis "get" Everett, not just by being an informant behind closed doors to the FBI, but she was prepared to give the Obama/Holder/Mueller et al cabal something much greater and more valuable. She and her client would capitalise on the sudden explosion of media interest and publicly Curtis would play the rat and victim at the same time. "Poor innocent snitch Paul Kevin Curtis was the victim of the dark-evil-genius" would be the narrative and Curtis would walk free and take advantage of the national platform. McCoy kept her promise and Curtis's national "snitch on Dutschke" tour began the moment he walked out of the jail, released by the Holder DOJ. This left Holder/Mueller team with the McCoy narrative that-"Poor innocent Paul Kevin Curtis was the victim of a rogue operation to frame him for the ricin attacks and the mastermind was J. Everett Dutschke." (McCoy even attempted to bolster this false narrative by filing suit against Dutschke for money).

While there is an overabundance of problems with that statement (starting with the fact that Curtis was far from innocent, he was *not* a "victim", there was no "framing" since he was, in fact, the mailer and there was no "ricin"), that became the 3rd narrative and the one Mueller and Holder had to stick with, since they felt they had already been too publicly embarrassed.

That narrative was fine with the rest of the cabal, as long as they could make the conviction, discrediting, maligning, destruction and silencing of Dutschke manifest. It did not matter how, the President simply informed Mueller and Holder to 'make it happen'. (This is a matter of factual record.)

Of course, there were massive issues with making the President's orders to convict Dutschke a reality, not the least of which included that Everett Dutschke had not even been arrested yet, he was still talking to the press and media, he was in discussions with super-lawyer Tony Farese regarding representation, who is very bright, articulate and not intimidated by DOJ conviction machine or the administration, he could and might be trying to leak the Tripoli File details to James Rosen or the file itself, and there was absolutely zero evidence that he was tied in any way to the actual mailing.

Plus, the Kevin Curtis FBI Informer "rat on Dutschke" tour was not going as perfectly as it should, primarily because whenever some national interviewer ("Good Morning America" or "Today Show" et al) asked Curtis a question, he would open his mouth. And Kevin opening his mouth has never equaled anything good.

He often said during interviews that he told the FBI, "I don't know anything. I'm clueless. I don't know anything about anything...but Dutschke did it!"

The two obvious problems (for the Holder prosecution team) was that: at some point Curtis might actually encounter a reporter who had more than one brain cell and thought to ask the next logical question—"well, Mr. Curtis, if you don't know anything and as you say you are completely clueless, then how is it possible you can blame Dutschke...or *any* body?"

Luckily for Curtis and Holder, no such reporter exists, or at least was not encountered during his blitz, because no one ever thought to ask the obvious question. Not one! The media had apparently gotten the message to sell the story, no matter how impossible, and ask no questions. The administration commanded, the media obeyed. Plus it left Mueller and Holder looking as if they had arrested the wrong guy (Curtis) in front of the entire world. The more Curtis did as McCoy had freed him to do, the worse it looked for Holder/Mueller with "egg on their faces", as one legal pundit stated. And remember, this was already Mueller's second chance, considering his failure during the 2001 Anthrax attacks which, though never solved, had resulted in the FBI prosecution of the wrong man (a CDC scientist whose life was so demolished by the intentionally destructive force of the FBI that it led to the man's eventual suicide). This "second chance" for Mueller to somehow "redeem" himself of his 2001 failures, he had already blown. Mueller was on his way to being considered a joke, and he could not afford to have blown his second-chance to his second-chance. He needed to do what Obama had commanded and 'make it happen' (Dutschke's conviction); even if that meant finding a way to make this third ("Dutschke framed Curtis") narrative work.

Because a 2013 media desperately wanted to be the date at the Obama dance, any narrative Holder/Mueller contrived would suffice, no matter how many times it changed. The entire strategy would be "trial by media and no due process", as Lara Logan characterises their tactics. In public, and to the defence, the Holder DOJ and the Mueller FBI would and did fabricate claims of evidence and suppress any document that would later prove their lies. The cabal would count on the complicit press and any journalist that did not act as Obama political operatives would fall into line and follow anyway.

The "evidence" about the making would be made up and no one would know any better. The evidence of the mailing would be completely avoided, since it did (and still does) prove that Curtis, alone, is the mailer. Yet somehow the DOJ spin would need to remain that "the reason that all the evidence points to Curtis is because somebody else did it."

What?

They were publicly invested in the claim that Dutschke "framed" Curtis, yet because the evidence shows otherwise—everyone better just forget all the mailing evidence that had already been presented (in court and under oath) during the Curtis hearings...the DOJ/FBI certainly was not about to remind the press that they had already sworn multiple times that Curtis was the mailer...now if only the media would play along and stay focused on the making and not ask any questions...especially about the mailing ("just report what and how we tell you, it is your job to demean, discredit and destroy Everett Dutschke").

The press did as they were bid.

Of course, they really had no choice. In regards to the mailing it would be an impossible thing to make the case—that the impossible had happened. Impossible is the only correct word to use because any reasonable person with even half a brain could see that it was an absolute impossibility for Everett (or anyone but Curtis) to have been the actual mailer of the KC letters; and because the DOJ knew Curtis was the mailer (as a matter of record) then the topic of the mailing became no longer relevant. What could the FBI/DOJ possibly try to present? How could they possibly make it look like Dutschke sent the letters? They couldn't...because it was impossible.

In regard to the judge that Curtis targeted with the KC letters: Remember the FBI did not reveal the fact that she had previously sentenced Curtis to jail for his armed assault on the Tupelo D.A. until April 20th or so, during the Curtis hearings and after his arrest. Until the FBI testimony no one knew about Curtis's previous incarceration by the hands of that judge. Did J. Everett Dutschke somehow dig that up and feed it to the FBI? No, he learned of it at the same time everyone else did, when the FBI revealed it in court. Did Everett simply remember that Tupelo assault and sentencing from way back in 1998 or 1999 or whenever it happened? No. It was not publicly known then and Everett knew nothing at all about Tupelo until he moved there, years later. In 1998, Everett was far away, surrounded by chiggers and future spies near Williamsburg Virginia, oblivious to any petty courtroom drama of a Mississippi town he did not live in or have any connection to, of a man he did not know existed. So there is no possible way for Everett or any other person to have simply guessed that this woman, a judge who was merely executing a sentence on a criminal (Curtis) in her courtroom who was guilty of a violent offence, would be the logical target for Curtis in order to "frame" him with one of the 2013 KC letters. How could someone have just randomly picked her name from thin air and then write this one local woman would be the subject of Curtis' ire? The population of the town is only about 50,000. The odds of picking the exact person from it would be, then 50,000:1! Is Dutschke *that* lucky? If so, he should live in a casino. How could the Mueller team have even attempted to explain it?

Coincidence?

As to Senator Wicker (another recipient of Curtis's KC letters), remember that the FBI revealed, along with Capitol Police who interviewed Wicker's staff, that Curtis had previously corresponded with Wicker before (even outside of the wedding harassment) and each time about Curtis's belief of the "black-market body-parts" scheme of politicians and hospitals—the same topic as the KC letters. Is there any possible way for Everett Dutschke to have possibly known that? Did Everett Dutschke get Senator Roger Wicker's mail? It was not Dutschke who told the Capitol Police that Curtis had written about this rubbish before—it was Wicker's Senate staffers who told the Capitol Police that. And even then they only did so *after* the 2013 KC letters! Did J. Everett Dutschke work on Senator Roger Wicker's DC staff? No. He did not. Is there any way for Everett to have known that Curtis had written Wicker before and what those letters were about? Was Everett Dutschke reading the Senator's mail? No. He was not. Such a thing is not only impossible but preposterously impossible. But because the mindless media allowed the Holder prosecution team and the Bob Mueller FBI to completely change the subject from the mailing to the making, the sycophantic press did not bother asking the simple question that an average two-year-old would have thought to ask. The "press", all of them, should be ashamed for willingly blinding themselves to obvious and gaping holes in the Holder/Mueller "framing" narrative. How could it be that this could have been missed when the "framing" narrative was literally being repeated on every single cable and network news broadcast on the planet and in every major and local newspaper when the disqualifying issue of the absurd theory is so blatantly obvious that even Stevie Wonder could see it?

A willing blindness by the "fourth estate" is such dishonest and biased manipulation of the public that it violates the rights of every American citizen, as (2020) Lara Logan describes the media's behaviour. The press might reply that it is not their job to defend Dutschke. Well the fact is, it is not their job to become an Obama/Holder/Mueller/Comey tool and convict Dutschke either, is it? ("Trial by media with no due process"—Lara Logan). If the same worldwide media who blindly reported the impossible "framing" narrative had actually done their job as the "government watchdog" (instead of that administration's lap dog), and press the cabal on this matter—how would the cabal have attempted to explain it? Did their "framer" just make a lucky guess? If so, then he should sally again to the casino. What other explanation could the cabal come up with?

Another coincidence?

It was revealed by the FBI that the 2013 KC letters to Wicker were signed "This is KC and I approve this message" (kind of odd way to conclude a letter, but whatever). It was revealed by Capitol Police that Curtis had also concluded his previous correspondence to Wicker the same way. In fact, it was a search of "KC" constituents that rang the bell of Wicker's staff. The only person outside of Wicker Senate staff that could have known how he wrapped up his posts would be Curtis himself. Everett did not work on that staff or read Wicker's mail. And yet once again, though the FBI, in fact, recognised such a remarkable detail in court during the Curtis hearings, they conveniently cast aside and conveniently "forgot" this detail as soon as the Obama/Brennan/ State Department/Mueller/Holder/Sigler/Lamar/Thomason cabal changed gears to finger Dutschke; and instead of the media puppets reminding the Puppet-Masters of the details that they once highlighted, the servile press simply allowed the cabal in their convenient "forgetfulness", aiding and abetting the cabal's criminal suppression of the suddenly no longer important integral details.

Now, there *are* news outlets that one would expect would dutifully report exactly how and what the government expects, and without bothering to question any (even not so obvious) prevarications. There are such media lemmings willing to help the government to pretend. Those kinds of news outlets are generally found in Moscow or Beijing or Tehran. But the 2013 press, who chose to seek political favor and the schadenfreudean joy of destruction over seeking truth, proved itself to be best-suited to be a mimic of the state-controlled media of those countries—certainly no better. Of course, this was good news for the cabal. How could they have answered?

That, though there was no way of knowing that the previous Curtis letters to Wicker were signed "KC" (which is odd) then the "framing letter" must say the same was a fortunate lucky guess by Dutschke? More luck like that? Again, casino. How else could the Mueller FBI have described such an amazing repeated fortune?

Another, another coincidence?

What about the Obama KC letter? Curtis was a proud Democrat. His Facebook page was private to friends only and thus not viewable to Everett Dutschke who is not a friend and likely not the least bit interested. The FBI revealed that just like Wicker, Curtis had mailed President Obama previously about his "body-parts" delusional beliefs. The 2013 KC letters seem to be about the same topic voicing frustration that Obama had not paid Curtis any attention on the matter. The 2013 KC letter was Curtis's chastisement to Obama for treating the delusional Curtis like a cockchafer by ignoring him and his odd delusions. Is there any way Dutschke could have known that Curtis, a Democrat, could feel that way about being rebuffed and ignored by the President of the United States? Is there any way Dutschke could have known that Curtis had been ignored by the politician in the first place? Is there any way that Dutschke could have known that Curtis had ever written Obama? Even if so, is there any realistic way for Dutschke to know what Curtis's subject matter was in Curtis's correspondence in order to then replicate the subject matter in faking ("framing") a later frustrated letter? The answer to all four of those questions is a resounding and obvious "No", since the answer would require a fifth question. Did Dutschke get, open and read all of President Obama's mail? No, of course he did not. (Nor does the president.) Yet, once again, though this detail of Curtis's previous correspondence and subject matter to the President, Curtis's frustration over being ignored then showing his frustrations in the 2013 KC letters, was a key detail to the FBI in its testimony during the Curtis hearings, they quickly swept the importance of those details under the rug and the press aided them in doing so. This was another lucky break for Holder et al since there would be no logical explanation of how Dutschke could have possibly duplicated such a detail except to claim that it was another lucky guess. Dutschke, then, must have more fortune than a bag of dry cookies in a Chinatown restaurant. What amazing luck! He must be a slot-machine's worst nightmare! How else could the cabal explain Dutschke's remarkable ability to have chosen yet another right person, right frame of mind and right subject, all of which unlikely in the first place?

Another, another, another coincidence?

And, just as with the previous Curtis correspondences to Wicker, Curtis's previous correspondences to President Obama ended "This is KC and I approve this message" (well, *of course* you do—you *wrote* it!). And, just like the 2013 KC letter to Wicker, Curtis signed his KC letter to Obama, the FBI revealed, with the same closing that he had in his previous mailing to the same man. So the obvious question here is precisely the same as with Wicker. Is there any way Dutschke could know that Curtis (or any human being) would have closed his previous mailing to Obama in such a strange and exact way, especially considering that no one actually ends a letter in such a fashion? It is unthinkable. In order to duplicate such an unexpected and exact closing, Dutschke would have had to have known what to duplicate. Did J. Everett Dutschke use secret ninja skills and sneak into the President's secure mail facility in the dark of night, search out any post from Paul Kevin Curtis and review the contents in order to learn how best to duplicate Curtis' previous adieu to the leader of the Free World? ("A-HA! Now, I've got it! I will be sure *not* to use "sincerely" like everyone else does, when the later letter is crafted."). Perhaps Dutschke employed one of his CIA friends to bribe a presidential mail sorter to tell him if Curtis's previous mailings to the Commander-in-Chief were signed in a special way. NO. Those things did not happen. Nor did Curtis make it known publicly or privately who he had written, what he had written about or that he does not sign off his previous letters in the same manner that the rest of the world does—with a simple "sincerely". Everett, never having received a letter from Curtis, was as cognizant of Curtis's previous letter closings as Obama was. Which is to say not at all, since neither Dutschke or Obama had ever bothered to read any letter from the simpleton and thus could not only have not known, and not guessed but not imagined it.

How did the media address this impossibility?

They ignored it.

Another, once important detail, became suddenly unimportant when the Holder DOJ and Mueller FBI waved their wands at the media to forget.

Hypnotized by the Obama Administration's blinding halos, not a single reporter thought to commit the egregious sin of questioning the holy myth on this (or any) detail. If they had dared, the administration could only have suggested that Dutschke had again just guessed lucky, like really lucky. Wow, Dutschke must search all day long for four-leaf clovers for such luck. He has more fortune than Jeff Bezos. How else could they explain it?

Another, another, another, another coincidence?

To even know that such an idea as "framing" Curtis (the narrative Mueller had stuck himself with) could even be a viable idea, one would have to know that Curtis had done this very thing before as he did with Reverend Mike Hicks. As a recap, Reverend Mike Hicks refused Curtis when Curtis had written to Hicks hoping to hijack Hick's congregation so he could bombard the church-goers with his delusional "body-parts" beliefs. Curtis's retaliatory scheme (since what he thought was "ricin" was not available to him at that precise moment) Curtis sent a follow-up mailing to the man of God, this time attaching a news article about a sliced up preacher who had been assaulted in a knife attack. Now, having recapped, this previous event by Curtis (on Reverend Hicks) was completely unknown until the FBI revealed it during the Curtis hearings in late April 2013. Thus no one on the planet could have duplicated the Hicks offence by Curtis into an Obama, Wicker and a judge without knowing of the original, which was unknown to anyone but Hicks and Curtis. In other words, no one could set about to "frame" Curtis using his previous modus operandi without knowing Curtis's previous criminal actions (replacing Hicks with KC letter targets). And no one knew that retaliatory mailings was Curtis' thing because it had not been revealed by the FBI until *after* the KC letters had already led to Curtis's arrest. It was the FBI, not Dutschke, who pointed out and recognised it significant that Curtis had, in fact, already done this kind of thing before. This is another key detail that Dutschke could not know until everyone else did. Which was only when the FBI revealed in court that Curtis was simply repeating his previous criminal actions. They rightly highlighted the importance of this detail during those hearings. Yet it was another detail that Mueller had to sweep under his own crowded rug, pretending it was no longer important enough to mention to the Dutschke grand juries (from whom this was another detail suppressed by the prosecutors and FBI) or to the media who had previously understood its importance, yet now "forgot" about it. If the prosecutors, for example the lying spinster Chad Lamar, had been asked, he would have been forced to stutter that "it was just Dutschke's luck that Curtis had done this before". More of Dutschke's amazing luck! The Holder team, including spinster Chad Lamar, must think Dutschke kept a leprechaun net within his reach at all times. No one in history had ever such a string of amazing lucky guesses. The only alternative to Lamar's potential "Dutschke has a leprechaun net" theory would be that there simply was no logical explanation...thus—.

Another, another, another, another, another coincidence?

To try to portray that the "framing" narrative ever had any validity at all qualifies the 2013 press as criminally complicit in the myriad lies and manipulations of the Holder DOJ to force the populace into swallowing an impossibility. Anyone who could possibly believe a physical impossibility is either intentionally ignorant, legendarily stupid or belongs in the same cracker box as the heavy-medicated, delusional Elvis-impersonator Paul Kevin Curtis.

But because Bob Mueller was already very skilled at looking completely ridiculous by that point, it would not have actually hurt him much more if the press would have asked about the return address indentations since he had already become the laughing-stock of the DOJ (and the entire country). Recall that the KC envelopes had no return address printed on them, but they did have the indentations of previous Curtis return addresses that had been written on the envelope above them in the stack of envelopes. Addresses that Curtis had written years earlier had pushed through and left indentations that were only discovered years later by the FBI forensic laboratory on to the KC envelopes themselves. Some of the addresses, the FBI determined through questioning Curtis' family, were over a decade old. Just because Curtis's family may have been able to recall where Curtis had lived Circa 1997 to 2004 (it was never made clear in court documents or FBI notes any exact dates) does not mean Everett Dutschke would have recalled such a thing. Dutschke did not know Curtis even existed until 2007 and never knew (or cared) Curtis' address then, after or prior (or when the indentations were made). Everett Dutschke did not move to Tupelo until years afterwards, it would be impossible for him to remember an address of a person he did not know, in a town he also was not yet familiar with at all. Having already addressed the time-machine theory—it is a safe bet that Dutschke did not build a time-machine then utilise the contraption to travel backward a decade to seek out a person he did not know in a town he did not know, then steal the man's envelopes and return to the future...or, the present. There would be far better uses for a time machine then to waste a second on pilfering Kevin Curtis's postal supplies, even if one regains that second. Judging by the span of address indentations, Paul Kevin Curtis retained possession of his own stack of envelopes over years and without any fear they'd been pinched by the time bandit. While Bob Mueller may not, personally, believe in the temporally-transient thief theory, one might think that he actually does since there was not a single thinking person in the press to say—"Now...wait a minute!" And again, this startling detail, well documented and specifically highlighted in court by the FBI in April of 2013, suddenly lost all its worth when they changed their focus from the mailer (Curtis) to instead focus on Everett Dutschke. It was as if the FBI said, "Hey worldwide media! Do you fellows remember all that stuff we told you and in court in April? Right, all those things we said were just so important? Yeah. Well...forget all that! Yeah, just pretend we never said it, okay? Right, do us a favor and just drop all that and don't ask us about it because it would be a real hassle for us to explain it now that we are swapping out culprits and we really can't. Soooo...would you news reporter types be a dear and forget what evidence you and I have already reported? Evidence is no longer important. Thank you, so much."

The remarkable thing is, that is exactly what the press did. It was much more fun, apparently, for the 2013 press to stop reporting actual evidence and instead jump into the ever-popular game of demolishing and smearing someone. Evidence and facts and details are too droll anyway, so bollocks it all; let's rather play "lambaste an innocent." It was as if the press responded by saying "Let us forget all that reporting of facts and details nonsense and pretend we are all American law enforcement. Here, we will be the wallopers and Everett Dutschke can play Rodney King." True to form, the press then decided to ignore the once-important details so they could collude with that administration's DOJ and become the lynch-mob wing of the FBI. This made the bag-eyed Mueller breathe a sigh of relief since he had no logical answer for why this evidence was also pushed from public view to be hidden under his new quite lumpy rug but to suggest that perhaps Dutschke (without a time-machine) just got lucky. Dutschke must be made of rabbit's foot. How else could the cabal have even tried to explain it?

Another, another, another, another, another, another coincidence?

Even if someone desperately searches for some manner of justifying a single impossibility, how silly does it make someone appear, who is headlong trying to justify multiple impossibilities. But since the 2013 press was eager to put logic aside for the venerated deities of the administration and cover their eyes to the blindly obvious problem with the narrative, the cabal, who was growing past its original core members, decided it could risk going further out on a limb.

Recall that the content of the KC letters reference to each of the targets the title of Curtis's 2011 anti-government "body-parts" conspiracy theory book ("Missing Pieces"). The primary subject of the book revolves around his deep belief of the Tupelo hospital packaging up barcoded chunks of refrigerated people (not an exaggeration) for sale "on the black market". (Incidentally, where is this darkly pigmented retail outlet? How is the parking there? Does this place run any specials or place coupons in the Sunday paper that can be clipped? Does this shop have a Christmas lay-away plan for kids? Why is it black? Can't they paint it in a brighter color? Periwinkle perhaps, maybe fuchsia?). Apparently, the issue of the KC letters is the exact same as not only the previous correspondences to both President Obama and to Senator Wicker but also the same as his 2011 book, which he referenced in the 2013 KC letters. But in Mueller's strange world, perhaps that is another, another, another, another, another, another, another coincidence.

But here is where the "framing" theory departs from bizarre-land and into pure lunacy. Recall that on April 8th, 2013, the letters were mailed. Then AS the KC letters were travelling to Curtis's various targets he created a photo file of a very specific, unique key phrase on his computer, claiming the copyright late the very next day. He then posted that picture file phrase onto one of his primary (of many) Facebook pages, just above his previous anti-Obama and his new gun-photo posts, for his friends to see. Nowhere else on the internet at that time was that exact phrase, which *he* specifically claimed to copyright on April 9th, 2013, specifically written. The only other place that key phrase was written as is was *inside the KC letters* which had just been sent, hours prior, and were at that moment travelling to his targets.

According to the cabal's latest version, of the now weaponized against Dutschke, DOJ tale—J. Everett Dutschke "framed" Paul Kevin Curtis. The *only* way in which that could happen is that if J. Everett Dutschke somehow knew on April 8th (then written it onto the KC letters and then sealed it into the envelopes which had been inexplicably stolen from Curtis a decade earlier) the exact word-for-word key phrase that Paul Kevin Curtis had not even thought of or "copyrighted" yet (until April 10th). Think about it for a moment. It is truly insanity. The unique key phrase was mailed. Curtis then, over the next two days claims credit and "copyrights" the exact phrase (that his "copyright" literally states that *he* thought of and put together) *as* the same key phrase, that *he* just "thought of" was in transit, already, inside envelopes.

No one but Curtis could know the key-phrase in his head that he would "publicly copyright" on April 10th. No one but the mailer would know the key phrase written into the three April 8th KC letters. Both key phrases are word-for-word the same. The key phrase he "copyrighted" on the 9th (10th posted publicly), was the same as the mailed KC letters from the 8th.

For any other person to know on the 8th what another person— specifically Paul Kevin Curtis—would suddenly later think-up and "copyright" the next day, word-for-word would require not just the deep previously-well-used but not-yet invented time-machine of the envelope bandit, but the telepathic gift of Professor X as well.

Is there *any* way for Everett Dutschke on the 8th to have possibly known Paul Kevin Curtis was *going* to think on the 9th? Does Dutschke have ESP?

Even more impossible is the timing of it...not only would the all-powerful Dutschke have to know exactly *what* unique key phrase Curtis would copyright, or think of, Dutschke would also have to have been able to time the mailing so perfectly that the KC letters (with that unique key phrase in them) would actually already be in transit, just <u>before</u> Curtis publicised that he'd thought it up. Dutschke would have to know, somehow, not what Curtis *had* posted on Facebook, but what Curtis was 3 hours later *going* to post on Facebook. This warrants repeating—this is two impossibilities, not one. The first is the key phrase. The second is the timing. For Dutschke to be the "framer" means he would have to know in advance exactly what Curtis was going to later post, but exactly when Curtis was going to post it!

If it was the other way around, it would be a remote but conceivable possibility. If Curtis had posted and copyrighted the unique key phrase on the 8th, then the mailer could have immediately copied it, but the timing would still be wrong. He would have already posted it before the letters would be in transit. However, that is not how it went. Curtis copyrighted and posted the key phrase that existed only inside sealed letters that had already been sent, within hours from the sending.

Once again, this was another matter that the FBI was smart enough to highlight during the Curtis hearing but slick enough to know they needed to hide when they switched to prosecute Dutschke. If these factual details were so important on April 20th, during the Curtis prosecution, how did the same exact "important" factual details suddenly become unimportant only one week later?

Where was the press on that one?

Here the world could clearly see more details that made it obviously impossible for anyone but Curtis to be the mailer, yet there was not one single person on NPR, CNN, MSNBC, ABC, CBS, New York Times, Washington Post, LA Times and every other newspaper, broadcaster and website in the world (including Fox News) that had courage or the mental acuity to simply look at the already testified factual evidence to question why the cabal's very own previous evidence was suddenly again swept under Bob Mueller's very dirty and overcrowded rug. Not one.

The press, in not "pressing", failed, committing malpractise. The timeline is not open to interpretation or twisting. The timeline evidence *is* the "smoking gun" of the mailing. And yet the cabal got away with claiming the utterly physically impossible "framing" narrative *because* of the 2013 press.

Even those normally liberty-oriented talkers (Beck, Limbaugh, Hannity, Levin) just let this sail by. Red flags all over the place, and even they did not bother to publicly notice that something "smells funny".

In the current (2020) moment, the same liberty-minded radio talkers are acting as if they are in an outrage that the cabal (Obama, Brennan, Clinton/Abedin, Holder, Comey, Power, Mueller et al) has set someone up, reported falsehoods to the sycophantic press and weaponized the FBI to prosecute and demolish a patriot to cover-up their own misdeeds. Where were they in 2013 and 2014 when the same exact cabal (as a matter of record) was doing the same exact thing to Dutschke? And the Dutschke case is worse, much worse.

Limbaugh calls the 2020 revelations of the cabal's "Obamagate", the biggest scandal in FBI history, as if they have never done this before. Sorry, Mr. Limbaugh, but Operations Crossfire Hurricane and Operation Razor were only possible because the same cabal of people (even more) had learned they could get away with it, emboldened by their success (and the media silence) of Operation Dojo, against Dutschke.

Levin states that the FBI's behaviour in Operation Crossfire Hurricane and Razor (the lies, manipulation, unmaskings, entrapment and coersions) are "disgusting" and "sick" and "if they can do this to Flynn, Papadopoulos, Page, Trump, Manafort, Stone and others, they can do this to *anybody*." Mr. Levin, they already did. You missed it. Where were you? Where was your outrage when the same exact people did the same thing the first time they did it?

Glenn Beck stated in 2020 of the weaponization of the Justice Department, "that administration misused the Justice Department," the American public has been lied to and that "our country cannot survive" (though Beck used the words "our Republic") and that no real system of justice can function this way. That is funny, Mr. Beck. That is exactly and precisely what Mr. Dutschke said the *first* time these same people did the same thing. In May of *2014* at the sentencing hearing. CNN was there. NPR was there. AP was there along with all the other media who not only watched the same cabal drown due process, fairness and liberty that day, but aided it as they held America's head under water until the bubbles of hope stopped rising. Where were you that day, Mr. Beck? Had someone put a stop to the cabal at that moment, the egregious abuses of power would not have happened in 2016-2020. (Especially since Dutschke was disarmed of something particular that would have ensured that Clinton would not have been the nominee, Obama would have been sitting quietly on his hands and Brennan irrelevant). To pour petrol on the blaze, Mr. Beck, it was *you* who later called Dutschke an assassin—without actually looking at any of the evidence (since suppressed). That did not help. So Glenn, welcome to the party, at least, but you are late.

Sean Hannity currently and frequently states that the bad apples in the FBI are few. He claims that they are 1%. That 99% are the outstanding "brave men and women in uniform who put their lives on the line every day..." blah blah blah. He would have people believe that the "dirty cops" are limited to the few "at the top echelons of the FBI". Even though people who actually know better, such as Sydney Katherine Powell (who may well be the actual savior of the U.S. Republic for exposing the truth), have actually told him, even on-air, that this is not true. It is, as she told Sean, "top to bottom." Mr. Hannity, you could not be more wrong. The tactics that you are so "shocked" by, are commonplace. The FBI and prosecutors train in them, practise them. There are actual manuals teaching these "shocking the conscience" tactics. There are monthly magazines prosecutors subscribe to sharing these tactics. The "dirty cops", Sean, are *not* the minority, they are the overwhelming majority. It is understandable that you, Sean, feel the political pressure to treat law enforcement as if saints, but that is so far from the truth that it is as wacky as the Progressives you chide for wanting a Police State.

This is one of the areas that conservatives consistently stay intentionally naïve about. The only Republicans that are anywhere close to constitutional on this issue are not the conservative Republicans but the Libertarians. If the cabal of the bad actors of Operation Crossfire Hurricane and Razor angers you, then the same cabal's same actions (three years prior to 2016) should have done the same. Will the American media ever issue an apology to their readers, viewers and listeners for their failure to report or even investigate what was right in the front of them? Such an "investigation" would not have been difficult at all. Simply compare the FBI's trumpeted events regarding the mailing (that *they* told the world and the court was so important making them one hundred percent certain Curtis was the mailer) against the complete lack of even a peep of evidence regarding the mailing *after* Curtis and his attorney (McCoy) made their deal. The evidence was so compelling (regarding mailing) on one day—simply comparing any *new* evidence (regarding mailing) to that on the next day. There was no "*new*" evidence regarding the mailing. So the comparison would have been easy. So where, then, is the media's apology?

If history is a guide, then it is easy to see that the media lacks the moral integrity to offer it.

Not only did that administration weaponize the entirety of American law enforcement, in a massive mobilization, but they also weaponized the press. That administration "went all out" as they involved the Capitol Police (which was first and the cabal scheme was to allow that to happen in a "natural" chain reaction), the US Secret Service, the Federal Bureau of Investigation (Mueller/Comey), the actual military (National Guard), the Lee County Sheriff Department (Johnson), the Tupelo Police Department, the Pentagon (Fort Detrick and Tampa drone Command Center), the NSA, the Justice Department (Holder), the National Security Division (Sigler), the Booneville Police Department, the US Postal Service, the Department of Homeland Security (Brennan, at first then CIA), the Department of Health and Human Services, JTTF, Centers for Disease Control and Prevention, the Department of State (Clinton/Abedin), the Director of National Intelligence (Clapper), the National Security Advisor (Rice), the National Security Council, the Environmental Protection Agency, the US Marshal Service and probably a Girl Scout or two. Though the cabal began as just a small handful of Oval Office frequents, by the time it was all over there was an army of, literally, thousands involved in some fashion or another in Operation Dojo's objective to "get Dutschke". But even those thousands, all force multipliers, were smaller than the force multipliers of the weaponization of the press. A thousand major to local news outlets were all scrambling against each other to see which could repeat each other first. Even Al-Jazeera got in on the act. Social media platforms, such as Facebook and Twitter became mini-news sites of their own reaching as many as the broadcasters. The number of media that jumped onto the gang-lynching bandwagon is far too long to list, but reached all 320 million Americans and then some. This means that because there was no counter-narrative allowed (Dutschke and his attorney had been silenced by executive order of the administration), that the "framing" yarn was the only thing spun. Through their weapons, the fawning and willing press, that administration was able to paint Dutschke as a traitor and a terrorist. The US marshals reported that Dutschke was being mailed death threats, but since he was not allowed any communication in or out by any person, he would never even know.

The sinister picture painted by the administration was entirely *not* familiar to those who actually knew him. But that did not matter, the objective (since January, actually) had been to smear Dutschke to the masses, poisoning the minds of the 320 million in the population against Dutschke so that he was discredited. Discredit and smear him so severely that individuals who once revered him would begin to doubt even themselves and either refuse to support him or would actively join in on the collective kicking of the man, perhaps even taking active measures themselves to aid in this smearing (a few did just that). The objective was to ensure that he had absolutely *zero* credibility with the populace. Those in the populace, trained by culture to treat anyone with a badge as if worthy of temples, were childishly naïve to the fact that the escalating smear and prosecution campaign as enhanced by the media was nothing but an inflated version of the usual practiced tactics of law enforcement and prosecutors. In short, the gullible public did not know any better. And without a counter-narrative, the impossible stuck.

It was and remains utterly impossible that Dutschke committed the crimes he was accused of in 2013. Particularly the mailing. Not improbable. Not unlikely. But impossible. But if there remains any number of the media with a shred of integrity, it is never too late to do the right thing. It may be too late to prevent the phony "investigation" and prosecution of 2013, but there are plenty of "right things" that could still be done—and a person's gut should guide them, though their head, logic, should guide them better (forgiving that simple logic was in short supply in 2013).

At this point, considering the *actual* details, anyone who still believes in that administration's portrayal of Dutschke or the entirely physically impossible narrative they publicly sold—either has a vested or political interest in their own involvement or should ring their psychotherapist presently because they are, in fact, loony.

Why is the mailing so important? After all, it is the minor crime of the allegation, right? The mailing of "threats" is a five-year maximum sentence. But the development of a biological weapon, a violation of the war-crimes treaty signed by hundreds of countries, is a primary crime of the allegation which carries a maximum sentence of life imprisonment. So, in the scheme of things, isn't it true that the mailing part of the allegation does not matter? No. Of course not. And for multiple reasons. One is that it is so easy to show how the administration's narrative was an absolute lie. In the likely actual scheme of the cabal, which will be detailed more later, Curtis was supposed to be collateral damage and go to prison with Dutschke as a co-conspirator. However, two things got in the way of the cabal's primary scheme. Mueller was not told that Dutschke was the administration's real target until after the investigation proceeded naturally and identified Curtis as the mailer with 100% certainty, in court, and under oath. The other? McCoy's insistence that her client (Curtis, who she likely was equally certain was guilty of the mailings,) walks free and does the dirty work of the "framing" narrative for them as the trial-balloon of the phony narrative.

Another reason that the mailing count matters is because it was all the evidence and details of the mailing that got so quickly pushed under the rug just as the Holder DOJ and Mueller FBI hypnotised the zombied press— (Uhhh...just pretend you never saw any of that...), and the fawning press obeyed, turning instead to the full-on destruction of Everett.

Another very, very important reason that the "mailing crime" is more important than the "making crime" was that there never was any actual "making" crime to begin with. There was no "deadly-toxin" at all. The mailing crime was the only actual crime. The charge of developing a biological weapon was bogus from the get-go. For starters—actual ricin would not be a biological weapon, by law, it would be chemical, even if it was the real deal, as with the Libyan product. Also, because there was absolutely nothing "deadly" or "poisonous" about the KC product, it does not fit the legal definition that the treaty was written for. As far as the making goes—there is no crime. A fact pointed out early on by one of the sole skeptics, Judge Andrew Napolitano of Fox News which led even Sean Hannity to recognise, on-air, that the only remaining crime would be the mailing, and then only if considered a threat. So because there is (legally) no actual crime of "developing a biological weapon" (if the actual, written law had been followed), then the mailing, and *only* the mailing (Curtis) matters. Leaving only the mailer as a criminal. A mailer who is obviously *not* Dutschke.

The primary reason the mailing is important is because that is key to the entire 2013 narrative(s) which makes one wonder what on earth kind of crack the media smoking when they forgot all about the mailing by 2014.

No thinking person could believe that Dutschke "framed" Paul Kevin Curtis for the mailing of the KC letters, in the face of overwhelming evidence of Curtis being the sole culprit of the mailing. And a thorough review of every one of the post-convictions filings as well as the sentencing transcripts would lead any analyst to the conclusion that there were two people, perhaps more, involved—though the mailer was still Curtis. Those narratives, which have generated buzz, but not much more, will be described, and a few worthy ones explored.

But there were others, based not on evidence but "motive".

One story which was tossed about only grew legs based on the quickly-written history which was that Dutschke acted alone and that it was a real assassination attempt. One variation of this tale claims that Everett Dutschke is a racist and tried to kill the first Black president. Anyone who has ever known Everett at all knows how completely absurd that theory is, but Americans can only handle simple narratives like that in their news. That theory was a simple enough "elevator-pitch" that it suited the American taste, but it also appealed to the sad yet angry "social-justice" dreamers who desperately search for anything they can label as racism. This also meant that it was not a theory that was objected to by the community-organiser that "occupied" the White House as catering to the theory meant perpetuation of a dual-narrative.

Another variation of the narrative was that Dutschke attempted to assassinate Obama because he was a black Democrat. What both of these variations fail to account for is that the other two targets of the KC letters were, in fact, white. One of them, Wicker, was not only a well-known Republican Senator, but considered a friend of Dutschke who had even gone far out of his way to help the Senator on multiple occasions (one accounting included Dutschke filling two chartered buses full of his small army of Tupelo people to travel and rally for Wicker at a speech on an indian reservation hours away). Both of those popular but reckless variations have led to the actual endangerment of Dutschke, not just exemplified in the death threats against him that the US Marshals intercepted, but in his phony labeling as a racist (a common tactic of mindless "progressives"). This label not only caused black militants to threaten, but it caused the opposing white militants to equally facilitate, which is equally dangerous. Because neither side bothered to consider the significance of the other KC letter target (white and Republican), since Americans are averse to thinking too much, there are some who still perpetuate one variation or another.

Another variation of the same flawed premise is that Dutschke attempted an actual assassination of Obama because he recognised Obama as a domestic threat to the United States and its way of life, or even in retaliation for his egregious and cowardly hand-off of responsibility to Hillary Clinton on Benghazi with catastrophic results, or Dutschke's discovery of a disgusting re-election scheme by Obama to capitalise on a pre-election Benghazi hostage situation. Even if the underlying facts behind such an assassination motive in the series was there, it would still be utter nonsense. There was no actual assassination attempt of any kind whatsoever. Any thinking person would only need to consider three things: One—The President does not open or even view mail addressed to him, thus he never would have been in contact with any "deadly poison with no known antidote". There is a White House mail-sorting facility especially designed for that (although *Curtis* certainly thought Obama would open and read *his* mail—as evidenced by his frustration that he was being ignored by the President). Two—There were two other recipients of KC letters, one inconsequential and one, a friend of Everett's. Three—There was no "deadly poison". In fact, the Fort Detrick analysis clearly shows the product of the KC letter was specifically engineered to NOT be toxic.

The "assassination" attempt variation was being perpetuated even years later and on such wide-reaching media as the overnight AM "Coast-to-Coast" radio, but without even a bit of consideration to the factual disqualifiers of that theory.

The variation that the Mueller (2013) then Comey (2014) FBI crafted and sold to the public and the press was that Dutschke "framed" Curtis in retaliation for Curtis's on-line harassment and negative posts about Dutschke. This holds no water either. First—Dutschke was not the mailer. Curtis was. Therefore only Curtis was in charge of the mailing. That alone dispels the Mueller variation. Second—Dutschke would have had no clue what Curtis said about him on his Facebook page because, as the FBI itself discovered, Curtis's privacy settings excluded Dutschke from even knowing it existed. The FBI *knew* this fact prior to crafting their narrative so this was another way in which their contrived version was an outright lie. Third—The variation is the progeny of the variation crafted by Curtis's ex-wife who claimed to the press that Dutschke was retaliating is part of some on-line feud.

This opens to a quick exploration of *that* narrative—some sort of "on-line feud". This stuck in the press early because it was uttered early by Paul Kevin Curtis's ex-wife who tossed them a quick statement without thinking. There was no "on-line feud" between Dutschke and Curtis. A "feud" over what? Dutschke had no dealings or associations with Curtis that the ex-wife could point to. The American media was too lazy to look for any evidence at all of some "on-line feud", which would have been easy to do because an "on-line feud" would be...well...somewhere on-line. Where is it?

This "on-line feud" theory cannot stand because there is absolutely no evidence online anywhere that Dutschke ever paid any attention to the unemployed self-described "Elvis impersonator"...anywhere. There was plenty of evidence of the other way around—in fact, Curtis had an obsession with Dutschke and any others who he believed were part of his "black-market-body-parts" beliefs, or anyone who "covered up" the issue or thwarted Kevin's publicity-seeking.

A "feud", by definition, cannot be one-sided, and because there is no evidence that Dutschke ever even noticed Curtis on-line. There was no "feud", a fact that early-on press would have easily discovered had they bothered to look instead of taking the ex-wife's clueless and quickly-tossed speculative as if gospel. Because the early-on press ran with that casually mentioned conjecture, the later press (also too lazy to bother looking) merely reprinted the earlier guess that was printed, because that's what the press does. Instead of laying out details and *thinking*, they just repeat each other.

The problem is and has always been, that there is a lot of noise in this case. Too many people, too much press, too much speculation saying too many things that are so disjointed and incongruent from the actual event and the actual details, that it is easy to shout anything into the noise. The facts, the truth and the actual details get so lost in the noise that people are quick to accept (and already inclined to accept) anything, anyway, even when the narrative is so incredibly impossible. To truly do an analysis of the case, one really must sit down and look at each individual claim and each individual bit of evidence and each detail completely separately to determine how it all fits together and which dots actually connect. The cabal's narrative was all there was. They started with that, their big picture, and fed that to the press without any details, and worked backwards. But an analysis does not begin with a finished blurry narrative full of noise, people are left to fill in their own blanks without details. And in this case, there were way too many DOJ claims made along the way that either contradict or ignore previous DOJ claims or are entirely made up. This is why mathematicians solve an equation one small operation at a time to arrive at the final solution. If the individual parts aren't right then the solution will be wrong as well—in this case, the individual bits presented are contrived, contradicted or ignored making arriving at their predetermined solution impossible.

There's another theory, which makes the most sense—which is simply that Everett Dutschke was the maker of a completely innocuous, non-toxic product and Paul Kevin Curtis was the mailer of it. Indeed, not only does all the evidence actually point to this theory, it is known that the FBI believes that this is true but suppressed their knowledge and the final evidence of it from everyone, including the press. Meaning that the FBI lied to the media.

Why the media does not seem to mind whenever prosecutors and LEOs lie to them is an absolute mystery. If certain politicians even exaggerate something, even just for effect, the media has a proverbial cow and go wall-to-wall coverage in their tantrums calling those certain (targeted by media) politicians "Liars". Why do they not do the same with the FBI or DOJ? Why do they not resent being lied to, especially on the big matters? It is reliably so that Hillary Clinton could say that her opponent, Bernie Sanders, was actually a large potato that was secretly colluding with extraterrestrial clown farmers and the media would not only believe it but distribute and repeat her talking points the next day. If Mr. Obama were to have claimed that he just raised the dead, healed a leper and walked on water, half the American Press Corps would fall in line to claim that they witnessed such an event, the other half would bring to him their first-born children for sacrifice. It is baffling that the very people who label themselves "trusted news sources" do not care a bit about trust. The foundation of relationships is trust. How is it that the media continues to have a relationship with the FBI and DOJ who lies to them as a matter of routine? Especially in this case when the FBI got caught in some of their lies and called out with documented evidence by Dutschke during the plea hearing when he tried to withdraw to go to trial. And how is it that the plebe media does not yet understand that it is their perpetuation of lies to the public that is the cause of the public's drastic erosion of trust in the press?

American media still treats the public like peasants. And why shouldn't they? In their mind, aren't they just as immune from any consequences for their lies? Just as judges lack the courage and willpower to hold prosecutors and law enforcement to any rational or legal standard (which guarantees they will continue to lie and violate the Constitution in courts), journalists know that the peasantry lacks any power or ability to hold them to account for lying, or worse—ignoring the truth. Journalists, in the aggregate, no longer follow the truth, they follow their like-minded agenda. Who would make them do otherwise?

Because no one will ever hold the FBI to account, they continue to lie to the press in this case, even by withholding the stunning evidentiary truth.

The FBI seized in 2013 a letter written by Everett to his wife, Janet. In this intercepted letter, which was slipped into a 15,000 page discovery document dump, Everett informed Janet of when Curtis actually received possession of what Curtis thought was ricin. This letter was in the FBI's possession nearly the entire time. They actually have someone at the FBI who is capable of actually reading, thus they not only knew how Curtis got the product of the KC letters, but they knew the details of *when* Curtis got it, *where*, the time of day (night) and why Curtis was led to believe it was ricin! And just like the January 18th text that Everett sent to Paul Kevin Curtis's brother Jack Curtis, the FBI did not even acknowledge that they had this information. These details, like all the evidence of the mailing and the evidence in the form of their own lab analyses, however, did not fit into the narrative they were told from the highest levels of government (literally) to sell.

And since the letter contradicted their narrative, then it, too, had to be ignored. Swept under Mueller's rug.

Bob Mueller's rug, under which was swept critical details of the case, bears a striking resemblance to the carpet in the Oval Office.

This opens the discussion of a growing common variation of the theory. And this is truly unfortunate, but while all the primary focus of this book is thematically about detailing the ignominious perversion of the justice system and the corrupt targeting of one man, it is likely that a portion of the readership will ignore the bulk of all the research that has gone into that and all the elaborations of the prosecutorial wrongs from what the American justice system advertises (through the press) to instead walk away remembering only this next part. It is, unfortunately, probable that this next part is exactly *why* some readers picked up this book in the first place. To some, the next bit is likely the part they have been waiting for; dangerous, because this next bit, as laid out, might serve only to fluff their own confirmation bias and such readers will then have missed the point and theme of this body of work.

So to those readers who have been "chomping at the bit" to get here—be forewarned. Do not read this next portion then place this book aside and go for a lie down. Interest only in what happened prior to Dutschke's arrest does not enlighten you one bit about the ills and wrongdoings of the manipulative use of the US Department of Justice for political attacks and the unconscionable schemes and maneuvers used by the Department of Justice. The thrust of this book is about those DOJ schemes that were directed from the top of the administration for Dutschke's targeted prosecution and smearing. *That* should remain the reader's focus even though the next part which is included because, as the intelligence analysts who piece this together conclude, actually began several months before both Dutschke's actual 2013 arrest and before the law enforcement smear campaign began.

The following variation on the theory is included now with the caveat that how it all came about is not separate from the later prosecution, because it is actually part of it. The prosecution and predetermined conviction of Dutschke was but one portion of a much larger scheme. That is the reason for its inclusion here and the other places where you find this intelligence analysis variation, are but click-bait websites who offer only "how it really happened" but without any context. Those websites, discussion forums and 3 minute radio segments do nothing to provide anyone the full context which should be considered.

And finally, this warning must include the particular point that the course of details and events is not a simple plot. There is no way to detail the analysts' deductions in a compressed manner. There is no "elevator pitch" for minds that require simplicity. Leaving out details leaves only a grey void in which people will fill in their own ideas. Keep forefront that intelligence professionals do not begin at conclusion then search for whatever fits that conclusion, casting away inconvenient contradictions. They begin at the details, some of which may seem far out of reach of any final conclusion, then assemble what known details exist, look at the pattern of intel and then suggest, "this is what the intelligence indicates". There will always be grey areas, which simply subtracts from the confidence level of the deduction. But an analysis to the point of deduction is not a conclusion, because to say "conclusion" and to even think that way (such as how LEOs and prosecutors think) is a dangerous and backward manner of thought which prejudices judgment of any details that arise after such a "conclusion" is decided in one's mind. Prejudicial thought is the exact opposite of intelligence-gathering and analysis. Prejudicial thought is the guiding force of law enforcement, who have proven time and again, to not be reliable or accurate.

This variation should begin with two sets of details—one set involving Paul Kevin Curtis's past, his tendencies, his historical actions, and present; another set involving the same with John Brennan.

As was revealed in court transcripts as the FBI testified, under oath, and in both magazine and radio interviews of Paul Kevin Curtis, he was a public whirlwind of constant anti-government accusations. In books, radio interviews and countless internet posts his public accusations were a dog's breakfast of accusations leaving no government official or agency unscathed. Among them: he would accuse the CIA of poisoning the American population (for whatever purpose) by using jetliners to drop (mind control) chemicals, claiming that these "chem-trails" were not the normal condensation trails caused by jet engines. He claimed that intelligence agencies and "Barney Fife-type" law enforcement was tapping his phones and monitoring his computer activity, claims that makes him sound like exactly the paranoid-schizophrenic that he is (although it did not help when a senator from SSCI, intelligence committee, did reveal to reporters that "he is known to us." This likely was more a reference to Curtis' harassment of those and other members of Congress and government agencies, not the other way around). Curtis claimed that agents "blew-up" his car in an effort to apparently kill him. He was publicly claiming that his house was burned down as a warning. Of course, there was the constant and loud accusations against the Tupelo hospital, that had fired him from his janitorial job mopping the floors, and politicians of the "body parts" rubbish he believed in, as well as anyone he believed was an agent of the "cover up". He actually publicly stated that the US government struck him a deep personal blow in retaliation by engaging in the successful operation to assassinate…his rabbit. These were but a few, and it was always something. There was always a flurry of bizarre anti-CIA anti-government besmirchment in his harum-scarum custom.

One would think that the events of the worldwide focus on the 2013 KC letters might have stunted his drive to continue being the agitator-in-chief. Indeed following the press conference arranged for him by the lawyer who finagled Curtis's deal-made release to began his "blame Dutschke" media tour, just after he announced to the CNN cameras and the press gaggle that he was eager to give lawyer Christi McCoy "a foot-massage" for her successful deal-making, Curtis did inform the gaggle that he was done with his illegal anti-government agitations, which McCoy had rightly convinced him to relabel as "activism" because, as she explained to him, it sounds more acceptable to the public. "Activism" almost sounds noble—like "community organising". What she was trying to do there was avoid the use of the word "terrorist activities", knowing Curtis's history, as the word "terrorism" was already beginning to be used. Her objective was to label Curtis's acts as the protests of an "activist" and simultaneously label Dutschke a "terrorist". She advised Curtis that he was the one who personally had to step up to the microphone to renounce his "activism" and then reaffirm that by using the word at least twice in order for the press-bots to actually catch it for their own regurgitation.

Under advisement, he did so and included the other elements she prepared for him which was to state that his newborn freedom was because the wonderful government administration proved that the system works (which is what one is obligated to say). Nevermind that he had spent his life railing against it.

Then he embarked on the "blame Dutschke" blitz, as McCoy had arranged (there is no intel available on how well Curtis performed her "foot rub") and he mostly stayed within the acceptable boundaries of what she had (tried) set for him (to the extent one could expect, considering that it was Curtis). He was told by her to stop any prattling that was anti-government, reminded of how lucky he was to be released and even to remove his previous controversial posts and practically become invisible and act like a good boy for a change. His interviews though, began slowly drifting back into his old ways, magazines, radio and internet. He assisted and consulted with a documentary filmmaker who was capitalising, she thought, on the national interest with the documentary movie and he even agreed to assist her in promoting the movie with the publicity tour for the movie release. She probably quickly regretted his assistance, considering the interviews became outlandish, self-serving and counterproductive to anyone but him. He used it all as a resume-builder (while remaining unemployed) and by 2017 had written another book, this time entirely about Dutschke, "Most Dangerous", full of total fabrications and mistruths. This all culminated in the revival of his anti-government ways.

Paul Kevin Curtis took to federal court in a lawsuit, seeking money, suing 15 "John Does" for the 2013 KC letters arrest and prosecution. Specifically, Curtis's court case lays out his belief, his narrative, that poor, little innocent Paul Kevin Curtis was the unwary, blameless victim of a rogue operation to "frame" him for a biological weapons war-crime attack against the highest levels of the United States government and the mastermind was J. Everett Dutschke. In Curtis' cash-seeking litigation, <u>Paul Kevin Curtis v. John Doe 1-15</u>, he blames 15 agents for his "wrongful prosecution" and inability to seek gainful employment. Though the agents' anonymity was protected as "John Does", there is one person who is outed in the 2017 decision of federal district Judge Bobby Pepper. That person—the only one named—is "Everett Dutschke", not surprisingly. Judge Pepper laughingly had thrice dismissed Curtis's lawsuit. (McCoy did not represent Curtis in his attempt to use the court to extort the money he seems incapable of earning. Instead Curtis was ironically represented by Tupelo Attorney James Moore, who had previously represented Dutschke in his purchase of a newspaper and contracts collection from the satellite business). The general variation behind Curtis's (failed) lawsuit ("Curtis was the innocent victim of a rogue operation to "frame" him for the ricin attacks") which, in part because of his lawsuit, is the model that will be explored here, putting aside that a majority of the individual details of his filing are completely fabricated. This includes that he couldn't (thus did not) admit in his filing that *he* was, in fact, the mailer—a commission of perjury in the denial of the overwhelming evidence. This lawsuit is also an example of how foolish the Department of Justice was to make a deal with McCoy (Curtis's solicitor), who also was frustrated that her advice to Curtis was not long heeded, since Curtis is incapable of keeping his word; not a surprise since his word means nothing and his head space is a fantasy-land of deceit. One could say that the DOJ deserved it from making deals with the devil, but since Curtis's lawsuit is not anything anyone cares to pay any attention to, and because it will never actually got anywhere, his lawsuit is of little consequence, a minor inconvenience, like a slapped mosquito to the DOJ. And because that particular Department of Justice is no longer in power anyway, his antics are chimerical at best. He was better off when he was acting as the FBI's jailhouse snitch. Instead of not being in prison, himself, he should be thanking the deal-making government, not trying to sue its agents (and ex-agents). Paul Kevin Curtis, however, still sadly lives a life that is actually worse than prison. Prison would be, for him, a lateral move. Curtis's current frivolous lawsuit efforts show that he still does not yet seem to realise that he was but an insignificant sacrifice pawn in a much larger game.

The analyses used here are social network analysis (which has nothing to do with on-line platforms), link analysis and pattern detection (DM) combined with time-series analysis that necessarily reaches as far back as is known for establishing personality patterns for all of those who are involved, clustering with their level of involvement and hopefully presented here with the right amount of visualisation that anyone can follow or understand the complex nature of the operation. This is not a news report, this is not journalism for the mass media, this is not a novel. This is intelligence as a work-product with little effort to refine the message to the catered-tastes of popular writing. This is not by or for the politically correct, so it is perfectly okay to elicit, or for the reader to experience, the emotions and attitudes conveyed, because attitude and emotion are undeniable truth and reality of life. Emotions and attitudes are real, unlike political spin or biased news which tries to sound as much like a textbook as it can in order to hide their bias. This book is years of work-product and is not pretending to be a textbook. So if the reader becomes uncomfortable with the writing style of this book, then that reader is using the wrong psychological lens to view it. This book is not a term paper or a research paper awaiting peer review. If a reader is engaged in this book as an exercise of reviewing footnotes and indexes in order to engage in debate over conclusion—then the authors kindly inform such a reader that they really do not care, and that such a purpose should be recognised as pointless and from a wrong perspective. This book is a presentation of intelligence that highlight the deliberate and corrupt practises of a particular group of abusive men using a single case to do so; it is *not* a book of conclusions.

You, the reader, are free to draw your own conclusions, but the factors that are part of the equation from which you will calculate your sum will necessarily include the relevant emotions and assessments (analyses) of any one person's character, which may make you uncomfortable, but intelligence is not for the weak. It is not designed for comfort. Assessments of character are essential to analysis and determining a level of confidence in the analysis (if it helps you to call that a "conclusion", then feel free). In a courtroom, often a person's established character is not allowed. The world seems to currently lean toward the idiom of thought to *not* make some "presumptuous" and "prejudicial" assessments and that everyone gets a trophy. But the fact is— character matters. A person's established pattern of behaviour and thinking is, in the intel world, critical to determining or predicting future behaviour and thinking; or in this case, figuring out after the fact how something happened by considering that person's norms.

Every person thinks a certain way. Every person operates a certain way. Knowing that a person has a (sometimes unintended) signature to the manner in which they operate aids in determining who is behind an operation. It is an "action bias" (often called "modus operandi", though that overused phrase is not encompassing enough). Action bias leads to predictability, which is dangerous in the field of covert action, although it is a boon for the analysts as it helps figure it all out. As far as covert field work goes, there is an old adage, "predictability gets you caught".

Someone should have reminded John Brennan.

It is important for the reader to know that there's absolutely nothing honest about covert field work. In John Brennan's day, the CIA covert operations in the field (aside from the technical officers, security officers, and support officers) were of the Directorate of Operations but are now called Clandestine Service, a more apt though less genteel name. The reason that anyone who retired from the DO (now CS) is thrice-divorced, paranoid and is constantly calculating is because that is how they were permanently "rewired" to think. John Brennan is not someone who is wired to think like an analyst or support or a "normal" person. To him, *everything* is an op. And who knows, perhaps he was SORT-ed there because he was already that way when the CIA accidentally hired him.

The word "accidentally" is used because even Brennan, himself, has publicly stated that he was "shocked" when the CIA actually hired him after they learned that he was, in fact, an actual voting communist, and at a time during America's history when that sort of thing would have been a security disqualifier. Brennan, despite that, schemed his way through the Langley bureaucracy (a politics of its own) to eventually become the Chief of Station in Riyadh, Saudi Arabia. perhaps, in some eyes, he was a good fit since Brennan himself is also, in fact, Muslim.

His time there was not free of controversy, and FBI CTC agent (John Guandolo) publicly states that Brennan was recruited (during his conversion to Islam) by foreign operatives—proving that he is "completely unfit" for the CIA. An intelligence operative that is so weak that he gets recruited by competing intelligence operatives? That is the man who Obama chose as his personal advisor then later appointed to the head of CIA, repaying favors. While he was the Chief of Station in Riyadh, Brennan was presented with two visa applications of Saudi men that had been previously denied. Reversing the denial, Brennan lifted the CIA visa hold and then issued the two Saudi men their visas to America. Those men did, in fact, use their visas to the United States, overstayed them, and never returned to Saudi Arabia.

The reason the two Saudi men did not return on the expiration of the visas which Brennan issued after reversing the hold on those very two men, is because those two Saudis were dead. The men died when they hijacked planes, then flew those planes into buildings, killing thousands on that same day.

It was Brennan who opened the visa door to them. Brennan.

This might have been part of the reason that there are indications that the CIA did not fully trust John Brennan. The relevant example here is that John Brennan was never informed at all about ███████ ███████ in 20█ which took place in ███!

Brennan's controversies aside, it is still important to remember these two things: One—as mentioned before, there is no such thing as a noble CIA operation. No matter what the objective is, nothing is off the table. Bribe. Extort. Fulminate betrayal. Misdirect. Steal. Hire a prostitute for a set-up. Start untrue rumors. Plant a false news story. Crash your car. Get them really inebriated so your target crashes *his* car. Convince your target to commit a crime, then go "rescue" him. Lie to his wife. Frame someone. All the while smiling at your target who thinks you are his friend. Leak to the press. Then repeat it all. It may not sound nice, and it isn't. "Nice" is for the analysts. Fieldwork, the recruiting and other operations conducted by the C/Os is not for Mr. Nice Guy. Everything listed above (which is a fraction) is the daily activity, every moment, every second of it. This is the necessary world they live in. Creating leverage over a person is the air they breathe. And they learn during their prolonged agent recruitment training at The Farm (and now elsewhere), "Everyone has their price. Everyone has their Achilles heel. Once you've picked the right target your job is to find it and exploit it."; Two—a John Brennan operation has a recognisable smell to it.

A John Brennan planned PACE operation bears certain "Brennanesque" trademarks. A signature style. There are certain expectations one should know when determining if Brennan was involved, and a primary among them is that it will be dirty, and it will not leave a speck of that dirt on him. When Brennan's hands are all over a dirty deed, sanctioned or not, he will not leave a fingerprint, which is handy, of course, for his adamant denials later will be unyielding. If the attention ever turns to him, he will label the suspecting person as absolutely batty and be the most convincing person on the planet in doing so. It is impossible to adequately explain to someone, and it is not an exaggeration to describe it exactly as Dutschke himself has described his C/O "friends". They are so good at what they do that "they can convince a man to chew his own arm off." One should never forget this is the stock from which Brennan is spawned, because it is easy for "normal" to people to think that field-intelligence officers are also "normal". They are not. However, a dossier of Brennan ops will show predictable (sloppy) commonalities.

It is a signature of Brennan to create an event, perhaps a crime or scandal, that does not actually exist. Make it appear as if a crime has been committed, a "frame-job". Other "Brennanisms" include—lying to the press. Enlisting others to take over the "dirty work". Smear the target, especially with some sort of sexual allegation, (those really stick). Discredit the target to ensure nothing he ever says will be believed. As bad as these sound, it should actually come as a relief that there exists this kind of person who can do these things in service to their country, because sometimes these things really need to be done, whether it is palatable to the people or not. CIA is no exception. This is why it is best that most Americans simply don't pay attention to how the sausage is made. Just avert your eyes and enjoy the sausage. Pretend these things need not be and are not done in civilised society. So such activities, in service to their country's national interest, should not be disparaged. It is necessary, like it or not.

The problem, however, is that certain people truly have replaced "national interest" with their own. In 2012 two people held nearly god-like power to command masses that were and are undeniably notorious for considering only their own self-interest (one in the Oval Office, one at the State Department) and were surrounded by those who, in their own self-interest, had no problems going to extremes to preserve that power. Power protects its own. Apologists and party sycophants (media included) are incapable of being impartial enough to admit that both have a long history (Clinton to a much greater extent) of being willing to sacrifice the pawns of the peasantry, and anyone not actively in their inner circle of footmen is but peasantry. So it is when those Brennanesqe operations are turned onto the political threats to the controlling powers that it becomes a problem.

For example, after John Brennan left CIA, the first time, and formed his own company, he directed an operation, even though a private citizen at that point, for the 2008 (then) Senator Barack Obama (running for president) where he "hacked" (used the known back-door access) the State Department's passport database to scrub clean the file of presidential candidate Obama from any record of Obama's politically problematic travel history. This was, in fact, why the candidate hired Brennan's "company" in the first place. As part of the operation, Brennan tampered with Hillary's database record, too… just so that it was not so obvious that Obama's problematic data did not seem like the target. Buttering up Hillary's record made the "hack" (though the news reported it as a hack it was not a "hack". Just unauthorised, illegal access) appear as if *she* was the target, a throw. And that's how it was leaked to the press (to the press through intermediaries is another brand and trademark), but that was just typical Brennan misdirection. It looked like one person was the target (in this case, beneficiary), but the *real* target was *not* who was reported, but it was Obama (the fellow who hired him) all along.

Any reader that is thinking ahead might consider that the authors are presenting the variation that President Obama was behind the "hit" on Dutschke and that Obama was repeating 2008, once again enlisting Brennan to handle the logistics on how to discredit and silence Dutschke. And that Obama, in this version, was pulling the strings of his powerful weapon of intelligence and law-enforcement.

That variation would not be groundbreaking, as numerous websites have already postulated exactly that theory—Obama targeted Dutschke before Dutschke could target Obama, then Obama used his White House adviser Brennan, and Mueller, to coordinate the attacks on Dutschke then rewarded Brennan with the posting to head the agency he once worked and left (CIA) as the DCI in 2013. Obama was the leader from the Oval Office.

But that would be wrong.

While this postulation is not new, it is entirely backwards.

From Obama's point of view, if Dutschke was not going to damage his re-election between September 12th, 2012 (his return from Libya) and November (election day), then Dutschke wasn't going to do it at all. Following the November '12 re-election, Obama felt invincible, certainly impervious to anything that J. Everett Dutschke could throw at him. There was no intelligence that indicated Dutschke had met with anybody he wanted to about the Tripoli File, only Congressman Nunnelee. As long as Dutschke was discredited, and as long as Obama had the fawning media in his pocket (he did), there was nothing to fear.

But that is not the primary reason that Obama was not the man behind the hit on Dutschke. And that version suggests that Obama was the ringleader and calling the shots.

He wasn't.

He was not capable of it. Obama is a wide "platitude" without any experience whatsoever thinking logistically. Obama was not a powerful puppet-master who had a weapon of mass destruction, in the likes of John Brennan, at his side.

It is the other way around.

The reality is much, much worse. Much more sinister.

It was John Brennan who was the puppet-master, and with a President under his thumb. Obama was never actually pulling the strings, Brennan just let him think he did—and always from the shadows, just how he likes it.

There is no disputing that John Brennan personally had the President's ear. The superfluous job title of Special Advisor to the President on Security and Counterterrorism (officially under DHS) does not even fit onto a business card, but there was little need for Brennan to hand out his business card in the Oval Office. It was not just that Brennan had undiluted influence over Obama, that part is obvious, it is more like Obama needed Brennan around.

For example, it was more recently learned that Brennan was a fixture in the Oval Office during the key meetings in the scheming against General Flynn, Trump and the others (Crossfire Razor and Crossfire Hurricane). And at that point (2016-January 2017) Brennan had been appointed as DCI (took the oath of service over something *other* than the Bible!). Has anyone bothered to ask *why* Brennan was at those meetings? Didn't he have an agency to run? The head of the CIA is *not* supposed to be hanging around the Oval Office waiting for meetings to come along. The DCI does meet with the President when needed and if needed, but only then. The DCI is *not* the presidential briefer, there is and has always been a person designated for that particular service that may fall outside of the PDB. In fact, Michael Morell (DCI before Brennan and cover-up of Benghazi) was once, earlier in his career, the CIA presidential briefer. Considering what was being discussed, Brennan had no business being there. By December 2016 and January 2017, Crossfire Hurricane and Razor had already been turned over to the dogs. It was then an FBI, that means a criminal, investigation.

Therefore, Brennan's involvement in any of the "Crossfire" meetings was not only improper, it was completely illegal!

The law, as explicitly written by Congress which codifies the long-standing CIA Charter, is very clear. Title 50, chapter 15§403(d) "powers and duties" (3) specifically states that the CIA (Brennan) "Shall have *no* police, law enforcement powers" and is a law still in-force to this day (50 USC§3036(d) "The DCI shall...have *no* police, subpoena or law enforcement powers or security functions"). The very second it became "criminal investigation", Brennan should not have been present. In fact, because the CIA is legally theoretically forbidden to even coordinate with the FBI, the CIA cannot provide "Intel for use as evidence" to law enforcement or FBI. The CIA is *not* in the law enforcement business, so the entire launching of the operation, which was a covert intelligence entrapment scheme (signature of Brennan) involving attempts of infiltration, bribes (to Papadopoulos), electronic and human espionage (SIGINT and HUMINT), utilising foreign assets originally recruited by CIA, then the entire premise of the "Crossfire" operations was an illegality from the onset. (Yet that *is* a Brennan signature)

If the FBI, or any other cop, wants to do a criminal investigation, they can gather their own damn evidence, which should not be hard since they have warrant-rubber-stamp FISA and district court judges in their pockets.

The Crossfire operations, however, are a step-by-step clinic on a Brennan operation. very exemplary of it, providing a great deal of enlightenment here. Obama, the "community organiser", could never be sophisticated enough to match even Brennan's level of predictable sloppiness. This kind of thing is far above Obama's head (Comey, too). Half of the United States (in 2020) really want desperately to believe there was no such thing as a Crossfire operation and the other half wants Obama himself to be exposed as the ringleader.

Both halves are wrong.

Obama was personally responsible *in title only*.

The reason that Brennan was present in all of those meetings is because he needed to be certain everything went exactly as he wanted it to go. Obama, acting as the conductor of the orchestra, was/is completely incapable and unqualified to conduct such an orchestra. "Community organising", such as it is, while rife with shadowy and underhanded political conspiracy, is nowhere near the level of training or experience of even a first-year CIA C/O or CST who is still under their 45-day program manager. The constitutionalist pundits on the right should be more careful before attempting to accuse the 44th president of being the "organiser" of the coup attempt of 2016-17, and the individual "hits" on targets associated with the Crossfire Operation, because the tactics involved are so far outside of Obama's ability, reach and comprehension that is painfully obvious to any analysis that he, the President, was but a patsy; a tool for someone who actually did have the skill to logistically build, work and then execute such a complex plan as the Crossfire Operations. As a comparison, Obama was essentially nothing but a rubber-stamp in the same manner that a judge is usually nothing but a rubber-stamp for the law enforcement bureaucrats called prosecutors. President Obama was merely playing a role, a role of "being in charge" at the meetings and the Crossfire hits because it was *his* office. While Brennan's hands (not his own) were getting dirty (such as Lisa Page, Peter Strzok, Comey, McCabe et al) the appearance of formality, sanctioning the Operation Crossfire events (i.e.— Page/Strzok text: "POTUS wants us to keep him posted") through the Oval Office might have led the President, himself, to *think* he was in charge, but it was just because it had been Brennan buzzing in Obama's ears the entire time. Obama's inability and inexperience to clandestine operations at this level cannot be understated. He was too much of an amateur.

Although, as a brief aside here, it must be noted that every single attempt at actual diplomatic relations met with such utter failures that it is a miracle that the NSC did not run such a coup on him. His failures were a catastrophically stupid and revealed him to be such a bumbling novice at world affairs that he was truly dangerous to the U.S. "A public nuisance who confounds his ambition with his ability" (Ambrose Bierce). And disqualifying him from dabbling in world affairs. It was Obama's fault alone that relations with Israel deteriorated. Only that President could have found a way to screw up that relationship (for example—referring to ISIS as "ISIL", an anti-Israel lingo that the moronic press blindly followed). Four-star Phil Breedlove was told by POTUS-44 to stop talking to Grasinov, because the President was never sophisticated enough to see the value in back channels that were not his own. And then, among many others, is Libya. Nowhere else in history has there been a bigger mess made by the United States than that administration's clueless bumbling of Libya, long before even the Benghazi events.

And the Benghazi events did not occur in a vacuum. Though the disgusting cover-up of the Soleimani organised "attacks" deserves its own chapter in some other books since the White House/State Department-led "cover-up" is a crime onto itself of historical proportions, what occurred prior to the criminal cover-up warrants scrutiny. The "attack" itself.

The "attack" was never a protest (over an American video is that no one saw) that grew. No one takes days to set up and properly site mortars onto a target (the US compound in Benghazi) or bring night vision goggles to an after-sundown "protest". The fact that the Obama Administration (Secretary of State led) thought the American public was so stupid should have insulted every American (though the American plebe media *still* has yet to criticise the administration for trying it) with the attempt to sell the phony narrative of a spontaneous protest against a video (another attempt by that administration to "shame" normal Americans for being so racist and anti-Islamic). The "attack" was, in fact, an attempt at a hostage-taking of embassy staff and a US Ambassador. The attempted abduction was foiled, therefore spoiled (by the CIA's GRS team) the intended hostage killed and then the CIA team left stranded, by orders of the administration. The small CIA group in Tripoli was not properly mobilised to timely help, not in a direct manner, and DOD was intentionally "stood down". The final foreign rescue team was a team coordinated entirely by the local CIA officers there in Libya, not from DC and the exfil team was *not* even Americans, they were Libyan. The failures of defending the US personnel were not failures, they were intentional criminal refusals to defend, protect and rescue the GRS, CIA and Diplomatic Corps—that crosses the line into absolute treason. Why did the Commander-in-Chief shrug-off his duties that night and decide to sacrifice the ambassador and the patriotic CIA men so that he could instead go upstairs for a lie down?

Because it was his plan that no one in the compound be alive to tell the American public what actually happened that night. Or rather, it was Brennan's plan endorsed by Obama. PACE. Brennan knows how to think that way. Obama does not. Primary plan was to have the security so lax, that the Ambassador and staff would have been easy pickings for Soleimani's Ansar Al-

Sharia militia allies. This was greatly aided by the refusal of the Secretary of State to bolster the DS staff to where they asked for it to be and on numerous occasions. Clinton's denial of the multiple requisitions for DS resources was (intentional to) making the ambassador a "low-hanging fruit" for attack. That was Brennan's manipulations with both Clinton (who may not have been privy to the ultimate Obama objective of having an election year hostage crisis for him to successfully resolve) and with...Soleimani himself. Did the Ansar Al-Sharia militants in Libya guess at when and where the ambassador would be? No. They were given intel and were *not* an unsophisticated and uncoordinated rag-tag collection of angry rejects. They were methodical, calculating and had days of surveillance and preparation with a fortuitous date (September 11th, of 2012) already pre-selected and chosen.

The abduction under the primary plan was foiled. By who? CIA. Specifically the arrival of the CIA-GRS contractors to add more "meat" to protection. GRS officers are not the spy-types. They are not C/Os engaged in recruiting foreign assets (agents). GRS is not interested in espionage or the deal-making of the C/Os. They are different than other field officers (the T/Os and C/Os or even SAD types). GRS agents are all ex-military, usually SEALS or Rangers with their heads on swivels, who think not about—"How can I get my hands on the intel I want," But instead about—"What, where, who and when are the military threats." Their arrival meant that the Brennan/Soleimani's next step—A. Alternate plan was in effect which called for a heavier force for attack. In this alternate plan, lives could be lost. This could make things problematic, for Obama—not for Soleimani's Libyan proxies. And this is what they did.

The attack with a heavier force resulted in the inability of the attackers to snatch and seize the ambassador, who had his own force that was able to fight back but unfortunately resulted in the Ambassador's death.

This means no kidnapping. No hostage. This triggered the C-contingency, which was—leave no one alive. This part of the plan required that the President do nothing, say nothing, order nothing and enact nothing. The idea being that if left without assistance the smaller GRS/DS force would be overrun and eliminated by the overwhelming numbers. The compound would be Obama's CIA Alamo. (Brennan/Obama vs Petraeus)

It did not work out that way and the smaller, and entrenched force was *not* overtaken. It was *not* the Alamo. The men lived to tell about it, or at least what they thought they knew of it. All records of "stand down" to U.S. potential assistance seemed to have disappeared (which was common for anything which might implicate that particular administration) and in the fog and noise of it all came the denials of it. What the Clinton State Department (and by association the Obama White House) did not consider is the possibility that every bit of SIGINT was being collected not just of foreign transmissions, but there was also a record made of all US transmissions as well, even everything back and forth at night from a location in Tripoli. A record which would be easily added to a memory card along with the other extremely significant intel that had been retrieved earlier that very day. That memory card—even before the Benghazi transmissions were added would become an unwanted, yet highly hunted prise. A prise which could have been the perfect weapon that if it had been deployed by the right person at the right time would have sent shockwaves through the world and several different (not merely the U.S.) governments.

During the Benghazi attack, a State T/O was killed. There were only two *new* people in Libya acting as a T/O on that day. It would have been a jolt for Clinton (and Abedin), Brennan and Michael Morell to have seen Dutschke among the personnel and Libya as they would be among the very few that could have gained access to that information. One was a State I.T., the other a non-State contract. Why was Dutschke not in Benghazi doing COMSEC? Because they had a guy for that who was among the best in the world and because Everett was not (on) officially there for that. He was meeting with someone and never left Tripoli. Was it anticipated that Everett (a green badger on a single gig) would have been in Benghazi by Brennan and Clinton/Abedin? In other words, was there another bonus "hit" placed on Dutschke.

It is plausible, but not likely.

At that moment, Dutschke would not have held the weapon (file) and would not have been of any political consequence at all to the administration as a whole or any individual in that administration. The idea that Dutschke would need to be a target would be extremely premature since at that precise moment he was a total non-factor, a person of absolutely no consequence washed-up and burned ex-spy who was meaningless in the scheme of things. He was already, in some ways, less than nothing and harmless to the administration since Dutschke's 2008 revelations of the Chinese links to the presidential campaign collusion and meddling in the election were paid no heed at all. And his reputation of getting beaten constantly by the Chinese (incursions into sub-Saharan Africa) and his 2004 discoveries of al-Qaeda influence and interference on behalf of John Kerry were soundly ridiculed due to above-deck officer "super agent" Larry Kolb's opposing theory of the Al-Qaeda-affiliated donations. Simply put, at that exact moment Dutschke was completely unimportant since he did not have the Tripoli File because it did not yet exist. That's the one thing that would have (and later did within 24 hours) made Dutschke politically perilous and was not known prior to the Benghazi attacks by anyone.

In Obama's mind, he had the perfect weapon in John Brennan. Someone who could carry out nefarious political operations, worldwide and with connections and experience that Obama, himself would never be able to coordinate. And the President who had been at war with certain factions of the

CIA, having the FBI/DOJ arrest and prosecute CIA officers dropping like flies, had a former CIA insider, Brennan, to aid him.

Just like the Brennan 2008 "hack" into the State Department data files for purely political purposes, just like the much later Brennan ordered wiretapping (electronic surveillance) members of the opposing party US senators and press, and just like the later Crossfire operations, were all done for the sole purpose of securing and preserving political power, party domination, and harming political opposition. This is another operational bias of Brennan, a predictable and potentially problematic one.

Which brings us back to Flynn and the Crossfire operations.

The now-infamous Crossfire meetings in the Oval Office were discussions by a like-minded gang of men (and women) who were planning a "hit" job utilising both the intelligence agencies (DCI and DNI). And the FBI/DOJ was the hitman. The goal was the political destruction of an enemy (the incoming Trump Administration) and the targets to be eliminated included General Michael Flynn (who had long before learned RUMINT Hillary Clinton puppeteering millions from a Russian nuclear agency, then arranged the sale of enriched uranium to Iran when Flynn headed the DIA) through an entrapment scheme (Brennan signature). The reason that Brennan was in those meetings is that they were *his* meetings. They only *looked* like they were Obama's meetings. They were not NSC meetings (though the VP and some NSC people were present) because the DOJ and FBI is *not* NSC. They were not IC meetings because the NSC and DOJ are not IC. The meetings were a hodge-podge of hitmen who thought Obama was a shot caller. Brennan (DCI in 2016-Jan 17) had no business in Oval Office meetings, except that Brennan (and only Brennan) had to ensure that his own president (Brennan's perfect weapon) did not screw things up and to "officially" offer Obama advice from the "intelligence community" although legally that job would have fallen to another man present in the Crossfire cabal, the flatulent James Clapper. And there was no way in which Brennan would allow Clapper to stink up the Crossfire operations.

These meetings must have been somewhat tortuous for the Crossfire cabal with Clapper in the room since they had to keep the door closed and there are no windows in the Oval Office which actually open. It is likely that the FBI Yeti, Jim Comey, might have escaped lung injury since he is a million metres tall and his oversized nostrils might have been safely above the famous Clapper cloud. Susan Rice would likely have caught the worst of it, thinking perhaps the White House was under chemical weapons attack. VP Joe Biden was likely searching for a corner of a round room and wondering if he, himself, was the causation of the gassy fog.

Regardless, as before mentioned, Brennan's mere presence in any Crossfire meeting and his participation in the early (pre-LEO stage) was illegal for the aforementioned statutory reasons. But it is again, his signature. Create an event, a covert intelligence operation "frame" job—then the LEOs are brought in on cue. Add another Brennan trademark misdirection for flavor and whip it up.

But Brennan's criminality goes deeper.

Every single one of the Brennan operations (some documented, some not) were intended to influence the President or intimidate a political threat or for some sort of political gain. Brennan's coordination of others (Clapper, Comey) to leak were attempts to influence the media and public opinion.

This (again) makes the puppet-master, John Brennan, a criminal in the literal sense. The Intelligence Reform and Terrorism Prevention Act of 2004 statutorily enacted other portions of the CIA charter (back) into law and regulation. 50USC§3001—reads as follows under Section 2-13: "Limitation on Covert Action—NO covert action may be conducted which is intended to influence U.S. political policy process, public opinion, policies or media"

This can be found at 73 Fed reg. 45325 (July 2008)

Brennan operations, including the Crossfire Operations from the Oval Office, violate 50 USC§3001 to the letter and without question. Operation Crossfire Hurricane and Crossfire Razor were not the first, in fact, by then Brennan and the very same cabal (adding in Clinton/Abedin and Bob Mueller) had already had plenty of practice and three years earlier... with Operation Dojo.

The "hit" put out on Dutschke.

Because each of these operations was coordinated within the actual halls (rooms) of power by the same shady figures, there is legally no need to determine exactly who did exactly what and sort it out for individual prosecution. Every one of the White House operations were violations of 18 USC§241, violating a citizen's constitutional right. And because they were all involved as a cabal they should all be prosecuted and imprisoned under the same theory used for the Bin-Laden and gang-related prosecutions. RICO.

The now-famous Susan Rice email from Susan Rice *to* Susan Rice which thrice states that Obama directs the operation/investigation to proceed "with the intelligence community and law enforcement *by the book*" is, in fact, an admission of the RICO crime commission. Because if anything was done "*by the book*" (as Rice wrote in a panic) then Brennan and Clapper could not be allowed anywhere *near* the meeting or the operations. Susan Rice never bothered to do a bit of legal research prior to her CYA email (Jan 20th, 2017) or she would have known that Brennan in the same law enforcement meetings is *confirmation* of a conspiracy (RICO—"two or more persons"—conspiracy) to violate 18 USC§241 at the least. It was a violation of law for Brennan to participate in or contribute to in *any* way the law enforcement operation of Comey's, no matter how it started (inside Brennan's IC connections), including the Crossfire operations. It was also a violation of law for Brennan to conspire (be part of the meetings) to "attempt to" "influence" the media, public opinion and the election (50 USC§3001-2.13). And with RICO—you get one of them on any crime then you get them all. RICO laws are dangerously draconian and illogical...but it's *their* laws, the same that *they* use to prosecute everyone else who has to live by them. Are they now above (or below) their own laws? Crossfire operations are, by definition, a RICO case. Every person in those Oval Office sessions is a co-conspirator. At any time any one of them *could* have said, "Okay, I am uncomfortable with the illegalities here...I am leaving," (except of course, for Biden who would have just walked into the closet). THAT would have been a better CYA then sending an email from and to themselves (that damaged her defence instead of helping it, since Rice did not know the law). Every one of them should all be on the same indictment as co-conspirators of RICO as the qualified John Brennan. If even one person in that room abused their power, they all aided it.

Note that before law enforcement could be brought into "notice" that a criminal (or CIC) investigation was starting, the stage had to be first set for the FBI to then act as if they noticed there was something to investigate. The FBI waited for a trigger and may not have known exactly what the trigger would be, to the details. In other words, an act had to happen for the actors playing FBI who were waiting in queue to come in on cue. That is classic Brennan ("wait until he is briefed by Jim, then *YOU* leak the dossier, you old gasbag" or "we're going to make it *LOOK* like this thing happened, see, even though it didn't. But it does not matter...as soon as we stage the crime, and the "framing" is done, that's when you FBI guys come on in. And don't worry about the media, we'll feed them misinformation which they will run anyway without question").

That is signature Brennan. That is his operational bias.

And *that* was also the premise of the convoluted Operation Dojo. The objective, the President (Obama), and the Secretary of State (Clinton) needed to neutralise the man who controlled all the myriad of information of the Tripoli File. The man who had already shown he felt no compulsion to merely turn it over. Since he could not be bought and could not be turned, he must be otherwise incentivized to do so or the dogs of hell would be released on to him.

What the President and Secretary of State may or may not have known is that the imps of each (Brennan—the devil on Obama's shoulder and Abedin—the devil on Hillary's pantsuit shoulder pad) could finally fulfill their long-term (2002) interest in evening the score for Rabita Trust, a payback for Operation Vengeance. In retrospect, Operation Vengeance served no purpose to the US since the entire MWL and Rabita Trust fund structure did just fine, financially, even without the donations from the three uber-wealthy financiers (except but to perhaps give the ██ ██ family a purge of its 3 members that caused such an embarrassment).

The doctrine of "crippling the finances" of Al-Qaeda, and the networks and organisations that supported it sounded reasonable, and needed to be tried, but the "crippling" effect was mediocre at best, save some noticeable effect in sub-Saharan African division where terrorism was more of a consumer of funds then a donor and where the few donors were fewer and easier to discover. In the grand scheme of things—"crippling the finances" (including through the extreme measures of 2002's Operation Vengeance) just didn't work. But Muslims have a long memory and 2002-2013 is not so long. With Brennan (the Muslim blacked out from the 2002 Operation Vengeance) in Obama's ear and pulling the strings, and with Abedin (whose family was directly affected financially, and daughter of Saleha Abedin) it would be the culmination of their long-term hunt, their unmasking of Dutschke in 2011 would finally pay off.

It would be a classic Brennan operation with all the key Brennanesque features. The hardest part would be the primary entrapment scheme itself, but Brennan was very experienced at it (and would continue to do it, repeating his tactics later in the Crossfire operations). Begin with smearing accusations, enlisting others, then ramp it up. Using an intermediary, aided by Dutschke's previously suspected experience, find a way to enlist Dutschke into transferring the same chemical weapon as the Libyan product of 2012, to someone. It did not really matter who, because development (and sale) of a chemical weapon would violate the treaty, triggering the FBI investigation. It only mattered if Dutschke thought that the person that was to take possession had become a target worthy of being a target. In other words, Brennan's operation began with convincing Dutschke that he was part of an operation himself against the target that involved National Security. From Brennan's point of view it was a simple entrapment operation, the kind that CIA actually does all the time for leverage, the kind Brennan preferred, and Dutschke himself would do all the work. All that was necessary was for Dutschke to develop and manufacture the product according to the Libyan specs and transfer to the target and then it is over. Simple. Entrapment done (just like other Brennan Ops). The selection of Paul Kevin Curtis as the mark and patsy was not a difficult choice or sales pitch for the intermediary to make to Dutschke. Dutschke could easily be convinced that Paul Kevin Curtis probably crossed some line somewhere, especially after Curtis's 2011 book capitalising on Dutschke's unmasking and Curtis' naming Dutschke as a "cover-up" agent.

The authors believe that intermediary was a trusted mentor-ish friend by the name of Kar-Mun Wong who Everett Dutschke had twice visited in California in recent times. It is unknown whether Wong knew that what Brennan presented, then what Wong presented to Dutschke, was actually believed by Wong to be true, or if Wong was let in on the fact that it was a setup by Brennan.

The evidence of the lab reports and court transcript suggest it might have been the latter and either Wong tipped Dutschke off; or if the former then Dutschke was suspicious because one thing is for sure, Dutschke (if he ever was the maker) executed a double-double-cross on Brennan of his own.

Just as Brennan used Operation Dojo (entrapment scheme against Dutschke) as the model for the later Operation Crossfire Hurricane (entrapment scheme against Trump campaign), and Crossfire Razor (entrapment scheme against Flynn), Dutschke had a model to use, too. Operation Merlin (the operation that Mueller/Holder used to imprison CIA officer Sterling). If nuclear plans were going to be sold to Iran, then make sure they are *not* actual viable plans—*but make them look convincing enough.* Brennan, who was *not* CIA in late 2012, tried to stage Dutschke to execute "Operation Kentucky Rain" (not the real name) which was a fake op, thus a double-cross on Dutschke. Dutschke, however, obviously did *not* follow the Libyan specs and when Curtis was finally compelled to acquire the product (which he did directly and *not* through Curtis's go-between as he was "supposed" to—also a red flag for Everett) Curtis got what he thought was a bona-fide Libyan product. Just like in Sterling's Operation Merlin Russian nuclear plans to Iran, Dutschke knew it was all but a matter of salesmanship. The transaction, according to the suppressed FBI discovery, almost had an audience—Janet, Everett's wife. She had just left work late that night and swung by Everett's office briefly. He was still there, then briefly departed for Kroger across the street for eggnog (it was during Christmas time) just missing the awkward transfer. If the records in the FBI's possession are accurate recountings, it was about 10:30 pm.

As far as Everett was concerned, at that point he was done. Finished with the operation (Kentucky Rain) but in his own way, and as the evidence shows, without any possibility of anyone actually being in danger. Whatever Curtis chose to do with the product afterwards was entirely on Curtis. Dutschke, from then, would have absolutely no way of knowing exactly what Curtis would attempt to do. Everett Dutschke had no associations with Curtis, himself. So when the New Year rolled around (2013) he would have had no possible way of knowing that the January hearings of the House Committee could possibly have been related to the phony Operation Kentucky Rain.

Brennan was waiting for the cue to know/prove Kentucky Rain had been done in order to call in the dogs, sic them on Dutschke neutralising him according to the plan of Operation Dojo. It should have been just that simple. But Everett did not know anything about any cue to trigger the LEO leg of the scheme.

Everett, however, did not wait to create controversy and send a shiver through the upper echelons when the White House and State Department (while in full Benghazi damage control) got wind that he was trying to renew his push to meet with Turry and John Mills. Although by January (10th) it seemed as though Everett had no intention to leverage or leak the Tripoli Files, his renewal of efforts to meet with, perhaps confront, certain people came at a time that was incredibly alarming to the administration as the actual, full-on and public Benghazi hearings were about to dominate the news cycle. Hillary Clinton's testimony before the same people must have incensed Everett, ("What difference, at this point, does it make?")

Regardless, Brennan began to enact his (A) alternate plan which was to use DOJ/FBI pressure on locals to ameliorate, destroy and discredit Dutschke, ensuring that *he* would be so ostracized as to be persona-non-grata, thus unable to credibly release the damaging in Tripoli File. Dutschke might have been having second thoughts, evidenced by the January 18th, 2013 text he sent to Paul Kevin Curtis's brother, Jack Curtis, that day that Everett was with his radio engineer siting for the future FM station, following his stepson's dentist appointment. It is literally within 2 hours of that text that the pressure began.

Though the FBI captured every text of Janet and Everett's mobile phones, even using some of Janet's texts against Everett in Thomason's testimonies, that one text to Jack Curtis was hidden, suppressed from discovery after the prosecution began in earnest (May 2013). Amazing how the U.S. Federal Bureau Investigation under Mueller and Comey seemed to "lose" only that one text, the one that was relevant, yet they had all the others that were not.

Funny how things at the FBI just...go missing.

Oh well...just a coincidence, right?

Everett would not have known that a (monitored, without warrant) text he sent to Jack Curtis was in any way related to the escalating personal and legal attacks and did not discover until March that the mounting accusations were by people specifically (and familialy) attached to the very same LEOs that were later a documented part of Operation Dojo (with the exception of one aberrant person who was just pressured to join the "Kick Dutschke" bandwagon). But one thing Everett did recognise, surely, was the April breaking news just after the Boston bombing. And he was likely *not* too surprised to learn from that wall-to-wall coverage what Paul Kevin Curtis had done with the "Kentucky Rain" product that Curtis thought was ricin. If KC letters triggered the FBI response, as Brennan intended as he and Obama watched it play out for a while before informing Mueller. It is likely that Holder already knew.

Once the FBI dogs, waiting in queue for the trigger, were unleashed, they would wreak havoc in their usual way and, as outlined in the other chapters, there was nothing honest about anything they did. From that point forward, Brennan's only coordination was to imply and push about the Tripoli File and bury Dutschke in a drowning sea of surveillance including the MQ-1 Predator drone—all of which Everett thrice slipped. Other than that,

Brennan's job was done at the moment. It became a "criminal investigation" for the FBI to take over (also signature Brennan).

Everett might have thought that by switching the product from the intended deadly chemical weapon of assassination to an inactive and harmless decoy product that he had double double-crossed and outsmarted Brennan. Even if he had, it did not matter. Mueller did not care, he was told (while in the Oval Office with the President and Holder present) to make sure Dutschke got convicted ("make it happen"). Embarrassed multiple times by Everett, Bob Mueller likely did not need such prompting.

When James Everett Dutschke was finally indicted for "Developing a biological weapon," John Brennan was again rewarded by Obama (just as he had been after the 2008 "hack") by being appointed to the office he'd wanted all along, this time replacing the Benghazi-ridden Michael Morell as a Director of the CIA, the same agency that did not quite have full faith in Brennan, that he'd left years before, attaching himself to Obama's coattails like a parasite. This was the perfect opportunity for Obama, too. With his man, Brennan, as the DCI (not that Morell wasn't, he certainly was), Obama could better revamp the agency to cater to his liking (doing his bidding) and would have less trouble from those meddlesome professionals of national intrigue. Brennan took the oath of office and was sworn in as DCI, not over a Bible like everyone else, but because he is Muslim he swore in over...something else. For the first time in history, a Muslim was in charge of the Central Intelligence Agency. One of Brennan's first acts as DCI was to issue the edict that the word "Jihad"; cannot be used in CIA document anymore when referring to Muslim terrorists and militant extremists as well as other similar adjustments in language. CIA had now become Muslim-friendly, with Brennan at the helm. It had just become an extension of MWL, just like Al-Qaeda; only instead of being funded by Rabita Trust, it was funded by the American taxpayer.

Under Obama/Brennan, CIA would become an agency competing against the US Air Force to become the Top Gun of drone strikes. Instead of the complex mission of gathering and analysing intelligence, the wayward CIA became a video game. If Hillary Clinton had been elected, there is little doubt that Brennan would have remained the DCI and Comey at the FBI and both organisations would be political tools, a perfect weapon, for her use at her disposal. As bad as the agency abuse during the Obama government (which competes historically with LBJ's abuses), Hillary Clinton (with Huma Abedin at her side) would have been even more extreme. The '16 election, which was based in part on "draining the swamp", *did* result in ridding the nation of Comey at the helm of FBI (though his influence still exists through the media and the hundreds of "little Comeys" still in the bureau) which is an improvement, plus the install of a worthy Secretary of State and a very, very worthy DCI. But the new heads of those agencies may well find that the "swamp creatures" are too entrenched and impossible to purge.

A good start would be to put every one of the cabal in prison and via RICO. Or in the Oval Office words of Barack Hussein Obama (April, 2013) when ordering the hit on Everett Dutschke, "Make an example out of him," or as he told Mueller about the conviction, "Just get it done, Bob." Quite frankly for justice to be "fair", then turnabout is "fair" play. And that means all of the Operation Dojo cabal (the same as the Crossfire cabal) must be tossed into prison for the same amount of time they sought with Dutschke—life. That is—Jim Comey, Bob Mueller, Barack Hussein Obama, John Brennan, Hillary Clinton, Huma Abedin, Chad Lamar, Sally Yates, Andrew Sigler and Stephen Thomason at the "top tier" of involvement. The rest of the cabal, via RICO association—McCabe, Boente, Clay Joyner, Jim Johnson, Dennis Montgomery, the patsy Paul Kevin Curtis, John Quaka, half or more of the media/press conspirators and a small list of duped citizens who knew nothing but tried to involve themselves in the fray anyway.

The narrative that the cabal and its complicit sock-puppets in the press chose to repeat ad nauseum meant that there were certain things that the Holder/Mueller/Comey prosecution had to make sure remained hidden. All of the evidence of the mailing, certainly, because *all* of it did, does and forever will implicate the crazy patsy Paul Kevin Curtis. He is, in fact, known by everyone, including the FBI, as the mailer and nothing will ever change that fact.

That is exactly *why* all the evidence they presented in court about the mailing of the KC letters, that even the press reported, was suddenly no longer talked about and the media went strangely silent about the very details they once shouted. But in addition to that, the reason the FBI "lost" the January 18th, 2013 text from Dutschke to Jack Curtis is because that would expose (perhaps *re*-expose) Paul Kevin Curtis' involvement, and *before* Curtis even committed the April mailings. Revealing that could have exposed the entire thing. Also the "intercepted" or "seized" letter from Everett to his wife, Janet. Had *that* been revealed, it would also have forced the prosecutors to deal with the details which are inconvenient to their narrative and the objective of Operation Dojo. All of those things were suppressed by the prosecutor (and much more) because the special prosecution team (given the command by Obama to "just get it done") would have been forced to acknowledge that Curtis is, in fact, the mailer (even though everyone knows this anyway), and they would have to stop pretending that he was not.

As far as Everett goes, if he actually *was* the mailer and had simply admitted it, the sentencing range would have changed (lowered) into a range that would have resulted in a far shorter sentence, somewhere around twelve years, because of the "Acceptance of Responsibility" which subtracts three "sentencing points" (the American sentencing determinations are a confusing and nearly arbitrary system of "points" which adds or subtracts, the sum of which results in a "range" of years). Because Everett entirely refused the "Acceptance of Responsibility", his refusal is in part what put him into a higher "category" of time. So even if Everett was innocent of the mailings, he had every incentive to *claim* that he was the mailer, just to cut his sentence in half. His refusal to claim that he was the mailer, his adamant proclamations that he was *not* the mailer at the stake of a much longer sentence, his denial to formally accept the "Acceptance of Responsibility" points and all of the actual evidence showing that someone else was the mailer (Curtis), is proof alone that Everett is not the mailer.

Furthermore, the maximum sentence for the mailings themselves was a five-year sentence. This means that, since sentences are concurrent (from the same "act") that the mailing counts (five years) sentences are already over.

The five-year *mailing* sentences fit *inside* of the "developing a biological weapon" sentence. So whether that longer treaty violation sentence was 12, 25, or life, it still would have covered and buried the *mailing* sentence. The mailing (5 year) sentences were of absolutely no consequence in time whatsoever since they did not add even a day. The mailing sentence (which started at the same instant as the biological weapons sentence), being much shorter, ran out long before the treaty violation sentence could.

So even if Everett was entirely guilty of the mailing, he would not have been sentenced to *more*. Not even a single day. So what then was his incentive when he refused to admit to the mailing that the prosecutors kept trying to "stick" him with? He denied it at two plea hearings, refused to admit to it on the "Acceptance of Responsibility" portion of the PSI, denied it in the "reading of the facts", objected to it in writing in the PSI response as a formal motion to the court, submitted a nearly 40 page statement in court denying it, then formally denied it in every single legal filing under penalty of perjury including habeas, a reply filing to the court, 2255 filing of 80 pages to the court, a formal reply, a formal motion for a reconsideration, motion for retrial, a motion to correct the record, a formal motion to the higher court of appeals, a formal reply to the 5th Circuit Court, the motion(s) for reconsideration, the second motion for rehearing en banc, and in the motion to the US Supreme Court— all under penalty of perjury as well as in at least fourteen separate interviews and statements, *and* to his attorney-of-record (Coghlan) he flatly asked, "Why are they sticking *me* with Curtis's mailings?", to which Coghlan shrugged, "Because they want this over with. This is the only way they'll do it." There has never been a more documented case of denials and insistence of innocence convicted by a plea agreement in history, ever. What more could he have done to deny the mailings? His refusal to lie in court and simply "say" that he was the mailer when he wasn't, resulted in a longer sentence.

This shows he was willing to go to jail for the truth. Most people would have simply said, "I'll say whatever you want, man," as Curtis did when he turned into a deal-bound FBI snitch, along with Dennis Montgomery and Christopher A. Stutsy, who were all willing to fabricate anything that their

LEO masters commanded, to win their freedom. That is no different than being a slave to the corrupt DOJ (*not* a benevolent master).

Dutschke, who showed he was willing to go to prison (and fight it from the other side of conviction) to fight for his beliefs. Doing the right thing is something forced upon us all by accident or circumstance.

James Everett Dutschke did not ask to be the bearer of the Tripoli File. If he had not met with his former contact in Libya and instead stayed that three days with his own family, safely on the other side of the planet, the contact might have eventually found some other trusted person. It would have been some other person's problem. Everett was merely collateral damage. It could have been anyone, but it wasn't.

Instead, Everett refused to agree to actually say he committed the "mailing" crime. The evidence proves he was right. He refused to admit that he "developed a biological weapon". The evidence shows that, even though he was "expected" to (Operation "Kentucky Rain") in defiance of Brennan, Everett did *not*. Therefore, there was *no* law broken by Everett and a thousand laws broken by his prosecution. The SAM order, written to silence him, was the most egregious of them all. He was willing to go to jail, while proclaiming his innocence at every step, as the actual record actually shows. Sometimes it is doing the right thing that costs the most.

The media has labeled him a traitor. Treasonous. A terrorist.

It was all fabricated. It was all made up and the actual details show it. But the media does not care about actual details anymore than the administration or the FBI or prosecutors did. "We came for a hangin' and we aim t'see one!"

J. Everett Dutschke, if the *real* narrative to be told, should have released the Tripoli File. He might still have been forced into his conviction, but he might have taken a few down with him, and hard. It might now be harder to "clean the swamp" of the cabal, most of which are no longer even in office. However, men and women who take the hit from the corrupt DOJ (especially the Obama regime) and weather it without breaking are heroes. THEY are integrity personified in the same vein as Martin Luther King Jr., Nelson Mandela, Gandhi, and Thoreau. From them, we draw inspiration.

John Kiriakou was beaten down by that administration's prosecution machine, his life and family destroyed and eventually sent to prison. He never deserved to bear the brutal attacks of the Holder/Mueller conviction machine, Yet everyone now sees the system for what it was. A political weapon. John K. was the collateral damage of the Obama symbolic trumpet-call to the fawning population that "torture is bad" (an unnecessary but popular statement) which required the symbolic sacrifice of someone. That someone was John Kiriakou (CIA officers make for easy convenient, popular targets). For his perseverance, suffering through the Obama/Holder/Mueller conviction machine, John K. is a victim, not a villain. He is inspiration.

K.T. MacFarland is a victim of that machine. K.T. MacFarland is inspiration.

General Michael Flynn is a victim of that machine. Flynn is inspiration.

Tom Drake is inspiration.

Jeff Sterling is inspiration.

Judy Miller is inspiration.

Everett Dutschke is inspiration.

Carter Page is inspiration.

George Papadopoulos is inspiration.

Even (swallow) Roger Stone is inspiration.

Attorney Jessica Raddack and Sydney Katherine Powell are inspiration. As long as he did not teach the Russians to do what the NSA was doing Edward Snowden is inspiration.

The narrative of all those listed above is not only unfair, it is entirely wrong and the opposite of the actual truth. Their fight against a DOJ that has unlimited resources and zero amount of propriety, decency, morals or intent to follow the law in pursuit of convictions, not truth. A DOJ that always wins, with a fight instigated over a political agenda, not truth.

The truth should be its own agenda.

As to that, though the analysts' version here has been previously speculated, first-appearing (oddly) on a linked story from Debka attributed (falsely) to Ann Fischer denying the SAD involvement or associations of the Libyan courier to Dutschke as being an agent of 8200, the earlier version of these revelations raised a question that on the surface seems valid but should be discarded as not relative or germane at all, which is this: (paraphrase from the Debka link) "If Brennan's entrapment scheme in Operation Dojo was so egregious, then how is Dutschke's similar role in Operation Kentucky Rain not equally as egregious?"

This is a false comparison. First—Dutschke did not *actually* run an entrapment (or "framing") scheme since he had no control or influence at all over what Curtis would do with the (harmless) product Curtis thought was ricin. Everett had no foreknowledge at all that Curtis would even do anything with it, much less something of ill-intent. That was entirely up to Curtis. Second—Dutschke was not law enforcement nor colluding with law enforcement. "Entrapment" ("framing") is a crime of law enforcement, not "crime" of an intel op. Third—the intentional detoxification of the 2013 decoy product itself meant that no "law" or treaty was being violated. It is *not* a violation of either the chemical weapons treaty nor the biological weapons treaty or any law to develop an entirely harmless (proven by the actual lab analysis) product (no matter how the field test reacts to it). Fourth—the motive of the Brennan/Obama cabal (*not* Obama/Brennan cabal) was an absolute abuse of power at the highest level, the worst abuse of power scandal in all of

American history (and one they would twice, to a lesser degree) attempt on a campaign, a transition, administration (all the same) and its individual members. Dutschke was not operating as an abuse of office, Brennan (et al) was.

Therefore the Debka link question is rubbish and there should be no attempt to equate the two.

Incidentally, although it may be unpalatable for American readers to learn and consider this, CIA "framing" tactics are commonly used to leverage a source to become a full-blown asset (agent), as with every other intelligence agency working HUMINT. Arrange for your foreign "friends" hand to be "caught in the cookie jar", then rush in and rescue your "friend" (maybe with a handful of pelf) and he is now indebted to you. This is, in fact, one of the most successful methods taught and trained for during "recruitment" training because everyone has their price, one much lowered when there is trouble. That is but one common application of "framing"; there are others but misdirection is not merely a tool of tradecraft, it is such a fundamental cornerstone of a trained C/O that it permeates their every action. A CIA officer cannot make a sandwich or sit in church or sing a song or brush his (or her) teeth without consideration of their indoctrinated curriculum, including misdirection. They are *not* normal people, imperatively repeated here. Their constant suspicions and constant recalculations draw upon "training" so deeply, at the cellular level that their abnormal, cunning cognitions are as instinctive as the right or left handedness of normal people. To someone like Brennan, his tactics are instinctive, therefore only sinister based on his motive and objectives. If the objective ends with causing harm to someone..."Oh well, so be it" to him. Which makes his role as the unseen puppet-master, perfect for his personality.

The arrogance of Obama only helped Brennan to allow Obama to play the role of being in charge of his own Oval Office plans and schemes. In other words, that President, when it came to operations like this, was already predisposed to abusing his office (through other lackeys), to punish and eliminate political criticisms (i.e.—Lois Lerner/IRS, firing I.G. Walpin for investigating an Obama friend, Mueller/Holder prosecution of John Kiriakou, Dutschke, Sterling, Rosen and many, many others); so because Obama already had the proclivity to abuse the presidency, he thought he was in charge of Operation Dojo (then later the Crossfire operations using the same people and tactics). Obama thinking that he was in charge was exactly how Brennan liked it. Neither of the two would have it any different.

The analyst's current reckoning of events, based on actual evidence, interviews and already known tendencies of the men and women involved and the 2013 yarn spun by the administration do not converge and exist separately. For anyone to actually believe in the latter, that is the fantastical impossible narrative that the cabal and the sock-puppet press spread, would require that one set aside the suppressed and hidden away evidence of the FBI, forget their previously testified critical evidence, refuse to see or acknowledge the operational bias of the key players that personally got involved into a criminal case, give inexplicable credence to physical and logistical impossibilities, have a certainty in the existence of time machines, be able to accept an absurd (and ever-changing) motive as well as hopelessly complex microtheories, ignore the actual and documented (and testified) *now* known history of Curtis himself (which FBI later ignored), mentally sweep critical details under the rug to pretend they are no longer critical, conclude that Everett Dutschke possesses supreme omnipotence including magic powers, ESP and telepathy; cast aside the original conclusions of the Secret Service, the Capitol Police, the Senate staff of Senator Wicker, Congressman Nunnelee's office, the Mayor of Tupelo, Curtis's own family members (originally), to some extent Curtis's own later filed lawsuit (Curtis v. John Does 1-15), Facebook, the FBI, a US Magistrate Judge and Reverend Mike Hicks and his congregation as well as anyone else who knew him. Remember, Curtis virtually announced (and dated) that he had committed the *act*. The *only* FBI testimony on record about the mailing was right (testified six times, under oath) the mailer of the 2013 KC letters was, in fact, Paul Kevin Curtis. No one else.

As to all that led up to—Dutschke, it is "concluded" with very high confidence, developed for Curtis a harmless product which, itself, does *not* violate the treaty and he could have had absolutely *no* possible way to know or influence what Curtis would, and ultimately did, do.

Anyone interested in the truth, that is it, leaving no holes, no blank spaces and even filling out the forgotten areas with explicit details including dates, times, people who are personally known to be involved and by name.

There are other assorted theories in the ether. But they are as substantial and as solid as Clapper's gas clouds. None have merit. One theory is that this case was yet another "harmless white powder" case. Rubbish. Those nonsensical "threat" cases are so common that there are about a hundred federal convictions a year for it. None of the cases have warranted the PDB, drones, massive military involvement, or personal documented involvement by the US Attorney General, President and the Director of the FBI himself.

One can be certain that when Brennan himself, Holder himself, Mueller himself, Comey himself, personally involved themselves in a case, it is *not* a run-of-the-mill prosecution or case. They do not send someone to be disappeared into the National Security Unit of the US Supermax for a measly "white powder" case. Although it is very, very rare, there have been other convictions of that treaty before (developing a biological weapon), the *only* person that has ever been in the ADX SAM unit for such a conviction remains James Everett Dutschke, the small but secret, non-communications unit comprised of nothing but spies and the world's top terrorists. That does not happen even with other actual rare convictions of "developing a biological weapon" and certainly not with the ubiquitous "white powder" threat convictions, that are "a dime a dozen."

It can also be said that whenever the FBI director(s) himself, the US Attorney General, the President and his personal advisor, any member of the NSC or Department of State personally involved themselves in a "criminal" case—it is not good and it is no good that they are up to. But when those exact people begin to conspire there is a reason for it. They are not meeting and talking about "police work" and being briefed on how it is going. They are meeting and determining how it is *going* to go.

The false narrative of the cabal (typical Brennan-plant a story) then use the planted narrative as reference into a perpetual disparaging of the target, prevents any counter-narrative etc) includes the commonly-thought and often-repeated claim that Dutschke admitted to the mailing and to "framing" Curtis. The actual record, however, shows that is not at all true. He *never* admitted to such a thing and, in fact, suffered his way all the way to prison, to the US ADX National Security Unit (SAM unit) constantly repeating that Curtis was in fact the mailer, not Dutschke, even chastising the entire courtroom including the media and the judge by asking "Why are you all still pretending?"

But as was stated in a CBS interview, by the Attorney General, "History is written by the victors!"

This is undoubtedly especially true when "victors" have won by cheating and by making sure no one can learn the truth, for when the truth is unavailable (because the SAM sequestered it from the press) then the common-folk will accept any myth that makes it to their unsophisticated ears.

It is documented fact that the players of the high-cabal: Obama, Brennan, Secretary of State (Clinton/Abedin), Mueller, Holder, Comey, Boente, Sigler, Yates, possibly Clapper, later Lynch, and countless other levels underneath them, all had crossed Everett at one point or another over a decade; most were directly involved in the 2013 Operation Dojo.

It is documented fact that the highest of these were all part of the PDB and it is likely that this part of the meetings were not actually led/controlled by Obama (though he may have thought himself in charge of the meetings) but by Brennan's manipulations which would have included manipulations of even Holder (AG) and Mueller (FBI).

It is documented fact that the (likely Brennan-contrived) narrative (which, in his typical fashion was "handed-off" to LEOs of FBI/DOJ) was somewhat "busted" when the FBI began running additional microoperations to add plea-pressure (coordinated by McCabe and primarily Thomason) which were patently false FBI claims (Brennan should have known the inept FBI would screw things up, as they do) and when the government's very own laboratory analyses debunked their narrative (Brennan and Holder did not foresee the possibility of Everett Dutschke's double double-cross of distrust against Brennan when Everett made sure that the 2013 Curtis received decoy product was *not* the same as the 2012 Libyan product).

It is documented fact that the instant the cabal learned of the final lab results which proved, as Everett had implied, that their claim of a "deadly" chemical weapon of assassination was a completely inert and harmless decoy version, that the FBI (Mueller) and DOJ (Holder) panicked (since their public claim was now proven false) and went into "cover-up" mode, issuing the executive SAM order.

It is a documented fact that the same people remained a part of the case even as Brennan was rewarded by Obama's appointment of Brennan as DCI to lead Brennan's former agency and Comey appointed to FBI director.

It is a known fact that Hillary Clinton had indicated to Brennan and Comey that she'd keep both men on when "her time" came.

There is one thing that Americans and the rest of the known world would do well to keep in mind—when all these specific people are involved (Obama, Brennan, Clinton, Rice, Comey, Mueller, Thomason et al), whatever is the official story is definitely *not* the truth.

Chapter 6

The SAM Prosecution — "Guilt" by Royal Decree

Now imagine, for a moment, that you are "arrested". FBI teams show up at your house, late at night, surround it and say you must go with them. You have not been indicted for anything, nor have you actually broken any law. You are held isolated. You are told that an attorney has been appointed for you, someone you've never met and do not know. You are given no paperwork, no "legal discovery" (casework), nothing but a roll of toilet paper. Your hostage-takers don you into orange prison scrubs. You ask to ring your spouse, the "answer" is "NO". Your mother. The answer is "NO". Your so-called attorney, the answer is... pause... "NO". You ask why you are being kept in such extreme solitary confinement. The answer is "We cannot tell you that." Your court-appointed attorney finally arrives one day and meets with those people in the jail that are on his "caseload" and allots each one five minutes. He has to get to lunch.

Your hostage-keepers finally toss you into a glass room with this solicitor who tells you that the Attorney General has been given the executive power of the President to hold you in such a fashion and has personally signed such an order stating that you can have no communication with any person at any time for any purpose, even through your attorney to any person because *he*, too, is bound by your new, sudden rules. "Can you call my wife," you ask, "Let her know that I am alive?" He answers, "No." I cannot contact any person on your behalf either. I cannot tell anyone that you said you "feel fine" or even tell the press, who is demolishing you, that you are innocent. If I do, then I go to prison for 10 years, just like Lynne Stewart, attorney for Omar Abdel-Rahman did and for a decade. This is the only communication allowed and you only have four minutes left."

"Four minutes for what?" you ask.

"Four minutes, now less than that," he answers, "to tell me what we do and how to handle your defence."

"Defence...against what?"

"Everything they accuse you of," he answers.

"What are they accusing me of?" you ask. "What the hell is going on here?"

Your lawyer then looks at his watch and sighs, "Lots of stuff. They say there's ten thousand pages worth of evidence. They are telling the press that evidence is overwhelming."

"Evidence of what? It is impossible. There is no evidence of anything! Let's see it!"

184

Your lawyer shrugs, "Well I don't HAVE it with me. And you're not allowed to have anything. If there's evidence that you think can be disputed or objected to in some way, then you need to tell me what it is."

"Dispute what? Object to WHAT? How can I dispute or object to anything that I've never seen? There IS none."

Your attorney reminds you that there are only three minutes left, then, "I can look at it for you. I'll tell you and show you what I think you need to see."

"You?!?" You ask. "No. I need to see it all. All of it. If they claim they have 10,000 pages of proof, then I need it. I am the one who needs to see it. You can't possibly know anything about any of it."

He shrugs again, "Well, they gave me some CD-ROMs, it is all on there. I am not going to print everything out. That takes time and I've got other cases. I'm just not going to."

You are shocked into silence. This man appointed to "help" you has just informed you that he does not *feel* like helping you. It would just be too much trouble. "This is my LIFE we are talking about here!" You say.

He shakes his head and sighs, "I suppose I could go through the CDs and print out a few things...I'll see you next week."

"Next week?!? What about tomorrow? We need to be in this room every day, for hours a day. What do you mean next week?"

"I have other cases," he reminds you.

"I don't care about other cases. Listen, have you ever gone up against these people before? Have you ever won? At trial"

"I do okay. Your judge appointed me for a reason."

"That's exactly my point. Have you ever beaten this prosecutor at trial?"

"Well, no...but they are offering you a plea. 40 years. Otherwise it is life in prison."

"I am over forty now! Forty *is* life in prison. We are going to trial. They can't get away with this."

The lawyer stands and buzzes the guard to bring in the next on his "caseload," "I'll see you next week."

The next week is exactly the same.

You are told the Attorney General's executive order is called a SAM order. You tell your lawyer to get rid of it so that you can be allowed to defend your case in the manner that has been long-since established as a minimum of appropriate since the current conditions do not even meet the minimum standards.

His answer is, "I have only been appointed to handle your federal criminal charges, no SAM order or any other stuff."

"It is all related! It is all the same!" you remind him. "Then get me a copy of this SAM order you and the Marshals claim exists. I want to see it. If *you* won't fight it, I'll do it myself."

"I can't give it to you or even show it to you. But I've seen it. The AG signed it himself. I've never seen or heard of such a thing before. Neither have the Marshals. But I can't give you a copy. You're not allowed to have anything."

"Then I don't even know such a thing exists."

"It exists. I've seen it."

"You say *you* have," you point out, "but I have not. Prove to me it exists."

"If it did not exist," your lawyers tells you, "they wouldn't be holding you like this."

"That is exactly my point," you tell him. "It's not right. This needs to be fought. And since *you're* too scared to do it. Then I will."

"It can not be fought. There is no process for disputing it."

"There *has* to be. We can't—I can't fight this case, especially *this* case by sitting in that cell with nothing but a roll of toilet paper. You know that cell is made of 347 concrete blocks...counting the halves?"

"You counted the blocks? That's good."

"No. I need to be working on this case. And we need to get rid of this SAM."

"But the President wants you convicted."

"I'll bet he does. That's why you got to fight it! Fight it. Like the way the system is supposed to work."

"They say they're going to remove that 40 year plea deal if you don't take it."

"THAT is not fighting! Screw them. I have to clear my name. We are going to trial, I told you before. Did you bring any casework, any of their evidence they claim they have?"

Your lawyer shakes his head, "You didn't tell me what to print."

"How can I tell you what to print and bring if I don't know what there IS to print or what any of it says unless you print and bring it first?"

"Soo..." your lawyer clicks his pen, "We just deny everything then? Times over."

Time is over. The next week goes exactly the same. So do all the next ones. Eventually, your appointed lawyer tells you that your wife has an attorney appointed to her, and the Justice Department is going to indict her. The press has been reporting lies about you and the "evidence" for almost a year. Nothing has happened because you refuse to sign their plea deal. Accusations keep coming. Your bank has frozen your account for the FBI (without a warrant), your friends and family are "turned" from helping you and all this— leaves you stuck with this attorney who is *not* representing you the way your own, personal, attorney would. But you cannot call or write your personal attorney. He is not allowed contact with you. And because you cannot go to the bank, you cannot get to your money to hire him anyway—not that it matters since the FBI has hijacked your accounts, denying you access. Your "appointed" lawyer is experienced in plea agreements, nothing more. He has never handled a case this high-profile. He has never handled a national security case. And, like every other lawyer, has never dealt with a treaty violation, especially the development of a biological weapon. The opposing prosecutorial lawyers have an unlimited budget and have enlisted every single agency in government (except CIA, who is silent, as always) and there are teams of lawyers working on the prosecution, each one with his own team of investigators, researchers, consultants, media spokespersons, paralegals, secretaries and their own budgets and resources. Your attorney, because of the SAM, cannot enlist any assistance at all so it is just him. Just the one guy, with a small-capped budget and zero experience or appetite for the case who does *not* consult with you, does not spend any time on your case and knows *nothing* about the actual written laws of which you've been charged. The only cases he knows are drug-possession, stolen cars and the like. The only defence he has ever used is surrender, waving the white flag of plea agreements.

You have been a sitting duck for a year and each time you refuse to capitulate to their plea agreement, they ramp up the pressure—adding some new accusation or claim, committing some new attack against your liberty, your person, your reputation or your family. Now that your attorney tells you they are about to indict your wife at the next grand jury, you sign the plea, hoping to fight the conviction on the other side and that they would drop the Attorney General's executive SAM order.

They don't.

You realise that the threat to indict and arrest your wife might have been a bluff, since their "evidence" was all a lie, just like every press report. You are taken to court for a plea (entering the agreement) and the media is all present, wall-to-wall, to witness the event. Your lawyer did not even arrange for you to appear in real clothes. You are brought in wearing the orange prison garb that says "guilty." The judge asks someone on the prosecution team to read what is called "statement of facts". You are advised by your lawyer that if you want the plea to stick, you have to agree with everything the prosecutor says about you.

The prosecutor reads aloud. It is all lies. Every bit of it. And you know that they know it and so does the judge and your lawyer who told you to just "go along" or you will be sentenced to life.

The judge asks you if what the prosecutor just read is true.

You answer, "Not at all!"

That wasn't supposed to happen. The press came to see a hangin'. You were supposed to just go along.

You are taken back to your concrete box. The SAM order is still not lifted. You tell your attorney you demand to see the laboratory evidence, because they lied to everyone including the press. Miraculously, he (eventually) returns in two weeks with copies of a few (not all) of the exculpatory evidence which proves they lied but says he will NOT print anymore since you signed the plea unless your wish is to withdraw. You are NOT yet convicted. But your "lawyer" is now refusing to help you defend your case because "you already signed."

"I'm not going through that discovery," he tells you, "the case is over."

Though you are not convicted. He steps out of the room and you stuff the lab reports he brought into your socks and hit the button summoning the guards. Your lawyer returns and says he will see you next week. He does not. Or the next. Or the next.

A report "for sentencing" (PSR) is prepared. It is all lies. Your lawyer does not want to object to any of it. You refuse, telling him he HAS to object to every lie in the prosecutor's report, which is all of it. He sighs and does so.

Many weeks later, you are dragged, in orange and chains, to court. The judge pays no attention to the objections, only whatever the prosecutor says. In doing so, the judge violates the law but she is in a hurry. There are other cases and the courtroom is now standing room only, it is so packed. So she won't be embarrassed by any "truth-telling" today. You have already informed your lawyer, after his weak performance at the last hearing, that you will speak for yourself. Despite that, he does speak, nonsense, and causes more harm than help. He has spent more time consulting with the prosecutors in this case than the principle, you.

You speak and assert your innocence no less than 25 times. Leaving no doubt that you are not guilty. Not once have you admitted to the prosecution's impossible narrative, or any of their claimed details because you cannot ADMIT to something you've not done. That would be a lie. So, to tell the truth, you are forced to deny everything. You try to withdraw from the plea. The hearing ends to reconvene (again) later.

The prosecution uses a trick to ensure the plea cannot be withdrawn. You are innocent. The judge, prosecutors, your appointed lawyer and the press don't care.

You are convicted anyway.

In your mind, now that they got the prosecution they were so desperate for, the pressure would be off and they would drop the SAM order, send you to a place where there are the legal resources and opportunity to fight the conviction on appeal, because sometimes second chances happen, especially since you are innocent of everything they have accused. Innocent people aren't allowed to stay in prison are they?

That relief does not happen. The SAM order remains.

You are specially flown to the highest security unit in the highest "Supermax" prison facility in the entire country and quickly learn, surrounded by other spies and some of the highest-level terrorists in the world, that that particular unit you are now a part of is also on a communications ban, everyone here has been sent here to be disappeared, everyone in here is in the Attorney-General's custody.

This is the SAM unit.

Unlike what you have seen on the telly, there are no prisoners in libraries learning the law. There is no library. You are not allowed any books that have been or could be shared. Unlike what you have seen in the movies, there are no inmate football teams playing football. Your limited "recreation" consists of the shackling of hands and feet and being shuffled into a large "dog cage" in an area which has no roof. THAT is considered "outside". Unlike the documentaries and dramatisations, there is no mingling or consulting with some "jailhouse lawyer" because there is just you. Unlike the telly, there is no writing a letter to a friend or lawyer to help you, there is no writing anyone. Unlike the films where some heroic attorney gets a phone call from a prisoner then takes up the prisoner's cause eventually winning the innocent man's freedom, there is no one heroic you can call and for three reasons—

1.) There are no heroes left in America since no one cares unless it is happening to themselves;

2.) You were flown here with nothing, no names, addresses, nothing at all;

3.) There are no phone calls. Not to an attorney, even your own attorney of record, not to the press, not to anyone.

This is the SAM unit; the one place in the country where the Constitution does not apply and the scant few cases ever filed against a SAM has proven that judges are afraid to touch it since every SAM must be a matter of "national security".

You are denied the right to counsel, or anyone who can intervene or help, because the objective of the SAM unit is not just to make sure you stay convicted by procedural denial, in daily practise, of due process, it is also to "disappear" you.

Your plan to "fight it on the other side of the conviction" is deflated. You demand that they justify these extreme conditions. You are reminded that you are on SAM. You demand to see their justifications for and proof you are on a SAM, a copy of it. After some prolonged nonsensical "administrative remedy" battle, their "proof" of the SAM is to then type up a letter that tells you you're on a SAM. They do not provide you actual proof of the actual SAM. They do not give you a copy of it. They merely typed something up stating that you are under a SAM. You were told it was the last act of the outgoing Attorney General Holder, and endorsed by the FBI Director Comey.

As to the "justifications"? They fabricate on a memo a collection of lies, alleged "crimes" you are supposed to be guilty of though you have never been convicted or even indicted for any of the rubbish on their list. Some of the allegations are quite impossible. Because you know it is all made-up, you demand to challenge the baseless allegations on which the SAM is based. You are reminded that you cannot challenge anything. There IS no challenge to the SAM order.

Everything written above is not a hypothetical, conjectural, supposed or fictitious series of occurrences. Everything above is *exactly* what happened to Dutschke as documented. And even *that* is the truncated version. Devoid of the details of it all. The expanded telling of the reality of it includes details that should shock the conscience even further, if possible. Not only is this not hypothetical, it is real, and it is in America... "The land of the free." It is entirely unconstitutional in every regard, and because it is used in espionage cases, it is used on the very people who took the oath of service to protect the Constitution against such acts as this.

The SAM is an act of sedition. It is a tool of power, nothing more. Generally speaking—the SAM is an executive order which derives its power from the President that he grants to only one man, the Attorney General of the United States as appointed by him and approved by the US Senate, not a "deputy A.G.", not any designee or U.S. Attorney. Not even a U.S. federal judge has that "authority". The SAM is only invoked in "matters of National Security" according to the regulations 28 CFR§501.2 and 501.3. But it does not happen in a vacuum. Because the SAM is an extension of presidential power, this is not a tool that can be invoked behind the president's back. All of those that are cabinet-level (as the A.G. is) are acting on behalf of and with the approval of the President. But it is the Attorney General, himself, who writes and "enacts" the SAM. According to the regulations, the AG's SAM is not written by the A.G. with only the President's blessing alone. The regulations (28 CFR§501) require the written endorsement of the HEAD of a member of the intelligence community(.2) and the written endorsement of the HEAD of a federal law enforcement agency (.3), and no one else. No "deputy" or "assistant" director can (legally) suffice to endorse a SAM. There does not need to be any conviction or even an accusation. Just any person. Now specifically speaking—the President whose power was being used against Everett Dutschke was President Barack Hussein Obama. The Attorney General who was granted the SAM authority and wrote/signed the Dutschke SAM was Eric H. Holder. The "HEAD of the IC agency"—at the time was the Director of the CIA, John Brennan, (according to court filings) never even endorsed the Holder SAM (as .2 requires). The "HEAD a federal law enforcement" at the time (2013) was FBI director Robert Mueller, III, who *did* personally endorse the Holder SAM on Dutschke, and when Mueller resigned, the SAM was then endorsed (according to the regulations) by Mueller's replacement, James Comey. All this is a matter of record.

The National Security unit inside ADX-Supermax is a small unit of around only 30 people being held hostage, all with the similar commonality that they are, every last one on an active SAM order. Because SAM does not require a conviction, and because the Bureau of Prisons has absolutely no say-so, no power and cannot designate anyone *to* a SAM or *off-of* a SAM, everyone in the small unit is, legally, under A.G. custody, not BOP custody—which is one area in which things get murky. For this reason, this small "Supermax" Uber-secure unit is called the SAM unit. (Or "Special Security Unit").

The word "SAM" itself, is such a vague phrase that it holds no inherent specific meaning as it is an acronym of the very, very, very, very vague "Special Administrative Measures." They can stretch it to mean whatever the A.G. wishes it to mean.

It is critical to understand, in Dutschke's case, the exact timeline and specific timing of the SAM's imposition. It is also critical to realise that in a logical and factual world, where one is entirely honest about things, things happen for a reason. There exists cause and effect. In the "justice system", especially one run by the cabal at the highest level, there are no "coincidences." and the documented timing is exactly as follows:

- The FBI (Mueller) reports to the press in April that the KC letters are "laced with ricin, a deadly poison with no known antidote."

- The sock-puppet media compete with each other to see who can regurgitate that story the most, the loudest and the longest.

- Then, as early as May 2nd, which is *before* Dutschke's indictment, the government's very own lab analysis contradicts that claim. The DOJ prosecution team (Holder/Lamar/Sigler) and FBI (Mueller) hide this from the press, because it differs from what was already reported.

- The DOJ and FBI hide this from Dutschke and his first appointed attorney as well (Lucas).

- The press continues to report, loudly, the original claim, with no knowledge of the lab analysis.

- The FBI (Mueller) put FBI agent Thomason on the stand at the grand jury who never mentions the actual lab analysis. Thomason lies about the DNA and "ricin" on the dust mask while under oath. The prosecutors (Lamar/Sigler) suppress exculpatory evidence from the grand jury who thinks they have no choice but to indict.

- The media still reports, constantly, the original claim, now bolstered by the indictment which claims the 3 KC letters were "laced with" a deadly poison "to wit-ricin" as well as the dust mask claim.

- Not a single reporter or legal analyst in the country (nor Dutschke's own appointed lawyer, Lucas) noticed that the prosecutors indicted for a biological weapon instead of a chemical weapon (as "ricin" is legally defined).
- The media continues to report the original claim
- Dutschke insists on seeing the actual lab analysis and toxicity analysis of the product in the KC envelopes. The CDC analysis shows the "positive-swabs" were *not* positive! That is hidden by DOJ.
- Dutschke still insists the lab analyses will exonerate him. The analyses are still being hidden.
- The press continues to report the original claim
- Late at night on October 7th, 2013 Fort Detrick completes the long-awaited toxicity analysis on the KC product. It is *not* toxic at all. It does *not* cross the prosecutorial threshold.
- October 8th, 2013. The FBI (Mueller) and DOJ (Holder, Lamar, Sigler) see the Fort Detrick toxicity analysis and panic. They have been telling the press, judge, and Dutschke's lawyer for 6 months that there was a "deadly poison, ricin, with no known antidote", and the media obediently reporting the same. Dutschke has been insisting it was a lie the whole time and now the government's very own lab report proves that Dutschke, not the administration, was right. The twist (a Dutschke double-cross of Brennan's double-cross) was not expected. If this was to become known (and it would if Dutschke goes to trial) the cabal would be exposed as liars. If they give this to Dutschke (Lucas), as discovery rules require if going to trial, Dutschke would certainly give copies to the press, proving publicly that it was a lie, a sham, a farce, a disinformation campaign by the cabal, already skilled at it. This October 8th 2013 analysis cannot ever become known. What on earth is the cabal to do?
- October 9th, 2013. Less than 24 hours after the DOJ/FBI learns that their very own laboratories' very own documents destroy their narrative and the indictment, Eric Holder writes and signs the SAM order. All legal casework in Dutschke's possession is confiscated. Holder orders that Dutschke is not allowed any communications with any person whatsoever. Lucas does not sign the unconstitutional "SAM attorney affirmation", he withdraws from the case. Dutschke is tossed into near-torture conditions.
- Attorney Ken Coghlan is appointed to the case (signing the "SAM attorney affirmation"), yet Dutschke has no idea that any attorney whatsoever is "representing" him. The media never learned any of it.
- Dutschke still has no idea that any of the exculpatory lab analysis exists, and still demands it, proclaiming he is going to trial. This is an

obvious problem for the cabal who cannot be exposed as the liars they are. They ramp up the pressures and tactics. The press continues the original narrative.

- Coglan refuses to address the SAM restrictions of his client, believing that the SAM restrictions will be removed when Dutschke finally surrenders to the plea.

- Eventually (January 2014) a plea is forced from Dutschke, though he maintains his innocence even during the hearings (all of them) and in filed court documents (every single document filed). *After* the plea was signed, a few of the exculpatory lab analyses are seen (and stolen) by Dutschke, the CDC "swab" analysis produced *after* the sentencing, via FOIA.

The important event in the above document a timeline was a receipt of the final toxicity analysis of the KC letters themselves, which proved that the FBI (Mueller/Comey/Thomason) and DOJ (Holder/Boente/Sigler/Lamar) had, in fact, been lying to the press (and grand jury, and two judges) all along. Because the Mueller/Holder teams were too publicly invested in their phony narrative, the next day (Oct 9th) Dutschke was silenced and legally blinded by the SAM order.

Again, they learned the truth on one day—they ensured no one can find out about it on the very next day.

There are no "coincidences". The timing is clear. The impetus and intent was suppression of the truth, triggered on October 9th, by the administration's very own Fort Detrick analysis.

The press however, did not know any better. They never learned the truth for it was suppressed, snuffed out by the SAM. So the media continued, the entire time, to report only the lies. The lies they did not know had been debunked by the government's own labs.

Will the media now apologise to Dutschke or make any attempt to make right? Doubtful. To do so is an admission that they were, in fact, wrong... and at a time when a man's life was at stake. For them, what value can a man's life be when compared to their ego? Egos which might be bruised in any acknowledgment that they, the "Fourth Estate", had been desperate to do the dirty public bidding of men who had lost any semblance of humanity whence men became drunk on their own power.

The SAM is one (of many) egregious crimes by Holder and the rest of the cabal. But the media's failure to simply think for itself, its own unquestioning blind reporting of anything the exalted administration wanted, was ITS criminal acts. There was not a single thing that administration did in the Dutschke case that meets any standard at all of what Americans are taught is the cornerstone of justice. There is nothing they claimed that was actually true and the signs of it were everywhere. There were more red flags over this case than over a weekend used-car lot sale. Yet the media did not bother to make even the basic and obvious inquiries. Even *after* Dutschke read aloud from some of the exculpatory documents at sentencing, the sycophantic 2014 press characterised Dutschke stating his innocence, then reading the proof of it aloud, as "a rant".

So someone cannot state their innocence (a "rant") but it would be just fine to state their guilt? In other words, to the media, the lies from the administration (for over a year) were just fine, but not the truth from Dutschke? Really?

This was the media's failure, and it had permanent results. Consider this IF the media had done its job and exposed the cabal in 2013-2014, then the 2016-2019 Crossfire operations would *not have happened*!

It is *because* the cabal (the President, Holder, Mueller, Comey, Clinton/Abedin, Boente, Sigler, McCabe, Yates, Power, Rice, Lamar, Thomason, Brennan, Clapper, Strozk et al) was able to get away with Operation Dojo (and other things) before, that they viewed themselves as untouchable instruments of unlimited and unbridled power whose primary job is to protect itself and solidify more power. Certainly, they were emboldened with the case at which the media was manipulated and controlled in 2013-2014 (Operation Dojo).

And although the SAM order prevented either Dutschke or his appointed "lawyer", Coghlan, from communicating to the press, *that* SAM order alone should have caused even the most simple-minded (and they all must be) to ask, "Wait a minute! Something fishy is going on here. What are the prosecutors trying to hide?"

But they did not.

The end result is that the cabal kept it up, even *after* they were out of office and targeting others (2016-20).

Incidentally, the standard of what warrants a criminal investigation into "election meddling" seems to have changed simply because the cabal was now in control of that standard.

In 2004, when Dutschke (and others) found foreign (even terrorists) interfering (money) in the Kerry campaign, nothing happened. It did not ever become a criminal investigation.

In 2008, when the same thing was discovered, again nothing happened. No criminal investigation (for *that* campaign). Even worse 2012 malfeasance resulted in exactly nothing but shrugs.

Yet in 2016, all of a sudden everyone wanted to pretend that it actually happened, then it became a big deal.

Hm... Why?

Because the standards (in 2016) were set (now) by the very ones who benefited from the *actual* election frauds of 2004 and 2008. And once again, the media proved itself to be more interested in agenda than in fairness or truth.

Considering who he is, Dutschke did find clandestine means to contact a reporter, subverting the SAM, yet because it was not the kind of reporter that was at least bit interested in the actual details, nothing came of it at all. Here Dutschke was, risking further prosecution, giving a reporter the story of the century, giving someone a chance to break the story that no one else could get (because of the SAM) and *directly* from the source! But she did nothing with it. When this was, much later, discovered—DOJ officials personally visited Dutschke *at his cell* in the US-ADX and threatened to prosecute him for it. He dared them to (prosecution means court, which means discovery, which means public) They did not. It was all more bluster and lies (same as before).

A primary objective of the SAM was to cut Dutschke off from the media. It is important to remember that the Dutschke SAM order by Holder was written before there was (forced) conviction. The way that 28CFR§501 is written, believe it or not, does not require one. The target of the executive order for such extreme imprisonment ("disappearing") need not be guilty of anything. The regulation simply says "any person", guilty or not—crime or not. This sounds unbelievable, but it is not only true (and published) it is what happened.

The SAM is a clear violation of the US Constitution's Bill of Rights. The SAM violates the First Amendment Freedom of the Press. Of course, it is intended to do so, and such was the intent of the cabal in 2013. The Freedom of the Press, in the First Amendment, does not simply guarantee that the press is free to report what it wants (which was not a problem in 2013 since what it wanted to report is whatever the Obama cabal told the press it wanted to report), it also guarantees freedom of access of citizens *to* the press. Numerous Supreme Court cases have decidedly defended this interpretation—and so it is a matter of law. Constitutional law.

The most acute concern that the cabal had was that Dutschke would get information to a reporter (in fact, their original impetus for the entire scheme was that he had). In the case of Obama, Holder, Mueller, Comey, Yates, Brennan, Lamar, Thomason—it was of great concern that the press would discover that the entire Operation Dojo was a lie and that the lab reports which proved it would become public. The Obama regime would not tolerate such insolence as the reporting of the truth and Mueller/Comey's FBI feared any further embarrassment. As for the larger criminal syndicate of Obama, Hillary Clinton/Abedin, Brennan (and a bit of Morell) it was of great concern that Dutschke could/had/might get the Tripoli File into the hands of a reporter that still cared about the truth (if any still existed) which would have revealed such a massive shocking spree of related atrocities against America that would have caused the D.C. halls of power to crumble and sink into the sea like Atlantis. It was critical that no one in the press got access to the original Tripoli File or even an encrypted version of it. As long as Dutschke and his unenlightened attorney were kept from the media (illegal or not) the cabal would be safe. Meanwhile, they would continue to demolish his reputation and credibility so that no reporter would associate with him. The two reporters who Dutschke had preferred, the same two they thought he had already communicated with (Atkisson, Rosen) would find themselves targets of 2013 intimidation, harassment and professional attacks. (Even Rosen's parents were surveilled)

Because the SAM continued even *after* conviction, there was not a way for any interested media person to inquire directly with the source of any person in the SAM unit. As far as those in the SAM unit are concerned, to the media, all of them simply ceased to exist. This is by design. The entire reason the SAM unit exists (and to some extent, the CMU unit elsewhere) is so that no one outside that unit can ever learn the things that the SAM prisoners know. And they know a lot. That's *why* they are there.

Plus, in the media vacuum it was much easier for the administration to establish whatever narrative it wanted, even an impossible one, to become the "history" since there was no opposing narrative to worry about. The cabal's tale would become the accepted "version" propagated by the obedient mediabots, simply by default. When the other team does not show up to play the game (even if it is because they are held hostage somewhere) then they forfeit the game.

Considering that part of the pressure to sign the plea stems from the constant media barrage that has as its mission the severing of any and all support from any potential supporters by the constant smearing (that would, if against an average citizen be an illegal act of defamation), the media is nothing but a force multiplier of the prosecutors (who arranged for the SAM in the first place). The press is a tool of the FBI, and for some unknown reason, is either not smart enough to figure that out, too lazy to bother asserting its duty to be independent or simply not mind being used like a two-dollar whore because they have the same agenda. Since the press *is* a de facto part of the conviction machine (which is why prosecutors and FBI train on and count on how to manipulate them), then that is where much of the "dirty work" of the prosecution takes place. The press releases and whatever is the law enforcement equivalent of RUMINT do not require that either the authoring, leaking or gossiping agent be under oath (not that oaths or truthfulness matters in court anyway since prosecutors and FBI run the courts). Because of the immense power that force multipliers (the press) has, equal access is critical to fairness. In cases like this that are tried in the press, a trial by public opinion (and judges are not immune), no trial can be a fair trial since only one side is heard. (Too bad no one in the media possessed the integrity or courage to demand fairness. The SAM, if one considers it logically, is an attack *on the press* as well as the target).

Thus the violation of fairness by the total forced muting of Dutschke was a travesty of justice of biblical proportions, one that should be repulsive to any constitutionalist or fair-minded person of any integrity whatsoever *and* to every reporter in America, who have now proven that they did not fit the description.

The SAM is violative also of the First Amendment Freedom of Speech. But what good is the right to speak if no one else is allowed to hear it? Any other person has a right to write to or call his wife, his mother, his lawyer or even, as above, the press. Dutschke had not been convicted...of *anything*, yet no communication was allowed with any human being. This is the SAM. Why?

Because someone might listen, that's why. Because it cripples the defence, that's why. Because the cabal does not want fairness in this case, that's why. To guarantee a conviction, that's why ("just get it done, Bob"). If someone hears Dutschke, they might begin to use their brain and realise the entire thing is rubbish. Worse yet, they might start digging around and discover something.

To tell Dutschke, "you are not allowed, by order of this government, to say anything to any person," is the literal definition of a violation of freedom of speech. It does not get any more clear and obvious than that. And in writing! "No communication of any kind with any person." How can any of that regime's apologists possibly make any credible claim that the phrase means something other than what it says?

The SAM was violative of the First Amendment right to "petition the government for a redress of grievance." When the SAM order is written, that is it. It is over. The AG, on behalf of the President, is judge, jury and executioner. There is absolutely NO process at all in which someone can refute it (and even the courts, who are terrified to address the issue, have allowed it to be this way). No way exists in which to dispute it and no mechanism for even challenging it, either on its imposed conditions or "rationale". Even when rare SAM cases have been filed in court, the trembling judges have dismissed the case because the administration, in imposition of the SAM, has invoked the words "National Security", causing the judges to claim that the executive branch of government "has wide discretion." Apparently it is so wide that the Constitution fell into it, never to be seen again.

The SAM, by its nature, is an administrative act imposed upon an individual. Adverse administrative acts are supposed to be governed, by statute, by the Administrative Procedures Act (APA), which is supposed to impose and enforce constitutional strictures on all administrative actions. Supposed to.

There is no law, no statute passed by Congress which gives the President and Attorney General SAM power. In fact, there is NO statute, no law anywhere at which even mentions it. It can only be found as a self-given regulation where the executive branch awards itself such power to nullify the Constitution and statutory law. There IS a statutory law which requires a *meaningful* administrative remedy procedure, the APA. Statutory law is supposed to take precedence over a regulation. A law has been passed by the proper and representative process in both houses of Congress and been signed by the President. A regulation has done none of that. Thus a regulation, constitutionally, is not law. In matters of law, the actual written law is supposed to be what controls over an agency's self-written regulation. Supposed to.

The US Constitution, which "guarantees" in the First Amendment the right "to petition the government for a redress of grievances", is supposed to be the supreme law of the land. The SAM, however, has no process to meet that First Amendment "guarantee". Thus, there really is no "guarantee" is there? The Constitution, not a regulation, is supposed to be that supreme law. Supposed to.

American judges are not the bold champions of liberty that the American founding fathers intended. They no longer have the same mission. Instead of ensuring that the citizen is not trampled over by tyrannical acts of government, today's spineless judges are but a rubber-stamp to tyranny. There may, now and then, be a scatterings of cases where a judge has a fit of conscience and proves that statement wrong, but those scatterings are a matter of instance not of generality. And those scatterings are becoming even more rare. The very SAM cases filed come from New York or Washington DC/Virginia (where a SAM is initially written), Colorado (which is where the US-ADX and the SAM unit is) or the unique Dutschke post-SAM filing in Arizona federal court. In every one of the very few SAM cases filed, it is easy to see that judges, ever-eager to award more power to DOJ and ignore constitutional protections of citizens, almost desperately search for reasons to dismiss such cases, usually by entirely misconstruing or ignoring the specifically raised issues the judge was tasked to address, proving that law is now irrelevant to judges.

The SAM violates the Fourth Amendment right from unreasonable search and seizure. This amendment to the Bill of Rights, the Fourth, includes "papers and effects" explicitly in the language of it. It "guarantees" that "shall not be violated." Yet when the SAM was written, the DOJ/FBI immediately "seized" Dutschke's legal casework, including privileged notes and letters to and from the previously appointed counsel (Lucas). Dutschke was *not* allowed to have any discovery and as the Arizona SAM filings reveal, even to this day, years *after* conviction (and the canceling of the SAM), the DOJ still will not return his own legal casework to his possession and control. Why? According to his attorney, inside that case work includes transcripts of the Curtis hearings, which demonstrate that the FBI knew with certainty that Curtis, not Dutschke, was the mailer and that testimony is under-oath FBI testimony. Anyone else in the world can access and print that transcript. Anyone but Dutschke, who is not allowed to have it. According to his attorney, inside that casework includes actual copies of exculpatory lab work which completely contradicts the FBI report, agent testimony of Thomason and every word the news media regurgitated. Any person on the planet can access, print and possess these exculpatory lab reports. Anyone but Dutschke, as the Arizona filings reveal. Privileged correspondence from his attorney? Nope. Can't have it. The exculpatory copy of the letter the FBI tried to conceal? Nope. Can't have it. The mobile phone records the FBI tried to conceal? Nope. Can't have that either. Well then, what can he have? Nothing that helps tell the truth, nothing that points to his innocence, nothing that reveals the FBI knew Curtis was the mailer, nothing that shows any FBI contradictions which leaves...really nothing.

Another egregious example of the Fourth Amendment violation will be outlined in a Fifth Amendment example below. But the idea, here, is that if a person is innocent and announces that he has documented proof of the innocence, or that an FBI agent lied, or the existence of any document which aids his case, then the FBI steps in and steals everything away leaving nothing but a roll of tissue behind, then the same FBI/DOJ had free reign to then (*after* their pinching the documents) say, "Oh yeah? Show us? Oh... you don't have it? Well then... too bad for you."

It is both unbelievable and inconceivable, and every other word of that connotation, that one does not have to be guilty of or even charged with a crime to be subject to a SAM order. There are approximately 330 million Americans and only a small handful of them have ever even heard of such a thing. The number of people in the country that are actually under a SAM order at any given time is 1:35 million or 1.000000002857143%. There is a much larger percentage of Americans that have won the lottery. There is a much larger percentage of Americans that have been struck by lightning. There is actually a larger percentage of Americans who are nuns who have won the lottery, and a larger percentage of bus drivers who have been struck by lightning. But nonetheless, it exists; not in some dark, oppressive dictator-run police state but in "Shining City on a hill," The United States.

It does not matter if Americans don't want to or refuse to believe it, it is real and it exists. And quite frankly, that tendency of most Americans to purposely close their eyes to uncomfortable realities is exactly how the DOJ/FBI wants it.

The SAM order is a violation of the Fifth Amendment right "to due process of law". It violates the critical "notice requirement" of due process. Although the SAM regulations (28 CFR§501.2 and .3) do state in writing that the AG is required to deliver to the SAM target the notification of exactly *how* the target, is a threat to national security, thereby warranting the SAM, it is revealed in Dutschke's SAM court case filings from both Colorado (where the ADX-SAM unit is) and Arizona that the SAM has *never* been delivered to him. Therefore he has never even seen it.

This is insane.

~~When one is written a ticket for a traffic violation, he is given a copy~~ of that very ticket. When an arrest warrant is executed, the arrestee is served a copy of that document. When one is indicted, the indicted person is served a copy of the indictment. These are documents that give notification of whatever the accusation is (and it must be specifically detailed to be valid).

Yet with the SAM order, at least as applied to Dutschke, this fundamental constitutional right was *not* observed. The Constitution (the supreme law of the land) requires it. The SAM regulation itself requires it. Yet how is Dutschke supposed to know it even exists if he has not even seen it? The court documents show that not only did the DOJ (Holder et al) conceal and falsify the SAM order, but they violated the Constitution (and their own regulations) never delivering it to him. The court filings make equally clear that both the judges that he took the case before had absolutely *no* regard (Zipps, Matsch) whatsoever for the statutory law (the APA requires that an agency follow its own rules), or the Constitution itself as both spinelessly dismissed "for lack of jurisdiction" (subject-matter). A Court's failure to recognise jurisdiction, according to long-established American law (Wheat) is an act of judicial treason.

Fifth Amendment due process is also violated by the SAM accusation's inability to be adjudicated. The SAM order Holder wrote on Dutschke alleges several "crimes", according to court exhibits and filings that refer to it. All of the allegations are rubbish and Dutschke has never been convicted (determined to be guilty) of any of the SAM allegations Holder wrote, despite that Holder wrote it as if Dutschke was guilty of the phony allegations in the SAM.

The American system of justice, it is taught, requires that a criminal allegation be properly alleged in an "indictment of a Grand Jury" (quoting the Fifth Amendment), then a determination is made in a court of law (a trial in which a judge/jury finds one is guilty). This has been the case in all of American history and every single person in the totality of American criminal jurisprudence has "enjoyed" that constitutional right. In order to find you, Mr. Citizen, guilty of a crime and then act accordingly against you based on your guilt, you must first be formally accused and then found guilty (by trial or plea). It has been so for every person that any government, local or federal, in the land has determined was guilty.

Every single person in the history of American law.

Every person, that is... except one. James Everett Dutschke.

For example, the SAM order, according to court attachments and a memo from the ADX warden (where the SAM unit is) reminds Dutschke that he was convicted in a jury trial in 2013 of a 2012 murder and dismemberment of an FBI agent. The "dismemberment", it states, involved "genital mutilation" of "the victim".

It even states that he was arrested for it "in September 2012".

Now that sounds particularly gruesome doesn't it? Especially the part about "genital mutilation". Whenever a LEO or prosecutor (Holder, in this case) wants to discredit and defame you, they always revert to some sort of sexual perversion. It need not be true, for just the accusation is revolting enough to poison the plebeian minds of the unquestioning masses.

There are serious problems with the accusation that the DOJ memo states is part of SAM. A glaring problem with it is that no such conviction exists! There was no such trial in 2013. In fact, if he was in jail and on trial in 2013, then how could he have committed the treaty violation of developing a biological weapon, the KC letters, for which he was arrested? That highlights a second problem with this SAM accusation, the "you were arrested in September 2012" bit. Court filings and other congressional testimony reveals that Dutschke was in Libya in September 2012, therefore making the alleged "genital mutilation" "crime" a complete impossibility as reinforced by the third problem with Holder's phony accusations, there was no 2012 arrest. Dutschke was not arrested for anything at any time or any place in 2012. The reason there is no record of such an arrest anywhere is *not* because it had been "agency scrubbed" to preserve security, it is because no such arrest ever happened. Dutschke was not arrested, or even targeted for any prosecution of any kind until 2013. This then makes the fourth problem with that particular phony Holder claim rather obvious. Where's the indictment for it? The DOJ memo even lists a specific name for a specific victim, Steven Campbell. Who the hell is Steven Campell? If such a person ever existed, if such a crime ever occurred, there *must* be an indictment for it somewhere…but there isn't.

It does not exist. Holder is a liar.

The Constitution's Fifth Amendment gives Americans the right to be free of false accusations. Because Holder simply proclaimed Dutschke guilty of the phony "murder" plot with all the trimmings of a good-old fashioned "genital mutilation", yet Dutschke had no way to defend against the Holder proclamation since there was no, and never will be any trial for the phony Holder claim, then Everett Dutschke has been denied due process to defend against it. Holder simply proclaimed it so, according to the DOJ memo, and thus it is so -no trial, no due process, no truth required.

But that is not the only proclamation the Holder SAM made about Dutschke. He also decreed that Dutschke is guilty of "intimidating witnesses", according to the SAM court filings. This, if true, would actually be a crime. So the question is simply—"Who?"

In other words—"What witness?", because in any of the Dutschke 2013 counts (the actual ones), there are NO "witnesses" of any criminal behaviour by Dutschke of any kind (there were a lot of witnesses of Curtis's acts, but not Dutschke). So who was intimidated? How are they a "witness"? When did such a thing take place and where? These questions on "intimidating witnesses" should be easily answered: just check the court transcripts from when Everett Dutschke was on trial for "intimidating witnesses". Look for details that the jury "found" him guilty of what Holder states. There is a problem there. A big one.

There is no such transcript.

NO transcripts of this conviction exist because no such trial ever happened. Hm. Perhaps then, one could simply consult the indictment. The details answering those questions must be in there, right? Well, again, there is a problem. There is no indictment anywhere even alleging that Everett Dutschke "intimidated witnesses." But there must be, because "intimidating witnesses" is an obstructive crime. So he *has* to have done it, Obama's Attorney General said so! Which means that somewhere there is an indictment with James Everett Dutschke's name on it stating exactly who "came forward" (in this misleading term that LEOs like to use) to say "Everett intimidated me" because certainly Eric Holder, the highest law enforcement official in the land, would not just make it up. After all he's ERIC HOLDER, for Christ's sakes! He is Jim Comey's boss, so we *know* he must be a man of integrity, right? But no. No such indictment exists. Anywhere. It never happened.

But what about a criminal complaint? Maybe there is a police report somewhere showing who, exactly, claims they were intimidated? No and no. There is no record anywhere of any such thing. And now, since the Arizona court filings were specifically challenged on this (and all) of the "phony SAM claims" (using the exact phraseology of the motions) to provide such proof, the Department of Justice failing to do so, it is now a legally established *fact* that it is a lie. A false proclamation.

Not only was Everett Dutschke *not* guilty of "intimidating witnesses", just like the "murder/mutilation" claim, he was never even accused of such a thing!

However, according to the judges who took, then eventually dismissed, Dutschke's suit against the SAM (Richard Matsch and Jennifer Zipps), one need never be found guilty to be guilty. According to Matsch/Zipps, no trial or due process of any kind is necessary, meaning the Constitution is not necessary. According to Matsch/Zipps, their dismissal of the case means that the new standard is "Guilty by bureaucratic proclamation".

The Arizona and Colorado cases, under review, show that the purpose of the filings were a formal and public lawsuit by Dutschke to simply correct the record. A government "record", the SAM documents of Holder, and whatever DOJ documents which copy or depend on the Holder SAM documents, that merely declares that Dutschke is guilty of a list of criminal acts. Because he was never indicted, tried or convicted of any of those criminal claims, the case should have been an easy one. The judge (Matsch and Zipps) could simply look for records of the claims, and since no such crimes were ever established in any court of law anywhere (not even alleged), the quick and easy result of the lawsuit should have been the order from the judge to "correct the record", purging the false claims. The law (APA) requires it, including the Privacy Act (which requires that "*all* criminal claims in *all* government records be accurate"). The DOJ's very own policy and regulations require it (the APA again). The Constitution itself requires it since the government does not just get to proclaim someone guilty of something. There is supposed to be due process. There is supposed to be the Fifth Amendment which requires it. There is supposed to be a criminal court existing for the sole purpose of exploring such accusations. Supposed to be.

According to Judge Jennifer Zipps (AZ), courts are no longer necessary. Her dismissal of the Constitution should literally mean she is out of a job, and according to her, cabinet members now make criminal determinations by fiat. Judge Jennifer Zipps, with her one act, and her desperate desire to side with those who she thought held the power against one who does not (since Everett is but a mere, measly prisoner of no significance) has completely demolished the fundamental premise of the Constitution, and reversed 230 years of the one principle which is supposed to separate America from North Korea. Supposed to.

Zipps' shocking act could qualify her for such a dictator's tribunal as the record shows that not once did she even suggest that it is wrong for the government to merely decree someone guilty of a crime. There is not even a hint of suggestion by Zipps that the DOJ justified the claims by producing a court record from a criminal court or remove the phony claims. In fact, her vague ruling, which ignored both of the issues that were raised and the actual explicit law behind them, seems to suggest that she thinks it is perfectly acceptable for government records to contain false criminal claims of a citizen without ever taking it to court. Bizarre. In two of the filings, Everett Dutschke straight-up challenged the Department of Justice to indict him on the phony Holder claims specifically so that he CAN prove Holder a liar in public court, or as he so plainly wrote it, "Put up or shut up," ("meaning really indict me and then prove it or correct the record and purge the claims from the file").

They did neither. Worse, even Zipps, a presiding officer of the Court, repeated the criminal claims as if established in some court somewhere, as if true. For Holder or any other member of the cabal to disparage Everett is one thing, but a federal judge should know better.

Everett Dutschke is the one person in American history to be "held to answer" (using the exact language of the Constitution) for crimes of which he's never even been accused. This is a clear and obvious violation of the Fifth Amendment which specifically and explicitly prohibits the government from doing exactly that. Perhaps Zipps, Matsch and Holder should learn the supreme law of the land, namely the Fifth Amendment. Perhaps might one day the Constitution will become fashionable.

But that is not all. The Holder SAM (at least the 2014, Holder/Comey SAM) proclaims Dutschke guilty of a "copycat mailing" plot. It even includes fictional details of such a plot. Here again, is a problem. There is absolutely no record of guilt of such a thing anywhere. No court in the land has ever taken it up. The fact is that there was, at one point, such a "copycat mailing" and the person found guilty for it was the Vampire Diaries actress Shannon Richardson, not Dutschke. A scheme was put together by the FBI cads who wanted to fabricate a scenario that would negatively influence Janet, Everett's wife, against him. But in December of 2013 Shannon Richardson (Texas) pleaded guilty and was sentenced in early 2014 for the "copycat mailing" plot. Everett Dutschke, however, was not, which is why NO such convictions exist, once again making Holder's SAM claim, a lie.

But there is more. The Holder SAM, or according to the DOJ memo the Holder/Comey SAM of 2014, proclaims Dutschke guilty of some sort of "cell phone smuggling", whatever that means. Again, something he has never been convicted or indicted for. This strange "crime" not only has no record, but it is impossible to stretch into a matter of "national security" which is what the SAM requires, by its own regulatory definition. Were these alleged cell phones part of a specially encrypted network to the Russian SVR? Were they a new Inmarsat-1 reverse-polarity interlacing and multiplexed terminal system on an undetected frequency plexus for use by hostile intelligence services or Al-Qaeda or the Girl Scouts? One way of knowing what is special about these supposed spy phones might be to simply review the conviction papers of this strange proclamation of Holder/Comey. Of course the problem is there *are* no conviction papers because (again) there is no such conviction. Maybe someone could discover the nature of these magical and "illegal" phones by reviewing the transcripts of the trial for that charge. Except... reviewing that transcript is impossible since it does not exist, as there was no such trial. Perhaps, then one could learn more about these super phones and the dastardly, nefarious, malevolent scheme for the criminally illegal commerce by reading the indictment for this count. But as usual, there actually is no such indictment to review. Everett was never indicted for such a thing. The secret spy phone claim is fiction. Holder made it up. However, how can one defend against the claim that was never even formally alleged? It cannot be done *unless* it is taken to court, which even when directly challenged to do exactly that, the DOJ refused to do it. This is why it is a clear violation of the Fifth Amendment.

The Department of Justice does not get to merely state—"You masterminded an Intergalactic scheme to engage in illegal commerce with extraterrestrials who wanted to 'phone home'. And you are guilty of this crime because we say so. We can't take you to trial because... because... well, we just can't."

Such a thing is absurd on its face and unconstitutional. Yet there it is, right there by Holder's own documented hand and signature

(Holder/Yates/Mueller/Comey). Why is there no indictment for the secret, ghost phones plot that was so foul, so black, so malicious and threatening that it was a matter of "National Security" (SAM-worthy)? It does not matter. No indictment means no trial therefore no conviction. Without a conviction, the government, especially the Department of Justice, does not get to legally even make that claim. Either go through the legal process (Fifth Amendment) or the claim is not legal.

That is the way the system works. Or is supposed to.

In *this* case, Holder simply states it, proclaiming it to be so. It doesn't matter *who* makes the claim, it is not legal unless it has gone through the process. No process of any kind means it violates the Fifth Amendment, a matter of constitutional law.

But wait! There is more (as if all the above was not enough). The last time anyone checked, "Murder-for-hire" is a crime isn't it? Like—an actual explicitly written crime, right? The kind where people are sent to prison for. Aren't there people in prison right now for that very crime? Yeah? Well... funny thing—the Holder SAM (Holder/Comey) actually claims that Dutschke coordinated a "Murder-for-hire" plot, and *even* alleges details of it! Wow!

That is kind of a big deal. According to the 2014 Jim Comey—SAM order, signed and written by Eric Holder, the Attorney General of the United States (aided by Sally Yates), Everett Dutschke coordinated a "Murder-for-hire" plot against a poor, innocent, defenceless, virtuous, pure, harmless individual. The sinless and wholesome victim must be really, really brave to risk himself to "come forward" (the LEO phrase designed to bolster credibility of false accusers) despite the immense peril that it must have put the noble victim under to do so. Gosh. Everett must have been a really busy man to have found the time and resources to do such an atrocious and depraved felonious crime on the righteous and virtuous victim. It is but justice served for Holder to include the heinous act on the SAM. What makes matters worse for the dastardly Dutschke, is that the innocent victim of the evil plot was a federal agent! That, alone, warrants a life sentence in prison. That is *not* a crime which is left unpunished and certainly one that the Attorney General of the United States must take *very* seriously. That would be, in fact, an assassination. Thus the law would unanimously come down like the fist of God onto such an evildoer.

So who then is it? Who was the sweet noble soul who found some way to muster up the courage and grieve that fiendish villain, Everett Dutschke, was about to have him off? Well... according to Holder, and the SAM, the unlucky hapless victim of the wicked Dutschke was none other than... FBI agent Steven Thomason!

In case it is forgotten, Thomason is the same man who signed the arrest affidavit stating that Janet's texts (about burning her personal bills) meant that some other person (Everett) violated the international treaty against the development of biological weapons. Thomason is the same man who constantly harassed Janet via text, personal visits to both Dutschke home (after he arrested Everett and personally drove him to jail) and to her workplace and phone calls. Thomason is the same man who intimidated and cornered Janet's son; who then gave a conflicting statement claiming the new computer boxes, which have nothing to do with anything, that were full of Janet's bills and bank statements and burned, were instead thrown into a neighbour's garbage can. This is what is known as a "perjury trap", the same thing that General Flynn and even Martha Stewart were prosecuted for. Thomason is the same man who sought out Everett's wife, Janet, to always engage in the smearing of Everett, an unavoidable and obsession of topics with him. Thomason is the same man who signed the sworn affidavit implying that Janet's spring cleaning habits is direct evidence that some other (Everett) must be guilty of something. Thomason is the same man who lied in court that Everett had purchased rubber gloves, dust masks and alcohol at a dollar store (for the purpose of manufacturing a deadly poison) when he personally knew the FBI records of the receipts showed that the supplies were actually purchased in December 2012 by someone named Jaime McGrath, one of the black belt instructors of Dutschke's school. Thomason is the same man who personally lied in court claiming that the yellow flyer (a mailpiece from a Christian Music Festival) was "yellow paper found in Dutschke's residence" that "matched the yellow paper of the KC letters," knowing that the FBI's own laboratory analysis concluded that the completely irrelevant schedule of events that the festival organisers had mailed *to* Everett did *not* match "the yellow KC letters." Thomason is the same man who lied that the three swabs were "positive for ricin", by virtue of what the equally dishonest prosecutor, Chad Lamar, called the "gold standard" ricin-test, the flawed field test. Thomason is the same man who lied in court claiming the notorious dust mask was positive for ricin and Everett's DNA, though both had already been debunked by their own lab analysis. Thomason is the same man who lied to the grand jury. Thomason is the same man who arranged an in-jail entrapment scheme which fabricated recording and other "evidence" to negatively influence Janet against Everett. And when she was appointed an attorney who finally told Thomason to scram, Thomason is the same exact man who, Dutschke's attorney reported, threatened behind the scenes to prosecute *her.*

Her charges would have been lying to the FBI, obstruction of justice and conspiracy to develop a biological weapon. The false statement charge was one that her own son just handed to the FBI on a silver platter. By one accounting, the computer boxes were filled up with her old bills and personal bank statements which was tossed later into a campfire at a routine weekend gathering. By another accounting (of the boy's), he (the boy) had disposed of the boxes into a neighbour's garbage bin, instead of their own. Thomason's later perjury trap on the boy ignored the fact that Janet's spring cleaning had already filled their garbage bin and that she had apparently gotten permission from whoever that neighbour was to overflow to that one. Thomason's implication was that an attempt to put empty boxes into a neighbouring garbage bin indicated some sort of cover-up which, by its nature, is obstruction of justice. The boy's accounting and hers are not the same. One must be false. Thus the charge of false statements to law enforcement. If the boy was correct, then that means that the "burn pile" (as the prosecutors and FBI labeled it) was evidence of a sinister cover-up.

Unfortunately for the FBI, they likely actually knew that Janet's accounting was correct, not the boy's. That did not matter to Thomason, who was the same man who waited until Janet left for work, then he gathered another agent to intimidate and interrogate the inexperienced and naive boy. After Janet, his mother, was gone; pressuring him into saying what they wanted.

If the boy's word is true then Janet is guilty of at least two crimes and a case could have been made bolstering a third. But if the boy was merely mistaken, then she is guilty of nothing. This is one reason they did not want her, the boy's mother, around when they flashed their badges at the boy.

Thomason is that same man. The one who lied, used Janet's "evidence" to arrest Dutschke, then used the threat of prosecution of *her* to leverage him into signing the plea. But *before* the plea, months, in fact, Thomason is the same man who whined that the sinister Everett Dutschke was about to end him, according to Eric Holder's hand signed document, the SAM order. Mind you, a "murder-for-hire" plot against an FBI agent is an extraordinary claim. While it is not really a matter of "National Security", as the E.T. phone clearly is, thus unworthy of a SAM (it is not "terror attack" or an espionage risk), it is still such a serious matter that the details of it should certainly be disclosed here, as it should have been by Eric Holder, himself. Surely he referenced the conviction paperwork from the offence, right? Hm. There seems to be no paperwork to reference. This is because there was no conviction.

Wow! This again? Well, did Holder consult the trial transcripts? Perhaps the reader, here, would like to read some of the transcript excerpts. The press certainly loves sensational details they can tantalize the masses with. Maybe some of the experts the media used in its reporting of this extraordinary and infamous criminal act from trial or proceedings could be included here. But, as usual, such a thing is impossible. Because even though this is such an unthinkable and unignorable crime, there seems to be absolutely no record of any trial or legal proceedings of it.

What? How can that be?

One would think the murder of an FBI agent even an attempt, would be in the news. It would certainly be prosecuted and tried, especially with Dutschke. So maybe then the best place to find the details of the depraved, detestable and sinister deed against the chivalrous, heroic, angelic victim (Thomason) must be in the indictment for ths capital crime of the greatest severity. But...alas...there is no such indictment either. It was but another farce. A lie. A "hoax". No such plot ever existed. Of course it is hard to believe that the likes of Eric Holder, Bob Mueller, Jim Comey and Thomason, himself, could possibly stoop to dishonesty, being the "stand-up" goodfellows they portray themselves to be, but it is now documented and decidedly determined, in a court of law, that they are, in fact, liars. For again, the SAM claim was specifically challenged in the Arizona lawsuit Dutschke filed against Holder and the DOJ (the named defendants) to either take him to court and prove it, or correct the claims.

The defendants (Holder et al) did neither. The court records are entirely devoid of any record of this prosecution because it never existed. The Arizona lawsuit exposed the cabal as liars. The next question is, does anyone care? Judge Jennifer Zipps sure did not, even when the defendant failed to produce even a single document of adjudication of this capital crime that Holder himself claimed.

It is okay for the government, without any trial or indictment or anything, to declare that you are guilty of a crime—then act on that proclamation?

Anyone who would disagree with that unthinkable concept, the Constitution (the supreme law of the land) agrees with you.

The SAM order (Holder/Mueller/Comey) additionally makes other various false statements, the genesis of which was the very dishonest Chad Lamar, simply repeated by Holder and endorsed by Comey with the full knowledge and approval of the structural head of the snake, President Barack Hussein Obama; but none of them are truthful nor are "National Security", SAM-worthy either. In short the SAM is a Holder dossier of lies about Dutschke that the DOJ relied upon (and leaked) to disparage, discredit and otherwise act adversely against him. A phony dossier.

See a pattern here?

The Dutschke SAM was a Steele dossier before there even was a Steele dossier.

Only much, much worse.

- The Dutschke SAM, the dossier of phony claims, was not ghost written by an ex-intelligence officer, it was written by the AG Eric Holder, himself and with documented contributions by Bob Mueller (2013) Jim Comey (2014) with other corrupt lesser DOJ and FBI officials (Yates, Sigler, Lamar, Thomason) and approved by the President, using HIS executive power. Steele didn't even have that.
- The Dutschke SAM, the dossier of phony claims, was not paid for by the Hillary Clinton campaign (as Steele dossier was). It was actually paid for by the American taxpayers! U.S. citizen tax dollars were used

to author the document of utter fabrication designed to smear a fellow citizen and silence the truth (of the exculpatory lab analysis) in support of whatever actions the cabal would take, which would also be paid for by American taxpayers. The Steele dossier didn't have that.

- The Dutschke SAM, the dossier of phony claims, was not just a single document as the Steele dossier was. It was actually two documents spanning three years (2013, 2014 and 2015) with effects that still persist. The SAM was written by Holder and was endorsed by Mueller. When Mueller left office and was replaced by Comey, Comey endorsed one, packing in even more lies from Chad Lamar. The Steele dossier was a one-time thing.

- The Dutschke SAM, the dossier of phony claims, was used as the basis to mute and conceal the release and discovery and disclosure of the final toxicity analysis of the Fort Detrick National Bioforensics Analysis Center showing and proving that there never was an "deadly poison" that laced the KC letters, it would have proved that the entire cabal were liars. So SAM was a CYA move of sorts. The Steele dossier was not.

- The Dutschke SAM, the dossier of phony claims, was used as the basis to imprison into extreme solitary confinement, with no communication with any other person, ultimately sending Everett into the deepest darkest hole inside the deepest darkest hole to be "disappeared". The Steele dossier was not.

- The Dutschke SAM, the dossier of phony claims, was used as a basis to cripple a criminal defence so badly that no defence was possible. Though they knew it was a lie, the objective was to ensure that a conviction and a prison sentence followed, a possible life sentence, in fact. The Steele dossier did not, by itself, have that intended a serious consequence.

The Steele dossier, which was the *second* time this kind of operation had been run (Brennan) then taken over by the FBI (Mueller/Comey), was the diet version of their *first* operation of the same, the Dutschke SAM.

In short—anyone outraged about the Steele dossier elements and usage should be livid, red in the face about the far worse and previous iteration, the Holder SAM on Dutschke.

The other commonality of the two is that the only way either is currently known at all is the outcome of the 2016 election of Trump.

Dutschke was fighting for transfer from the USADX and it was the Attorney General Lynch (who to her credit quietly dropped the SAM when Dutschke challenged it to the OIG) that was fighting to keep Everett Dutschke *in* the Supermax facility. Had Hillary Clinton won, she had already promised Lynch that she would keep her on as the AG ("just don't investigate me or my email"). However, the election went the other way and as a result, Lynch was out. That left no one to fight Dutschke's transfer to a facility where the public can access him a little more readily and he would be able to better pursue justice and file in the courts, a valuable source of information for this book. It is a fact of temporance that the very week after the new presidential administration was inaugurated, Dutschke's transfer out of the ADX was approved. That is the indisputable timeline.

If Hillary Clinton had won the 2016 election, no one would ever have learned of the Crossfire Operations against Trump staff and Flynn. If Clinton would have won the 2016 elections, Lynch would still be AG and Dutschke at ADX, no one would ever have been able to learn of the Operation Dojo against the "disappeared" Dutschke, because he would have stayed disappeared.

By the time the 2016-19 Crossfire operations started, the cabal already had practice.

And that practice was a conspiratorial (RICO) violation of constitutional rights. The deprivation of constitutional rights by color of authority IS a federal (18USC§241) crime, it is just never prosecuted. This is because the same people who would initiate such a case (the DOJ/ FBI) are exactly the same people who committed the felony, and they are most certainly never inclined to "prosecute themselves". Never.

Another one of the constitutional rights that was violated by the cabal is the Sixth Amendment. The right to a speedy, public trial, to confront and produce witnesses and the right to counsel. Of those phony SAM criminal claims that Holder, in a government (DOJ) document, just proclaimed Dutschke was guilty—not a single one of Holder's lies of criminality was ever given the constitutional airing of a public or any other kind of trial proceeding. Even the bizarre murder/mutilation scheme outlined in the DOJ memo that states that Dutschke was "arrested in September 2012" for the plot never actually happened. The same memo claims Dutschke was convicted in 2013 of the plot in a jury trial, though there was no such conviction and Everett Dutschke has *never* been part of any jury trial, ever. Court filings that follow the SAM lawsuit make quite clear that Dutschke himself specifically demanded, and in the words of one filing—"I *dare* you, indict me" to be indicted and taken to trial for the myriad of made-up accusations.

For a government agency (DOJ) to "establish" guilt of a crime without any use whatsoever of any court system means there is no opportunity for the "established" (by decree) criminal to have disputed or defended against the decreed guilt (one cannot even say "he could not defend against the accusation" because, in most cases here, there was not even an accusation— just a decree of guilt of a crime). With no process for defence, literal defenceless, there was *no* trial ("guaranteed" by the Sixth Amendment), *no* confronting "witnesses" ("guaranteed" by the Sixth Amendment) no right to counsel ("guaranteed" by the Sixth Amendment). When guilt is declared (by the Attorney General, a person who *should* have known better) *outside* of the Courts (and Dutschke is the *only* case where this has historically happened), it violates these fundamental constitutional protections.

When the courtless guilt decree is then adversely *acted* upon by that very same entity (playing judge, jury *and* executioner) then that is evidence of willful intent of the previous constitutional violations and the adverse acts that follows (followed) *is*, itself, illegal. The adverse acts themselves are (were) deplorable criminal acts—in the case at hand, a conspiracy to commit a violation 18 USC§241, by its definition.

But who cares, right? Who's going to prosecute the DOJ and the FBI? The DOJ and FBI? ("We can get away with whatever we want. Who's going to stop us?")

This is not opinion or speculation. This is the documented in detail of how and what actually happened. In America. Not by some small-town, crooked, redneck, dirty Sheriff (though one did get involved—Johnson), but by the (literal) highest office holders in the land, as a matter of documented history. The constitutional violations could not be any more clear. And the violators (the criminal cabal who committed the clear constitutional violations) could not be any higher. Who is the President's supervisor? There isn't one. Who is the AGs supervisor? The President, who in the Dutschke case (Operation Dojo) was also explicitly involved as the de facto captain of the ship (though that navigator, Brennan, was actually the logistical leader-even after "hand-off" to the FBI).

In retrospect, Brennan, who was literally the only person in the cabal with any experience whatsoever in operational logistics, should have known that once it was handed off to the LEOs that they would screw things up. It is their nature. FBI director Mueller was never trained to think like an intelligence officer (as Brennan was), nor was FBI director Jim Comey or AG Eric Holder. None of them were ever actually real law enforcement. None went through Quantico or any other extensive LEO training, not even the beginner's orientation session that brand-new recruits go through. All three of the men were nothing but prosecutors prior to their appointments (though Comey, and to some extent Mueller, had a small stint "outside" of government just long enough to cash in on millions from Bridgewater, which really was but a money-laundering scheme from *government* contracts). So the three LEOs that Brennan handed the op off to (in typical Brennenesque fashion) were completely incapable of the proper subtleties of an intelligence op, since they think only in terms of "How can I get a loud and public conviction that will affirm my oversized ego?"

All these details herein are the actual occurrences, the raw intelligence, the estimation of it all is unavoidable, these were unconstitutional acts by the same cabal of the highest office holders in the land.

It is worth informing the reader that the division of the DOJ that runs the federal prison system, the Bureau of Prisons, has absolutely no authority in a SAM. Not a single person and not all persons of the Bureau of Prisons collectively can designate a prisoner into or out of a SAM unit. The BOP makes all the administrative determinations of which convicted/sentenced person is designated to which facility, unit, cell and bunk. The *only* exception to this is the very rare SAM prisoner. Those are *all* sent to the invisible SAM unit by designation of SAM itself which is controlled by only one person, and that one person only who is outside of the BOP—the United States Attorney General.

An interesting security note was added by the SIS into Dutschke's security file. After Dutschke's transfer into the SAM unit an FBI agent went through the extraordinary steps far outside his jurisdiction which are entirely unprecedented, to add special security conditions. That FBI agent called and convinced SIS to insert a security note that Dutschke had special training, including very high-level martial arts training, and was a MENSA member. Why would an FBI agent, whose job is to convict someone, care about which security measures are taken *after* someone is imprisoned? The purpose for the completely abhorrent post-conviction contact to the SIS was clearly simply to cause Dutschke as much inconvenience in the harshest and most extreme and draconian treatment of that prison, already the US Supermax facility, and to impose extreme daily scrutiny at a facility already hyper-monitored and in the very unit that is the highest security, highest monitored in the country. The FBI is under the DOJ, this is true, and so is the BOP. But why would this particular FBI agent, post-conviction, wish to make Everett's life even harder? Why would any FBI agents have any involvement at all with an SIS officer?

The answer to that question is simple. It was personal. This was made obvious in the security notes that the SIS officer, Turner, had inserted into Dutschke's security file. The insisting FBI agent submitting the information was none other than...FBI agent Stephen Thomason, the same agent who had been removed as "special" agent in charge of the Dutschke case after Thomason's malfeasance finally got out of hand, and was replaced by "special" agent, Brandon Grant (who, it may be, is not quite as sinister or stupid as Thomason).

Thomason, who has absolutely no jurisdiction, no say-so whatsoever outside of his own agency, took it upon himself to assert himself into a completely separate entity in order to affect any security assessment with the sole purpose of affecting Dutschke's day-to-day treatment. This is unheard of in the BOP. It is like your ex-mother-in-law bursting into the office of your ongoing IRS tax audit so she can tell the tax auditor what a bad guy you are, and they should give you the electric chair. Put simply, there is a reason that the FBI does *not* run the penal system. It is to deny exactly Thomason's behaviour. The SIS chief and the BOP warden should have both told

Thomason to go "pound sand" then referred him to the OIG for disciplinary measures since how the prisons are run is none of his business and Thomason has no authority to (even by request) any person's security file. This act, alone, speaks volumes; not about Dutschke, who is not privy; to either SIS or prison security profiles, but about Thomason himself and the utter depravity of his character. It is the kind of "move" that Jim Comey would be proud of, and *that* says something. It is most unfortunate to report that a law enforcement officer's level of professionalism is demonstrated to unveil that a person in such an (undeservingly) esteemed profession is such a petty, petty monster. Yet, there it is, as reported by SIS agent, Turner, to bear Thomason's name. That kind of arrogant beaming of modern-day FBI agents is truly sickening; they do not even bother to be ashamed of their malefactions and crimes anymore. In fact, the misanthropes almost seem to be proud of it. If such a thing was relevant or within his power, he (Thomason) would not have needed her (Turner-SIS) to "backdoor" such information into the file. It would have already been there.

Thomason's involvement from the beginning proved that he was the perfect grifter for a Holder/Mueller/Comey job in the service of Brennan/Obama. He was just the swindler they were looking for to help Chad Lamar dissonante, falsify and pervert the case itself while the cabal distorts and embellishes the narrative that their fawning imps in the press bedazzle the public with. Not a single person in the press even asked a single question about the SAM. They may not even have known about it. Not even when Dutschke was sent into the SAM unit.

As a result of the prosecutorial branches from the 2016-20 Crossfire/Mueller investigations and prosecutions, the smarter half of the country that was not intentionally blinding itself, acted appalled and upset by the PREconviction treatment of at least one of the Mueller prosecution targets. And that shock and anger was truly warranted as solitary confinement (which sounds much more benign than it is in actual practise), which is one of the actual tactics of "enhanced-interrogation", is and has been determined in courts to be "cruel and unusual punishment", especially if *pre*conviction or *pre*trial. So it is really tempting to ask that "smarter" half if their shock and anger was feigned outrage. There were several pundits, even the "constitutionalists" who made quite a fuss about that arrested man's treatment by the FBI, jailors and orders that the prosecutors had finagled. Were those "constitutionalists" faking it? Because...Where were they the *first* time around?

They were right to the point out to their vast radio, telly, print and internet audiences that it all is a violation of the Eighth Amendment. But where were they when the SAM did the same exact thing to Everett Dutschke in 2013 (and for *years* and to a much greater degree?) If they were upset over Manafort, or Stone, they should have been boiling in their own skin the first time Mueller et al pulled this tactic, by order of Holder using the President's power and multiplied a trillion times the conditions.

It is not true that a violation of the Eight Amendment is still a violation no matter what the name is? Even if that name happens to be James Everett Dutschke?

Descriptions of the SAM unit, itself, are impossible to find except through scant court cases. Simply because there are no public descriptions at all. Until now. The transfer of Dutschke from US-ADX into a more accessible (though still maximum) facility means an inquiry can be now made directly with the source, as any inquiries to associated staff yield only limited results. ADX prison staff feel they are proud about the physical properties of the uber-secure facility. Yet information about specific prisoners themselves, is very sequestered. If one asks about a specific prisoner at the ADX, the DOJ employees immediately clam-up. This is quite a shame because, although most Americans do not endeavour to care about anyone outside of their own lives (except for, perhaps, the Kardashians), they still have a right to know exactly what goes on in American prisons. It is that fear of interest that affects most Americans that keeps the population so naive about the realities of the system as a whole that leads to such absurd levels of ostracism by the uninitiated, plebeian public thinking of "a convict". Such willing blindness only feeds the false judgements and prejudices against the "convict" label. As a result, most people do not or have not yet realised that it is the hostage takers (the LEOs and prosecutors) and the hostage keepers (judges and prison staff) that are far, far, far more depraved than the vast majority of "convicts".

Consider this, How do you feel about tortuous murder? How would you react if you learned from the news tomorrow that some barbaric extremists had crucified to death a man in Alabama's backwoods. As the man hung there, bleeding and dying, the barbarians laughed and tortured the man, right in front of his weeping family. The news reporter who is (salivating over himself) reporting this tells you he cannot show you the video, for "it is far too gruesome". What is your reaction?

You are rightly appalled.

Then you discover that the crucified man, who was beaten and nailed down to bleed to death by the torturers, was accused of being a thief (just like the biblical crucifixion scene). Does that instantly change your reaction? Does that somehow mitigate your degree of ghast? Perhaps some say, "Oh, well… he deserved it then." (If *that* is your reaction then you are no less the barbarian). If there is any mitigation in your mind at all, then why? One man (allegedly) stole something, it does not matter what it is or the worth of it, but the other gang of men murdered someone. Leave out what "the law" says, this discussion is about a sense of conscience and humanity. From a human (not a legal) perspective, which deed is worse? The torturous murder of a human being or stealing an item?

It was not the thief who was a tortuous murderer. It was the jailors that did that to the thief next to Jesus (and Jesus himself). Who, then, is most worthy of a society's decision and disgust, if not the most depraved?

The value, the quality, of a society can be properly gauged by how they treat their prisoners.

The worst of mankind is not generally found in the "convicts", but the men (and women) who derive their daily affirmation for their constant interpositions asserting that the "convict" is somehow of lesser value than the sadistic barbarians who enjoy being the hostage-keeper. It gives the hostage keeper (jailor) a reason (though only a false sense) to pretend there is someone they are "superior" to, since the kind of person who seeks out such a profession is not exactly the creme-de-la-creme, not the best brightest, and they know it.

Valedictorians and those who earn high marks in school do not aspire to be a prison guard (or any LEO).

So the blackout that ADX employees have during interviews in regards to the prisoners, themselves, is unfortunate because it is the prisoners (i.e. the people) that are the interesting part. How they are treated, how they are forced to live, what they do and who and how they interact. That blackout is even more pronounced when the subject is any of the actual people confined in the national security unit at the ADX (SAM unit), because the blackout is the entire point of the unit's existence.

The description should begin with answering the question: "Who is in the SAM unit?" The legal answer to that nearly answers every other question. The legal answer is simple—anyone who is on a SAM. The regulatory qualifications of the SAM, which invokes national security objectives, weed this down to almost the right number for space available in the unit itself, which is small. It is essentially a prison inside a prison of around only thirty people. With the exception of about three individuals, the SAM unit is not a place of "convicts", meaning that the tiny population is not very representative of the prison population as a whole. Basing this on a period when Dutschke himself was on a SAM, and on what the regulations (28 CFR§501.2 and .3) require, it is easy to deduce what kind of person the US Attorney General determines must be "disappeared".

The SAM unit is a unit of spies and terrorists of the highest level, and some that fit in the grey area between those two. Leaving aside the aberrant three that *are* of the typical prison-type, everyone in the SAM unit is highly-achieved, highly-educated and high-profile. They are all the victims of a SAM-crippled prosecution for some type of actual espionage or terror-related case (or both). Problems never happen with the bulk of these prisoners because they, mostly, are quite civilised. It would be a stretch to think that the former US State Department diplomat, Myers, would be a rabble-rouser. He is an energetic, wise and knowledgeable but harmless older man.

Nosir Gowadia is, yet another harmless old man who is held in the most secure unit in the most secure prison in the US Why is he ankle shackled and handcuffed each day as he is escorted by multiple baton-wielding burly prison guards into a dog cage ("rec cage") in an area of the unit which has only a chain-link roof to simulate being "outside"? Is this little old man so dangerous? Gowadia is the designer of the B-2 stealth bomber, and in Dutschke's estimation has no business in a prison cell. As Dutschke (tried) explained in one interview, the intellectual contents inside a man's head cannot be the property, in its whole and in perpetuity, of any government, including the American government. If Gowadia had an idea, a new one, it is his right to sell it to whoever he wants to, as long as it was not the same idea he had bound to the United States (the B-2). If China, the country in question, wanted to pay the man to consult with them about *new* (*non* B-2) projects, whether it was a "stealth boat" or a "stealth missile" (which was a bogus accusation since it does not exist), then why was Gowadia not allowed to do so? It is *his* brain! No contract with the US government could possibly be valid which states—"We own everything in your head, everything that will ever be in your head, in perpetuity." Thus the old man's conviction was based on false and trumped-up allegations and evidence to begin with, no wonder the DOJ machine and Attorney General needed to hide it all. Everett's accounting was that they would often talk science when they happened to be in adjacent dog cages ("rec cages") and Gowadia would feed the sparrows that would come to visit him with bread that, instead of eating, Gowadia saved for his feathered friends.

A word on the specialisation of the SAM unit. Everything is custom monitored. Each SAM prisoner has at least one monitoring agency that constantly listens to everything that is said by the prisoner. For example, the "rec cages" to which some visit on their daily or weekly schedule are each separately monitored by a camera and a condenser microscope installed directly above each individual assigned cage can pick up every whisper. This is not for show. The video and audio feeds to a monitoring station that is constantly live monitored and recorded for real-time review by paid monitors and interpreters fluent in Spanish, Arabic and several other languages. This is one reason why the incarceration cost per SAM-prisoner is astronomical to that of a regular federal prison in a regular facility. Each prisoner's SAM monitoring agency is different. The standard FBI is common for them all, though the assigned agents themselves may vary. Additional agencies are CIA (which should not be since CIA is *not* law enforcement), DOD and others depending on each person's case. In Dustchke's case, the US Secret Service was an additional monitoring agency, but there is absolutely no indication that any Secret Service officer ever bothered or cared to involve themselves at all since they have better things to do (like their actual jobs). All SAM prisoners are monitored by the special polyglots hired by DOJ.

There are no radios at the ADX, including the SAM unit, so any news that a SAM prisoner receives is whatever is filtered through the political lens of the partisans of CNN, MSNBC who are incapable of delivering any news at all that does not carry the same political flavor. Fox News was added to the telly channels of the ADX's television system which they pipe into each cell for a prisoner's individual viewing. Any other news comes in the form of a daily delivered prison-customised USA Today.

The USA Today is provided, most likely, so that prisoners do not raise a legal stink about receiving their own subscription to their own hometown paper, to which they would otherwise feel entitled to after the lawsuit of SAM alumni Richard Reid (the "shoe-bomber"). So now, each SAM prisoner gets their own snipped up version of the USA Today. For every prisoner, the page with the "classified" advertisements is completely removed (the thinking is that someone could write up and pay for a "classified ad" message to communicate to a SAM prisoner). Then each is specifically redacted via scissors. For example, when former State Department Diplomat Meyers gets his USA Today, any story about Cuba is removed. When former CIA official Harold J Nicholson ("Nick") gets his, any article on Russia has been sliced right out of his copy. Whenever Dutschke got his copy of USA Today, it was nothing but holes where the articles had been of the CDC and other laboratories that were (2014-2016) shipping live Anthrax and other infectious agents. Any time any story specifically named a SAM prisoner (or even an affiliate), which did happen from time to time, the SAM prisoner's paper was obviously minus that article. Because there were numerous high-ranking Al-Qaeda members in the SAM unit, their papers frequently resembled something from a cat box. The SAM monitors are very skilled with scissors.

Likewise, they are extremely cautious even with communications between the hostages in their unit. That is the purpose of the condenser microphones which hang over the center of each "rec cage". Speaking to a nearby hostage in a different language is no obstacle, since the DOJ officers stationed in the SAM unit employ translators who are themselves multilingual. If they hear anyone "on the rec yard" saying anything that *they* deem is too sensitive, too classified or otherwise potentially dangerous, they will immediately and without any hesitation at all come snatch that person right off the rec yard, as Everett learned the hard way on two occasions.

The way the SAM unit is physically structured is described as a pair of upside "U" shapes, two-tiered with a pair of showers at one end and the guard station at the other. Though most ADX cells (which are concrete rooms with no metal) have their own shower, the SAM unit does not. Each prisoner has assigned "shower days" that require that a team of guards has to come and go through the absurd fuss of handcuffing, chaining and shackling the SAM prisoner in order to "escort" that shower-ready fellow the 11 feet to the shower cell, where the insane shackling is then reversed and the showering fellow is locked into the shower cell.

Plastic trays are delivered to each cell door at mealtimes through the door's "tray slot". As far as the food goes, the ADX is rumoured better than most for a variety of reasons, including that the food is *not* prepared by the same prisoners of that facility. In fact, the only "jobs" in the facility are "orderly" or janitorial jobs. The pay on these jobs is something close to slave wages. Dutschke claimed he was an "outdoor orderly" of one of the two larger rec yards (the roofless concrete area of big "dog cages") and was paid only $20. Not $20 an hour. Not a day. Not a week. $20 per month.

It would be almost depressing to witness that these men in particular, men of stature, men of eminence reduced to menial tasks. The downstairs indoor orderly was Everett's trusted friend Nick (Harold J. Nicholson). The upstairs indoor orderly was Ramzi Yousef. Seeing this above-deck senior CIA officer, and the revered and almost a legendary terrorist sweeping, mopping and buffing floors would be quite a conflicting sight. "Here is Nick, a man who through his skills and experience, an entire generation of CIA CSTs emulated whether they knew it or not. The man could have eventually run the entire agency, and now he's running a floor buffer", and "Here is Ramzi Yousef, the man who wreaked havoc on the world, was the *original* mastermind of 9/11, who was the first to attack the World Trade Center and the United States. And now the same government has him scrubbing showers"; it is all an immense irony. (Not coincidentally, the tiled floors and everything else in the SAM unit is the cleanest in the entire BOP by far, to a near hospital-grade standard.)

The ADX SAM guards themselves are a much more professional lot than in any other facility, in that they treat, personally, each imprisoned person with much greater civility than other facilities who must have been scraping the bottom of the barrel for staffing. The ADX SAM guards are likely more educated and certainly more experienced in interpersonal skills which eliminates tensions long before tensions become problems. While part of the equation is that this type of prisoner is a much more refined and dignified person, the other and equally important half of the equation is that the guards, themselves do not instigate any issues by an utter lack of people skills, so the result is a calm—almost serene environment.

That serenity is broken all at once, five times every day as almost half of the SAM population very loudly prays, almost battling to "out Muslim" each other in a near-competitive fashion. When 15 of the most devout Muslims on the planet all get fired up at once, each of them ensuring that all the others hear them above all the others, lest one doubt another's Islamic credentials, the remaining non-Muslims must put down whatever they are concentrating on and wait until the cacophonous dissonance of separate competing shouts to Allah have ended, for in their mind, the world must stop and there will be no concentrating on anything else. While there have been some efforts to at least pray "together", in unison, each of the Islamic devotees still does his own thing. Often the one trying to coordinate the intransigent heads is the diminutive El Hage.

El Hage was a calm and almost delightful tiny figure that Dutschke enjoyed discussions with who frequently was dragged to the hospital for force-feeding after his many hunger strikes. After four days consecutive tray refusals, the government shoves a feeding tube through your nose, down your throat and dumps Ensure into you.

Even when El Hage was eating, he wasn't. He often passed down his bologna packages, salisbury steak or hamburger patty down to Dutschke. The little man, it seems, is mostly vegetarian.

There is one man who does not pray or "rec" with the other Muslims, that is Zacarias Moussaoui, the man some have called the "20th hijacker" of the 9/11 attacks who did not make his flight and others have said was to be part of the UBL's "second wave". Both, to some extent, are true. He is sent to his own rec yard and is kept in a special area ("the Suites") because he is just too loud and disruptive in his default state of mind which is entirely out of it. If one can catch him at one of his moments of clear-headedness, then he has much to say as he knows quite a bit, but those moments are extremely rare.

In his correspondence with a radio broadcaster, Dutschke revealed that when he arrived at the ADX SAM unit, he found a "workout partner" in Farouk Abdulmutallab, "the underwear bomber", though he was soon transferred out of the main SAM unit to begin a "step down" process to the CMU ("communications management unit"). He was soon replaced just a couple of weeks later by the arrival of Dzokhar Tsarnaev, the "Boston Bomber", whose case had occurred just days before the KC letters. In Dutschke's long conversations with Tsarnaev, it became clear why the Mueller/Comey FBI had pushed Holder to write a SAM on the kid. As he informed Everett Dutschke, the entire story the press was reporting, as controlled by the FBI, was completely wrong. Dzokhar did not know everything that his brother Tamerlin was into, but he knew enough to know several of the connections the FBI had to Tamerlin. One of the things that stood out to Everett was Dzokhar's comment to him after the devout, Middle Eastern Muslims of the SAM unit tried to give the European Dzokhar a Muslim name ("everyone was named Abu-something-or-another") and Dzokhar told Everett, "Everyone is making all these (wrong) assumptions!"

The "official" story of the Boston Marathon bombing, as controlled by the FBI, should smell to high heaven, because it is *not* the full or true story; not at all. Which is why the FBI needed him either dead (they tried) or disappeared (the SAM). It would have been during this period that Everett, while merely talking casually to the other prisoners that the DOJ would have wanted disappeared, that he would have learned all about each of them and their cases and how the public story never, never matched with the truth.

Hence the government's need to ensure that no outside person would ever hear them speak. But Everett was not an outside person. Not anymore. Considered a national security priority for years, he was now one of them. In an unwitting, unwilling way Everett Dutschke had been able to infiltrate the secrets OF, and secrets IN, the Attorney General's unknown, shadow-prison. The prison inside of a prison.

It would also have been during this period that CNN and MSNBC and all other news media would have been loudly and angrily trumpeting the criminal behaviours of law enforcement. Police shootings and killing citizens in Ferguson, Missouri. Another man who was shot and killed by officers while he was in his parked auto as his fiancé filmed the murder-by-cop with her phone. The media displayed outrages during this time of another criminal shooting of a man who was shot *in the back* by an officer who was then unknowingly filmed as he approached the still bleeding corpse and "planted" his taser in the victim's limp hand so as to report that the man had taken his weapon. A grown policeman was filmed body-slamming a non-aggressive 12 year old swimsuited girl on the ground and "restrained" the skinny pre-teen swimmer who now had a concussion. CNN ran that police criminality on a loop and loudly lamented how wrong it was that there never seems to be any legal criminal repercussions for criminal cops. In New York City, not far from where MSNBC broadcasts, a citizen was murdered by a law enforcement officer by asphyxiation even as it was filmed by bystanders (who also did nothing to stop it). The media screamed to the public, sports figures began kneeling during the national anthem in protest of the misbehaviours of police (though that movement somehow morphed into something else). Female officers, seeing that the male cops could get away with murder, must have demanded equal treatment and two different female wallopers were filmed in two separate "motorists" incidents of cop-on-citizen murder (one would think this sort of thing would satisfy "feminists", especially since both of the dead victims of the badged-babes were men, therefore they inherently deserved to be murdered anyway). The nation rioted and the press (mostly) cheered on the riots and railed against the police's felonious criminal rampages. Even, as a Minneapolis citizen is slowly murdered on film by asphyxiation of an officer's knee, as other cops ensured that no bystanders could interfere with the murder, the 2020 media are unanimously clamouring to hold law enforcement to account for its misdeeds. But where were they in 2013-14? Why is it so that federal cops during the Obama Administration were allowed by the press to commit criminal acts, not just in the Dutschke case, but every single case in which a SAM was ordered is, by definition, a case in which the DOJ was hiding the truth. When the FBI/DOJ hide something, it is only because there's obviously something to hide!

Just as each of the law enforcement murders from that period were attempted cover-ups, such as the man shot in the back <u>before</u> the shooting officer planted his taser on the corpse, just as law enforcement in those cases all universally filed their own report shifting blame, denying reality and covering for each other—all denounced by the media; the obvious wrongdoings and cover up by the highest law enforcement and office-holders in the land should have garnered at least as much outrage. If it, according to the media, is such an atrocity and abuse of power when local officer Joe Blow (a white cop) commits a crime against a citizen, isn't it equally an atrocity and abuse of power when the President of the United States, the Attorney General and the FBI director(s) along with agents commits (by conspiracy) *multiple* crimes against a citizen then lies to cover it up?

Why isn't the media stirring up riots to discover the truth and protest every single prosecution and sentence of every single person ever put in the SAM unit?

In one interview, Dutschke expressed that the only SAM prisoner who ever deserved to be there "was Bob Hanssen", the former FBI agent who was also charged with espionage (for Russia), whose selling of intelligence to Russia actually lead to CIA agent deaths, unforgivable (as unforgivable as the 2012 Benghazi actions which were both directly and indirectly responsible for new stars on the wall. An event for which a SAM imprisonment should have been ordered for Secretary of State Clinton and two others, immediately and with no trial, no due process; just as was done with Everett).

If the press "cares" so much about LEO misdeeds, why were they so willing to look the other way and *aid* in the cover-up and perpetuation of a fabricated, impossible narrative? In the Dutschke case and every other SAM-related case. How could it be, in the mind of the media, local cops are bad, but federal cops are good? The answer is, again, unfortunately that the media is not interested in the truth and is willing to be led around by the nose by the FBI and DOJ because agenda trumps truth, to them.

"Never let the truth get in the way of a good story."

In the Dutschke case, the lies are documented. Easily proven. All one has to do is simply look and be objective. The "official narrative" does not match the truth. In the radio host's correspondence with Dutschke, he made it clear that his frequent discussions with America's highest-profile, hidden away prisoners quickly showed him that he was not the only one.

One surprise happened a while after his arrival to the SAM unit. The staff keeps close track of who knows who, who is affiliated with who and even who gets along with or "hangs out with" who. Someone entered (or re-entered) the SAM unit who Dutschke seemed concerned would recognise him. It was none other than ██ ██, the same man who had, years earlier, been tortured by the ██████████. Dutschke concluded that there at the ADX SAM unit, as he would discuss, usually scientific topics, with this former university professor, that ██ ██ simply never remembered the faces from the 2002 operation (the names were necessarily different). ██ ██ either did not remember Dutschke or was very good at hiding it. Either way, Everett personally knew that ██ ██ was never given a fair trial and that there was enough relevant truth about the man that could fill volumes, the FBI and media narrative (the same) about him was dramatically wrong that the difference was night and day.

The DOJ noted, as did SIS monitors, that Dutschke had no problem making friends with any of the other SAM prisoners who talked freely with him as if feeding an insatiable curiosity, which fits Dutschke's profile. More than a handful of people in Everett's real life, pre-imprisonment would notice that people who were not interesting to him were people he paid absolutely no attention to. "It was like Everett didn't notice them," was the assessment of Dr. Julia Baker, "like they were just a piece of furniture." Assuming this common evaluation is true, and considering that Dutschke spent an hour each day over a week, months and years talking and listening to the SAM prisoners is a testament that, to Everett at least, they were genuinely able to nourish or even fuel his further interest in them. All but one of whom it is reported was rather curmudgeonous to begin with.

Perhaps all the SAM hostages found Dutschke just as interesting as they all were very generous in helping him as much as they could. Or perhaps they all sensed that he might be the only way for them to finally reveal the truth to someone, anyone who would listen, since the SAM is designed to prevent the public from knowing anything about them.

Regardless, the staff did note that Dutschke made use of his time among these similarly situated victims of political prosecution by establishing quick friendships with some and deep friendships with others.

One of those cordialities had arrived from Guantanamo into SAM (AG custody, not BOP custody) who kept a quiet dignity about him that appealed to Everett right away. Ramzi Yousef introduced the man as Soleiman Abu Gaith (often spelled Ghayth). He and Dutschke were friendly to one another and Soleiman Abu Gaith's English is only slightly better than Dutschke's Arabic, so their conversations were slow and Soleiman Abu Gaith seldom left his cell (and refused the telly). The irony of their friendship to the guards, to SIS or anyone who truly knew the deep history of each, is striking. For here was Everett, who once attempted to sever the funding of the ██████ financiers of MWL and Rabita Trust that supported Saleha Abedin's IMMA and the IRO which funded Osama Bin Laden directly (which is the original operation that through a long chain of events certainly added to his much later downfall) making friends with Soleiman Abu Gaith, the very man who, as the spokesperson for UBL's organisation and chief recruiting officer for high-level Al-Qaeda operations, was the person in charge of allocating the very same funding where and how UBL needed it to go. Just as Soleiman Abu Gaith (S.A.G.) was a key target of Alec Station, second only to Osama Bin Laden himself, Everett was likely a key target (one of six) of the entire Rabita Trust/MWL network which is what later led to the illegal 2011 unmasking through insurance records, a task likely strongly urged by one of the remaining ███ financiers, Usayid Ahmed Ja'ara and most likely carried out by Brennan and the Secretary of State (Clinton/Abedin) for Saleha then tasked by Susan Rice for the unmasking leaks. Here were two men that, on the outskirts, had previously worked against each other, in adjacent "dog cages", expressing no animus toward each other. This, not the enhanced interrogation that SAG had been subject to, is a much more effective method of learning about a person, though time-consuming.

The reports are undoubtedly true that Everett's deeper friendships were with Ramzi Yousef and Harold J. Nicholson ("Nick" in the SAM unit). Although it is likely that none of the three ever revealed everything to each other, they were certainly close. A massive irony here is that following the 1993 World Trade Center bombing by Yousef (coordinated with his uncle, "the Blind Sheik"), Ramzi Yousef was most certainly on the CIA's radar, which means on Nicholson's radar, and yet here they are, peacefully co-existing together in the SAM unit as friends. As reported in one letter with a radio broadcaster, the first person who met Everett at the USADX was Nicholson, the second was Yousef, both of whom became Everett's inner-tighter circle, perhaps due to his affinity for intelligent conversations with intelligent people. Another irony is that both Yousef and Nicholson had already affected Everett, more than a decade prior. After Nicholson's arrest, a new policy was created that CIA instructors are never told the actual last names of CSTs, not in orientation, not during their interims, not at The Farm and not during language school. This was in effect by 1996, so included 97D. 97D was also directly affected by Yousef. Part of the explosives training included study of the detonation designs and urea-based chemistry which accredited Yousef by name to the CSTs. Of course, post SAM order, Dutschke now had direct and daily access to the engineer, himself. That would not be the only kind of conversation between them. If conversation is nothing but political or technical chatter, it would never hold Dutschke for too long. There would have to be much deeper intellectual and philosophical fruit in a person's brain to pick or Dutschke, by all accounts, would simply not pick at it. Indeed this squares soundly with Dutschke's writings professing that Ramzi Yousef is absolutely *not* the monster he is portrayed to be, no matter what his crimes or actions, and that Nicholson is one of the best human beings, and most trustworthy, he has ever met; both are assessments that, if they were not sarcastic, are the polar opposite of the public narrative.

And much, much more to them as a person, then one history book entry of their crime alone.

As any historical accounting or personal remembrances of Everett can attest, he wore a lot of hats and was never any one thing. Just as he expected other people... no that isn't right, insisted that other people rise to his intellect (seemingly ignorant of the fact that people sometimes are just the way they are)

223

he likely believed that everyone else was multi-faceted, so at least bonded with those who could offer him something to think about or ponder. And in the SAM unit, there was obviously much more going on with these people then some pronouncement of guilt. There was something more to each person, especially the ones Everett grew closer to, than simply a decree from some *other* person that "you are a threat to National Security." There must be more than just that, that they all had in common.

But the SAM environment is a constant reminder that someone else wants you silenced. It quickly reminds you that it obeys no authority, including The Constitution, in its furtherance of the goal of muting truth.

Despite that The Constitution "guarantees" access to the courts (Sixth Amendment), the exemption to that is the Attorney General's SAM unit. While Dutschke was challenging the SAM to the OIG, Nicholson thought to challenge some of the unconstitutional and unconscionable wrongful SAM restrictions in federal court (with judges who had demonstrated for years that they were too cowardly to address the SAM issues. To the few SAM judges, the less the public knew, the better). Any other person, represented by counsel or not (the SAM unit and the SAM itself *is* an AG ordered denial of counsel) as pro-se, any citizen, any person has a right to write and file any motion with the court.

Not so, apparently, in the SAM unit.

Nicholson's motion to the court, as is routine in the SAM unit, instead was first forwarded to CIA (the monitoring agency), who then redacted practically every relevant word in Nicholson's handwritten motion before sending it to the other monitoring agency (FBI) who finally forwarded it back to Colorado, then to the district court, with*out* informing Nicholson of exactly what was done. By the time that the SAM-apologist judge actually received Nicholson's handwritten filing, there was nothing of substance left to it. John Brennan (the DCI at the time) who was, in fact, the defendant in that lawsuit seeking injunctive relief to reverse Brennan's SAM impositions, made sure in the redactions—that Nicholson was unable to express to the court what he needed to express (violating the 1st, 5th and 6th Amendment). It was absurd!

There is *no* country in the world that operates a judicial system in that manner. NOT ONE! Except...the United States...a country run "by the rule of law"...except the supreme law (the Constitution) and any other laws some bureaucrat (Brennan) does not care to deal with.

To the cabal, laws are such petty, niggling things.

So the trembling judge, scared white-faced to dare question the invoked (by Brennan and Lynch, defendants) "National Security", actually allowed, permitted thus encouraging more of, the same illegality in his courtroom; a room where the law (the Constitution) is secondary now to the whims of the judge's masters.

Moreover there is a great deal of evidence that the CEG (Counter Espionage Group) and the FBI CIC (Counter Intelligence Center) have been and continue to intercept and tamper with the mail between Nicholson's parents and his foreign fiancé, without any open warrant. If it is on a FISA warrant then the FBI has no real justification for the FISA, making the warrant itself illegal (sound familiar?). Tampering or interfering with the mail, no matter what/who the entity (even if DOJ) is a federal felony. But because the DOJ is involved in it, who the hell is going to prosecute it?

The DOJ? That's not likely to happen.

Prisons do it all the time. They simply trash incoming or outgoing mail and if ever questioned, the response, from the cowardly criminal prison staff is, "Can you prove it was sent?"

Since they made it vanish, they know there is no proof, they disposed of it! The only proof was either the incoming or outgoing letter, the one that "vanished". Try to take them to court on that (or any) issue and they transfer you to a hostile prison, mooting the court case.

Of course, under a SAM, since there is no mail to speak of except court filings, it is important to know that those, too, are tampered with. In regular prisons, the staff will "sit on" your incoming legal mail (to "investigate whether or not it contains contraband) long enough for you to miss the reply deadline which results in automatic dismissal. Such underhanded and cowardly tactics are the ploys of dishonest and small-minded worms, but it is not only common, it is expected. *That* is the DOJ that the American people do not know exists. *That* is the real DOJ, which is the opposite of the organisation the public is told they must respect.

What is worse, unthinkable, is in the Nicholson case, his mother (in her 90s) is *not* and was never "acting as a foreign agent" thus any "surveillance" on her, including the mail surveillance, is entirely a constitutional violation (First and Fourth) as she has never been convicted of anything. This is the same exact situation of the remote, hacking ("surveillance") intrusion into Dutschke's mother's desktop PC and the search of Dutschke's father's Texas ranch, a violation of First Amendment (privacy) and Fourth Amendment (search/seizure). This should outrage every American who does not want a police state.

This proves that the DOJ never gives up. Once they have killed the horse, they continue beating it. In the Dutschke case, the unwarranted thus illegal searches of Dutschke's parent's properties (computer/home) was conducted as operations to recover a specific item (the Tripoli File) though they pretended it was for something else. In the Nicholson case which occurred in 1995-97, the information that he allegedly gave to the Russians during the Clinton Administration would be, at this point, decades-old and yet they are still surreptitiously surveilling Nicholson's near centenarian mother as if, any day now, they will find "it". Because after nearly three decades of illegal

FBI behaviour, they are looking for something specific, as in the Dutschke's parents situation. They would not simply be just looking "for something to find". The FBI (weaponized) seems to love turning its sights on people's parents. In 2010, when the Obama cabal went after former CIA Officer Jeff Sterling, they also began to prosecute journalist James Risen and surveilled Risen's tight COI in very Carnivore (the shared intel program) fashion. In 2013, the cabal thought Dutschke had been in conversations with Fox News's James Rosen, perhaps even thinking that Rosen was the one Dutschke had sent the Tripoli File to. The FBI then began surveilling Rosen's parents (with no valid FISA or other warrants). These are facts of actual known history for which there is no explanation.

The Police-State apologists of the plebe, sock-puppet media might say, "Well, the feds are just looking for any evidence of the crime." This explanation, even though it ignores the illegality of the searches themselves, which by themselves *are* criminal acts violating 18USC§241 and RICO conspiracies to do the same, is an explanation that possesses no logic whatsoever and is as likely as *zero* chance. In the Dutschke case, of developing a biological weapon, are the apologists suggesting that the feds were hoping to locate a super-fast, high-capacity multitube GSA rotor conical centrifuge inside of his mother's desktop computer? In Nicholson's case, are the LEO apologists suggesting that Nicholson went to his ancient mother and said, "Here Mom, these are the top secret plans for our invasion of Russia and the list of moles we have inside. Hold on to these until 2022 then give them to Vladimir for me, okay? And this is great meatloaf, mom."

Rubbish.

But it gets worse. The Clinton Administration, with Janet Reno as AG tossed GS-15 CIA officer Harold J. Nicholson in prison, trumpeting the conviction, hoping it would distract from the other many, many scandalous abuses of power (some of which Reno and the FBI was the direct causation). He had all his good time and would have been released around 2016, his sentence concluding. In 2011, the Obama Administration, with Hillary Clinton a very prominent figure in it (preparing herself for the 2016 election which belonged to *her*; it was *her* destiny, dammit), decided that would be a problem and they had to ensure Nicholson would *not* get out of prison. So they went to work. On his son.

The FBI (Mueller) and DOJ (Holder) were going to indict, prosecute and imprison Nicholson's son (just as they did with the Dutschke's wife and Flynn's son), forever wrecking the life of Nicholson's son. The charges were petty, paltry and not really based on much of anything. But there is one thing the Nicholson family (unlike most Americans who stay willingly blinded) knows is that when the conviction machine turns its aim towards any person, all it does is destroy lives. The machine is unstoppable whether it gets a conviction or not. Though the federal conviction rate is 98% (that number alone tells you it is not a "fair" system), the rate of destruction is *over* 100%, since lives that are collateral damage are affected even outside of their target. The case was nonsense. The Nicholsons have learned that does not matter.

It is a fact that they came to Nicholson, who was *in prison* already at the time (2011) and leveraged *him* to plea to another eight years imprisonment (a period of time that would have covered Hillary Clinton's 2016 election and 2020 re-election), then they would drop the bogus wrecking-ball poised to demolish his son's life. Keep in mind, here, no matter whatever they alleged his son had done, was done outside of prison-where his son lived; and that Nicholson, himself, lived *inside* of a prison, and not merely *any* prison either, but a special unit with communication restrictions. Yet somehow, the offer was—"You agree to...uh...let's say money laundering and...uh...acting as a foreign agent or something like that—do another eight years and keep your mouth shut, and then Bob and Eric will just...you know...forget about wrecking your son."

Did anyone in the 2011 media bother to raise an eyebrow and object, "Wait a minute... something's wrong here! *That* guy over there is accused but *this* guy is in a prison. How can *this* guy take the fall for *that* guy?"

No. Not a peep of any logical query was heard from the 2011 press.

Tactics like that are common in the DOJ, especially during that particular administration. CIA officers were target practise.

How do you convict a guy who is in prison for some (illusory) thing that (did not really) happened outside of prison? Same as anyone else, threaten to imprison a loved one. That isn't their first tool in their queue but it is a reliable one... because it works.

And it did.

THAT's the DOJ. And because Nicholson was on SAM, and remains so, he couldn't really defend himself or speak the truth.

The effect is the "the defendant" is, mouth duct-taped shut as the judge asks "do you have anything to say in your defence?"

The defendant, gagged to a mute, glances over to see the FBI (Mueller) and the DOJ (Holder) aiming guns at his loved ones who (wife, son) then shakes his head. "No?" The judge asks, "nothing to say in your defence? Well, guilty then". Then the sock-puppet press reports, "Well he's guilty. He admitted to it."

Apparently those Gestapo tactics are just fine with the press.

Law enforcement, which normally includes the criminal court, should never be political, yet SAM prosecutions exist! There's a whole unit full of them, and a small alumni of past SAMs (mostly inside the CMU). But for some unknown psychological reason, people (and the media are just people) choose to willingly pretend it does not while at the same time allowing themselves to be outraged and condemn when it happens in North Korea or in the old Iraq of Saddam Hussein. No one wants to think about political criminal (phony) prosecutions, but some of the tactics are the same even for prosecutions that are not.

Once a prosecution is complete, if it was a corrupt prosecutor (they all are) the next step is the appeal process. Normally, this is where the convicted then gets to point out to a judge where the prosecutors and FBI lied, where his trial attorney failed or even how the judge himself screwed up the case in the judge's inherent bias for the prosecutors. This step is critical because it exposes the problems in the system, for the convicted who actually have the courage and willpower to do so. The appeal is not only a right of all Americans, it is a duty. A duty of anyone who believes in or has even taken an oath to uphold and defend the Constitution, which *cannot be defended by passivity*. It is at this critical stage where it gets highlighted exactly how the law was not followed, almost always by police, often by the prosecutors and very often by judges themselves who simply don't care. This is also why judges (and prosecutors) avoid whatever issue is raised in the appeal to instead pretend the convicted raised a different issue (because they don't want to address the actual, raised problem since it only shows that they screwed up). The judge, dishonestly feels obliged to then address the pretend issue instead of the actual raised issue. This is why they never have to fess up to "errors" which were likely intentional anyway. That process, while usually pointless since the deck is stacked, is a critical process and one in which someone has the right to hire an attorney if they don't wish to do it themselves. There are attorneys who specialise in it.

Everyone has a right to hire an attorney, that is... unless you are on a SAM.

"The...uh...Constitution doesn't apply to those disappeared people." Since every person has the right to hire a lawyer, but Dutschke, who was on a SAM and was not allowed to contact anyone in order to hire them; how then, could Dutschke (or Nicholson or Gowadia or Meyers or any of them) exercise that right?

He can't. He couldn't.

He was constructively denied that "guarantee" of the supreme law of the land! This is another way in which the Sixth Amendment is violated by the SAM.

Every single person who was convicted on a SAM must have their convictions overturned. Every single person who has filed an appeal while on a SAM must get another chance with representation.

SAM orders are the most extreme measures imaginable by Americans, and to most Americans is actually unimaginable. With a normal criminal prosecution the deck is already very heavily stacked in favor of the prosecutors (so much for "fairness"), there is no such thing as a "fair trial". But a SAM prosecution is more akin to a "witch trial" from the 1600s.

"So we bound the lass up, hands and feet, called her a 'witch' then toss her into the deepest bit-o-the lake. If the girl floats, then she's a witch so we drown her...but if she sinks to the bottom and drowns...well then maybe she wasn't really a witch."

There is no defence allowed when on a SAM. If one is ever so unfortunate as to find oneself as the legal counsel for a SAM prisoner, beware. The lawyers who "represent" such people are bound to nearly the same terms, unlike any other attorney for any other person.

In this way, the American DOJ gets to "legally" interfere with contracts, which is an unlawful act, so that they can (do) intimidate that attorney away from proper representation.

Here is an example any person in America can hire an attorney to ACT on his behalf. An attorney can open or close a bank account for his client. An attorney can secure a copyright for his client. An attorney can represent the client in a contract negotiation. An attorney can represent a client in court. These are all things an attorney is supposed to be able to do. It is his *job* to represent the client, as best as he can.

Unless your client is on a SAM.

Then *you* are, too, and the Department of Justice then gets to tell you what you can and can not do and exactly how you can represent your client. This is no joke. This means the attorney is *not* free to best represent the client at all.

There is an example of this that makes the point. And it proves the point that the DOJ takes the SAM very seriously.

Counsels of a SAM prisoner are *not* free to represent the client in the way that *any* other attorney can because if the DOJ, who is always both the opposing party in the case but is also who issued the SAM, does not pre-approve every aspect in detail of (what is under normal circumstances privileged) communication then the attorney is imprisoned.

Sound believable? It shouldn't, but it is the truth, as was publicly demonstrated already in the case of attorney Lynne Stewart who represented SAM prisoner Omar Abdel-Rahman. Through his counsel, Stewart, Abdel-Rahman negotiated a ceasefire with the Egyptian government (and a ceasefire is a good thing, right?). When Stewart made a comment of Rahman's response of the ceasefire to a reporter, she was prosecuted by the "fair" DOJ and then flung into prison herself to serve a 10 year prison sentence.

10 years in prison... for representing her client.

For what? The cease-fire? How is an Egyptian ceasefire, which saves lives, somehow counter to America's "National Security"? Was it for representing Rahman to a reporter? Yes, according to DOJ (who is the entity of the SAM) such a thing jeopardizes "national security"! Wow! (Remember that the sole purpose of a SAM, must be, purportedly, an essential requirement to protect "national security").

This is not, as the Stewart case proves, simply a matter of some bizarre *veto* power of the DOJ over the opponent's defence (*that* would be egregious and sinister enough), *this* is much, much worse somehow than even that.

New York attorney Bernard Kleinman, nailed it as he challenged the SAM by saying Eric Holder and the DOJ was "waving the well-worn flag of National Security".

It has been publicly noted that prosecution and imprisonment of an attorney could result from as simple a matter as counsel telling the SAM prisoner's family member, "Your son is feeling better today."

According to Eric Holder and the Department of Justice, *that* deserves incarceration. Just ask Lynne Stewart.

Other than a miniscule few, Americans have absolutely no clue the SAM exists and no one would believe it if they were told, as now. The response would be "certainly not *here*...not in *this* country."

And one *should* be incredulous at the learning of it. Because it is entirely antithetical to everything Americans think they know of their country and would be outraged if they heard of such an injustice in any other country. Iran? Well, Americans could believe such a thing goes on there. North Korea, Maybe. But *not* America! Certainly not! No way!

But it does.

And although federal judges are deathly afraid of it, and wouldn't think to even touch it with a metre stick, they are powerless anyway. A judge cannot enact or implement or even order SAM ended. It has nothing to do with a judge, even if one had the courage to even pretend outrage over the practise. If a judge wanted to start a SAM on someone, he couldn't. If he wanted to stop one, he couldn't. So none have tried. They just spongily go along with the administration, without question. Nor does anyone in the press have the courage to question it, because, in part, some of the SAMs were originally written by Janet Reno and Eric Holder and Loretta Lynch, who will forever get a free pass for law-breaking by the media. Perhaps that excuse is, "Well, if Obama wanted this feller under a SAM then thurr musta been a good reason fur it. After all, he's the-gubment and we kin trust him."

Which means most Americans can excuse anything as long as it isn't done to them. In America, there is an entire industry designed around whipping the population into a frenzy about something to extort political favors from the government or often to fuel a hatred of a group of people against some other group or political party. Although there are a myriad of issues and organisations, no one has perfected the extortion tactic as well as the "social justice" industry has. The "social justice" (which sounds so noble, for who would argue against "social justice") advocates have one job and one job only which is to go about pointing fingers at everything and everyone declaring it all to be "racist." This tactic stirs up the usually anti-white sentiment of Black voters and the phony guilt of white voters. The objective, just prior to elections, is to label one party as a "racist" party and the other as the benevolent advocates who protect people against racism.

Because American voters, and the American population as a whole, is so media-programmed, they all fall prey to the parasitic scheme every single time it is deployed, never bothering to think for themselves, never recognising that it is always one political party who is always doing the pointing and never recognising the significance that it happens prior to elections. Like the Star Wars Jedi "mind tricks" on the feeble-minded, the "community organisers" find they have *no* problem in moving people, enlisting the media at large to the "their cause", extorting concessions and outright graft from government and government programs and even generating their desired hate toward their political opposition. This perpetuates and self-generates so that there is always some person or group of "outrage" people in the queue to take up the advocacy.

Another example is that there is always an advocacy for starving children. Or both sides of abortion. Advocacy for veterans of certain wars. Advocacy for water preservation. Trees have Advocates. Shivering dogs in cages have advocacy groups. So do spotted owls, polar bears, a worm found only near one lake, whales, homeschooling, religious sects and groups, business owners, midget children of unwed pirates and even the weather. Yes, the weather and climate has countless advocacy groups for which each tornado, rainbow, cloud and tsunami is mostly assuredly thankful for. For without mobs of emotional people who are so willing to reach into deep pockets (usually someone else's pocket) then hurricanes would run out of cash. And then what? Chaos.

But there is *no* advocacy group for those on SAM. The one group of people in America who are literally being oppressed in ways that not even a spotted owl or polar bear could dream of, are suffering bigger injustices than anything ever experienced and it is happening in a sanctioned way by a government agency. NO crime needs be committed or even formally accused for the highest officials in the land to order SAM imprisonment. It just happens. It does not happen "because someone is black" or "because of a crime" or "because of an intelligence leak" or "because an extensive ties to terrorism" or "because of a conviction" even. There is no "because" with a SAM order. The President simply wants it so the Attorney General makes it happen. It is that simple. There is no fighting it. There is no due-process. Their mere invoking "national security" immediately shuts down any questioning or debate, and not that question or debate matter because the unfightable decree simply IS.

There have been political accusations that "Trump is a dictator." The fact is, President Trump did not order Dutschke's SAM. That was entirely during the Obama Administration. As was Nicholson, and others. The SAM literally is the most dictatorial move that is conceivable. The SAM-like power of an executive branch through the DOJ is the *exact* kind of abuse that American conservatives criticise China and North Korea for. It is the *exact* power that American liberals feign that they are horrified to see in those same countries (while at the same time surprisingly secretly pining for it). Only the American libertarian Republicans have warned people against this kind of Orwellian nightmare, yet even they (the libertarians) have no clue that that very nightmare already exists, secretly among them in the "land of the free".

Perhaps none have a clue because they willingly stick their head in the sand hoping not to see it, lest they then be burdened with the knowledge. Those leaning Right blind themselves intentionally to it because such knowledge would shatter their constant drumbeat of their worn-out old tune of America being so great and so just and so fair and the law enforcement officers are so pure of heart and the noblest creatures on earth. The American Right has (far too) long worshipped at the Church of Coppers, and changing a religion is a very, very difficult thing to do. The Right does not wish to admit that their precious DOJ is holding the rest of America hostage.

The American Left-leaners cover their eyes and try hard not to see such things for several reasons. One reason is that it confuses them. Each time an Obama-era political prosecution occurred against some wayward and completely undeserving target, the Left would have been forced to acknowledge, thus admit, that the instigator was one of their own. They would also be forced to then admit that nearly the entire conviction machine is comprised of Left-leaning swamp-dwellers. The creatures of the sinister apparatus are but bureaucrats; parasites who pad themselves with government checks, government pensions, government hours, and government protections. And the Left, who know such infiltrations were always part of their plans, seem to find it conveniently unpalatable that this necessarily includes "law enforcement" and the DOJ, who *are* the government and *are* the ones holding hostages. Additionally, the Left would be forced to admit that because the prosecutors and LEOs are their own, creatures of the Left, that their other primary schemes would be exposed. Because it is important to the Left to constantly separate people and claim that *only they*, the Left, can protect Blacks or gays or illegal aliens or women or whoever it is today the Left can convince is so inept in life that the only reason that someone isn't a king is because the evil-white over-privileged male has its foot on some unsuccessful person's neck. Imagine how damaging it would be for people to finally realise that the person with his foot on the neck of the poor Black, illegal alien, "transgender" woman/man/pronounless entity could only be one of *them*, a creature of the Left—that permeate the DOJ top to bottom. And if the Left cannot tantrum about Racism or Gay-o-phobia or "Allah phobia" (in that order), then they are stricken silent into a panicked confusion. And they really cannot whine about "institutional" or "systemic social injustices" if others realise that it is *they*, the swamp-lefties, who *are* and have *been* the institutions and systems. Besides, the Lefties intentionally bury their heads in the sand because if they acknowledge that the SAM power exists, which mirror and magnify the injustices they publicly complain of from other countries, they then would feel compelled to *pretend* to fix this, an actual and real injustice and they are not in the business of *actually* fixing real injustices...only the pretend ones (racism etc). Plus, though one would think that their overwhelming sense of guilt would make them eager to highlight and address the SAM abuses which take place right under the noses of the Leftists, they have nothing to gain from it because the tiny number actually affected can no longer legally vote and there is no pile of money at the end of that rainbow for the Left to plunder.

The records show that Dutschke remained unrepresented during his SAM, even as he fought against it with the OEO and OIG against Lynch and continued even after, as did Nicholson. Nicholson and Dutschke's court filings were both pro-se, self-represented, handwritten filings. Even if they had wanted to hire an attorney who would have been willing to sign on to the SAM "Attorney Affirmation" the way that Lynne Stewart did for Rahman, neither Nicholson or Dutschke could have even tried to hire anyone because they were not allowed to try. For when you do not know a name or phone number or address of a lawyer and you are not allowed to ask for a name, number or address *nor* are you allowed to call or write or communicate in any way with one.... What can you do? One isn't going to magically appear in your cell.

How on earth is that compliant with the Sixth Amendment right to counsel? It isn't.

This is not speculative. Included here, in this book is the proof in the form of notifications that were sent *to* Ken Caghlan, who *was*, in fact, Dutschke's actual attorney of record in the KC letters case. As these notifications show... Dutschke's Sixth Amendment right to his own appointed counsel was denied and it is now a documented fact. The notifications informed Dutschke's attorney of record that he, Ken Coghlan, was "not approved to correspond with" Dutschke, SAM prisoner, and that Coghlan's correspondence was being rejected and sent back. Dutschke would never know what was in the letters or that any letters existed.

Coghlan, Everett's lawyer, was not the only one to receive such a "rejection". Others who tried to help or contact Dutschke received similar rejections "You are not approved to correspond" with the SAM prisoner, including the filmmaker who made the one-sided documentary movie about the case, who was informed that Everett was not allowed to correspond with any member of the news media as her notification cited 28CFR§501. THIS violates the First Amendment—Freedom of the Press. So now someone who was *not* ever on the SAM and did not sign on to it in any way, the movie-maker, has had *her* constitutional rights violated.

This country, this DOJ, not some other place, not some other group, is who denied counsel (now documented). It is not the SS, the Gestapo, the brownshirts being revealed here, it is the United States and its Department of Justice during the Obama Administration under Eric Holder (then Loretta Lynch) as endorsed by Bob Mueller (later Jim Comey) and the others of the Obama criminal syndicate. Like it or not, these are the historical facts.

That administration, its leader hypersensitive to the image he wanted to portray therefore intolerable of anything that could tarnish that image, was vindictive and used the DOJ (and its associated media thugs) to often dispose of dissent. Just after journalist Dinesh D'Souza exposed the political reality in a documentary film of the corruption, hypocrisy and *real* injustices that persisted even in the Obama administration (at his direction), the cabal targeted D'Souza. It took no time at all for the Comey FBI, as directed by the very same cabal, to arrest the man who dared document that Obama was a fraud. As the Comey FBI searched, seized and dug for a reason to imprison this man who had dared to criticise the "Dear leader Obama", they found a way to latch onto a routine and personal campaign contribution which was all that Leftist DOJ puppet Preet Bharara, one of the reliable swamp prosecutors, needed to squeeze out a conviction against Dinesh D'Souza, sending him to prison. Let that be a lesson! No one criticises the Supreme Leader, Barack Hussein Obama!

Considering that this weaponization and mobilization of the DOJ, as documented in his case (United States v D'Souza) was just to teach a lesson to others, in the administration's vengeful drive to "get even" with a harmless documentary filmmaker...what limits would the same administration's cabal place on themselves in the face of a *real* threat to their power, their offices, their very legacy and even to their own freedom? The Tripoli File, would not have merely been a slap, as a documentary was. The Tripoli File would have been the fist of God slamming down onto the Sodom of Washington DC, forever devastating the legacy of half of the administration, possibly even leading to war and definitely resulting in a complete disruption that would have tested America's breaking points.

The SAM power *is* the very example of the extremes that the administration (or any administration) will go to to protect itself against serious political danger. While entirely reminiscent, as described, of the very same tactics of the "evil" countries (and in some ways is even *worse* than what those countries do), the SAM abuses are but only one step down from outright summary execution (a power that, in America, is currently reserved only for the Clintons, historically).

Most reasonable and logical people agree that someone who actually knows a man personally is a proper judge of the man's character instead of someone who does not know the man at all.

By all accounts, everyone who actually and personally knew Everett Dutschke knew him to be inspiring and influential in every sense of the word, not some dark and sinister intriguer as he was painted by those who never even met him. Jim Comey, who had never before bothered to even say "Hello" or shake Everett's hand, and Comey's "special agents" knew absolutely nothing about Everett's character, neither did the Holder special prosecution team who had never spent even a minute with the man. Yet it was *they*, these men who had no inkling of who they were actually dealing with, and no care, who were the same men selling to the world an image of Everett that they wanted to portray. While those who had actually met him should have known better and had the courage to stand against the false image by simply speaking the truth, the rest of the world never had that opportunity... because of the SAM. With only one narrative, one portrait being reported, the false one the cabal wanted, the rest of the word (who had no idea that the true Everett Dutschke was being silenced and suppressed by the SAM, written by the very people that wanted him tarnished and disappeared and selling the false narrative) was left only with the false portrayal. The SAM, which shut down all opposition, and in every sense, is the perfect weapon by the high-level syndicate.

Given the, now documented, fact that the administration was perfectly willing and comfortable to lie to the public, the "defence", the press and even the judge about actual evidence- why wouldn't they do anything but the same of their targets very character? They can. They did.

At this point, any breathing person who thinks that particular administration would never do anything like that (although it is a documented fact that it *did* happen and exactly as described) and that exact cabal of individuals would not ever conspire against a patriot, hide the truth, enlist the media to gin-up public animus against that patriot, label him as a traitor and weaponize every agency and asset to that political end as a person intentionally breathing the bias fumes of willful naiveté or simply has not been paying any attention at all. A country's intelligence agencies must be allowed its secrets. A country's law enforcement must not.

It should not be left entirely to 2020 A.G. William Barr and prosecutor John Durham to "do something" to rescue America. Each and every person in the country has the power to publicly indict the corrupt cabal (as the cabal did with Dutschke) to the population and to every single person within their circle of influence as the press did to Dutschke in 2013-2014. While it is true that an individual American citizen may not have the same influence as the New York Times, CNN or any of the other Obama controlled media outlets, it is wrong to do nothing.

Glenn Beck describes it (July 2020) almost religiously, "God will not forgive our silence," and encouraged support for "Someone who was willing to go to the gallows to tell the truth."

J. Everett Dutschke *was* exactly that person.

As a thorough review of the court transcripts clearly shows, Everett was not the least bit shy about telling the truth. It is equally obvious that particular administration was desperate to shut the truth down and keep Everett, and the truth, hidden away. For that is specifically part of the explicit intent of the Holder SAM. It is also plain to see that the judge of the case, Sharion Aycock, was fearful of too much of that "truth" nonsense in *her* courtroom, whatever the special prosecution team (Sigler, Lamar, et al) wanted was "how it was going to go." Americans should immediately revolt whenever any LEO or prosecutor (or DOJ) seeks to keep anything silent, it indicates that the reason they are trying to hide something is because there is something nefarious to hide. In Dutschke's case, it was worse—because that administration (from the highest) ordered that they weren't just hiding something, they were hiding *everything* and from *everybody* (then filling in the blanks with their own impossible contrivances). American's failure to themselves and the beginning of their downfall was marked by that very moment where every citizen should have stormed the streets in support of Everett Dutschke. If a child in some future generation asks his great-grandfather "What was the moment when Americans stopped being Americans, Pa-paw?" His only proper answer must be, "We had a chance once to prevent the collapse of the Republic, child. We failed to stand up for it when Everett Dutschke was imprisoned but we all looked the other way. I'm sorry, dear, but we could have saved it since that's when the enemies of the Constitution, some of whom were in power then, realised that they could get away with anything."

There will be a few critics of this book, swamp creatures of law enforcement or media, who will say "I don't believe that," or "this can't be true," or will stick to whatever their 2013-2014 story was since no one wants to be revealed to the world as wrong or complicit. Those critics have a choice, either open their eyes and minds to the documented reality or admit to the world that they are, in fact, the "domestic enemies" of the Constitution and the very country based on it.

For all practical purposes, though they were but fawning tools of the cabal, the media really is part of the RICO-worthy criminal syndicate of the Obama Administration. Their deeds, now being exposed (not just by this book but by the DOJ and a suddenly aware and interested investigative few in alt-press), it is now much easier to see (understandably painful to accept, but the reality is) that everything the cabal presented—especially "criminally"—is completely backwards and the opposite.

Everett Dutschke is not a traitor.

They are.

Chapter 7

Questions — An assorted Miscellany of Minutiae

Although the CIA had tried early developmental programs that have mostly failed, Everett Dutschke had expressed, as early as 2007, that he believed such programs could be successful and that was one of the things the Russians and a few other nations got right. In the white paper shared with "Miss Peggy" ███ (who complained to Kathleen ███ she was the wrong person to share it with) Dutschke expressed that exofficers or recruiters tend to become possessive of potential CIA recruits, especially for CSTs and analysts. His proposed solution to that, according to the internal abstract, was formalising the informal practise of cooperation between recruitment officers embedded in different organisations. Different, instead of opposing. This would be successful, he presented, as it was the accidental model he was familiar with and indeed it is historically true that recruited applicants are a lower churn than unrecruited applicants since the "fit" can be determined over periods of a decade or longer instead of during just an interview process. Recruitment officers (some exofficers) can not only take the time to find the potential "jewel in the rough," but even predevelop that jewel until a reliable program manager takes over; thus multiple recruiters over time can not only discover and monitor potentials not just through college, but as young as age 11 (the Russians were known to begin grooming in their early developmental program as young as seven).

Dutschke's 2007 paper is only relevant to 2013 because at the time of his 2013 arrest, and the FBI's 2013 confiscation of documents, they seized several files of exactly this sort; individuals from within his organisation with descriptions for "use of sound judgment", "dedication", "technically competent", "driven to superiority" and "proficiency to learn" as well as additional personal details for the candidates. One promising candidate had been developed from youth to medical school, another high achiever had learned foreign language to a conversational level all on her own. At least three of the "seized" files showed fresh entries, as if still considered active and high levels of proficiency for referral. Several other files, however, seem to have lost Dutschke's interest for whatever reason, as there were no recent entries at all. These, if Dutschke's judgment was sound, are now all a loss to their country, and unintended casualties of the Dutschke prosecutions, as well as a loss to the potentials themselves whom Dutschke could have guided and paved their path toward the 'five signatures' which have high level of CIA outreach and engagement and into the arms of one of those recruitment officers that prepare them for success, all without the candidate ever even knowing. For his own

237

part, Everett wanted the program to show results to prove that, even outsourced, such an early developmental program was feasible, practical, reliable and even preferable, and that the primary reason such programs had not produced much fruits before was that they were not properly "staged" to naturally flow from step-to-step of a normal person's life. Whether or not his staged approach would yield something different will now never be known. His 2007 contention that these candidates, already tested, tried and proven long before they are sworn-in, would be light years ahead of anyone else who EODs at the same time. Though others in that organisation remain active, Dutschke's 2013 arrest obviously means that he will never get the chance to prove it.

There are still questions that to this day remain unanswered, though not through lack of seeking, sometimes intensely. Some of those who could aid in the answers are either "unavailable" for one reason or another (including unexplained, unexpected deaths), unwilling to provide any answer (CIA FOIAs have responded with—"Executive order 13526—the CIA can neither confirm nor deny... such records currently and properly classified and is intelligence sources and methods... protected from disclosure", which is obviously not very helpful), or are questions that depends on the answers to other questions. But the simple fact that some inquiries have been met with outright claims by some of no involvement actually dispel the "official" narrative because it keeps "passing the buck" around to someone else until there is no one left to "pass the buck" to, which makes no one responsible for anything. The few that "accept" any responsibility (some few at the bottom) are the same tiny handful who have proven themselves to be liars already by either denying documented facts such as the lab reports or by fabricating additional crimes and accusations from thin air which they know have been never proven, could never be proven and/or has never been properly alleged. That same tiny handful also appear to elevate themselves to stratospheric heroic status in their fantastical version as if they saved the world and act as if *they* (these FBI agents such as Thomason and DOJs Lamar) were the ones calling the shots and dragging Mueller, Holder and Obama along (and later Comey and Yates) which is doubtful; yet even if that is true—and especially so, would show that not only is the "official narrative" that the mind-numbed press reported not only completely false—then the whole fiasco was not planned and coordinated (by the cabal on record) and then foiled by the truth and botched but was somehow instead a haphazard, clown show of bungling ineptitude from the beginning.

In *that* scenario, the one with Thomason and Lamar calling all the shots, then a clueless Eric Holder merely personally signed himself onto the case, slobbering the whole time since he is just so easily controlled by the omnipotent Superman hero, Thomason; in *that* scenario, the President of the United States led the PDB on Dutschke and allowed his executive orders on Dutschke because he was so star-struck that the greatest heroic figures in human history, Thomason and Lamar, actually thought Obama worthy enough to allow him to briefly tag along with those cool gents; and that the humble, modest, and unpretentious Obama was so very deeply flattered that the lofty Thomason would deign to include him. How exciting! In *that* scenario, Bob Mueller (and Holder and Obama) did as Thomason commanded and cared nothing at all about reputation and was such a pure figure that he would never allow any political influence whatsoever to taint his deep integrity.

Yeah, sure!

So it is possible that some questions will never meet up with any satisfactory answers, which leaves these details for continued speculation. The only good news is that the blanks are not yet filled in with actual intelligence or not critical. The remaining questions are more like curiosities. It's true, however, that often curiosities lead to a great deal of personal satisfaction, but not much more than that. Just as often, though, curiosities that are followed end only in more questions, more curiosities. For example—For centuries humanity longed to land on the moon. Then, decades ago, it happened. Men touched down on that orbiting rock and said, "Hip hip hooray! We did it!" (Or some such rubbish). They drove around for a bit, traffic was rather light. Played golf. Skipped and jumped and picked up some rocks, since there were a few extra lying around and it was questionable whether earth had enough. Or perhaps it was running out of rocks and needed to borrow some from the Moon; we will never know because no one has ever been curious enough to conduct a rock census for an accurate count (or perhaps those that have, never got a chance to complete it). They sipped on Tang and when all was done one spaceman turned to the other, raised an eyebrow and, feeling a bit let down by it all, asked—"So... now what?"

Some of the questions about the 2013-2014 phony manufacturing of a terrorist (that isn't any such thing) or about Dutschke himself are a bit like that "now what?" kind of moment. The answer does not really "move the needle" or add much light to it all. Some are massive philosophical questions which, if answered, would progress humanity a million years. But at this point, these are but questions. Questions answered not in ink but in sketchy pencil. A few of those speculations, however, are so severely sinister and so criminal that the gravity of which is of such monumental proportions that it could easily be said wars have been started over less, countries have fallen and entire empires been stripped of their leaders and beheaded for their betrayals not just to their country, but to all that make us human.

While this is not necessarily advocating any beheadings of "world" leaders (moot since no longer in office anyway) two of those speculations will be addressed, here, and for the very first time.

In addition, there are other curiosities that presented themselves later, a flurry of almost unrelated false claims that were presented *after* the "piling on" phase began. For a time, it was quite vogue for the media to print untrue tales told about Everett by people who simply did not know him, some patently false. Everyone wanted to jump on the "wallop Dutschke" bandwagon for a while which certainly delighted Holder and the gang since *they* weren't yet coordinating such attacks on Dutschke, they had their own character assassination campaign and when unsolicited plebes jumped aboard it only added momentum to the fervor.

One thing is for certain, it certainly made Everett furious. It was the little and insignificant lies that upset him as much as the big ones, as was discovered by Dr. Anne-Marie Hackenwerth when trying to discover why some people were attacking her friend. Her interviews of previous staff at the Oxford jail uncovered a recalled conversation between two former guards, one a female guard named ▮▮▮ that Everett seemed to confide in about the GQ article. He was angry at the authors of the 13 page feature and of his portrayal in it.

One thing recalled by Hackenwerth was Everett's outrage over accusations of some sort of romantic interest in Paul Kevin Curtis' ex-wife, the chatty agent, a claim that *she* made to GQ. The ex-wife of Curtis claimed to GQ that Everett had expressed a fancy for her but she turned him away citing that "he's short and hairy", (GQ printed.) Dutschke, as recalled by the she-guard, Kevyn, was red-faced over that one. "She's a liar!" He'd told the guards, "I would never even give that hunchback little troll a second thought!" The claim does seem to be incredibly thin since the ex of Curtis is barely 5ft tall if that—thus no one is actually "short" to her. Every photo of Dutschke available shows him very short-haired and clean-shaven including a photo of him with President George W Bush where he appears at least an inch or two taller. Indeed all of the official government records, of which there are many including multiple drivers licences which list him as 5'11, thus an inch above average. This patently untrue claim seems to come from nowhere and since it is not germane in any way to the specific details of the 2013 KC letters mailed by her ex-husband, Paul Kevin Curtis, it seemed the entire purpose for its inclusion by GQ was as a blatant cheap insult.

Another sinister insinuation from the same article raised his ire. GQ added a feature of song lyrics they presented as a song Dutschke had written entitled "Too Young". The obvious objective by GQ was to try to display Dutschke as perverse. What they did *not* disclose to their readers is that that song was simply part of a demo library compiled by Dutschke for producers who pitch various songs to various recording artists. That is how the music industry works. What GQ presented (lyrics and all) as a song that Everett had written was *not* written by him at all, but by a very talented female British songwriter who deserved exposure, named Lee. The song "Too Young" is actually *hers*, as can be seen on her YouTube channel "mental moomin." But of course, GQ did not bother to tell its readers who the actual songwriter was.

Dutschke was obviously not very happy with that portrayal. But it was not the only one. Another similar example directly to and printed by GQ dealt with an accusation of "public indecency", that is instead some sort of "voyeurism" on the part of the neighbourhood hoodlum peepers, though GQ did not bother to mention that bit of legality. Nor did they bother to ask any of Everett's lawyers—Wayne Housely, Tony Farese or Lori Basham who could have informed GQ that a person cannot be convicted of such a crime in absentia. A simple inquiry to the court in 2018 reveals that the actual court records show that there *is* no such conviction. GQ included the claim to simply aid in the smearing which added to the sensationalism and interest of the case. Court documents obtained in 2018 reveal that the original accusation itself was but a farce and an attempt to discredit and pressure Dutschke and that Dutschke was never present for any such proceedings. No transcript of any hearing exists, only a public claim of a 2013 pronouncement of guilt apparently made without any "notice" or any presence of either the accused or his attorney. This means there was no valid verdict, just the pronouncement of a verdict of uncharged unindicted claim of conduct that was for the sole purpose of applying pressure and discrediting Everett, a typical tactic to ensure that anything someone says is not believed. This, according to the court documents, was never actually adjudicated (appeals are denovo) until 2017 when the absurd case was actually dismissed. But one would never know that by reading the newspaper or GQ or any number of internet websites who all falsely claimed, repeating each other, that Everett was somehow found guilty of public indecency (while in his own bathroom and bedroom if one looks carefully at the GQ details) inside his own home. The media used quite a bit of space and ink in trying to portray Everett as some sort of deviant, and the bizarre accusation *did* appear to have a freezing affect on anyone, even his close loyalists from stepping up to defend him, especially in Tupelo, Mississippi where everyone is constantly looking to point out and ostracise the "sinner of the week." Had either GQ or any of the other media outlets bothered to investigate for themselves, since no one else did, they would have easily seen that such a claim was impossible since there was, between the Point A of the detested neighbour's home and the Point B controversial window, a house in the way. Nevertheless, the newspapers, broadcasters, magazines and websites had already cast their bones and invested themselves heavily in 2013 so the question is: Did they bother to retract their defamations and apologise to Dutschke and their readers when the phony accusation was actually dismissed? They sure did make a big deal of it when they thought it was valid, front page—above the fold. So did they run a retraction front page-above the fold when the legal resolution turned out to be the exact opposite they reported? If a broadcaster spends quite a bit of time or if a newspaper spreads a lot of front-page ink reporting that such a thing happened, doesn't the broadcaster or newspaper *owe* to both the target and to its own news consumers to spend at least an equal amount of time and ink and meeting later that they "misreported" or that the same thing did *not* happen? Is it not ethical to retract with an equal amount of vorosity as was used to report a false event?

If so, then no one told the broadcasters, the newspapers, the websites or magazines. Because NOT a single one offered even a modest retraction. Not one. And at least in the retraction, the media could have actually shown actual documentation in the actual form of the actual dismissal which bears the actual signatures of the court and Everett's actual attorney, Lori Basham. In 2013, when the sock-puppet press was busy doing the dirty work as an arm of the prosecutors and investigators (who had found it easy to dredge up a detested neighbour), the media had absolutely no documentation and "went to press" or "went live" without having anything to actually show its viewers or readers. Yet now, when there actually IS documentation proving the dismissal instead of a conviction, the media has absolutely nothing to say. As a result, no one ever learned the truth, no one ever learned of the dismissal. Why? Because the media never reported *that*...a dismissal isn't seedy enough. A dismissal is boring. It is much more fun to create and fabricate monsters than it is to reveal that they don't exist.

Here is what the conviction machine, especially politically-oriented machines of personal destruction knows and what the media knows that the general public is entirely naïve to—To *really* disparage a target, to really discredit them so badly that no one would ever believe anything the target ever says (even if he claims 1+1=2) you toss some sort of sexual accusation at him. There is no need for it to be true, the accusation is enough. It does not matter what it is either, even if it's something that some individuals in the public are themselves guilty of, everyone...everyone will remember only that too. It will stick. Even if it is as innocuous as an affair (Bill Clinton, JFK) and harmless in the scheme of things, though LEOs always try to imply that it is much more monstrous than a simple affair, that will be first in people's minds tainting any evaluation of character. The accusation is all it takes. Which is why no one in the media bothered to later report the dismissal and that the accusation was yet another bogus, trumped-up tale with no actual, final adjudication behind it.

Considering that the cabal (from Thomason to Holder) did, in fact, try to make claims of a murder-for-hire where the alleged FBI "victim" was the very much alive and perjurious Thomason (in the Holder/Mueller SAM) and of a bogus 2012 September arrest/conviction for murder and "genital dismemberment", what on earth would prevent them from these lesser yet equally as disparaging fabrications? The answer is—nothing. Which is why they did it. It is, in fact, what they do. It is documented that the cabal lied about the SAM claims and it is documented that the other "conviction" is *not* a conviction. But the media, including GQ, decided it would be more interesting to cover the accusation, but not the adjudication.

Jennifer Williamson, Everett's long-term friend from well over a decade prior, and Dr. Hakenwerth knew better. Williamson noted, "Everett was very modest. He slept in a shirt and always kept one on. Two or three if possible. He wouldn't even change clothes in front of Victoria" (a small white kitten she had given him—circa 1998). When Paul Kevin Curtis, the actual mailer of the KC letters, began to immediately blast Everett (as per Curtis's "get out of jail" agreement negotiated by Christi McCoy), he publicly made the accusation that Everett Dutschke had been inappropriate with students that he had taught in his Taekwondo School in North Carolina. No one in the media bothered to expose Paul Kevin Curtis as a liar who knew nothing at all about Dutschke and his claim was another impossibility. Dr. Hakenwerth knew, though. Living in North Carolina, she knew that Everett had never even been to North Carolina, except for a brief, two week period for training of his own of a different kind- that was Moyock in 1998 or early 1999. He had never had a student there, he had never had a school there and had never taught a single class there. Curtis's public 2013—present accusation was yet another of his fabrications. But it had legs. For when even looney people say looney things, other looneys often repeat it like a wave. Even the FBI at one point made an inquiry (meaning Thomason) hoping there was truth to it, and went as far as to contact a few of Dutschke's loose associates who lived in North Carolina before they concluded it was so much rubbish that there was nothing there to legally pursue (although the public claim of an accusation was useful to them).

The word "legally pursue" is carefully chosen because they had no intention of preventing *others* from continuing to perpetuate the false story. It benefited them (Mueller's FBI/Holder's DOJ) for the general populace to think nothing but ill of Everett Dutschke and even if the DOJ/FBI itself, or LEOs were not making the claims they certainly weren't going to stop, and to some extent encouraged, any dispersions aimed at Dutschke, who because of SAM, could not defend against them.

Paul Kevin Curtis claimed to GQ magazine that he had written on the Oxford jail cell wall some sort of particular looney phrase. Had the magazine author bothered to simply check with the jailors, they would have known that was another lie. When the GQ article was released, two of the guards (one a supervisor) Mary and Lee, actually checked the cell and searched for Curtis' proudly claimed graffiti. It did not exist. They recall Curtis singing like a loon to the other solitary confined inmates and staff as if he was performing Jailhouse Rock to a fawning audience. While it is perfectly acceptable for Paul Kevin Curtis to make his fanciful claims that are nothing but lies to the very core since he is mentally insufficient and a complete loon (even the strongest of medications only 'help' if you actually take them), it's *not* okay at all for the press to perpetuate such destructive lies. Curtis lives in a crackerbox castle and does not know any better; *he* likely believes in the rubbish that escapes from behind his ever chattering chompers. The media, on the other hand, should at least feel some sort of obligation to its consumers to try to tell the truth. But the one truth that can be counted on is that they cannot be trusted to tell it.

After all the truth, to them, is just so boring, and gosh, personal destruction is just so much darn fun. Particularly, it is, when that total destruction is part of the explicitly ordered agenda of an administration that the media had been brainwashed into believing was the second coming.

So the truth of the accusations, which is that there was none, never got published—not by GQ, CNN, MSNBC, New York Times, LA Times, Washington Post, Huffington Post, Clarion-Ledger, Tupelo Daily Journal, Drudge Report, Fox News or *any* of the thousands or so other media outlets that mentioned such rubbish; and *all* of those news outlets remained so incredibly distracted by that "non-official" salaciousness and the "official" hyper-dramatic fable of the *actual* case that no reporter even gave a thought or did so much as lift a finger to examine the details, question the narrative or connect the dots of *any* of the underlying elements of the intrigue. Not one.

At what point is either the press or the American public going to learn that when the government (especially *that* one), and particularly anyone associated with DOJ/FBI says "Hey...look over here!" that it is a much better idea to look somewhere else?!

Wherever they *tell* you to look is *not* where the truth lies. Another open question is whether the Secretary of State (Clinton/Abedin) bothered to review the 2012 September personnel in Libya prior to Everett's very brief Tuesday visit and meeting, or if she (Clinton/Abedin) only discovered thus learned of Dutschke's Tripoli meeting *after* the recall. IF it was prior to the planned Benghazi attacks-then there is a chance someone thought he would have been in Benghazi instead of Tripoli, and could have been a convenient target for Soleimani's thugs (but it was the other *actual* State Department T/O) as part of the likely *pre*arranged attack—an attack that, no matter who knew what about whether Everett was there or not, was likely already known to a few American officials, stateside, in advance. Half of the cabal (not the LEO half) and a member of the NSC, intelligence suggests, knew it was coming, and expected the Ambassador (Stevens, who was CIA-friendly) to be taken hostage. It was, one way or another, a vicous and sinister betrayal of the CIA and its good men by the upper-upper-upper echelons of its sister, State Department and the Commander-in-Chief who, when his plan went sideways and the Ambassador died and the CIA officers (most) lived (neither of which was supposed to happen) completely turned his head the other way and acted very un-Commander-in-Chief-like. The two new stars placed on the wall at OHQ were the direct result of that President, that Secretary of State (Clinton/Abedin) and John Brennan (and a couple others) just as much, even more so, than the attacking thugs of Soleimani. They all have the blood of good men on their hands and should never be forgiven for their absolute betrayal of the unsuspecting CIA patriots.

So an open question is—How is it that Michael Morell was so willing to forgive all three (maybe four) of those responsible? Since the 7th floor CIA *did* hear intel of the plot. Certainly Petraeus (DCI at the time) learned of it afterwards and was *not* happy with that administration's sedition of a re-election scheme. Petraeus knew and recognised that this was the biggest transgression and near-treasonous act since the 1963 Kennedy assassination that installed LBJ and re-empowered the FBI. Petraeus was a (DIA/CIA) patriot and not eager to put the country through the pain of learning the truth of the Benghazi (coordinated with a paid-off-in-cash-Soleimani) attacks by Iranian players on Americans in Libya—but this was too much. The President (Barack Hussein Obama) and the Secretary of State (Clinton/Abedin) learned of Petraeus's discovery of their scheme and his fury over their clumsy cover-up ("spontaneous protest") and their flippant discarding of four American patriots; so the President did what he usually does—he unleashed Mueller's FBI dogs on the CIA man to bring down Petraeus and began a smear campaign ("Petraeus/betray us") when the real betrayal was Obama and Clinton/Abedin. The scheming Obama's way through it all was his shoulder imp-advisor Brennan. Petraeus's "official" departure story was an extramarital affair discovered by...? The FBI.

Because if there's one thing that everyone knows it is that an extramarital affair must result in the abandonment of high office... right, Hillary?

Never, never, never believe an "Official" story, especially when the FBI is involved.

Yet Mike Morell, who likely also learned as much as Petreaus, decided that the administration's manslaughter of good CIA officers was acceptable. In fact, it was *he*, Morell, that actually played clean-up during the later congressional inquiries in the matter when *he* was the acting DCI; just before Obama was appointed...? Bennan...who was just as much an Obama/Hillary sycophant who probably would have drunk Obama/Hillary's bathwater (bathwater that likely would have drawn by Abedin).

In addition to Obama's treason of his knowingly plotting with a state sponsor of terrorism (Soleimani—who ended up well paid for it all), the former "community organiser" was a fool for entrusting the Secretary of State (Clinton/Abedin) to "handle" it logistically. For, if anyone is capable of screwing things up, it is Hillary Clinton.

Note: throughout this book, the phrase "Secretary of State" is often accompanied by the parenthetical descriptive "Clinton/Abedin". This is because they act as, and in fact are, a single unit divided into two separate bodies—one quite pretty and bright, the other an evil, twisted, power-mad, angry, loony hag. The singular "unit" was admitted as much *to* Saleha Abedin herself when Hillary met with her in Riyadh. It might have been a smarter move to defer to Huma more and speak much, much less.

Regardless, by the time it was clear that there was trouble, and her complete abandonment of the good men who were only doing *their* duty (cleaning up the Libyan mess made by the very same administration, with participation from Turry and Sen. McCain) things had already gone through (as does everything she touches) and it was likely that only then did she review any kind of personnel list of all Libyan operations. The only other people of high enough clearance to know them all (including Dutschke's name) would have been very limited—Sec. Of State (Clinton/Abedin), Brennan (maybe), the President and Petraeus, (and possibly Morell).

Dutschke's name would have only meant something to two of them— (3 really) which would have been Clinton/Abedin and Brennan, (and possibly Morell). All of whom would have been frantically busy with their cover-up of the criminal conspiracy to manslaughter the officers (and Ambassador) to make sure there was no "blowback" onto either Obama or Clinton.

The FBI's removal of Petraeus, installing Morell, helped the cabal get away with it. The biggest tool in the arsenal—the press, who refused to take off their "Yes we can" socks and T-shirts.

Thus a day after Dutschke had met again with Nunnelee and the others, when Hillary sat before the committee in an open and scheduled hearing and shrugged, "What difference, at this point, does it make?" She really meant "What difference does our hidden manslaughter of CIA officers and shitty cover-up make, since we just won the re-election anyway? YOU lowly Congress people can't touch us. We are shielded by the press and our attack-dogs of the DOJ. You Congressional worms think we can't get away with murder? Yes we can!"

It is obvious why Brennan played along. Why did Morell? Since Dutschke's 2012 visit to Kar-Mun Wong in California and his continued correspondence with him was even somehow known and raised by the FBI (in SAM documents of Holder/Mueller/Comey), was it Brennan who contacted Wong to coordinate "Kentucky Rain" using Dutschke or was it Brennan to Morell to Wong to Dutschke? While the likeliest scenario is that Brennan made the connection himself ("Kentucky Rain" was not really its own operation but the pretense of one—in actuality was the embryonic stage of Operation Dojo) since Brennan had 'field' experience and Morrell did not. However, the fly in the ointment is that at the time (2012-2013) Brennan was *not* CIA and Morrell was. So why would Wong give a damn what Brennan had to say? Wong was known to be one of the wisest and smartest men on the planet and would easily see any pitfalls for Dutschke or traps that would have been set by lesser minds like Morell or Brennan, and Wong's mind combined with Dutschke's would guarantee caution. Whether the double-cross, "switch" from the Libyan ricin product to the decoy was Wong's suggestion, Dutschke's idea or both will likely never be known as both Wong and Dutschke both refused any details or even acknowledgement of coordination.

The other question is—how is it possible that either Mueller or Comey could have informed Holder about the Dutschke-Wong connection at all?

Senior FBI officers, even at that level, have no access whatsoever to those kinds of CIA records, especially if individuals who have been dormant "Not official" for so long. So how did this happen? The only obvious way, which is how it made it into the SAM order and PDB, was that it was leaked. Morell is not known to "allow" leaks, though it has likely happened. Brennan, on the other hand, considers it part of his stock-and-trade…because it is; sometimes "leaking" things that are not true, sometimes leaking (unmasking) things that are. If Brennan, then he would not ever do it himself, as he masterfully keeps his tentacles clean. If Brennan, then the leaker to the FBI was either the haloed one himself, the President, or the whiffy Clapper (who is quite known for his constant leakage). If Obama, then he has no qualms about doing it himself, since he knows Mueller and Comey are his house boys, or Susan Rice or Samantha Power. Although it was Susan Rice that was used in the 2011 Dutschke health records unmasking (of the 2002 operation), it is far less likely she had anything to do with revealing to the FBI the Dutschke-Wong connection and most likely the President himself.

Besides, there is yet another reason that it was likely the President who would have done such briefings with Mueller or Comey instead of Clapper as well. James Clapper was reserved primarily for *press* leaks, like Susan Rice was. Obama handled the DOJ and FBI man himself as a matter of temporal safety. In fact, the Secret Service might have required it as a safety measure. Follow, if you will, this reported this paraphrasing of Everett's supposition of events:

First, one has to remember that in dealing with the Wong connection, Brennan would not want to "burn himself", so *he* would rather not have Holder write, as he did, "Dutschke's associate in California" in the Holder/Comey SAM (which was likely also in the Holder/Mueller SAM on Dutschke). And Holder, who is himself about as useful as a football bat, does not "investigate" anything himself. Nor did Holder have access to any CIA networks himself and FBI's Carnivore access would not have turned up such a connection. So someone had to inform the FBI man personally, whether it was Comey or Mueller (earlier). Either way, it is either Comey (who is ½ wookie ½ fecal matter) or Mueller, whose brain has long since become but a pudding of sorts, which is why he carries an extraordinary large handkerchief, in case he sneezes, so he can catch—well, it kind of explains itself. Any bits of greyish matter that intransigently refuse to transmogrify into a loose porridge of lost cognition have long since petrified, like an ancient tree that fell millions of years ago when some brachiosaurus needed to scratch at on itch on his backside and unmentionables (petrified weed is not known for its cognitive agility). Whoever, whichever of the two it was would require quite a bit of time invested into making sure they understand any details at all. Which is also a reason why such passing of this simple information, that they considered critical to make it into the SAM, was not likely done within one of the typical meetings of the syndicate which had the entire cabal in the Oval Office at the same time, because anyone trying to explain (anything) to Comey or Mueller is going to require a lot of time. It would require—tal-king...re-al...slow (using small words) and a few illustrations. And if the entire treasonous syndicate *was* in the room at that time, then Joe Biden (sitting on a stool in the corner of a round room) would have been in possession of the West Wing crayons at the time, making it impossible for anyone to draw the requisite pictures for the petrified Mueller or distracted Comey (who was too busy staring at himself in the reflection off the French doors pondering how awesome he might look with a nipple piercing, longer bangs and corn-rowed hair). Although it is plausible that during one of the many moments that Joe Biden sat slobbering and staring at "purple" trying to figure out which end of the crayon tasted the most like grape soda, that Susan Rice or Brennan could have "borrowed" some of the remaining colors for Obama's picture for the "boys".

Of course the drawing of it would have to have been accomplished at the Resolute Desk itself; lest Obama risk Comey reaching down, snatching up "green" and drawing a picture of his favorite thing, himself as the Hulk...so Obama would have had to keep the crayons out of reach of Comey and likely drew a drawing of Wong and Dutschke then an arrow pointing between them. Because he was in a bit of a rush, since Biden was already sniffing at Susan Rice's hair and wondering where he left his pants, Obama had to sketch quickly and grabbed the first piece of paper he found for it, which was Donald Trump's birth certificate from Kenya.

So if that connection was disclosed during the April (2013) meeting of the cabal, there would have been too much going on and too many distractions. THAT was the meeting where Brennan's unofficial operation became ("handed off", Brennan Style) an "official" LEO matter. Which means that Obama's known instruction to Holder and Mueller of "make an example of him (Dutschke)" would have likely been immediately followed by his question to Holder, "Eric...did Bob hear me? Is he still alive? Check for pulse..." and then the drawing bit with the crayons.

Of course, having the only "purple" might have been a problem for Joe Biden who might have thrown a tantrum reminiscent of his memories of the gang leader "cream puff" or "cocoa krispies" or whatever the ruffian's "name" was. And Brennan knew that Biden had to be kept busy with something to play with, and aside from Jim Comey's teeth there were no shiny things in the Oval Office to hold Joe's attention, so Brennan might have had an idea.

Brennan, recall, did not know that the "deadly toxin, ricin, with no known antidote" might have been switched by Dutschke to an inactive and denatured decoy product of similar molecular proteomic structure but rendered harmless. During the April 20th meeting, Brennan still thought that the KC letters contained the actual Libyan product which, according to Dutschke's own House testimony, was in fact, the "deadly toxin".

248

And recall that the KC letter that was sent to Senator Wicker never made it to the actual laboratory at Fort Detrick for toxicity testing. So where did it go?

It could be postulated that when Brennan recognised that Biden was about to throw a hissy over his missing flavor sticks and needed something else to explore, then Brennan had the missing "ricin" envelope ready to go.

"Here, Joe... why don't you play with *this* for a while."

"Gee, thanks, John... an envelope! Can I lick it?"

"Sure, Joe. Make sure you do."

"You're such a good friend, John."

"Don't mention it, Joe...no, seriously...don't mention it...to anybody...understand?"

Because explaining things to Comey or Mueller requires a really long time and in a distraction-free zone, then the Wong/Dutschke connection was likely not the April 20th meeting, but later. And it likely was not the flatulent Clapper who took *his* time to do it in a full meeting of the cabal because of the physical risk to the President. Remember that the President is a smoker. Not cigars, like Bill Clinton (though it is uncertain whether Clinton actually smoked cigars or just...uh... played with them), but Obama actually lit up cigarettes (and whatever else he happened to find lying around). And keep in mind, then, that whenever Clapper was in the Oval Office with Obama, the Secret Service kept him on an egg-timer. In part because Clapper's "bodyman" always kept a spare set of trousers on the ready for his hourly changing and also in part because there are no windows in the Oval Office which can open (windows are purely for admiring Comey's reflection) and it was only a matter of time before the Anointed One, the Supreme Leader and World Saviour really started jonesing to "light one up." And for obvious reasons the whiffy Clapper was not allowed near an open flame.

(Although there was some CIA RUMINT about what had happened to Susan Rice's eyebrows once).

So no, the entire swarm of the cabal was most likely not present at that one particular meeting, though they were all amassed at the other. For this particular bit of intel was probably disclosed (slowly and with pictures) by Obama, himself, after Brennan had already slithered away. Plus there is, in fact, a pattern that Obama knew that he needed to scheme with either Mueller or Comey separately after the adults had left the room. (Brennan, who was usually the one who remembered to bring his brain to these meetings, also knew RUMINT that Obama could not leave the French doors open to "air out" the room Clapper was fumigating at the same time Comey or Mueller was in the Oval Office for fear the FBI men might run out into the street. DC has a leash law. And more than once the Secret Service had to chastise that saggy-eyed Mueller-hound and the Mastiff-Comey with a newspaper wack to the nose when they were caught hiking their legs in the Rose Garden). And... Scene!

Again, it isn't that the FBI's knowledge of the very secret Wong-Dutschke connection is important, it is just interesting. Certainly neither Wong nor Dutschke ever publicised it. A curiosity, that's all.

Just as it is obvious that limbs from the FBI (Mueller/Comey) who endorsed the Holder SAM and briefed the President all the way out to the farthest twigs and offshoots, such a thing can be traced in both directions. Thus, once the cabal handed off the operation to the LEOs (FBI/DOJ), every single person involved from twig to bough can be identified and all the way back to the White House itself. There were a great many twigs (Thomason, Quaka) that, like the corrupt tree itself, were poisonous, in-line with the nature of the tree itself (the result of a toxic and poisonous planted intent from the beginning), yet there were some individual twigs and offshoots that, strangely, were not. These non-toxic parts, perhaps the fruit of this tree, were more subject to sterilisation of the purifying sunlight, perhaps, than the sinister intent that ran like sap through the body of the corrupt cabal's objective. But, the reason these fruits weren't fed the toxic intent by the tree itself was because they might have been forced by their circumstances into honesty—a trait uncharacteristic of the cabal's tree. This is so because those circumstances were that their limited role was scientific in nature, which is less subject to intent. These are the inside the laboratories themselves; not the FBI agents who wrote and compiled reports and "conclusions" (since *reports* are still written with the bias of the corrupt objective, conviction, in mind. They are weapons for the agents disguised as impartial and scientific). The reality is that the actual laboratory technicians, not the objective-blinded and sinister LEOs who sadistically dream of putting people in prison but the PHD-level, knowledgeable technicians, the biochemists and molecular biologists and microbiologists from places in laboratories like the CDC's "bioterrorism unit" (BRRAT) and the National Bioforensic Analysis Center (NBFAC) National Biodefence Analysis and Countermeasures Center of DHS and the Chemical, Biological, Radiological and Nuclear Unit (CBRNSU "weapons of mass destruction unit") were not subject to the intent of the cabal...intent being conviction. People like Stephen Cendrowski PhD, Dr. James L Pirkle MD, PhD and Dr. Michael Farrell and Connie Fisher that might have been the only honest players in the entire thing, meaning of the entire "tree". The only honest "fruit" were the ones possibly "forced" into honesty because the science is what the science is, and is not subject to twisting. And that science turned out to be exactly how Dutschke claimed it to be from the very beginning and *not* how everyone in the cabal claimed it to be. However, no one heard Dutschke's call (SAM) since the media is but a parasitic vine of the tree and listened to and announced only what poison was shared with it, symbiotically, from the tree itself and to the rest of the world.

But it is good to know that there were a small handful, albeit tiny, group of people acting as individuals who did not succumb to the immense pulling pressure of the cabal, even if people like Dr. Pirkle, Dr. Ferrell and Dr. Cendrowski had only a limited role and still could have been even stronger in their language so as to not give any "grey area" for the cabal and prosecutors to twist. Although these professional men of science were technically employed by the monstrous conviction machine it is a wonder they were not fired for leaning their analysis toward the truth (no ricin on dust mask or envelopes; not Dutschke's DNA), since they were likely just supposed to play along with the Obama rules to instead falsify and lie (ala Thomason, Mueller, McCabe, Comey) about the results. Usually, the Supreme Leader, the Anointed One, his Majesty Barack Hussein Obama, just sacks any disobediants who dare speak the damned truth or has the unmitigated audacity to endeavour to think for himself, or who does not blindly substitute and sacrifice their own good and rational judgments for replacing by Obama's agenda (which was *never* about what was good for Americans). Just ask General Carter Ham (U.S. African command) who wanted to send in military rescue forces to save the lives of the American CIA patriots under attack in 2012 Benghazi but was sacked by Obama for it. Or ask Rear Admiral Chuck Gravette (Commander of the USS John Stennis Carrier strike group) whose decision to aid General Ham's efforts by providing any intel which could *save* the lives of those CIA patriots was actually considered insubordination which led to the Admiral's sacking. Don't all these people know they are supposed to subjugate their own oaths and their morals, virtues and character to the whims of the King?

The sacrifice knows no end, even the ultimate sacrifice. The entire reason that Chris Stevens agreed to aid in cleaning up the utter mess created by Obama/Clinton in the first place (along with CIA staff in Libya) is because they actually thought that cleaning up the disaster that Obama's "support the Muslim Brotherhood" strategy (which didn't work so well in Egypt, Libya *or* Syria, did it?) was actually the objective and that it even *could* be cleaned up. Little did Stevens know that Hillary Clinton personally selected him because, to her, he was expendable. He would, blind to her insidiousness by his own patriotism, dutifully march into the fray, armed with only a mop to sop up her (and Obama) own filth; never really knowing he was but a sacrifice, an ultimate sacrifice. The reason all those men went to Libya in the first place is because they believed in their overall mission, protecting America, and in their specific assignment, even if the specific assignment was just to correct and sanitize the contamination left behind by failed (and sinister) foreign policy making...they did not go there to be killed, humiliated and betrayed by these very same foreign policy makers.

Presuming that a portion of the Tripoli File includes the detailed intelligence of how Kasim Soleimani came to coordinate the 2012, September attack (including intelligence of specific contacts and a back door chain that led, in a near straight line, to Obama) what good would it do to release that small part of the Tripoli File today, considering that every person involved

(AND other operations) is out of office? This is to ask the same question as Hillary Clinton (from her January 2013 testimony), "What difference, at this point, does it make?" Remember that it was only a few days before that testimony that Everett sent his January text to Jack Curtis (which the FBI suppressed), which was the final trigger which led to his becoming a target (within hours) for prosecution. That few days was time enough for either John Mills or Mark Turry (or both) to have gotten back with him, if they ever did. That text already indicates that Everett had suspicions and that some sort of operation against Jack's brother (Paul Kevin Curtis) had *already* started...*prior* to the April 8th mailings. Considering that Everett's text to Jack Curtis is indicative in January that he seemed to warn Jack about a potential problem involving Paul Kevin Curtis months *before* the April mailings, then that means that, at least in Everett's mind, he thought some operation ("Kentucky Rain") was already under way and that he did *not* trust those he thought were involved.

Combine Everett's January actions, which is what pulled the trigger against *him*, with his previous meeting with Wong and his January 10th actions in DC where he buried the Tripoli File, it shows that he had already determined that the cabal was up to its neck in its own mess and the only way out, perhaps *his* only way out, was to swim through it. It certainly reveals that he'd entirely lost all faith and trust in the high office-holders involved and saw no clean path out of it. It also reveals that the Clinton testimony was confirmation to Dutschke of two things: A—That the intel of at least that portion of the Tripoli File was, in fact, real reliable (there was no way he could have entirely trusted the details. Otherwise, thinking perhaps it could have been false and misleading intel); and B—How high up the connections went (also— there was no way Everett could have completely trusted such claims or confirmed it until Clinton's January testimony). This means that Everett's text to Jack Curtis was both a betrayal in the minds of the cabal (which until that time he couldn't know who or what was part of it) and a recognition that *he* had felt betrayed. The recognition of betrayal led to his own (sending the warning). So did Everett consider that his warning to Jack would be enough? There are no phone records showing that Jack Curtis ever responded. Another open question is did Jack Curtis bother to pass the warning on to his brother (Paul Kevin Curtis) or discuss it with him at all?

Chances are he did not. IF Jack Curtis had discussed it with Paul Kevin Curtis, in January or at any time thereafter, then Paul Kevin Curtis would likely have *not* sent the KC letters. The FBI phone records originally showed that Jack Curtis was, in fact, sent the January 18th text, so that was a known fact. There was even a witness to the text (that friend of Jack Curtis who met Everett Dutschke in Jack's parking lot as the friend was loading the chair into his truck—it was Jack's friend who gave Everett Jack's number). So why then, did Jack Curtis choose not to discuss Everett's texted concern or at least mention it to his brother, Paul Kevin Curtis? IF Jack had simply done so then none of this would ever have happened. This is not to say that Paul Kevin Curtis's actions are Jack's fault, however. If all news and FBI reports are to be believed, Jack was the only of the Curtis siblings that would still associate with Paul Kevin Curtis, others having gone as far as to have the man arrested and even place "restraining orders" against Paul Kevin Curtis. But, according to reporting, Jack was very, very familiar with the fantasy world in which Paul Kevin Curtis lived, and he knew that his brother genuinely believed in the things that were utterly impossible and held a grandiose view of himself that led to his constant paranoia about being personally targeted by the evil, evil government to whom he always heroically stood against as a modern martyr.

Except, this time they're actually was a bit of truth to it. As the little boy who cried "wolf", and Paul Kevin Curtis was finally that little boy (even though instead of standing heroically he later sang like a canary...or more likely squawked like a lost budgie), and, as was already known to Jack Curtis, when someone is as much a nutter and as obtuse as Paul Kevin Curtis, he cannot truly be held to account for his actions. Even buffoons are not always at fault for their buffoonery when his limited ability to think rationally is curved not by will or by choice but by the unfortunate hand dealt to the man when nature itself cobbled together whatever detritus it could find to suffice as the smear of Paul Kevin Curtis's brain. There is a part in every sentient man that cannot help but feel quite sorry for a creature like that, especially when that creature is a biological brother. Perhaps it was because Jack, in fairness to him, simply could not have understood the significance since he had, he thought, seen it all before.

Regardless, Hillary Clinton's exact words—"What difference, at this point, does it make?" as any psychologist will tell you, is but an indictment of *her* since it really means "What difference, Congressman, does it make to *me?*" This was likely all the confirmation that Everett Dutschke needed to validate that that portion of the Tripoli File was credible, enough to show him that her callousness was not based on some inner sense of practicality, but was instead based on a genuine lack of curiosity about the genesis of the Benghazi attacks.

The lack of curiosity betrayed her as it flowed directly from the fact that she already knew the genesis of it. Her disinterest, which she fully expected the House Committee to share, was both her own mental barrier and a conversational barrier to any exploration of the attacks inception, which she *knew* already was *not* some anti-video protest. Had she not already known, in advance, of the attack—she would have approached the entire hearing in a different way. Had she not already known the full run of the Benghazi plan, she would not have been defensive in her very tone as these lowly congressman *dared* to question the complete abandonment, and by overt and active measures to ensure that abandonment, of the American CIA patriots who had fought for their very lives after being sent there, in the first place, to clean up *her* mess! And if she had not had foreknowledge and been complicit, her hearing demeanor would have been sorrowful.

The very small circle of people who knew of the Kasim Soleimani coordinated attack on Americans in Libya was very tight and no one (on the American side of the ocean) betrayed any of the others, proving that it never trickled down from the Secretary of State's office. Proving also that Huma Abedin, who knew and knows everything about every cell in Hillary Clinton's body, is fiercely loyal since she (like her mother) was no friend at all to Soleimani. Sometimes allowing the devil in your playground is for the greater "good" (temporarily).

Hillary Clinton's unknowing public hearing admissions, and demeanour, was Everett's affirmation that she was not only complicit, but a central planner, though not the architect, of it all. This likely highlighted the already strong compulsion to mistrust the Oval syndicate (which at the time did *not* include DOJ/FBI), a mistrust that must already have existed, as evidenced by his swap of the Libyan product for the counterfeit "ricin" before its December transference to Paul Kevin Curtis, a little more than a week before the hearings and three before Everett's text to Jack Curtis. The same sort of caution that Everett showed, reminiscent of Jeff Sterling's concerns in Operation Merlin, would have been better if contagious, so for that caution to spread would have required Jack Curtis to act as the vector. So why didn't he?

It is not critical, and it does not change any of the evidence...but it could have...because had he done so there would never be any evidence at all and the legal and public attacks against Everett would have eventually simply fizzled out.

But then, there is the possibility that Jack did. In which case, since Paul Kevin Curtis pursued it all, his way, anyway—leading to infinitely more questions. This possibility would require a near obsession by Paul Kevin Curtis with any and all things Dutschke, which is not beyond the realm of possibilities when dealing with Paul Kevin Curtis.

While it is doubtful that Paul Kevin Curtis gave a true accounting to his lawyer, Christi McCoy, it is likely that she knows full well that Curtis was, in fact, the mailer even if only because she is not an idiot and knows the evidence of the case, of the mailing at least. One thing is most certain, Curtis owes McCoy his life and the recompense of her rescue of the sap is worth far more than the "foot rub" that he publicly promised her during one of his odd moments before news cameras (odd for anyone else, really, maybe not so odd for him). Because although Paul Kevin Curtis immediately began to wail away to the FBI in his eager attempt to become their FBI snitch, he was doing so for free and getting nothing for his prattling collusion with the LEOs until Christi McCoy happened along and brokered his freedom in exchange. Until she came to his rescue, Paul Kevin Curtis was spit-shining the loafers of the lowest of the FBI thugs while simultaneously putting the handcuffs on himself. He even disclosed to the agents, willingly and without representation, several tales of his own long criminal history. Tales which always ended with some other responsible adult sweeping in to rescue (with pity), the poor sap who should never be held to account for whatever is his criminal act of the month, considering his extreme mental instabilities. In fact, Paul Kevin Curtis these days often regurgitates a woeful tale of his being "chained to the floor" for hours of intense FBI interrogation as they held him captive demanding answers. This frequent diatribe of his has come to be an irritant to the agents involved since they insist it was the other way around. No one was ever "chained to the floor" as Curtis falsely claims and it was *he*, Paul Kevin Curtis, that held *them* hostage (not in the physical sense, although the FBI *did* uncover the 1990s event where Curtis held a Chicago girl hostage at gunpoint).

According to the low-level FBI agents, Curtis just would not shut up. Since the FBI is too corrupt to capture interviews and interrogations on video (because it is harder to falsify videos than notes), they simply take written notes called 302s, which can later be altered to tailor fit their predetermined objective/narrative. The FBI agents who were trapped in the same room with the unemployed conspiracy theorist who claimed to be a professional foot doctor, Elvis impersonator, author of anti-government books and political 'activist' all rolled (loosely) into one split personality, all claimed that they would have run out of paper if they had not eventually stopped listening to his rantings. Paul Kevin Curtis seemed happy that he had a (small) captive audience. At one point, the note-taking agents just quit writing.

And according to them, though they did not understand the significance until Christi McCoy mentioned Dutschke in the Curtis court hearing and word to the street level FBI agents was passed down from DC that Everett Dutschke was the actual target of Mueller (and the cabal), Paul Kevin Curtis (the same chap who these days claims had no idea about any of it and was supposedly entirely clueless) actually told the agents immediately that it was J. Everett Dutschke who is responsible for the product that was used in the KC letters that they knew, and swore under oath, that Paul Kevin Curtis had mailed. Curtis had never claimed to the FBI men that Everett was the one who had put the letters in the post, he knew he couldn't. During the interview, he had, in fact, admitted that he had written to Senator Wicker and Obama before and even disclosed his previous mailing of the same type to the Reverend Mike Hicks. At that time, they were less interested in the maker and more in the mailer (Curtis), which is where the real *mens rea* (ill intent) lies anyway. That is, until the street-level FBI were told to forget about the mailer and instead focus on the maker; told that by their DC supervisors, in part because of the horse-trading by Christi McCoy. Although, Paul Kevin Curtis is much more like a confused donkey of some progressive decrepitude than a horse.

The anti-government conspiracy book by Curtis which flung accusations of black-market body-parts sales immediately followed the 2011 Rice/Power unmasking of Everett Dutschke using the insurance records produced after the 2002 helicopter crash. Jack Curtis was an insurance executive, but was not a broker for the same insurance company. Paul Kevin Curtis's ex-wife, who is the same one who allowed Paul Kevin Curtis into a closed meeting in order for Curtis to meet Everett, was an agent; but that meeting which was supposed to be about insurance coverage was also about a different company and it was years prior to Curtis's book. However at the same meeting, where Curtis had no authorization to be, was allegedly where Curtis claims that Everett refused to hear out Curtis' alleged information of the "body parts" issue. Curtis's feelings, as he had expressed it, was that Everett Dutschke was supposed to be the man to whom people specifically brought information *to*...or at least, as Curtis explains it, that's what was publicly advertised. In other words, "if OTHER people can bring Dutschke information, then I should be able to bring him THIS...", was Curtis's thinking. That idea of Curtis was what has led him to label Everett Dutschke now, for over a decade, as a "hypocrite" in public. In Curtis's mind, Dutschke's refusal to listen to Curtis was his way of saying that "my information was not good enough for him" stating that it was a "political" decision to protect the hospital (that had fired Curtis as a janitor) since the hospital was one of Tupelo's largest employers; and from that point forward Curtis believed Dutschke to be part of the cover-up of the hospital "body parts" plot and was protecting his political buddies from exposure of what Paul Kevin Curtis actually believes to be the truth.

So was the timing of Paul Kevin Curtis's accusatory conspiracy book and the 2011 unmasking a coincidence or did he have help? If not a coincidence, then Paul Kevin Curtis's attack against Dutschke, from 2011 and on at least, were already coordinated, and he had been a tool since the time that the cabal was but a few (two or three in ███ █████████ and three or four in the states with one local asset in the field). However, if Curtis's attacks on (and near obsession of) Everett Dutschke were entirely of his own design, if they were conceived from within Curtis's own empty head, then they got noticed by others; not just noticed by the hyper security-conscious officers and executives who (especially since the 2011 unmasking) had deemed such exposure to be a security risk (since no longer lily-white), but it also got noticed by the then small cabal, well over a year before the Oval Syndicate of the usual suspects developed the scheme which later became Operation Dojo. What this means is...*if* Curtis began his attacks on Dutschke of his own accord, then it was *he* who later, inadvertently and unknowingly gave the Oval Syndicate (Brennan) the idea which developed into Operation Dojo (which almost entrapped Curtis himself). This is the most likely scenario. ("Who can we plausibly use?")

So Paul Kevin Curtis, the fellow who claimed/claims to be frustrated that no one was paying attention to him, *was* actually being paid attention! He just did not know it. True, his issues were being paid no mind and were dismissed as quickly by everyone else just as Everett had dismissed them; and equally as true that no one believed the bizarre things that Curtis actually believed. But at that point when the security apparatus saw that one of their own (Everett) had become exposed (unmasking 2011) and people began to research the extent of it, Curtis was discovered. At that point he was considered dangerous by some (as Senate Intelligence Committee woman Claire McCaskill said—"He is known to us") and yet considered potentially useful to others (Saleha Abedin, Ja'ara, Naseef, Clinton/Abedin and Brennan), but noticed nonetheless.

Whereas Carter Page and George Papadopoulos were intelligent enough to escape the clutches of Brennan's attempt to turn them into his unwitting tool (circa 2016), Paul Kevin Curtis was decidedly *not* and would never realise such a thing.

In fact, he ended up face-to-face with the very same G-men that he claimed to detest, when it all came to a head, he became their chatty pet rat. A pet rat willing to say and do anything to please his masters.

So what happened to the tough-guy conspiracy theorist who liked to brag on radio shows how the government is his enemy and that it has been tried by law enforcement "Over 40 times" (he told interviewers) to lock him up and "None were successful"? What happened to the fellow who claimed to be standing strong against the oppression of the coppers?

Well…he folded, that's what happened. The second they came with badges and started asking him questions, he gleefully not only answered but chattered away to the FBI men so much that they couldn't get him to shut up. In the end, Paul Kevin Curtis (the mailer) cried hard for the FBI men to give him a plastic badge and join the rest of the rat-pack with Dennis Montgomery (rapist) and Christopher Stutsy (Fast & Furious thief). When the chips were all in, Curtis was the opposite of the stout "activist" he pretended to be on the radio shows. Instead, the man not only folded, he did not "stand up" at all. Hell, he practically cooked them breakfast!

Presuming that Paul Kevin Curtis was indeed an easy sell to make as a concern to national security, though not at a flash or priority level, to Dutschke, a valid question might be "How"? Paul Kevin Curtis used the media to claim that the CIA was "poisoning" the population with mind control "chem-trails" released airliners, so what? So he accused the US government of selling, in his words, bar-coded heads, hands, feet, elbows, intestines or whatever nonsense he claimed, so what? So he claimed the CIA (or whoever) blew up his car (without him in it?), burned down his house (without him in it?), and killed his bunny rabbit (Not a joke. He actually has *publicly* made such claims), so what? How is any of this of any concern to national security? How would such a sales pitch go?

Believe it or not, Curtis aside, this is actually a pretty common problem. In his particular case, it is a little more than a petty nuisance, as he portrays himself as an innocent victim, targeted for extreme measures because of his nonsensical beliefs. Paul Kevin Curtis is more than a mere meddlesome thorn. He is considered a festering sore of governmental distrust whose waste and rubbish feeds more than just the conspiracy theory flies but draws in the interests of others, the common folk, by constantly martyring himself as the innocent victim of non-existent government conspiracies. He is a present danger to the already precarious balance of trust.

Nevermind that Curtis's ex-wife has stated in interviews that the car probably just had an electrical problem which caused the explosion, and the house fire was possibly caused by a common kitchen fire, not arsonistic government agents, and that rabbits just die eventually (that's what living things do). It is highly doubtful that if any of Everett's friends would have detonated a vehicle bomb and missed their human target, lit a house aflame without their human target in it or worry about fuzzy rodents. There is no reason that either Paul Kevin Curtis or his bunny should be part of the disposition matrix at all. It is preposterous.

How would that conversation even go? The CIA director and the President would go before the Gang of Eight and say, "Based on actionable intel we launched a preemptive kinetic strike yesterday, gentlemen. The target, a known threat to America's interest, known as 'Snowball', was neutralised at 0900 with an armed Air Force asset MQ-1 piloted jointly from CAOC and Tampa by three Hellfire missiles in two passes as live monitored by the NRO and a SISOL from a 110 mile aerial view of the cage. I'm sorry that we could not brief you yesterday, gentlemen, on the elimination of this HVT rodent, but given the sensitive nature we needed to be sure that we could all breathe a sigh of relief that the furball was, indeed, actually eliminated. We are briefing you now because the Joint Chiefs and the NSC have just gotten word from the Combined Arms Center that the 902nd Military Intelligence Group confirms that nothing was left of the bunny but its charred remains. I apologise for the delay of the briefing...but don't worry, gentlemen, lunch is on me."

And since this chapter is but an assortment of related items that would not cleanly fit inside any of the other, more designated and specific chapters, here would be a good time to caution the reader not to feel any empathy towards Paul Kevin Curtis by thinking him in any way an animal lover. There is an event, most unbelievable, that disproves this idea. And when this is disclosed, it will surely seem as fictional as a comic book or cartoon character...and yet it is mostly assuredly a true event that actually happened. And it is advisable to read this next bit twice through as it is so fantastical that it will leave even the most expectant reader completely chapfallen in disbelief.

This true event will reveal Paul Kevin Curtis to be as friendly to animals as a cockchafer is to wood. Recall the posts Curtis made in his Facebook page just before he announced publicly this unique phrase he had just written into the 2013 KC letters. Specifically a few days just before, the posting of the photo of his new pistol and his caption "say hello to my little friend." Clearly he was feeling very, very confident in himself that weekend in April 2013... he was just about to mail off the KC letters (on Monday), but felt invincible and powerful just before that from Wednesday and Thursday into that weekend (the weekend just before his Monday morning mailing). So powerful the foot doctor-impersonator was feeling that he bragged on his new acquisition of arms to the world, and all his friends to witness his new-fangled 2nd Amendment power. "Say hello…" he said.

But that was not enough. Now that he was newly empowered, he would announce it to the world how invincible, untouchable and important he is on Monday, when he sent out the KC letters...except this guy, the self convinced superstar of a man was feeling so vigorous that he wanted to feel it now. Why wait until Monday, the letter day? Now would be a good time to demonstrate how strong and powerful he is (was). Now would be a really good time to shoot something.

Paul Kevin Curtis was far too broke to go on a safari hunt. And since he had Monday plans (mailing the KC letters) there really wasn't enough time to go on holiday so he had a lie-down and considered some options. There are some cats that roam around in his low-income, government-provided housing-project (the same damn government he lambasts on the media all the time, ironically), maybe he could fire off a few rounds and see if he could hit a kitty or two. They all have nine lives, right? Oh...but his neighbours might notice the gunfire and call the coppers. The wallopers would show up, blue lights flashing, and guns at the ready. Who needs that nuisance? Hmm... Maybe he could take a spin out to the country a ways and shoot off a few rounds at cows. That could be fun. But not very spectacular. He'll keep the bovine target practise in mind. Still feeling elevated about himself and seeing on Facebook that his online friends (people who limited any associations with him to the cyber world) had visited the visiting fair that had set itself up outside of the Tupelo Convention Center on Main Street, and decided he owed himself a treat. He considered brushing his teeth, but it wasn't a Tuesday yet, so opted instead to drive down Highway 45 a bit to see what all the commotion was about, he should not be left out of it.

Almost as soon as he arrived at the busy place, he knew he had made the right choice (but then how could that ever be in question since he is, after all, Paul Kevin Curtis) and that this fair was where he belongs. Fairs need clowns and he had just arrived. He was enthralled by the dog races since these dogs all had little monkey jockeys strapped onto their backs. The dogs didn't mind, though the monkey seemed to. In fact, the fuzzy little dog jockeys seemed too angry to care if the dog they rode on won their race or not. That didn't seem right to Paul Kevin Curtis. For if Paul Kevin Curtis was strapped into a Lhasa Apso or a Whippet saddle, he would want to win every race. Paul Kevin Curtis selected the least bored-looking primate atop of a long-legged mutt for the next race—and they were off! Well...off was more of a wish and seemed to have more of a grey area than a sudden beginning. According to witnesses, when the buzz announced the start and the starting gate fell, the dogs just sort of meandered about the course socialising with each other instead of launching into a full-on sprint. It was as if the racing canines had some catching up to do, as if they had not seen each other in a long while. Nor were the jockeys endeavouring to do their job of keeping the curs focused on their mission either. The simians seem to have just given up any attempt to control their mongrel steeds at all, some sat in their saddle (not as if they had a choice) with their arms crossed, glaring at each other, and their carefree dogs, either indifferent or annoyed at their assigned bitch or some other monkey's bitch, this included Curtis's selected racer. The jockey, wearing his tiny green tights with a lucky number "7" emblazoned across him glanced briefly at Paul Kevin Curtis as if to say "What's the point? We are going to lose anyway." It didn't matter how much Paul Kevin Curtis yelled at the tiny primate "Go!". It didn't matter how hard he pointed and gestured. The little jockeys had resigned themselves to the reality that the dogs were just going to mingle for a while and that the dogs thought that the mingling was the point. Number "7" was NOT going to be so lucky.

Except for the red-clad Number 12. That duo was not the fastest team, but was clearly the only dog that understood that all that canine hobnobbing was a bit too tedious for his taste and ridden by a monkey that liked to win. Since Number 12 was the only team walking through the race course, they won. It took a while, since there was no real running involved, but the moment Number 12 slowly crossed the finish line and won, Paul Kevin Curtis lost.

He thought maybe he should shoot a monkey right then and there. But which monkey should be shot? Jockey number 7, who caused him to lose or jockey number 12 who also caused him to lose? Maybe he should just shoot the lot of them. As he pondered and meandered about, he forgot entirely about cats, cows, dogs and monkeys.

And it occurred all at once. Not because he was forgetful (though he very much is), but because he happened upon the perfect target near the opposite corner of the fairs set up from the Monkeys Riding Dogs race course when he discovered the petting area. No, he was not going to shoot any of the goats, though he did put some coins in the feeding dispenser to dump some cheap goat food into his hands, and a few of them were nice enough to pretend to like him for a moment, as long as it took to munch the goodies that he offered. Which is quite a bit like prostitution when one thinks about it, explaining why the "better paid" goats are the ones that hang closer to the feed vending machine. ("Sure, I'll pretend that I like you for a minute or two... until you run out of quarters"). No, it was not the nannies and billys that piqued Curtis' shooting interest, it was... the elephant!

He had never shot an elephant before, at least not that he remembered. But, boy! That sure would be something to remember. WHO Could actually say they shot an elephant? Not many, that's who. Paul Kevin Curtis would be the first in his family to fell a pachyderm. His mother and the ghost of Elvis would be so proud.

He wanted to be sure he was one of the last to leave. He drove around a bit, scoping out the best angle. He decided that since the petting area was near the Main Street corner fence line that the massive quadruped would have to be targeted from the street that ran next to it, but there was a problem. If he set up nearby, he could fire at the mammoth through the chain-link fence but someone would surely hear the shots and call upon the coppers who would respond very quickly since the Sheriff's department is but a block behind the Convention Center one way and the police station one block on the other way. Logistically, it had to be a drive-by shooting, in the style that black people sing about in their music. If Paul Kevin Curtis positioned his auto just right, he could fire off a few shots before quickly angling his vehicle toward Main Street, turn left and be on Highway 45 heading north towards Corinth in the blink of an eye, long before 911 picked up the phone to even respond. Close to midnight, still feeling good about himself, though nervous, this is exactly what he did. There is no way to know for certain how many times Curtis pulled the trigger that night, some witnesses said 3 but one bullet hit the young jumbo and he bellowed loudly. Shaking with excitement and fear, Paul Kevin Curtis stepped on the pedal and fled the scene.

The poor elephant was terrified and bleeding from his shoulder. He was supposed to be a beloved animal, one that people paid to see and pet and feed and if they were lucky, even ride on. He was a circus attraction and had never been in a gunfight before. The fair staff did not think to immediately check their pachyderm, believing the gunfire to be something else. For usually when a person hears gunfire his first thought isn't, "Go check the elephant." They did, though not straight away, and panicked. By then, Curtis was long gone. The "Savings" petrol station on that very corner caught Curtis' white SUV fleeing the scene on its security video.

The veterinarians were called, as were the police and Sheriff's Department. Though that would not have mattered since Tupelo police had never dealt with an elephant shooting before... for them, this was the first, and since the Sheriff was Jim Johnson, the extent of the "investigation" by his investigators and himself was to merely make sure that none of HIS guys could get pinched for it. In Johnson's mind, there's nothing wrong with shootings and killings and even beating as long as Johnson and his thugs were in the clear for it. The local newspaper jumped to cover the shooting and everyone was concerned for the fair attraction. Tupelo residents raised money, though it is still unclear why, and some Tupelo churches even prayed for the calf who pulled through and, after surgery, was all right.

Curtis, however, was still on top of the world. And he had successfully gotten away with the 2013 KC letters AND shooting an elephant in the city. Who could say THAT? Not many, that's who. (As told by Curtis to a former "friend" of his who no longer associates with him)

Alas, it would be wonderful to say that the event never happened, for one has to feel badly for the other (though it might have saved the life of a cow or a couple of monkeys), but it was an unfortunate true event. The good news is that there seems to have been no more pachyderm shootings in Tupelo since. A goal for the Tupelo Chamber of Commerce and the city council was to make Tupelo an elephant safe zone after that, efforts which, judging by the crime statistics since then, have been celebratedly successful. At last check, the tourism board might have considered a sign proclaiming "Welcome to Tupelo—no elephant shootings since 2013!"

All this discussion of the elephant target practise seems too ridiculous to be true, but it actually gets worse—or better, depending on one's perspective. Recall that the last time Curtis had gotten in trouble for his gun in Tupelo, and almost precisely at the same time, was when he assaulted the district attorney with a (different) pistol years prior. The same assault that a judge sentenced him to a year in jail for who happens to also be the VERY SAME judge that was about to receive one of these KC letters in the mail! On TOP of that, the FBI was consulted about the elephant shooting... This is the point where the reader may simply toss down this book with an incredulous eye-roll and proclaim, "I give up!" Just as the dog-racing monkeys had decided that they had had too much.

There was, in fact, an FBI agent who was sent to Curtis' flat (government provided housing unit) to disarm him and make sure there were no weapons there which could cause another injury like the one to the petting zoo elephant. Would the reader care to guess which FBI agent admitted, after having to correct himself when he falsely stated he had never been to Paul Kevin Curtis' "residence" or met him? According to court transcripts that "special agent", the one who admitted actually entering Curtis' home and "clearing" that same very pistol and then removing it was none other than... Stephen Thomason.

It was, as a matter of record, Thomason that unloaded and removed the elephant-shooting pistol from Curtis' "home." Funny how things all interconnect in the most bizarre ways, isn't it?

While this part of the true story of the KC letters and the fraudulent prosecution and making a terrorist of Everett Dutschke has no direct connection whatsoever to Rabita Trust, or the three financiers or the concealment of exculpatory lab work, the elephant story is so curious and so novel that it had to be included in this book somewhere. So although it isn't really relevant, it is still a kind of unignorable sideshow that its inclusion, unnecessary, is warranted because, at this point, the reader deserves the whole truth, and it's just plain fun. City elephant hunting was not a pressing issue of National Security, but it is revealing, on a serious note, of exactly what kind of person had gotten noticed and selected as the tool for Brennan's scheme.

That scheme, it might be said, was not as much about the elimination of Dutschke (though the 2002 score was not yet settled, apparently) and more about preventing any disclosure of the Tripoli File, which would have eliminated the Secretary of State (Clinton/Abedin) chances at a 2016 presidency and would have sent that 2013 administration into immediate impeachment hearings (ironically) as the true nature of the Benghazi collusion would have made Watergate look like a petty offence. This would have made the handsy Biden the "president", which would have been fine for any puppet masters that would have survived the purging that would have taken place. The one thing the 2013 Oval Syndicate had going for it was that it was part of a larger cabal which included the DOJ (Mueller/Holder/Yates/McCabe etc.) which would never have prosecuted any of them for anything no matter what. The only people that the Justice Department (cabal) was interested in prosecuting were the good guys. Just ask Jeff Sterling, Sharyl Atkisson, John Kiriakou, Thomas Drake, James Risen, James Rosen and the Associated Press CEO Gary Pruitt to whom Obama replied "I make no apologies" citing (predictably) "National Security". These people, victims of the cabal's weaponization of the DOJ, learned the hard way that the American justice system is, indeed, multi-tiered and that a certain political class was not only immune from prosecution but also insulated (by the media) from scrutiny. That immunity does not apply to everyone, especially when that particular regime was in power. One only needs to look at the recent Crossfire related prosecutions and cases (candidate and President Trump, Manafort, General Michael Flynn, Page, Papadopoulos, Roger Stone and so on). The perfect example of which is General Flynn. Furthermore, to anyone who might even begin to question what extremes that administration would go to in protecting their interest, only one needs look at the Flynn case to see that the destruction of a man was but an expendable, collateral damage to their greater ends of protecting their interests. People, including General Flynn, were but throw-away souls and disposable to the whims of Clinton and Obama and the cabal. But the entire Flynn case, indeed the entire Crossfire trove of operations could have easily been prevented and never would have happened in the first place if the cabal had been stopped. That stoppage should have been the Dutschke case.

Same prosecutorial misconduct. Same judicial abuse. Same weaponization of the DOJ and the very same cast of characters (except that

Dutschke had Eric Holder added into the mix, Flynn did not). If there had been a heroic figure like Flynn's attorney Sydney Katherine Powell to stand, unafraid and unintimidated, against the cabal in 2013 with Dutschke (and against even GREATER abuses) as there was with Flynn in 2020, then the cast of characters would have been exposed and rendered powerless instead of emboldened to later repeat a diet version of the Dutschke attacks/operations on Flynn. But it is clear that the conspiracy to violate a citizen's constitutional rights (18USC§241) with a fraudulent prosecution, investigation and public smearing was an operation that the cabal was skilled at performing and even those at the very top knew how to weaponize the system to deal with someone that threatens their political interest. Just as when Obama told Mueller (April, 2013) and Holder to "make an example out of (Dutschke)", the President revealed himself to be complicit in the using the system as a gross abuse of power. (Not speculative. An actual quote.)

In the recently declassified Oval Office meeting notes of Peter Strzok (FBI-National Security Division), it is revealed that it was Obama himself who specifically directed Comey to "Use the right people... to get it done." That is a direct quote from the FBI's-NSD, Strzok's notes as attributed TO THE PRESIDENT of the United States!

Now what exactly did the President, Barack Hussein Obama, comment mean exactly when he said that to his lurch-like co-conspirator Jim Comey? Who are "The RIGHT people?" What this shows is that Obama was fully cognizant that choosing loyal people who, like Comey and Obama, are willing to do whatever it takes to really destroy, discredit and convict someone was key. Obama, by using those exact words (if Strzok notes are accurate), was saying, "We don't want anyone who will follow the law. We want swamp creatures who are willing to go with fabricated and planted news stories, lies, pressure, family, threatened witnesses, concealed evidence, created phony accusations. People like Stephan Thomason. THAT'S who we want on this case, because our priority isn't truth, it is destruction and conviction. Find THOSE people, Jim! Put THOSE people on the case."

Obama's exact words to Comey, as recorded in Strzok's notes, are important not just because words have exact meaning ("Use the RIGHT people") but also because he meant those exact words. That's one sentence, alone, as it was exactly phrased should tell the world what is the truth about Obama, and that his abuses are intentional acts. This is the kind of thinking— that certain citizens are disposable to the whims of protecting his personal political interest and ego—is the kind of thinking that is associated with Russia, China and North Korea, where a citizen, and the truth, is of zero value to a political office holder. Iran, Venezuela and Cuba are not even as malignant as the Obama Oval Office, a malignancy which has spread to the Secretary of State (Clinton/Abedin), who obviously viewed citizens, even heroic CIA-GRS officers, as nothing but disposable rubbish to be discarded for her entertainment or advancement. Or perhaps the malignancy had spread the other way, from Clinton to Obama, or perhaps Brennan had infected them both, but it does not matter. The cancer that was that administration's not just apathy but hostility towards its own citizenry could have and should have been stopped at the Dutschke prosecution. The portion of America that still had brains were outraged in 2020 over the abuses and weaponization of the DOJ and even the judges during the Flynn case (the brainless have actually encouraged the abuses). Where were those same voices in 2013, the FIRST time the same cabal fraudulently destroyed a patriot on fabricated claims (and with a SAM "prosecution" at that)? Where was Mr. Hannity, Beck, Limbaugh and Levin then? They did not even notice. Why? Because Everett was not a president and cared not a hoot about the politics. Nor did he ever ask for the Tripoli File which made him a target to begin with. Had the so-called constitutional scholars, freedom-lovers and Doctors of Democracy bothered to pay attention THEN, then the entire later Crossfire nonsense would never have happened. AND the appointed and timid Ken Coghlan is a far, far cry from the brave and fearless Sydney Powell.

There may be an interesting parallel which returns the story full circle, nearly back to the start. While Everett Dutschke has expressed that he generally has little confidence or trust in DOD, one exception to that might just be General Flynn, himself. The reason for that being twofold. First, Flynn was not just some gun-toting, grenade-tossing general... he was DIA, An intelligence officer. TO Dutschke that might be different... closer to the CIA then some missile-jockey. Second, Flynn, DIA at the time, might have been privy to exactly what happened to and who was responsible for the death of Sa'ayd Al-Sayidi (2006) and his team (the man who, in part, rescued Dutschke and his own team in 2002... notwithstanding the crash). It was reported that it was US military who claimed to have found those (?) responsible for Al-Sayidi's assassination and turned that man over to the new Iraqi government. In fact, it is very, very likely that very incident was in front of Flynn's eyes, and more than once.

It would have been Dutschke's contention that the Al-Sayidi team killing, which was NEVER the "ransom-kidnapping" it was purported to be, but was an outright targeted-killing. Intelligence, that Flynn would have been privy to at the time, would indicate that Al-Sayidi's team was shot, execution-style, on the same day in the very spot where they were taken. That, for one, indicates a hit, not an attempt at a "ransom." It would be hard to believe Flynn did not know more about it, certainly more than Dutschke (as CIA was mostly out of the loop by then), and in fact Flynn may have even known the importance of Al-Sayidi or any of the back-channel ties; but he has to know, has to remember something.

In retrospect, the execution of Sa'ayd Al-Sayidi and the others seems like an obvious retribution of the ███████. this was their way of telling

Dutschke and CIA, "okay, you took out three of us (in 2002), so now WE will take out 15 of YOU." (And even then, in 2006, ███████ was not certain that anyone had survived the helicopter crash) for THAT is the way that they do business.

It is here and it is with that that the author now advance a never-before expressed statement, and one that will be incredibly controversial. As long as there is anyone who disagrees with a person there is always someone who can consider unsubstantiated conclusions to be nothing but gossip. However, some things leave no overt substantiation, but a trail of breadcrumbs means there is something to follow to a location. Part of the purpose of clandestine activities is to ensure that there ARE no details which can lead to conclusions to a conclusion, thus assessments are often made without documented "evidence." This is how intelligence analysis works and why it is necessarily different from courtroom evidence. (Put simply, covert ops leave no evidence)

For example, an intelligence analyst would state with strong confidence that some birds have eaten from the bird feeder that an agent reports is now empty of seeds. Thus, the birds like it and will return expecting more, so the proper investment is to purchase more of the same seeds. The agent did not actually witness birds eating, yet now the analyst to whom he eventually reports now knows the appropriate course of recommended continued action; purchasing more of the same, to get the birds to return.

This would not be acceptable to "court of law". The "conclusions" that were drawn by the analyst (birds like that seed) and the analyst's recommended course of action—purchase more of the same bird food) would be considered by a government solicitor, a prosecutor... a lawyer, to be "meritless" and by a judge as conclusions "having no merit".

"Where", such absurd court dwellers would say, "is the notarized documentary evidence that the birds actually like that seed? Or for that matter, the agent has provided no valid documents proving that it was birds in the first place. The wind could have carried it off. Secondly, there is NO established court precedent that shows that the proper procedure for such a scenario might be to purchase more bird seed. Therefore the agents and analysts are denied as frivolous."

This kind of nonsensical thinking is why there are very few lawyers in real intelligence work and very little real intelligence in lawyers.

To the rest of the logical, rational and reasonable world, it is obvious that the intelligence accessments ("conclusions", if you will) are spot-on. The birds eat the seeds. The birds like the seeds. The birds will come back if the seed is replaced. But brainless people, such as lawyers or the vast majority of the press can only "agree" with such "conclusions" only if it fits with their predetermined conclusion to start with. And THAT is given to them by

266

someone else (or by groupthink) who TELLS them which conclusion to make, and to reject. They lack imaginative intellect.

All of this is given as an example in order to state that the authors here, now, are for the first time in this book about to assert something, and something quite controversial, that there is no "direct evidence" of.

Everything else in this book, including the flatulence of James Clapper, is either already known or established or there are direct dots to connect, even if hazy. This new assertion, however, is not. And it is not based on anything concrete because those involved intentionally left no breadcrumbs to follow. It is far from gossip.

Those that read any further can either choose to accept this bombshell of an accusation or they can choke on it. It will not change anything either way, and there is just as little "evidence" to disprove this conclusion as there is "evidence" which proves it.

So accept it or do not accept it, the reader's acceptance will not factor into it at all. The accusation, however SHOULD be taken not as baseless speculation but as a matter of absolute fact—.

The murder of the 15 men, one of whom was a rescuer of Dutschke's 2002 team, was a group assassination that was knowingly planned out and coordinated with the direct involvement and resources of Wa'el Hamza Jalaiden and Saleha Abedin, the mother of Huma Abedin. It is doubtful that Huma Abedin, the most successful espionage agent in history (who has penetrated farther into the US government than anyone else but Brennan) and John Brennan did not know. It is likely that Hillary Clinton herself, Huma's mark, even knows. Saleha Abedin, by association and coordination, is a conspirator in a mass murder. She was not the one who pulled the trigger, but UBL was not one of the pilots who weaponized America's commercial aviation either.

On September 12th, the new Bush doctrine made no distinction between the terrorists and anyone who harbors or supports a terrorist. Saleha Abedin is not merely "connected to" the killers that the US military finally caught and turned over to the new Iraqi government, she had a direct hand in it. Some of the intel used to identify Al-Sayidi and the other targets of her assassination, furthermore, came directly from U.S. sources... it HAD to, because only Americans knew how to complete the information the ██ ██ had extracted from ██ ██. And there were only two people who could access exactly that intel with any direct or back-channel to Saleha, John Brennan and Huma Abedin (through Senate channels). The most likely candidate being Brennan (even as "Analysis Corp" the intel contractor of McLean) who would have known who to work to get it.

Because the gunman who was captured by the US military in 2009 WAS a known member of AQAP which is a terrorist designated group. By the Bush Doctrine and the DOJ standards at that time (2006), anyone who aided him is also a terrorist. Anyone who "provides material support" is a terrorist. Providing a target (Al-Sayidi and his team) is "material support". Therefore John Brennan, who relayed American intel to Saleha Abedin (or whoever is his handler) IS a terrorist. NOT Dutschke.

Saleha Abedin and John Brennan, using Rabita Trust finances (Naseef and Ja'ara) ARE, by conspiracy, mass murderers. The 15 men who were executed by AQP gunmen in Anbar Province would be alive today were it not for Saleha Abedin and John Brennan. They were good men with loving families. Al-Sayidi's daughter, Maha Sa'ayd, would not have had to grow up fatherless, without the man who was an inspiration to her, if it was not for Brennan and Saleha Abedin. Saleha's entire network (Naseef, Jalaiden and the rest) are but a vast criminal organisation that must be treated at least in the same way the American patriots were treated. Attacked. Smeared. Prosecuted.

Jeff Sterling. Tom Drake. Steven Belvin. John Kiriakou. Nasir Gowadia. Everett Dutschke. Jeffrey Prather (Fast and Furious). Michael Flynn. Carter Page. George Papadopoulos. Dinesh D'Souza. Roger Stone and even Donald Trump. Not a single one of those men has betrayed their country in any way, not one has committed an act of mass murder. Yet the media sought out to destroy them all because that administration told them to.

Meanwhile, Saleha Abedin mother of Huma Abedin has gotten away with the mass murder of (at least) 15 people.

They left no fingerprints at the scene. There is no direct recording as absolute proof. There exists no sworn testimony for court. So it will be easy for John Brennan and Saleha Abedin to simply dismiss this accusation as mere speculation.

But such dismissal won't bring Maha's father back to her. This assertion is not to be casually dismissed or waved away. The execution-style murder of 15 men, all in succession is a very serious matter, especially those men. But because that execution did not happen in Baltimore, Chicago, Atlanta, Detroit or St Louis, and the executed men were not black, so the American media does not need to pretend to care. Apparently, to the American press, only black lives matter, especially when the killer is, by conspiracy, Saleha Abedin.

Where were the protests? Where is the clamouring for justice? Why isn't someone taking over downtown Seattle demanding that Hillary- friend of Huma's mother, Saleha be arrested along with Obama-friend and her co-conspirator John Brennan? Is murder suddenly considered okay (as long as Al-Qaeda does it)? Where is CNN? Is it okay for a mass murderer to stay free but Michael Flynn has to be tossed into a prison?

And on this very matter, it is most likely Flynn (and some in the DIA) actually DO have the "smoking gun" details that directly connect Saleha Abedin to the murders. It is THIS kind of information that made Flynn a danger to the Obama creatures of the swamp (remember, he was not a mere combat General but forever an intelligence officer. DIA is always at war, even when America is not). While the cabal did not silence Flynn by slamming a SAM order on him and shipping him to the National Security Unit (SAM unit) as they did with Everett, he was still rendered silent by the prosecution itself. That does NOT mean Flynn does not know which rocks to turn over that might expose swamp detritus. He does. Perhaps Flynn one day can turn over the rocks that conceal the details linking Saleha definitely to the killings. But one thing is clear—the DOD "official" story (a "ransom kidnapping" by a single gunman) is just as bogus as a 2013 KC letters "official story" by the DOJ.

In 2007, when that the mass execution happened and the bodies of 15 men were left in an Anbar Province ditch, Everett Dutschke was on the other side of the planet trying to piece his life back together and ready to teach his new students in a new class in his new school as part of his new life, and he was powerless to help a friend or prevent bad people from doing things that were harmful to Americans. But Everett, too, is an American, and that was harmful, in some hidden ways, probably devastating to him. Barack Hussein Obama had barely been a sitting senator for two years, Clinton/Abedin biding her time in the Senate, Brennan, like Dutschke, was but a green-badger then, and aside from the organised murder of Al-Sayidi and his team, things seem to be getting safer for America and for Everett, who could begin to take his life back. The world would turn just fine. America's enemies looked to be dwindling.

It did not last. Almost as soon as 2009 began, the dormant cancer of domestic angst began to metastasize to different parts of the American psyche. Americans, themselves, began spawning their own domestic and internal enemies. Long-dead issues suddenly sprouted like weeds and quickly spread as if fertilized by the new administration who seemed to have a parasitic need of their own to feed on the new internal strife now being created between and amongst its own people. Perhaps those issues were always there, as fungal spores waiting for the right and most complacent and ripe environment to spur a growth in their infection and Americans were just too complacent or inobservant to notice them. Whichever the case, the malignant weeds found the next eight years was the perfect ground to take root and dig their pathological roots so deeply into America's soil that it may now be impossible to remove them and excise them.

The symptoms of America's sickness includes the willingness of the Department of Justice to become a political tool of unstoppable power used to kill and destroy others in service of itself. As Sydney Powell has pointed out, the potential for misuse and abuse of that tool has always been there, the conviction machine is NOT the pure of heart and noble mechanism that it is advertised to be. It has long been corrupt and, as she puts it, a licence to lie by those who operate within it. But for the last decade that corrupt machine has grown to insurmountable proportions of both audacity, moxy and sheer barbarity into a cannibalistic monster that feeds on its own people, sharing the bones and blood of its spoils with an ever-hungry parasitic media. Once targeted, There is no escape. The DOJ has become far more dangerous, a far greater peril to the American population than terrorism ever was (and the irony is that citing "terrorism" is, in part, how it got there). The US Department of Justice and all localized versions of it, are terrorists. And try as they might, the 45th president, Trump, and the Attorney General, William Barr, may not be able to clean it up, as they claimed as their goal. It is likely too deep and too far gone. Biden certainly will never even bother trying.

Although recent cases, all Trump related, have exposed it to some extent, the one case that remains the exemplary case of the worst corruption of people and process remains the fraudulent prosecution of James Everett Dutschke. No other case in modern history has as much a blatant perversion of justice as that one.

This is not to say Misters Barr and Trump should not have tried. Failure to do anything is the same as encouraging it.

The irony of it all is that the empty-headed nutter, Paul Kevin Curtis, was actually right in the KC letters themselves, at least in sentiment, when Curtis himself wrote, "To see a wrong and not expose it is to become a silent partner to its continuance". So at this point, for President Trump and Attorney General Barr (and subsequent administrations) to NOT reverse all that had been done during the Obama cabal's reign of terror would be the same as Trump joining Obama in his purpose and legacy. Whatever the current president chooses to do, however he chooses to undo the wrongs of the cabal that targeted Dutschke (the very same cabal that targeted him, albeit with an even lighter touch), at least now the truth of the Dutschke matter is known, disclosed here for the first time publicly. The entire prosecution was a sham. An intelligence operation which was handed off to the LEOs in 2013, then fed to the media for its red-meat consumption. It was all a fraud. Phony. Or as Mr. Trump calls it, "fake news". It didn't seem to matter then because no one knew the concealed truths.

Now you, the reader, do.

It was all corrupt and phony from the beginning (and even BEFORE that). Presently, there is a social push (the Left does not bother "nudging" anymore) to eliminate police all together and a backlash from the opposition to expand it. Both sides are, as usual, wrong.

Those on the Right argue "Who will keep us safe from criminals if the police are abolished?" This argument does nothing to address the REAL issue that it is often (very, very often) the case that the criminals ARE the police.

So the real issue that both sides, polarized as they are in America, should actually realise as their common accord is "How do we prevent people of poor character from becoming LEOs in the first place?" This should be coupled with the same, "How do we prevent people of poor character from becoming prosecutors?"

The rationale is simple. The system is only bad because it is being abused (by people of poor character). The system, as a structure, is fine. It is the people who run it that make it corrupt. The reason that LEOs and prosecutors are abusive, reckless and dishonest IS, in part, because there is no accountability (ever) in court or anywhere else for their actions. And that is indeed a big part. But the primary reason that LEOs and prosecutors are abusive, reckless and dishonest is because they are abusive, reckless and dishonest people.

If you do not want snakes guarding the hen house, then stop hiring snakes. However, refraining or changing the equation is not a simple thing. Though the equation itself is simple ("Garbage in. Garbage out". Americans say). Corruption is what should be expected when corrupt people are hired for the job. The solutions are not so simple.

To start with, there is no apparatus that can discern the men (and women) of good character from the batch of liars, thieves and finks that currently make up the LEOs and prosecutors (or the "conviction machine" as Sydney Powell popularized it). There are laser thermometers, that can check a person's temperature, 12 lead EKGs that can diagnose cardiac problems and a blood test that can identify nearly every problem conceivable, but there is no diagnostic analysis that can tell someone, "You have Holderitis"; or "This person has Kamala Harris syndrome"; or "You have a chronic case of the Muellerenes" (which is a severe form of autism); or "You have Obama disorder" (a combination of oversized larynx and a chronic fecal impaction caused by the jamming of the entire media into the rectum); or "That person has been infected with Brennanococcus" (which causes skin to become scaly, vampiric bloodlust, microcardiopholy, forked tongue and an impulse to deny everything); or "Thomasonosis" (symptoms include halitosis, sclerotic grey matter, factophobia, fibbiphelia, chlamydia, gynophobia and a severe case of micropenis); or "He is diagnosed with Clapperliosis" (loose sphincter); or "This is a clear case of Hillaremia" (characterized by total lack of regard for any human being, psychopathic and sociopathic behavior, heartworm, mad cow disease, necromania, crooked spine and a very Thomasonosis-like micropenis); or "This guy is a Bideneptic" (which really means he's been dead for quite some time of foot and mouth disease yet someone simply forgot to inform the old chap that he has already passed on); or "I hate to inform you, you have chronic Comeyolepsy" (fascination with self, blind obedience to secret Kenyans, progressive demylinization of white and grey nerve cells, more fascination with self, whooping-poots, megalomania, gigantism, hairy palms and loss of eyesight, pica, beriberi, fecalocephalus, syphilis, mange, treason pox, crappipholia, narcissism, sadism, and a bizarre obsession with orange balls).

In fact, the problem is publicly known. Recently, former beat-cop turned Secret Service agent turned political commentator Dan Bongino stated, "Let's face it. With what cops are paid, and how little they are trained, you're not going to get the philosophers and scholars". To Sean Hannity, Bongino added, "You're not going to get the PhDs (to become cops)." Basically, the pool of people that WANT to become LEOs is rich with candidates of poor character. Bongino was right, but he failed to suggest any means of vetting out the riff-raff from those of better character. (And the Riff-raff, Mr. Hannity is FAR greater than "the 1%". Garbage in. Garbage out).

One solution is to eliminate "qualified immunity" and create serious criminal sentencing enhancements for LEOs who violate the Constitution while in uniform. Currently, they are NOT actually on duty "to Protect and Serve" unless they are "Protecting" their own arses and "Serving" their own sordid desires. If they, as a profession, are truly to be thanked for their sacrifice then the staffing should consist of people who truly DO put others (not their badged buddies), the citizenary as first. Otherwise, there is nothing to "thank" them for. It is disingenuous. The solution, one way or another, must involve accountability. Courts should hold police to a higher standard, eliminating any and all differences and presumptions of truthfulness... or AT LEAST hold LEOS to THE SAME standard as everyone else. Currently, judges aid in cover-ups and fraudulent prosecutions, concealment of exculpatory evidence and acts as praetorian guards to the conviction machine. Currently, judges allow themselves to be part of the prosecution. Currently, American judges are the puppets of the cops. THIS is the primary reason that the change should begin at the entry point, not at the finality point. That is to say that because it is far less likely that judges can or will ever change their malignant thinking and leanings, the easier change is to prevent (majority) bad apples from ever bringing fraud into the courtroom by preventing them from ever having any involvement in the first place. It is easier to ensure and keep a controlled environment by planting only good seeds then to later try to weed out the garden especially after the weeds have already taken over.

Good luck, America, figuring out how to do that.

Perhaps all judges, prosecutors and LEOs should live INSIDE the prisons they send people to so easily. THAT would solve the problem overnight. Furthermore, convicted felons should not be excluded from juries. Prosecutors eliminate such potential jurors because they want only the naive who are still brainwashed into believing that LEOs are pure, prosecutors are infallible, the courts are fair and everything works exactly as it does in the tele. Such people are much easier for prosecutors to manipulate than those people who know what to look for and know the law better than the general population... convicts. Those who have seen how the system actually works (which is the opposite of how it is advertised) are the people who have been through it, convicts. And the entire jury pool should be comprised of THOSE people, the ones who KNOW how it all works, not those who don't.

The practise of a jury to be able to examine and cross-examine witnesses directly should be utilised. There is no constitutional or statutory prohibition against this practise. And juries have the right to demand the truth in order to make a "beyond reasonable doubt" decision. Such a practise ought to be required, in fact, until the point that no unanswered juror questions exist. Witnesses, especially criminal defendants, should insist on it.

Every time an American prosecutor makes any attempt to suppress any evidence whatsoever, he should immediately be taken out back of the courthouse and be forced to listen to an atrocious combination of the Spice Girls, REM, The B-52s and Drake (all verified PSY-OP and torture techniques) while being continuously walloped with a cold fish. If a prosecutor is trying to hide something, ANYTHING, then the jury and judge should automatically presume it is exculpatory and mitigatory and therefore the suppression is dishonest and unfair, rendering the entire proceeding void.

There should be no such thing as "procedural bar" to any issue of appeal. Judges who, on appeal, misconstrue any appellant issue, or prosecutors who mischaracterise an issue raised by an appellant should be immediately imprisoned for life, then upon their expiration and internment, dug back up and imprisoned again, all the way wearing pink and castrated since they obviously lack the balls to address whatever issue was actually raised. If an appellant raises an issue, prosecutors and judges should have the courage to address THAT issue instead of pretending it was something else raised then addressing the pretend issue. What are they afraid of?

LEOs who are on the witness stand should be hooked to a polygraph that administers a severe and prolonged electric shock when a deceptive answer is given. This response should also include their children and mother who are strapped together in clear view of the testifying officer, and receiving the same shock at the same time. The trio (the testifying officer, his offspring and his mother) should first be fed copious amounts of liquid laxatives before the testimony, forced to wear white pants, and all that broadcasted live on their Facebook pages for their "friends" to witness. For "special" agents like Thomason, quite a few "likes" will result from the very messy spectacle. And the judge should have to be the one to clean it up.

In fact, such an event would become the new betting sport with the Vegas odds-makers. Courts could sell tickets and broadcast rights to the new hit show entitled perhaps, "Truth or Whoops"; or "Scatological Jeopardy"; or "Name that Dung"; or "Stool or No Stool".

Since it seems to be expected that FBI agents are going to lie, even under oath, and always encouraged by judges to do so, at least the rest of the world can chuckle at the gutter entertainment of the banality once a Thomason-like agent's testimony goes off with a bang.

Congress should immediately act to implement these changes.

To return to seriousness for a moment, there is a better chance of tightening the screening as there is the abolition of police; and there is a better chance of passing legislation that regulates vetting procedures than there is of purging courtrooms of the masses of prosecutors and judges who value political convenience over actual law, justice and fairness. Some things could make it through Congress easier than other things because Congress, on both sides, is packed with people too fearful and cowardly to actually conduct such a purge.

The problem remains, there IS NO means, no viable test that can actually tighten the screening. Until then, America is left to fill its "justice system" with the dregs of the moral scrapings from the bottom of the integrity barrel. Bongino was courageous to admit that the best and brightest ("the PhDs and philosophy majors") matriculate elsewhere. Interestingly enough, the "best and brightest", an organisation that requires good character and university degrees and original and logical thinking is CIA. Proving that the cream rises to the top (THERE, Mr. Hannity, is where your 99% rule applies—the 1% being Morell, Brennan, Sensi and Hirschfeild and a few others of still high intellect but bad intent).

Until such a "test" is developed... good luck.

CIA and the Department of State had always had a beautiful relationship together... until the Obama/Clinton treasonous actions of September 2012. That was when several of the CIA officers had the audacity to stay alive and protect the compound in Benghazi. According to the original arrangement between the Soleimani-backed Ansar Al-Sharia militia and whoever in the U.S. government (Obama/Clinton), the GRS was not supposed to put up such a fight against the attacking militia. Hillary's State Department (only at the highest levels) knew that CIA officials (at the highest levels) and a few CIA counterterrorism analysts knew this. The animus that Obama and Clinton felt for (former) CIA director, Petraeus, filtered down the State Department ranks through the diplomatic corps and bordered on hostile.

In 2013, one year *after* the 2012 Benghazi attacks, Everett Dutschke was sitting in a jail cell in Oxford, angry that one man could go through so much and care so deeply about his country, yet a few people, a corrupt handful had manipulated the country into calling him a traitor, treasonous and a terrorist. It was, without a doubt, the men (and women) in the highest office of the land who had weaponized DOJ to do what they learned could not be done otherwise. In addition to Obama's success at intimidating and imprisoning not just CIA but anyone who deigned to insult him (such as Dinesh D'Souza), using the DOJ to keep the CIA "in line", the State Department got in on the kicking as well.

As Dutschke sat in a 2013 jail cell awaiting trial for "Developing a Biological Weapon", on the other side of the planet; inside the Tripoli compound near the airport in the city Everett was a year prior, the CIA officers and analysts held a bonfire memorial to recall the failure (betrayal by Hillary and Obama, really) of Benghazi 2012. That night, September 11th *2013*, the bonfire even reflected on the importance of that date, the high-treason betrayals of specific individuals and agencies (that resulted in both the 2001 and 2012 attacks) and even renewed commitment of the CIA officers present to continue their often personal sacrifices to defend and protect their country in spite of it all. According to the NSA officer that was assigned to that post, the Tripoli group, led by the security team leader, all sang "Amazing Grace" spontaneously. The CIA group etched two stars into the Tripoli compound wall to commemorate the two CIA officers who in 2012 had for (in Benghazi) as they protected the lives of Hillary's State Department employees.

The Tripoli State Department corp took offence at that 2013 Tripoli bonfire memorial. In 2014, when the Libyan civil war between factions became hostile toward the U.S. (Obama wanted a continued presence to both try to clean up his Libyan mess and to look like he was not "retreating"), the Zintins could no longer protect the Tripoli compound. CIA security began a chock convoy self extrication, abandoning Tripoli. The evac was intensifying (burn and shred protocols), in the 130 degree climate (54 degrees C), State Department staff supplied ice cold water, but they withheld that relief from the CIA staff, reserving the momentary refreshments for themselves, without regard for even the GRS (CIA) staff that would keep them safe during the upcoming 26 hour evac over rough terrain. This was a tiny betrayal in the large scheme of things, but this slight showed THAT PARTICULAR State Department's true colors. (Everett had told Williamson in January 2013 "You cannot trust THIS State Department"). The 2014 CIA group, patriots to the end, quickly got over that snub and kept to their task, laser-focused.

But the State Department staff was not finished revealing themselves. Just as the State Department had NOT shared something as simple as cold water with the CIA, at a final destination point at an airfield in southern Tunisia, when the State Department prepared a makeshift meal, guess who was left out... guess who was excluded from simply eating... CIA personnel. This was not merely an affront, it was unthinkable. The State Department staff should have been falling to their knees in gratitude to the CIA group that had just (once again) saved its arses and gotten them to safety, 26 hours (by back roads) away from all the fighting and attacks. Though most of the diplomatic corps flew out, the CIA officers still had work to do as they had to get their Tripoli (armored) autos to the US Embassy in Tunis. Their long—long, extreme hot day had not yet ended. The dashboard thermometer showed 140 degrees Fahrenheit (60 degrees Celsius), yet when the CIA family arrived at the Embassy in Tunis with some State Department personnel the U.S. Ambassador told the CIA group that they were NOT welcome! To the ingrateful State Department of Clinton/Kerry, the CIA was not even worth a

"Thank you"... same as Benghazi. "The Marines could stay, the Tripoli diplomatic corps could stay, but the CIA has got to get the hell out of here." There was barely time for a nap before the flight arrangements were made. The Ambassador made sure the embassy door hit the CIA officers in the butt on the way out. The CIA's analyst, who had been the hardest worker in Tripoli and had forged what she thought had been a good relationship with State was baffled. There was no one, no one more dedicated to the Libyan assignments and missions than her. She was the one who held daily and open briefings, even when not much was going on (though there was always something going on). Booted. How's THAT for inter-agency cooperation?

Did anyone in America report any of this to the American public? No. They did not. The American media was too obsessed with Obama's personal involvement and subtle dog-whistling by the Left to stir up racial division after the George Zimmerman acquittal (who shot a man, Trayvon Martin, who had been assaulting and attacking him). And there was no way the 2014 press would ever tell the truth of the Obama (Clinton/Kerry) State Department.

Considering the amount of time and training of Mensa-member Dutschke since his childhood, it would be easy to say he was the perfect weapon.

But in this tale, there is more, much more to consider. The product he is accused (and convicted) of developing, ricin, is—for its purpose—the perfect weapon, leaving no traces and no definable post-mortem diagnosis. The media, as eagerly allowing themselves to be the tool of mass and total destruction by that particular administration as Rush Limbaugh stated, is the perfect weapon. A personal network of the most powerful people in the world, a cabal, conspirators who are untouchable and above the law, is the perfect weapon. The weaponized Department of Justice, with its overwhelming, unlimited resources and a licence to lie are a perfect weapon. And religious disguise to cover a well-funded terrorist network is a perfect weapon. Well and highly placed spies embedded next to high office is the perfect weapon. The executive order of a president, as personally carried out by the Attorney General of the United States, the Eric Holder SAM order on Dutschke, endorsed by Mueller and Comey, which silenced and muted him and convicted him unconstitutionally and "disappeared" him into the dark, National Security Unit, the AG's private prison, is the perfect weapon (since NO defence is allowed). This SAM unit, itself, inside of the US-ADX Supermax is the perfect weapon. The prosecutors' threat, in this case, to prosecute Everett's wife (Janet) and their additional public pressures was the perfect weapon. A judge who is always but a prosecution's rubber-stamp is the perfect weapon. A corrupt FBI agent who is allowed to lie and fabricate without consequence and influences the media attack dogs and overzealous prosecutors is a perfect weapon. But if this has all shown us anything, it has shown us this; the power of the Office of the President of the United States, bolstered by blind obedience and high on its omnipotence, is the perfect weapon.

It never mattered that J Everett Dutschke was provably innocent. He never did and, it seems never will, get the chance to actually present the now discovered truth to the court. For when the President wanted someone convicted, that was it. There was no discussion, there would be no dissent. There is never, not even with the Crossfire operations run by the very same Oval Office syndicate and cabal against Trump associates, not even with the treasonous coup attempt, never been a prosecution in American history as corrupt and egregiously unconstitutional as the 2013-14 fraudulent prosecution and making a terrorist of J Everett Dutschke. There has never been a more sinister media hit-job and it remains the most monstrous perversion of justice in American history without question.

It is time for the American public to acknowledge it and it is the duty of every citizen to recognise (King) that "an injustice anywhere is an injustice everywhere". Every citizen incensed by the anti-Trump cabal's attempts with the Crossfire operations (Operation Crossfire Hurricane and Crossfire Razor) should be twice as angry about the very same cabal's execution of Operation Dojo to frame an innocent man (by claiming HE was "framing" someone else) and by planting false claims in the press, falsifying warrant and arrest affidavits, fraudulent claims to judges, grand jury, courts, media, defence counsel, intimidating family and ultimately refusing to drop the plea that was fraudulently obtained by the same intimidation. A SAM is unconstitutional in every sense of the word and so is a SAM prosecution. Not even the Crossfire operations went that far.

It is not merely a right of all Americans to be angry about such manifest injustice, it is their right to demand something be done about it. It is their right to demand reversal of the SAM conviction of an innocent man and quite frankly, it is their duty to urge every person they know to demand the same. Americans are screaming, these days it seems, at the top of their lungs that they demand a justice system that is fair. Surely "fairness" is fairness, regardless of skin color. "Fairness", then, must include that innocent people are not in prison (by SAM or by trial). Although most Americans did not even learn of the National Security order and directive to convict Everett Dutschke without due process (invoking the President's power under 28 CFR§501.2 and .3), as signed by Holder himself, but if someone claims to be "a constitutionalist" or care about "civil liberties" guaranteed by the Constitution, then it is time to rally against the SAM which suspends a single, targeted person's constitutional rights. That rally does not mean silently putting this book down, it means decrying the practise of the SAM (and the Dutschke SAM conviction) through clenched teeth. People must learn. They cannot do so by osmosis. The time to talk, shout, share, post, call, discuss, report, demand, fight for beliefs held-dear is now. Proof is in deeds and actions.

Morals and virtues are not genuinely held, they are but a weak charade if not matched by "Something attempted, something done" (Longfellow). Silence is not a feat of courage.

This is a chance for Americans to find ways to creatively demonstrate that they believe what they claim to believe.

The America of virtue and integrity is worth fighting for. The time has come to prove it. A perversion of America was planted and for nearly a decade it flourished and grew. That weed must be pulled and the perversions reversed. This includes reversal of the conviction of the cabal's target, including and especially J Everett Dutschke. Not a terrorist, but a patriot.

2002

July 202
Operation
Vengeance

Escape aided by
Sa'ayd Al-Sayid

Helicopter Crash
Insurance
Med records created

Insurance med
records

2004

Terrorist support of John Kerry
US Presidential campaign
discovered.
CIA Larry Kolb narrative twists and
defeats Dutschke narrative
No criminal charges

2006

May 2006
Mass assination of Sa'ayd al-
Sayidi, Ahmed Ali and 14
teammates Iraq

2007

2008

Former CIA/COS John Brennan's new
'consulting' company—"Analysis Co"
hired by Obama campaign. Hacks into
State Dept passport records to scrub
Obama file

2009

John Brennan rewarded by Obama
w/White House appointment

Sec of State
inquires into
'02 operation

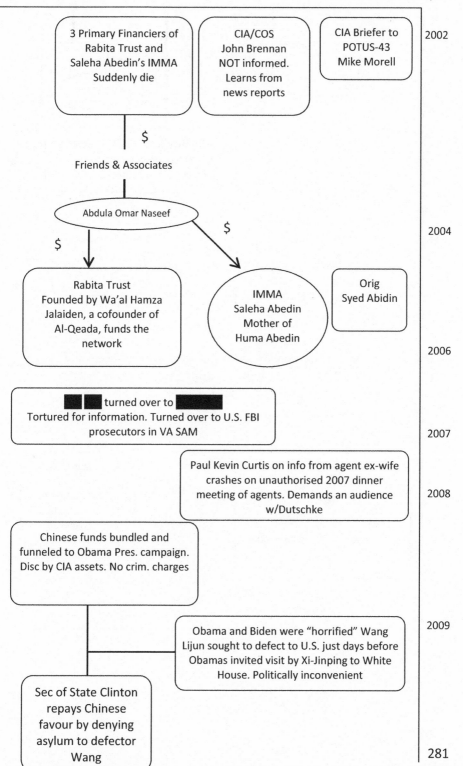

3 Primary Financiers of Rabita Trust and Saleha Abedin's IMMA Suddenly die

CIA/COS John Brennan NOT informed. Learns from news reports

CIA Briefer to POTUS-43 Mike Morell

$

Friends & Associates

Abdula Omar Naseef

$

$

2004

Rabita Trust Founded by Wa'al Hamza Jalaiden, a cofounder of Al-Qeada, funds the network

IMMA Saleha Abedin Mother of Huma Abedin

Orig Syed Abidin

2006

███ ██ turned over to ██████
Tortured for information. Turned over to U.S. FBI prosecutors in VA SAM

2007

Paul Kevin Curtis on info from agent ex-wife crashes on unauthorised 2007 dinner meeting of agents. Demands an audience w/Dutschke

2008

Chinese funds bundled and funneled to Obama Pres. campaign. Disc by CIA assets. No crim. charges

2009

Obama and Biden were "horrified" Wang Lijun sought to defect to U.S. just days before Obamas invited visit by Xi-Jinping to White House. Politically inconvenient

Sec of State Clinton repays Chinese favour by denying asylum to defector Wang

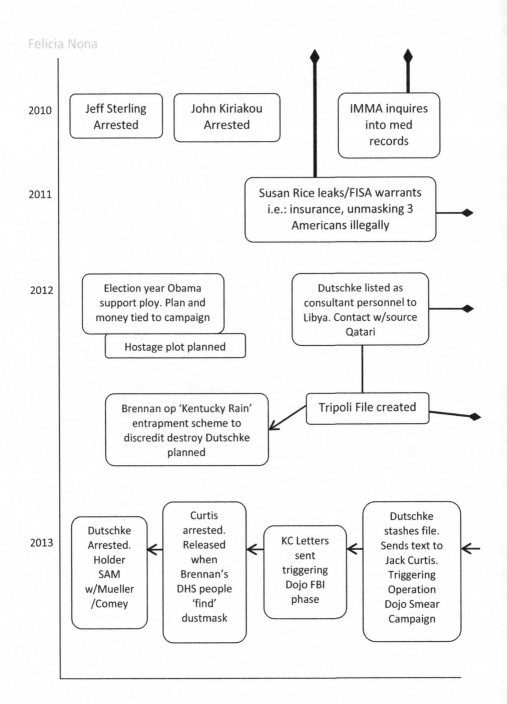

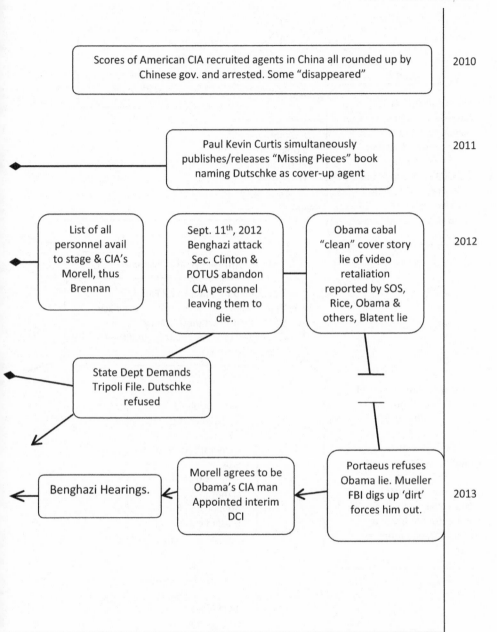

Scores of American CIA recruited agents in China all rounded up by Chinese gov. and arrested. Some "disappeared"

2010

Paul Kevin Curtis simultaneously publishes/releases "Missing Pieces" book naming Dutschke as cover-up agent

2011

List of all personnel avail to stage & CIA's Morell, thus Brennan

Sept. 11th, 2012 Benghazi attack Sec. Clinton & POTUS abandon CIA personnel leaving them to die.

Obama cabal "clean" cover story lie of video retaliation reported by SOS, Rice, Obama & others, Blatent lie

2012

State Dept Demands Tripoli File. Dutschke refused

Benghazi Hearings.

Morell agrees to be Obama's CIA man Appointed interim DCI

Portaeus refuses Obama lie. Mueller FBI digs up 'dirt' forces him out.

2013

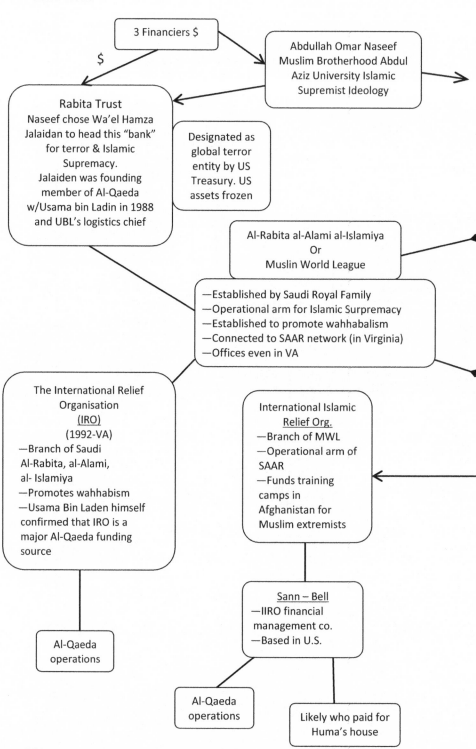

IMMA
The information and propaganda wing of the Islamic Supremacy. This would be their "spy network", disinformers and public relations center all rolled up into one entity, Naseef originally placed Syed Abedin at head. Now Saleha Abedin & family

$

Donor > Tariq Ramaden "Muslim Scholar' donated to terror groups. Banned by Bush in 2004 from U.S. In 2010 Sec. Clinton lifted ban

<u>SAAR Network — based in VA</u>
—"Safa Group" — raided by Feds (x15)
—Complex network of companies, Islamic 'charities' and NPOs to conceal activities of members & contributors
—US ICE alleged is giant money laundering operation to finance terror groups
—>100 groups — funds held offshore
—Some SAAR orgs. Real, others only paper

American Muslim Alliance (LA-1994)
—Serves as PAC
—Supports Hamas
—Donated $50G to Hillary

<u>Muslim Public Affairs Council – MPAC</u>
—501 c(4) — holds/supports terror rallies
—Affiliated withMuslim Brotherhood
—Hosted Hillary at convention

United States District Court Judgment
(United States of America V. James Everett Dutschke)

This document was part of a filing by the DOJ & Attorney General as defendants in the Colorado lawsuit by Dutschke against the SAM.

This filing by the AG/DOJ shows that the conviction/sentence for Dutschke is for violating the international treaty against developing a BIOLOGICAL weapon, not the treaty against developing a chemical weapon, which was the specific product that administration alleged (ricin). This is a fraudulent prosecution, conviction and sentence.

Had the law been followed, according to CWCIA statutory requirements, any violation alleging ricin (a listed/designated chemical weapon) MUST be investigated/prosecuted under (18 USC 229), a completely different statute enforcing a completely different treaty than the Count 1 you see here (18 USC 175).

Case: 1:13-cr-00081-SA-DAS Doc #: 81 Filed: 05/28/14 1 of 6 PageID #: 456

AO 245B (Rev. 12/03) Judgment in a Criminal Case
Sheet 1

UNITED STATES DISTRICT COURT

_____ Northern _____ District of _____ Mississippi _____

UNITED STATES OF AMERICA
V.
James Everett Dutschke

JUDGMENT IN A CRIMINAL CASE

Case Number:	1:13CR00081-001
USM Number:	15536-042

Mr. Kenneth H. Coghlan
Defendant's Attorney

THE DEFENDANT:

X pleaded guilty to count(s)   1, 2, 3, and 4 of the Superseding Indictment

☐ pleaded nolo contendere to count(s) _____
which was accepted by the court.

☐ was found guilty on count(s) _____
after a plea of not guilty.

The defendant is adjudicated guilty of these offenses:

Title & Section	Nature of Offense	Offense Ended	Count
18 U.S.C. § 175(a)	Developing, Producing, Stockpiling, Transferring, Acquiring, Retaining, or Possessing a Biological Weapon	04/17/2013	1
18 U.S.C. § 871(a)	Threats Against President	04/16/2103	2
18 U.S.C. § 876(c)	Mailing Threatening Communications	04/16/2013	3
18 U.S.C. § 876(c)	Mailing Threatening Communications	04/17/2013	4

The defendant is sentenced as provided in pages 2 through   6   of this judgment. The sentence is imposed pursuant to the Sentencing Reform Act of 1984.

☐ The defendant has been found not guilty on count(s) _____

X Count(s)   5 and 6 of the Superseding Indictment   is/are dismissed on the motion of the United States.

It is ordered that the defendant must notify the United States attorney for this district within 30 days of any change of name, residence, or mailing address until all fines, restitution, costs, and special assessments imposed by this judgment are fully paid. If ordered to pay restitution, the defendant must notify the court and United States attorney of material changes in economic circumstances.

May 19, 2014
Date of Imposition of Judgment

Sharion Aycock
Signature of Judge

Sharion Aycock, U.S. District Judge
Name and Title of Judge

May 21, 2014
Date

FBI Laboratory CBRNSU
(Chemical, biological, radiological, nuclear laboratory)
Date: April 27, 2013

The Mueller FBI/Holder DOJ's public "smoking gun" claim to the court and press was their sudden "discovery" of the dust mask from a public garbage bin that contained traces of "ricin" on it, same as the KC letters, such as the (Q-11) Holland envelope.

The press, media and courts continue to this day to parrot the claim by the administration's FBI/DOJ. Notice the date.

This document proves that the entire claim was a lie and had always been a lie since BEFORE the indictment of Dutschke.

The FBI knowingly presented the lies to the court and to the press and was "basis" the warrant, arrest, indictment and SAM conviction.

Not only did they know prior to indictment there was no "ricin" on the dust mask as they claimed, but the FBI's very own laboratories knew that the judge's envelope (Q-11) did NOT contain "ricin", according to their very own analysis.

U.S. Department of Justice

Federal Bureau of Investigation

Washington, DC 20535-0001

To: FBI Laboratory ECU- Attn: Rebecca Reynolds

From: CBRNSU- FE Neel Barnaby

CC: CBNRSU UC Lora Gioeni, CBRNSU PM Les McCurdy, CBRNSU FE
       Christa Mason

Date: April 27, 2013

Re: 279A-JN-2819332- Trace Evidence Collection Screening Results

On April 26, 2013, the trace evidence collections from following items of evidence listed below were screened for the presence of Ricin by the National Biofoensics Analysis Center, Ft. Detrick, MD. Ricin was not detected on any of these items. Based on these results, these samples are deemed cleared for entry into the FBI Laboratory.

If you require further information please contact FE Neel Barnaby (CBRNSU) at 703-898-7012 or FE Christa Mason (CBRNSU) at 703-906-2334.

Trace evidence collections from   [7 total tubes]

FBI Lab# 130417001 ADW
Q11   Envelope (NBFAC.130418.0001.0004)   [2 tubes]

FBI Lab # 130425001 ADX

Q420 Dust Mask (BT220, NBFAC.130425.0001.0010)   [3 tubes]

Q422 Dust Mask (BT218, NBFAC.130425.0001.0012)   [2 tubes]

Respectfully,

Neel Barnaby

Page 1 of 1

1:13CR81 Discovery
LAB-000125

Fisher, Constance – DNA

Part of the Obama cabal's "smoking gun" claim was that the magically discovered dust mask (by Brennan's then Homeland Security agent just at the moment they needed a "basis" for arrest and prosecution under SAM), which they falsely claimed contained "ricin" also conveniently contained Dutschke's DNA. This claim was seriously damaging and the court and media ran with it, repeating it ad nauseam for a year and continuing to this day. Note the date.

This document proves that the claim by the Mueller FBI/Holder DOJ was knowingly false from the beginning as is documented by the FBI's very own DNA laboratory. This notification by the FBI lab to special agent Grant specifically and explicitly states that Dutschke was *ex*cluded by the FBI's very own laboratory as the dust mask's DNA source.

Yet agent Thomason lied to the magistrate judge (Alexander) on the arrest warrant and testified, also under oath, at a hearing and grand jury (x2) the opposite. Magistrate Alexander, Judge Aycock and even the grand jury was NEVER shown this exculpatory evidence; neither was the press.

The date of this notification from the FBI lab, notice, PREdates the indictment(s), proving the Mueller FBI/Holder DOJ knew their DNA claim to the court and media was a lie (or at best questionable) from the start, yet they concealed it.

The detailed analysis further showed that the DNA was XX chromosomes, therefore female and (Dutschke is XY).

FISHER, CONSTANCE L. (LD) (FBI)

From:	FISHER, CONSTANCE L. (LD) (FBI)
Sent:	Thursday, May 02, 2013 4:37 PM
To:	GRANT, BRANDON (JN)(FBI)
Subject:	279A-JN-2819332 --- CLASSIFIED

Classification: CLASSIFIED
==

Dear SA Grant — I have been assigned to this case for mitochondrial DNA (mtDNA) examinations.

My report on the hair(s) from the dust masks and the buccal sample from Dutschke (he was excluded as a source of the one hair we were able to get a profile on) is in review. Please let me know if you have any questions — my contact info is below.

Thanks
Connie Fisher
mtDNAU
703-632-7579 (desk)
703-632-7573 (fax)
Constance.Fisher@ic.fbi.gov

==
Classification: CLASSIFIED

FBI Laboratory
Date: April 27, 2013

With both the DNA claim and the "traces of ricin" claim invalidated by the FBI's very own laboratory, the entire "smoking gun" claim of the dust mask was equally invalidated.

This was hidden from the press (and the prosecution from the judge) so that the phony dust mask narrative was perpetuated, and was hidden from the grand jury and falsely represented by FBI agent Thomason.

As long as the public believed that lie, Judge Aycock would play along. And the Obama-ordered SAM, issued by Holder and endorsed by Mueller, then Comey (adding Yates and Boente), ensured that Dutschke (and his attorney) could not refute anything that the prosecutors ever said and was even kept from any knowledge of it.

The SAM aided the administration's (now obvious) lie and resulted in the most successful cover-up in history as Dutschke remains imprisoned to this day for developing a biological weapon, based, in part, on the now-debunked "smoking gun" claim of the now infamous dust mask.

CLASSIFIED

Results of Examinations

Mitochondrial DNA sequences were obtained from the Q420.1 hair from Q420 dust mask- blue and the K24 buccal collector from JAMES EVERETT DUTSCHKE. The mtDNA sequences obtained from specimens Q420.1 and K24 are different. Therefore, JAMES EVERETT DUTSCHKE can be excluded as the source of the Q420.1 hair.

There was insufficient mtDNA present for a DNA sequence to be obtained from the Q422.1 hair from Q422 dust mask- white.

No other mtDNA examinations were conducted.

Methodology and Interpretation

DNA is extracted from each sample and portions of the control region of the mitochondrial DNA are amplified using the polymerase chain reaction (PCR). The amplified regions are sequenced using fluorescent dye-labeled chemistry. The sequences obtained are aligned and compared to the rCRS. Differences between the sample sequence and the rCRS are noted by nucleotide position and DNA base. The annotated profiles for all of the samples are then compared. Matching profiles may be searched against the mtDNA population database currently available to the FBI Laboratory (CODIS + mito Popstats version 1.4, CODISmpPop_4000v2) to provide an upper bound frequency estimate.

Mitochondrial DNA cannot be used to identify an individual because mtDNA is maternally inherited and all maternally related individuals are expected to have the same mtDNA profile. Also, unrelated individuals may have the same mtDNA profile within the sequenced range.

The following interpretations are possible for sequence comparisons:

CANNOT EXCLUDE:
If samples have the same sequence, or are concordant (share a common DNA base at every nucleotide position, including common length variants), they cannot be excluded as coming from the same source or maternal lineage.

INCONCLUSIVE:
If sample sequences differ at a single nucleotide position or if they do not share a common length variant, no conclusion can be reached as to whether they originate from the same source. If

Page 2 of 3

130425001 ABL

CLASSIFIED

1:13CR81 Discovery
LAB-000311

W

CDC Memorandum Pirkle

Among the Mueller FBI's phony claims, as made by the FBI agent Thomason, was that several items (3) had "swabbed positive" for ricin. This included a sink drain trap from Dutschke's office building and a hammer that had allegedly been moved by his wife, Janet, and her friends (without Dutschke even around), to a storage building owned by her friend.

The "field test" (a PCR reaction test) was allegedly "positive" or "reactive" for ricin on these swabs.

However, what was never made part of the discovery was the June 25th actual analysis by the CDC on the so called "positive reaction" swabs. Whether the omission from discovery was inadvertent or intentional is unclear. But considering the trove of other malfeasance committed by the prosecutors and FBI on this case, in it not a surprise that the CDC Memorandum detailing analysis of the 3 "reactive" swabs by the Bioterrorism Rapid Response Advanced Technology Laboratory from the Director of Laboratory Science, James Pirkle MD, PhD and Dr. John Barr to Dr. Michael Farrell (Research Microbiologist) was only obtained years after Dutschke's conviction by a FOIA process.

As the memo states, the swabs were NOT positive at all. In fact, the scientists concluded that *analysis was simply not even possible*. Dr. John Barr, who was a peer-reviewed expert on ricin, was beyond proficient in ricin detection methods and had co-authored numerous published studies showing the FBI's PCR "field tests" woefully inadequate. In this CDC report, the mass spectrometry assay concludes "NR" (NOT Reactive), which is the exact opposite of Thomason's under oath testimony of the swabs.

Another FBI/DOJ lie of their cover-up exposed by FOIA.

Ricin Health Service
Centers for Disease Control
and Prevention (CDC)

DEPARTMENT OF HEALTH & HUMAN SERVICES

Memorandum

Date   June 25, 2013

From   Director, Division of Laboratory Sciences

Subject Measurement of ricin and RCA120 in 3 environmental samples from the Bioterrorism Rapid Response and Advanced Technology (BRRAT) Laboratory of CDC/NCEZID.

To   Dr. Michael Farrell
        Research Microbiologist, BRRAT Laboratory
        Division of Preparedness and Emerging Infections
        National Center for Emerging and Zoonotic Infectious Diseases
        Centers for Disease Control and Prevention

Measurement of ricin and RCA120 (a protein with 89% similar structure to ricin) has been completed for three environmental samples. In addition, ricin activity has been determined for each sample. Analyses used established analytical methods in our laboratory. The samples were analyzed for ricin, RCA120, and ricin activity using liquid chromatography tandem mass spectrometry (LC-MS/MS).

Unfortunately, due to the presence of bleach in these samples, analysis of these samples was not possible. The bleach in the samples resulted in sample degradation, making them impossible to measure. Bleach treated samples have never been tested by CDC mass spectrometry based methods, and the low area counts of the internal standard spiked into these samples indicate sample degradation.

Quality control samples spiked with ricin and RCA120 and a matrix blank were used to verify the method. QC results for all analytical runs were reviewed and approved by a quality assurance officer. Results are provided in the attached table.

Any questions concerning these results should be directed to Dr. John Barr (770-488-7848).

Sincerely yours,

James L. Pirkle, M.D., Ph.D.

Number	Ricin Mass Spectrometry Structural Assay	Units	RCA120 Mass Spectrometry Structural Assay	Units	Ricin Mass Spectrometry Activity Assay
TMDJ-012-SW	NR*	ng/100 uL	NR*	ng/100 uL	NR*
TMDJ-022-SW	NR*	ng/100 uL	NR*	ng/100 uL	NR*
TMDJ-031-SW	NR*	ng/100 uL	NR*	ng/100 uL	NR*

Dr. Cendrowski
Memorandum to Christa Mason

This is the final analysis from Fort Detrick, the National Bioforensic Analysis Centers "National Biodefense Analysis and Countermeasures Centers" by Stephen Cendrowski PhD. This document, proving that the two tested KC letters were not the "deadly poison with no known antidote", Also it is the proof that the Mueller FBI/Holder DOJ and the entire world wide press had been lying to the American public the whole time, and that Dutschke did, in fact, tell the truth.

The standard for chemical weapons in the United States requires at least 90% purity. However the law for prosecution under CWCIA called the "Round to Zero rule" for Schedule 1 chemicals (ricin) actually carries out to even less than single digits. Specifically, the prosecutorial threshold required for prosecution can be as low as 0.5%; which carries, as you can see, all the way to the tenths position, one position past the decimal.

Think of a prosecutorial threshold, in the manner explained in the court-filed appeal documents, as the same as a DUI prosecution. If one does not "blow" over the legal limit, there can be no prosecution.

The chemical weapons statute, requiring half of 1% (0.5), could not have been used by Holder/Mueller since the toxicity (by percentage), as Dr. Cendrowski's analysis here shows, simply does not come anywhere NEAR the prosecutorial threshold. This document, as shown, even displays the percent PAST the decimal point and tenths is ZERO.

Even carrying the number (to the tenths) at the decimal point, it is proven here that there was no legal way to prosecute for the development of the decoy product. So what did the cabal do? How to cover for their lie? Lie more. They fraudulently indicted and prosecuted under the wrong statute, and the willing media and judge aided them in their massive unprecedented fraud.

Memorandum

To: Christa Mason

From: Stephen Cendrowski

Cc: · James Burans

Date: October 7th, 2013

Re: NBFAC.130417.0001 and NBFAC.130418.0001

Case samples from NBFAC.130417.0001 and NBFAC.130818.0001 were tested by the NBFAC Immunology/Toxinology department for active Ricin. The active Ricin for each sample was estimated based upon results from the Ricin Cell-Free Translation (CFT) Assay and reported below relative to the mass concentration of the total sample received for testing.

The percent of active Ricin for NBFAC.130417.0001.0001.0001.0001 was estimated to be 0.0 %

The percent of active Ricin for NBFAC.130418.0001.0001.0001.0001 was estimated to be 0.0 %

Approved:

Stephen Cendrowski   _October 7 2013_

Stephen Cendrowski, Ph.D.   Date
Immunology/Toxinology Manager

For Official Use Only   1 of 1

EXHIBIT
B

1:13CR81 Discovery

§6771

The law, as written and enacted by the CWCIA, is very clear and its definitions specifically designates ricin to be prosecuted under the correct statute of 18 USC§229 (Chemical weapons). Law be damned, the Holder DOJ and special prosecution team (National Security division Sigler) instead pretended that the "chemical weapon" (what they alleged was ricin) was a biological weapon and prosecuted under §175.

As can be seen here, 22 USC§6771(c), the CWCIA, as passed by Congress into law, prohibits exactly that kind of fraudulent prosecution since it further defines what could even qualify as a "biological weapon".

Any grade school student with even mediocre marks could easily tell you that "bio" means life. A living thing. (Anthrax-biological.) Everyone should now well understand (post-COVID) what a biological weapon is. In fact, the distinction is easier when using the previous and military terminology, "Germ Warfare". It makes it easier to understand.

The special prosecution team that Holder cobbled together for the fraudulent prosecution to do the dirty work of the Obama cabal apparently was completely clueless to what any fourth grade student understands... or they were intentionally dishonest. There is no other choice. Either they were ignorant to simple science AND this written law (which is a problem) OR they were not and it was an intentional fraud (a bigger problem).

In retrospect, it is an easy distinction. One cannot catch "ricin" from someone else, like a COVID-19 virus. Ricin is NOT biological. Not in science. Not in law. §6771(c) explicitly defines "biological agents" in such a way that "ricin" is clearly excluded. That dishonest administration, prosecution, media and judge did not care. The law be damned. Science be damned. Conviction (by SAM) was more important.

"This Act", referred to in this section is Division I of Act Oct. 21, 1998, popularly known as the Chemical Weapons Convention Implementation Act of 1998, which appears generally as 22 USCS §§ 6701 et seq. For full classification of such Act, consult USCS Tables volumes.

MISCELLANEOUS PROVISIONS

§ 6771.   Prohibition

(a) **In general.** Neither the Secretary of Defense nor any other officer or employee of the United States may, directly or by contract--
    (1) conduct any test or experiment involving the use of any chemical or biological agent on a civilian population; or
    (2) use human subjects for the testing of chemical or biological agents.

(b) **Construction.** Nothing in subsection (a) may be construed to prohibit actions carried out for purposes not prohibited by this Act (as defined in section 3(8) [22 USCS § 6701(8)]).

(c) **"Biological agent" defined.** In this section, the term "biological agent" means any micro-organism (including bacteria, viruses, fungi, rickettsiae or protozoa), pathogen, or infectious substance, or any naturally occurring, bio-engineered or synthesized component of any such micro-organism, pathogen, or infectious substance, whatever its origin or method of production, capable of causing--
    (1) death, disease, or other biological malfunction in a human, an animal, a plant, or another living organism;
    (2) deterioration of food, water, equipment, supplies, or materials of any kind; or
    (3) deleterious alteration of the environment.

(Oct. 21, 1998, P. L. 105-277, Div I, Title VI, § 602, 112 Stat. 2681-886 .)

© 2017 Matthew Bender & Company, Inc., a member of the LexisNexis Group. All rights reserved. Use of this product is subject to the restrictions and terms and conditions of the Matthew Bender Master Agreement.

301

Supplement No. 1 to part 745—Schedule of Chemicals

The Schedule 1 list of chemicals that are specifically defined as a Chemical Weapon, thus are legally to be controlled by the Chemical Weapons treaty and enforcing statutes and regulations instead of the entirely separate Biological Weapons treaty (and its enforcing statutes and regulations) where ricin is NOT, is a well defined list of those Schedule 1 chemical agents, including "ricin". That is duplicated numerous times into statutory and regulatory code. There really is no way for any legally competent person to miss or misunderstand exactly that.

At NO place in law or regulation is "ricin" listed as a biological weapon. It has been specifically designated by Congress, the CWCIA and by the nearly 200 different nations of the international treaty as a chemical weapon.

Since chemical weapons are (by law) required to be investigated by the FBI and prosecuted under 18USC§229, yet the Mueller FBI and Holder DOJ intentionally used 18USC§175, the biological weapons development statute instead—the question becomes "Why did the Mueller/Holder team intentionally and fraudulently indict for an inapplicable and invalid statute?"

The answer is because by the time of the indictment, they knew that the Libyan product had been swapped by a harmless, non-toxic decoy but "the ball" had already begun rolling so they needed to avoid the toxicity threshold "Round to Zero" rule that comes with the correct, chemical weapons, statute.

Their bait/switch fraudulent swap went unnoticed by the court, press and counsel.

SUPPLEMENT NO. 1 TO PART 745 -- SCHEDULES OF CHEMICALS

	C.A.S. Registry No.

Schedule 1

A. Toxic chemicals:

(1) O-Alkyl ([<--] C[10], incl. cycloalkyl) alkyl (Me, Et, n-Pr or i-Pr)-phosphonofluoridates

| e.g. Sarin: O-Isopropyl methylphosphonofluoridate | 107-44-8 |
| Soman: O-Pinacolyl methylphosphonofluoridate | 96-64-0 |

(2) O-Alkyl ([<--] C[10], incl. cycloalkyl) N,N-dialkyl (Me, Et, n-Pr or i-Pr) phosphoramidocyanidates

| e.g. Tabun: O-Ethyl N,N-dimethyl phosphoramidocyanidate | 77-81-6 |

(3) O-Alkyl (H or [<--] C[10], incl. cycloalkyl) S-2-dialkyl (Me, Et, n-Pr or i-Pr)-aminoethyl alkyl (Me, Et, n-Pr or i-Pr) phosphonothiolates and corresponding alkylated or protonated salts

| e.g. VX: O-Ethyl S-2-diisopropylaminoethyl methyl phosphonothiolate | 50782-69-9 |

(4) Sulfur mustards:

2-Chloroethylchloromethylsulfide	2625-76-5
Mustard gas: Bis(2-chloroethyl)sulfide	505-60-2
Bis(2-chloroethylthio)methane	63869-13-6
Sesquimustard: 1,2-Bis(2-chloroethylthio)ethane	3563-36-8
1,3-Bis(2-chloroethylthio)-n-propane	63905-10-2
1,4-Bis(2-chloroethylthio)-n-butane	142868-93-7
1,5-Bis(2-chloroethylthio)-n-pentane	142868-94-8
Bis(2-chloroethylthiomethyl)ether	63918-90-1
O-Mustard: Bis(2-chloroethylthioethyl)ether	63918-89-8

(5) Lewisites:

Lewisite 1: 2-Chlorovinyldichloroarsine	541-25-3
Lewisite 2: Bis(2-chlorovinyl)chloroarsine	40334-69-8
Lewisite 3: Tris(2-chlorovinyl)arsine	40334-70-1

(6) Nitrogen mustards:

HN1: Bis(2-chloroethyl)ethylamine	538-07-8
HN2: Bis(2-chloroethyl)methylamine	51-75-2
HN3: Tris(2-chloroethyl)amine	555-77-1

| (7) Saxitoxin | 35523-89-8 |

(8) Ricin

CFR   1

© 2017 Matthew Bender & Company, Inc., a member of the LexisNexis Group. All rights reserved. Use of this product is subject to the restrictions and terms and conditions of the Matthew Bender Master A

09813025

Supplement No. 1 to part 712—Schedule 1 Chemical

According the CWCIA, the Chemical Weapons Treaty, the statute "enacting" that treaty (which the Supreme Court said is invalid) and the federal regulations and statutes that regulate the Chemical Weapons Treaty and statutes, "ricin" (which is what was alleged in the Dutschke case) is specifically and explicitly a "chemical" weapon, not a "biological weapon".

By law, ricin is a chemical (Schedule 1), which would require prosecution under 18USC§229. In fact, 18USC§229 itself identifies "ricin' as under its legal purview, explicitly defining it so at §229F.

Dutschke, however, was prosecuted under 18USC§175(a) which is for "biological weapon" development.

The Holder DOJ intentionally used the wrong statute, the wrong law to prosecute Dutschke. Dutschke's attorney, who had never handled a case like this before (no one had), didn't even notice that the wrong law was being used, nor did the entire American press. The judge, Aycock, didn't care and convicted (via SAM) Dutschke anyway, despite that the indictment (citing an inapplicable law) was invalid, thus the conviction that followed was equally invalid.

SUPPLEMENT NO. 1 TO PART 712 -- SCHEDULE 1 CHEMICALS

Supplement No. 1 to Part 712. -- Schedule 1 Chemicals

	(CAS registry number)
A. Toxic chemicals:	
(1) O-Alkyl (<=C[10], incl. cycloalkyl) alkyl (Me, Et, n-Pr or i-Pr)-phosphonofluoridates	
e.g. Sarin: O-Isopropyl methylphosphonofluoridate	(107-44-8)
Soman: O-Pinacolyl methylphosphonofluoridate	(96-64-0)
(2) O-Alkyl (<=C[10], incl. cycloalkyl) N,N-dialkyl (Me, Et, n-Pr or i-Pr) phosphoramidocyanidates e.g. Tabun: O-Ethyl N,N-dimethyl phosphoramidocyanidate	(77-81-6)
(3) O-Alkyl (H or <=C[10], incl. cycloalkyl) S-2-dialkyl (Me, Et, n-Pr or i-Pr)-aminoethyl alkyl (Me, Et, n-Pr or i-Pr) phosphonothiolates and corresponding alkylated or protonated salts e.g. VX: O-Ethyl S-2-diisopropylaminoethyl methyl phosphonothiolate	(50782-69-9)
(4) Sulfur mustards:	
2-Chloroethylchloromethylsulfide	(2625-76-5)
Mustard gas: Bis(2-chloroethyl)sulfide	(505-60-2)
Bis(2-chloroethylthio)methane	(63869-13-6)
Sesquimustard: 1,2-Bis(2-chloroethylthio)ethane	(3563-36-8)
1,3-Bis(2-chloroethylthio)-n-propane	(63905-10-2)
1,4-Bis(2-chloroethylthio)-n-butane	(142868-93-7)
1,5-Bis(2-chloroethylthio)-n-pentane	(142868-94-8)
Bis(2-chloroethylthiomethyl)ether	(63918-90-1)
O-Mustard: Bis(2-chloroethylthioethyl)ether	(63918-89-8)
(5) Lewisites:	
Lewisite 1: 2-Chlorovinyldichloroarsine	(541-25-3)
Lewisite 2: Bis(2-chlorovinyl)chloroarsine	(40334-69-8)
Lewisite 3: Tris(2-chlorovinyl)arsine	(40334-70-1)
(6) Nitrogen mustards:	
HN1: Bis(2-chloroethyl)ethylamine	(538-07-8)
HN2: Bis(2-chloroethyl)methylamine	(51-75-2)
HN3: Tris(2-chloroethyl)amine	(555-77-1)
(7) Saxitoxin	(35523-89-8)
(8) **Ricin**	(9009-86-3)
B. Precursors:	
(9) Alkyl (Me, Et, n-Pr or i-Pr) phosphonyldifluorides e.g. DF: Methylphosphonyldifluoride	(676-99-3)
(10) O-Alkyl (H or <=C[10], incl. cycloalkyl) O-2-dialkyl (Me, Et, n-Pr or i-Pr)-aminoethyl alkyl (Me, Et, N-Pr or i-Pr) phosphonites and corresponding alkylated or protonated salts e.g. QL: O-Ethyl O-2-diisopropylaminoethyl methylphosphonite	(57856-11-8)
(11) Chlorosarin: O-Isopropyl methylphosphonochloridate	(1445-76-7)

CFR   1

© 2016 Matthew Bender & Company, Inc., a member of the LexisNexis Group. All rights reserved. Use of this product is subject to the restrictions and terms and conditions of the Matthew Bender Master Agreement.

BP-S327.058 Returned Correspondence U.S. Department of Justice
Date: August 14, 2014

This is the "rejection letter" that was sent to the filmmaker, Melanie Addington informing her that Dutschke was not allowed "any communication with any member or representative of the news media", disallowing HER 1st Amendment right as well as his. She, as a documentary movie-maker/reporter, has not only the First Amendment right of Freedom of Speech (but not with Dutschke), Freedom of the Press (but not allowing Dutschke to tell her the truth) and Freedom of Association (as long as she's not associating with Dutschke). As of this letter clearly shows, Addington's rights (as well as other reporters who tried) were, in fact, violated along with Dutschke's as the Bureau of Prisons cited in the national security based "Special Administrative Measures" (28 CFR§501.2&.3) that were written by Holder. At THIS date—it was the Holder/Mueller SAM still.

BP-S327.058 **RETURNED CORRESPONDENCE**
U.S. DEPARTMENT OF JUSTICE   FEDERAL BUREAU OF PRISONS

TO: (Sender-See Return Address)	FROM: (Institution)
M. Adointon 1210 S. 16th St. Oxford, MS. 38655	United Sta

RE: (Inmate's Name and Register No.)	DATE:
Dutschke, J. #15536-042	8-14-2014

SUBJECT: Correspondence Returned to Sender

On 8-7-2014, Inmate Dutscke James received two incoming letters that was not from his immediate family, the mail was from a friend. Due to the Special Administrative Measures it states that Communication with News Media the inmate shall not be permitted to speak, meet, correspond, or otherwise communicate with any member or representative of the news media in person, by telephone, by furnishing a recorded message, though the mail, his attorney, or third party; or otherwise. All mail that is being seized shall be referred to the FBI or USSS and the inmate shall be notified in writing of the seizure of any mail.

The rejection of this correspondence is in accordance with the Federal Bureau of Prisons policy on Correspondence≡ as published in Title 28 Code of Federal Regulations, Part 540 and in the Federal Bureau of Prisons Program Statement on correspondence, Special Administrative Measures Pursuant 28 C.F.R. 501. You have the right to appeal this rejection by writing the Warden in care of the above address. The inmate to whom you addressed your correspondence has been notified that this correspondence has been returned to you and of his or her right to appeal the rejection.

Thomas B. Smith, Associate Warden Programs

(Printed or Typed Name and Written Signature of the Warden)

BP-S327.058 U.S. Department Of Justice Federal Bureau of Prisons
Date: July 13, 2015

Dutschke's appointed attorney of record was Kenneth Coghlan of Oxford's Rayburn-Coghlan Law Firm. This "rejection" letter from July 13th proves that Coghlan, Dutschke's attorney of record, was not allowed any communication at all with his own client, denying Dutschke his Sixth Amendment right to counsel during the appeal of the also unconstitutional SAM "conviction".

This is the letter attorney Coghlan was sent when communication was tried.

BP-S327.058

MAY 94

RETURNED CORRESPONDENCE CDFRM

U.S. DEPARTMENT OF JUSTICE

FEDERAL BUREAU OF PRISONS

TO: (Sender-See Return Address)	FROM:
Rayburn Coghlan	United States Penitentiary Administrative Maximum P.O. Box 8500 Florence, CO 81226-8500

RE: (Inmate's Name and Register No.) DUTSCHKE, James Everett 15536-042/H	DATE: July 13, 2015

SUBJECT: Correspondence With Inmate Returned

Your correspondence to the above named inmate is being returned. This correspondence was not delivered to the inmate because you are not approved to correspond with this individual.

The rejection of this correspondence is in accordance with the Federal Bureau of Prisons policy on "Correspondence" as published in Title 28 Code of Federal Regulations, Part 540 and in the Federal Bureau of Prisons Program Statement on correspondence. You have the right to appeal this rejection by writing the Warden in care of the above address. The inmate to whom you addressed your correspondence has been notified that this correspondence has been returned to you and of his or her right to appeal the rejection. Any inquiry concerning this rejection will need to be referred to the following address: Federal Bureau of Prisons, ATTN: FOIA, 320 First Street, N.W. Washington, D.C. 20534.

B. True, Associate Warden BT/rjm
(Printed or Typed Name and Written Signature of the Warden)
Record Copy - Addressee (with Correspondence); Copy - Inmate; Copy - File (with copy of Correspondence)
(This form may be replicated via WP)   Replaces BP-327(58) of FEB 84

BP-S327.58 U.S. Department of Justice Federal
Bureau of Prisons
Date: July 15, 2015

The Holder SAM order which informed Kenneth Coghlan, Dutschke's attorney, that NO ONE was allowed any communication with Dutschke, even though Dutschke was lawyer Coghlan's client ("this inmate is not authorized to correspond with you"), under presidential executive power that Obama extended by regulation to one man only (28 CFR§501.2&.3), Eric Holder, was also then extended by Obama to Holder's replacement, Loretta Lynch. This July 15th attempt by Coghlan to aid in the critical appeal process resulted in this, yet another rejection letter from the DOJ's Bureau of Prison to Coghlan. This is a copy of what Coghlan received. Dutschke couldn't receive mail from Coghlan during the multiple year SAM or even knew anyone had mailed him at all since communication is entirely disallowed.

Dutschke later managed to challenge the executive SAM order against him with the OEO/OIG and it resulted in Loretta Lynch's quiet dropping of the Dutschke SAM.

BP-S327.058

MAY 94

U.S. DEPARTMENT OF JUSTICE

RETURNED CORRESPONDENCE CDFRM

FEDERAL BUREAU OF PRISONS

TO: (Sender-See Return Address) Rayburn Coghlan Law Firm, PLLC	FROM: United States Penitentiary Administrative Maximum P.O. Box 8500 Florence, Co 81226-8500
RE: (Inmate's Name and Register No.) DUTSCHKE, James Everett 15536-042/H	DATE: July 15, 2015

SUBJECT: Correspondence With Inmate Returned

Your correspondence to the above named inmate is being returned. This correspondence was not delivered to the inmate because this inmate is not authorized to correspond with you.

The rejection of this correspondence is in accordance with the Federal Bureau of Prisons policy on "Correspondence" as published in Title 28 Code of Federal Regulations, Part 540 and in the Federal Bureau of Prisons Program Statement on correspondence. You have the right to appeal this rejection by writing the Warden in care of the above address. The inmate to whom you addressed your correspondence has been notified that this correspondence has been returned to you and of his or her right to appeal the rejection. Any inquiry concerning this rejection will need to be referred to the following address: Federal Bureau of Prisons, ATTN: FOIA, 320 First Street, N.W. Washington, D.C. 20534.

B. True, Associate Warden BT/dh

(Printed or Typed Name and Written Signature of the Warden)

Record Copy - Addressee (with Correspondence); Copy - Inmate; Copy - File (with copy of Correspondence)

(This form may be replicated via WP)   Replaces BP-327(58) of FEB 84

Felicia Nona

Felicia Nona

Made in the USA
Las Vegas, NV
15 February 2022

43944658R00187